Management Level

Paper P2

PERFORMANCE MANAGEMENT

EXAM PRACTICE KIT

To

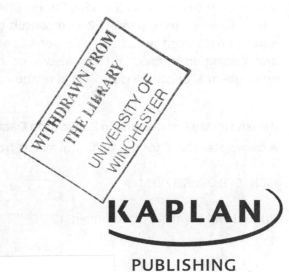

CIMA

PUBLISHING

KAPLAN

PUBLISHING

Published by: Kaplan Publishing UK

Unit 2 The Business Centre, Molly Millars Lane, Wokingham, Berkshire RG41 2QZ

Acknowledgements

We are grateful to the Chartered Institute of Management Accountants for permission to reproduce past examination questions. The answers to CIMA Exams have been prepared by Kaplan Publishing, except in the case of the CIMA November 2010 and subsequent CIMA Exam answers where the official CIMA answers have been reproduced.

British Library Cataloguing in Publication Data

A catalogue record for this book is available from the British Library

ISBN: 978-0-85732-994-3

Printed and bound in Great Britain.

CONTENTS

Section

Key features in this edition

In addition to providing a wide ranging bank of real past exam questions, we have also included in this edition:

- Paper specific information and advice on **exam technique.**

- **Guidance** to make your revision for this particular subject as effective as possible.

- Enhanced **tutorial answers** packed with specific key answer tips, technical tutorial notes and exam technique tips from our experienced tutors.

- **Examiner's comments** reproduced from the Post Exam Guide with the kind permission of CIMA.

You will find a wealth of other resources to help you with your studies on the following sites:

www.EN-gage.co.uk

www.cimaglobal.com

INDEX TO QUESTIONS AND ANSWERS

INTRODUCTION

This new Paper P2 has now a different shape and emphasis to the old Paper P2. Two complete sections – financial information for long term decision making and the treatment of uncertainty in decision making – have been moved from the old Paper P2 to the new Paper P1.

The replacement material in new Paper P2 has come from the old Paper P1, namely in section C budgeting and management control (20%) and section D control and performance measurement of responsibility centres (20%). The new Paper P2 has much of the traditional management accounting material concentrated in one place. Note that the skill levels of this transferred material are generally at a higher level than before. This is likely to make this paper a challenge in terms of the technical knowledge and problem solving requirements. Students will need to ensure that their basic knowledge of costing techniques is well established before sitting this paper.

KEY TO THE INDEX

PAPER ENHANCEMENTS

We have added the following enhancements to the answers in this exam practice kit:

Key answer tips

Many answers include key answer tips to help your understanding of each question.

Tutorial note

Many answers include more tutorial notes to explain some of the technical points in more detail.

Top tutor tips

For selected questions, we "walk through the answer" giving guidance on how to approach the questions with helpful 'tips from a top tutor', together with technical tutor notes.

These answers are indicated with the "footsteps" icon in the index.

SECTION B-TYPE QUESTIONS

Pricing and product decisions (30%)

ANALYSIS OF PAST EXAM PAPERS

The table below summarises the key topics that have been tested in the new syllabus examinations to date.

Note that the references are to the number of the question in this edition of the exam practice kit, but the Pilot Paper is produced in its original form at the end of the kit and therefore these questions have retained their original numbering in the paper itself.

	Specimen 2009	May 2011	Sep 2011	Nov 2011	Mar 2012	May 2012	Sep 2012	Nov 2012	Mar 2013	May 2013	Sep 2013
Pricing and product decisions											
Relevant cash flows	Q6			Q6	Q6		Q6				
Strategic, intangible and non-financial judgements in decision making								Q5			
Marginal and full cost recovery for pricing decisions	Q5			Q1			Q6				
Optimum mix analysis								Q6		Q6	Q6
Linear programming								Q6	Q6	Q6	
Multiproduct breakeven analysis, and charts		Q6			Q6	Q6	Q7			Q4	
Pricing decisions (algebraic)		Q1	Q1								
Pricing decisions (tabular)						Q7					
Pricing strategies						Q7					
Joint costs allocation/ further processing											
Cost planning and analysis for competitive advantage											
Value analysis			Q6	Q3							
JIT, TQM, theory of constraints											
Kaizen, CI ,cost of quality		Q3	Q3	Q2	Q2		Q4	Q4			
Learning curve	Q2			Q1	Q1		Q1	Q1	Q1	Q2	Q1
ABM											
Target costing	Q5										
Lifecycle costing		Q2	Q2				Q5				
Value chain	Q1									Q2	
Gain sharing	Q1										
ABC, DCPA, DPP	Q4								Q3	Q1	Q3
Pareto	Q4										

	Specimen 2009	May 2011	Sep 2011	Nov 2011	Mar 2012	May 2012	Sep 2012	Nov 2012	Mar 2013	May 2013	Sep 2013
Budgeting and Management Control											
Feedback and feedforward	Q3			Q4	Q4			Q2	Q4	Q3	Q4
Rolling budgets/ZBB											
Responsibility accounting; controllable and non-controllable costs		Q5			Q2		Q3				
Ratios: profitability, liquidity, asset turnover											
What-if analysis and the use of spreadsheets											
Out-turn performance and advanced variances	Q2	Q4	Q4								Q2
Behavioural issues and participation	Q3							Q3			
Non-financial performance indicators											
Balanced scorecard and beyond budgeting			Q5	Q5	Q5	Q2	Q2		Q5	Q5	
Control and performance measurement of responsibility centres											
Cost, revenue, profit and investment centres		Q7			Q7						
Presentation of financial information representing performance			Q7	Q7					Q7		
ROI and its deficiencies; RI and EVA as alternatives	Q7										
Transfer pricing theory										Q7	Q7
Use of negotiated, market, cost-plus and variable cost based transfer prices; dual prices and lump sum payments	Q7	Q7	Q7	Q7	Q7		Q7	Q7		Q7	Q7
International transfer pricing											

EXAM TECHNIQUE

- Use the allocated **20 minutes reading and planning time** at the beginning of the exam:
  - read the questions and examination requirements carefully, and
  - begin planning your answers.

  See the Paper Specific Information for advice on how to use this time for this paper.

- **Divide the time** you spend on questions in proportion to the marks on offer:
  - there are 1.8 minutes available per mark in the examination
  - within that, try to allow time at the end of each question to review your answer and address any obvious issues

  Whatever happens, always keep your eye on the clock and **do not over run on any part of any question!**

- Spend the last **five minutes** of the examination:
  - reading through your answers, and
  - **making any additions or corrections**.

- If you **get completely stuck** with a question:
  - leave space in your answer book, and
  - **return to it later.**

- Stick to the question and **tailor your answer** to what you are asked.
  - pay particular attention to the verbs in the question.

- If you do not understand what a question is asking, **state your assumptions**.

  Even if you do not answer in precisely the way the examiner hoped, you should be given some credit, if your assumptions are reasonable.

- You should do everything you can to make things easy for the marker.

  The marker will find it easier to identify the points you have made if your **answers are legible**.

- **Written questions**:

  Your answer should have:
  - a clear structure
  - a brief introduction, a main section and a conclusion.

  Be concise.

  It is better to write a little about a lot of different points than a great deal about one or two points.

- **Computations**:

  It is essential to include all your workings in your answers.

  Many computational questions require the use of a standard format:

  e.g. income tax computations, corporation tax computations and capital gains.

  Be sure you know these formats thoroughly before the exam and use the layouts that you see in the answers given in this book and in model answers.

- **Reports, memos and other documents**:

  Some questions ask you to present your answer in the form of a report, a memo, a letter or other document.

  Make sure that you use the correct format – there could be easy marks to gain here.

PAPER SPECIFIC INFORMATION

THE EXAM

FORMAT OF THE EXAM

Number of marks

5 compulsory questions which will be **predominantly computational**:

Section A : Five compulsory medium answer questions, each worth 10 marks. Short scenarios may be given, to which some or all questions relate.	50
Section B : One or two compulsory questions. Short scenarios may be given, to which questions relate.	50
	———
	100
	———

Total time allowed: 3 hours plus 20 minutes reading and planning time.

Note that:

- The Performance Management examination will primarily test the skills of comprehension, application and analysis using verbs from levels 2 – 4 of the CIMA verb hierarchy.

- You will be expected to use all of your knowledge and skills, gained from your study of the Performance Management syllabus, to explain and apply the various concepts about which you have learned.

- The scenarios used in this examination are based on real life, though simplified, and prepare you for the Strategic level examinations..

PASS MARK

The pass mark for all CIMA Qualification examination papers is 50%.

READING AND PLANNING TIME

Remember that all three hour paper based examinations have an additional 20 minutes reading and planning time.

CIMA GUIDANCE

CIMA guidance on the use of this time is as follows:

> This additional time is allowed at the beginning of the examination to allow candidates to read the questions and to begin planning their answers before they start to write in their answer books.
>
> This time should be used to ensure that all the information and, in particular, the exam requirements are properly read and understood.
>
> During this time, candidates may only annotate their question paper. They may not write anything in their answer booklets until told to do so by the invigilator.

FURTHER GUIDANCE

As all questions are compulsory, there are no decisions to be made about choice of questions, other than in which order you would like to tackle them.

Therefore, in relation to P2, we recommend that you take the following approach with your reading and planning time:

- **Skim through the whole paper**, assessing the level of difficulty of each question.

- **Write down** on the question paper next to the mark allocation **the amount of time you should spend on each part.** Do this for each part of every question.

- **Decide the order** in which you think you will attempt each question:

    This is a personal choice and you have time on the revision phase to try out different approaches, for example, if you sit mock exams.

    A common approach is to tackle the question you think is the easiest and you are most comfortable with first.

    Others may prefer to tackle the longest questions first, or conversely leave them to the last.

    Psychologists believe that you usually perform at your best on the second and third question you attempt, once you have settled into the exam, so not tackling the bigger Section B questions first may be advisable.

    It is usual however that student tackle their least favourite topic and/or the most difficult question in their opinion last.

    Whatever you approach, you must make sure that you leave enough time to attempt all questions fully and be very strict with yourself in timing each question.

- **For each question** in turn, read the requirements and then the detail of the question carefully.

    Always read the requirement first as this enables you to **focus on the detail of the question with the specific task in mind.**

For computational questions:

Highlight key numbers/information and key words in the question, scribble notes to yourself on the question paper to remember key points in your answer.

Jot down proformas required if applicable.

For written questions:

Take notice of the format required (e.g. letter, memo, notes) and identify the recipient of the answer. You need to do this to judge the level of financial sophistication required in your answer and whether the use of a formal reply or informal bullet points would be satisfactory.

Plan your beginning, middle and end and the key areas to be addressed and your use of titles and sub-titles to enhance your answer.

For all questions:

Spot the easy marks to be gained in a question and parts which can be performed independently of the rest of the question. For example, writing down due dates of payment of tax, due dates for making elections, laying out basic proformas correctly.

Make sure that you do these parts first when you tackle the question.

Don't go overboard in terms of planning time on any one question – you need a good measure of the whole paper and a plan for all of the questions at the end of the 20 minutes.

By covering all questions you can often help yourself as you may find that facts in one question may remind you of things you should put into your answer relating to a different question.

- With your plan of attack in mind, **start answering your chosen question** with your plan to hand, as soon as you are allowed to start.

DETAILED SYLLABUS

The detailed syllabus and study guide written by the CIMA can be found at:

www.cimaglobal.com

POST EXAM GUIDES (PEGs)

After each sitting, the examiners and lead markers produce a report for each paper outlining what they were looking for in the exam, how it related to the syllabus and highlights in detail what students did well and the areas that caused problems. This feedback is extremely useful to help you to focus on producing what the examiners want and thus increase your chances of passing the exams. The PEGs for P2 can be found here

http://www.cimaglobal.com/Students/Exam-preparation/Management-level/P2-perfomance-management/Post-exam-guides/

APPROACH TO REVISION

QUESTION PRACTICE IS THE KEY TO SUCCESS

Success in professional examinations relies upon you acquiring a firm grasp of the required knowledge at the tuition phase. In order to be able to do the questions, knowledge is essential.

However, the difference between success and failure often hinges on your exam technique on the day and making the most of the revision phase of your studies.

The **Study Text** is the starting point, designed to provide the underpinning knowledge to tackle all questions. However, in the revision phase, pouring over text books is not the answer.

The **online fixed tests** help you consolidate your knowledge and understanding and are a useful tool to check whether you can remember key topic areas.

Revision cards are designed to help you quickly revise a topic area, however you then need to practice questions. There is a need to progress to full exam standard questions as soon as possible, and to tie your exam technique and technical knowledge together.

The importance of question practice cannot be over-emphasised.

The recommended approach below is designed by expert tutors in the field, in conjunction with their knowledge of the examiner and their recent real exams.

The approach taken for the fundamental papers is to revise by topic area. However, with the professional stage papers, a multi topic approach is required to answer the scenario based questions.

You need to practice as many questions as possible in the time you have left.

OUR AIM

Our aim is to get you to the stage where you can attempt exam standard questions confidently, to time, in a closed book environment, with no supplementary help (i.e. to simulate the real examination experience).

Practising your exam technique on real past examination questions, in timed conditions, is also vitally important for you to assess your progress and identify areas of weakness that may need more attention in the final run up to the examination.

In order to achieve this we recognise that initially you may feel the need to practice some questions with open book help and exceed the required time.

The approach below shows you which questions you should use to build up to coping with exam standard question practice, and references to the sources of information available should you need to revisit a topic area in more detail.

Remember that in the real examination, all you have to do is:

- attempt all questions required by the exam

- only spend the allotted time on each question, and

- get them at least 50% right!

Try and practice this approach on every question you attempt from now to the real exam.

EXAMINER COMMENTS

From looking at the post-exam guidance, the common mistakes are as follows:

- misallocation of time

- running out of time

- showing signs of spending too much time on an earlier questions and clearly rushing the answer to a subsequent question

- Not relating the answer to the scenario/context of the question.

Good exam technique is vital.

THE P2 REVISION PLAN

Stage 1: Assess areas of strengths and weaknesses

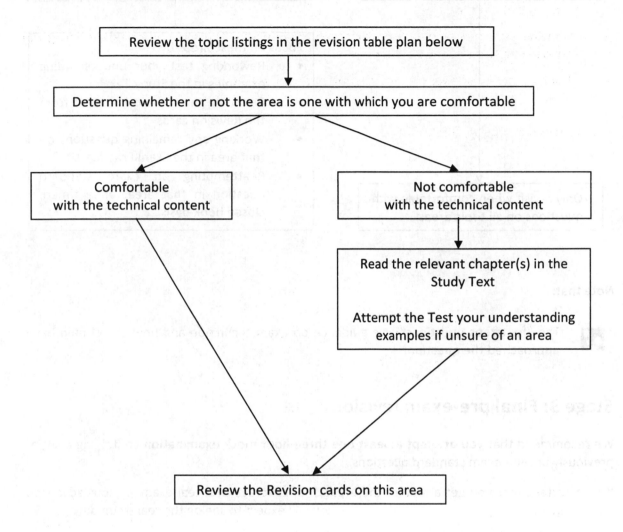

Stage 2: Practice questions

Follow the order of revision of topics as recommended in the revision table plan below and attempt the questions in the order suggested.

Try to avoid referring to text books and notes and the model answer until you have completed your attempt.

Try to answer the question in the allotted time.

Review your attempt with the model answer and assess how much of the answer you achieved in the allocated exam time.

Fill in the self-assessment box below and decide on your best course of action.

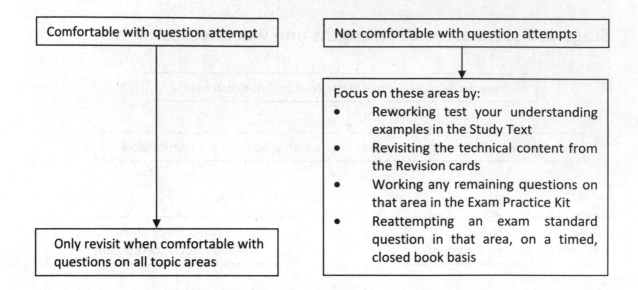

Comfortable with question attempt	Not comfortable with question attempts

Focus on these areas by:
- Reworking test your understanding examples in the Study Text
- Revisiting the technical content from the Revision cards
- Working any remaining questions on that area in the Exam Practice Kit
- Reattempting an exam standard question in that area, on a timed, closed book basis

Only revisit when comfortable with questions on all topic areas

Note that:

 The "footsteps questions" give guidance on exam technique and how you should have approached the question.

Stage 3: Final pre-exam revision

We recommend that you **attempt at least one three hour mock examination** containing a set of previously unseen exam standard questions.

It is important that you get a feel for the breadth of coverage of a real exam without advanced knowledge of the topic areas covered – just as you will expect to see on the real exam day.

Ideally a mock examination offered by your tuition provider should be sat in timed, closed book, real exam conditions.

THE DETAILED REVISION PLAN

Topic	Study Text Chapter	Questions to attempt	Tutor guidance	Date attempted	Self assessment
CVP analysis	3	9	A quick review of the key role of 'contribution' in decision making but more importantly, a good question to review multi-product CVP		
Decision making and relevant costs	4	83	Fundamentals of relevant costing and an example of a favourite decision-making situation.		
Linear programming	5	86	Establishing constraints and solving a LP problem is key to decision making		
Learning curves	6	23-28	A popular exam topic, guaranteed to form part of the exam. There are many questions on this area. Start with question 23, a basic warm up question. Build up to questions 28 which is more demanding past exam questions on this area.		
The pricing decision	7	6,7	Optimum pricing and the application if key pricing formulae are a guaranteed examination topic.		
The Modern Business Environment	8	11,12,13	Important modern-day management accounting theory areas that will help you practise narrative answers to exam questions.		

Topic	Study Text Chapter	Questions to attempt	Tutor guidance	Date attempted	Self assessment
Costing Techniques	9	21,24	Another popular exam topic, guaranteed to form part of the exam. Target Costing has been examined recently and a comparison with standard costing seems to be a favourite		
Advanced Activity Based Costing	10	42	Be prepared to perform calculations as well as explain the pros and cons of ABC compared to a traditional absorption costing approach.		
Principles of Budgeting	11	66,58	Budgeting and controllability need to be well rehearsed for this exam. Likewise, more modern alternatives to traditional budgeting are likely to come up .		
Budgetary control	12	63	You must be familiar with the key concepts of control and the different techniques that can be employed.		
Responsibility Centres	14	122,123	The usefulness of various performance measures within a divisionalised structure is also a likely contender in the exam.		
Transfer pricing	15	131,130	Fundamental issues relating to transfer pricing, and the different ways of setting up transfer prices are a core syllabus area.		

Note that not all of the questions are referred to in the programme above. We have recommended an approach to build up from the basic to exam standard questions.

The remaining questions are available in the exam practice kit for extra practice for those who require more questions on some areas.

MATHS TABLES AND FORMULAE

PRESENT VALUE TABLE

Present value of $1, that is $(1+r)^{-n}$ where r = interest rate; n = number of periods until payment or receipt.

Periods (n)	Interest rates (r)									
	1%	2%	3%	4%	5%	6%	7%	8%	9%	10%
1	0.990	0.980	0.971	0.962	0.952	0.943	0.935	0.926	0.917	0.909
2	0.980	0.961	0.943	0.925	0.907	0.890	0.873	0.857	0.842	0.826
3	0.971	0.942	0.915	0.889	0.864	0.840	0.816	0.794	0.772	0.751
4	0.961	0.924	0.888	0.855	0.823	0.792	0.763	0.735	0.708	0.683
5	0.951	0.906	0.863	0.822	0.784	0.747	0.713	0.681	0.650	0.621
6	0.942	0.888	0.837	0.790	0.746	0705	0.666	0.630	0.596	0.564
7	0.933	0.871	0.813	0.760	0.711	0.665	0.623	0.583	0.547	0.513
8	0.923	0.853	0.789	0.731	0.677	0.627	0.582	0.540	0.502	0.467
9	0.914	0.837	0.766	0.703	0.645	0.592	0.544	0.500	0.460	0.424
10	0.905	0.820	0.744	0.676	0.614	0.558	0.508	0.463	0.422	0.386
11	0.896	0.804	0.722	0.650	0.585	0.527	0.475	0.429	0.388	0.350
12	0.887	0.788	0.701	0.625	0.557	0.497	0.444	0.397	0.356	0.319
13	0.879	0.773	0.681	0.601	0.530	0.469	0.415	0.368	0.326	0.290
14	0.870	0.758	0.661	0.577	0.505	0.442	0.388	0.340	0.299	0.263
15	0.861	0.743	0.642	0.555	0.481	0.417	0.362	0.315	0.275	0.239
16	0.853	0.728	0.623	0.534	0.458	0.394	0.339	0.292	0.252	0.218
17	0.844	0.714	0.605	0.513	0.436	0.371	0.317	0.270	0.231	0.198
18	0.836	0.700	0.587	0.494	0.416	0.350	0.296	0.250	0.212	0.180
19	0.828	0.686	0.570	0.475	0.396	0.331	0.277	0.232	0.194	0.164
20	0.820	0.673	0.554	0.456	0.377	0.312	0.258	0.215	0.178	0.149

Periods (n)	Interest rates (r)									
	11%	12%	13%	14%	15%	16%	17%	18%	19%	20%
1	0.901	0.893	0.885	0.877	0.870	0.862	0.855	0.847	0.840	0.833
2	0.812	0.797	0.783	0.769	0.756	0.743	0.731	0.718	0.706	0.694
3	0.731	0.712	0.693	0.675	0.658	0.641	0.624	0.609	0.593	0.579
4	0.659	0.636	0.613	0.592	0.572	0.552	0.534	0.516	0.499	0.482
5	0.593	0.567	0.543	0.519	0.497	0.476	0.456	0.437	0.419	0.402
6	0.535	0.507	0.480	0.456	0.432	0.410	0.390	0.370	0.352	0.335
7	0.482	0.452	0.425	0.400	0.376	0.354	0.333	0.314	0.296	0.279
8	0.434	0.404	0.376	0.351	0.327	0.305	0.285	0.266	0.249	0.233
9	0.391	0.361	0.333	0.308	0.284	0.263	0.243	0.225	0.209	0.194
10	0.352	0.322	0.295	0.270	0.247	0.227	0.208	0.191	0.176	0.162
11	0.317	0.287	0.261	0.237	0.215	0.195	0.178	0.162	0.148	0.135
12	0.286	0.257	0.231	0.208	0.187	0.168	0.152	0.137	0.124	0.112
13	0.258	0.229	0.204	0.182	0.163	0.145	0.130	0.116	0.104	0.093
14	0.232	0.205	0.181	0.160	0.141	0.125	0.111	0.099	0.088	0.078
15	0.209	0.183	0.160	0.140	0.123	0.108	0.095	0.084	0.079	0.065
16	0.188	0.163	0.141	0.123	0.107	0.093	0.081	0.071	0.062	0.054
17	0.170	0.146	0.125	0.108	0.093	0.080	0.069	0.060	0.052	0.045
18	0.153	0.130	0.111	0.095	0.081	0.069	0.059	0.051	0.044	0.038
19	0.138	0.116	0.098	0.083	0.070	0.060	0.051	0.043	0.037	0.031
20	0.124	0.104	0.087	0.073	0.061	0.051	0.043	0.037	0.031	0.026

Cumulative present value of $1 per annum, Receivable or Payable at the end of each year for n years $\dfrac{1-(1+r)^{-n}}{r}$

Periods (n)	Interest rates (r)									
	1%	2%	3%	4%	5%	6%	7%	8%	9%	10%
1	0.990	0.980	0.971	0.962	0.952	0.943	0.935	0.926	0.917	0.909
2	1.970	1.942	1.913	1.886	1.859	1.833	1.808	1.783	1.759	1.736
3	2.941	2.884	2.829	2.775	2.723	2.673	2.624	2.577	2.531	2.487
4	3.902	3.808	3.717	3.630	3.546	3.465	3.387	3.312	3.240	3.170
5	4.853	4.713	4.580	4.452	4.329	4.212	4.100	3.993	3.890	3.791
6	5.795	5.601	5.417	5.242	5.076	4.917	4.767	4.623	4.486	4.355
7	6.728	6.472	6.230	6.002	5.786	5.582	5.389	5.206	5.033	4.868
8	7.652	7.325	7.020	6.733	6.463	6.210	5.971	5.747	5.535	5.335
9	8.566	8.162	7.786	7.435	7.108	6.802	6.515	6.247	5.995	5.759
10	9.471	8.983	8.530	8.111	7.722	7.360	7.024	6.710	6.418	6.145
11	10.368	9.787	9.253	8.760	8.306	7.887	7.499	7.139	6.805	6.495
12	11.255	10.575	9.954	9.385	8.863	8.384	7.943	7.536	7.161	6.814
13	12.134	11.348	10.635	9.986	9.394	8.853	8.358	7.904	7.487	7.103
14	13.004	12.106	11.296	10.563	9.899	9.295	8.745	8.244	7.786	7.367
15	13.865	12.849	11.938	11.118	10.380	9.712	9.108	8.559	8.061	7.606
16	14.718	13.578	12.561	11.652	10.838	10.106	9.447	8.851	8.313	7.824
17	15.562	14.292	13.166	12.166	11.274	10.477	9.763	9.122	8.544	8.022
18	16.398	14.992	13.754	12.659	11.690	10.828	10.059	9.372	8.756	8.201
19	17.226	15.679	14.324	13.134	12.085	11.158	10.336	9.604	8.950	8.365
20	18.046	16.351	14.878	13.590	12.462	11.470	10.594	9.818	9.129	8.514

Periods (n)	Interest rates (r)									
	11%	12%	13%	14%	15%	16%	17%	18%	19%	20%
1	0.901	0.893	0.885	0.877	0.870	0.862	0.855	0.847	0.840	0.833
2	1.713	1.690	1.668	1.647	1.626	1.605	1.585	1.566	1.547	1.528
3	2.444	2.402	2.361	2.322	2.283	2.246	2.210	2.174	2.140	2.106
4	3.102	3.037	2.974	2.914	2.855	2.798	2.743	2.690	2.639	2.589
5	3.696	3.605	3.517	3.433	3.352	3.274	3.199	3.127	3.058	2.991
6	4.231	4.111	3.998	3.889	3.784	3.685	3.589	3.498	3.410	3.326
7	4.712	4.564	4.423	4.288	4.160	4.039	3.922	3.812	3.706	3.605
8	5.146	4.968	4.799	4.639	4.487	4.344	4.207	4.078	3.954	3.837
9	5.537	5.328	5.132	4.946	4.772	4.607	4.451	4.303	4.163	4.031
10	5.889	5.650	5.426	5.216	5.019	4.833	4.659	4.494	4.339	4.192
11	6.207	5.938	5.687	5.453	5.234	5.029	4.836	4.656	4.486	4.327
12	6.492	6.194	5.918	5.660	5.421	5.197	4.988	7.793	4.611	4.439
13	6.750	6.424	6.122	5.842	5.583	5.342	5.118	4.910	4.715	4.533
14	6.982	6.628	6.302	6.002	5.724	5.468	5.229	5.008	4.802	4.611
15	7.191	6.811	6.462	6.142	5.847	5.575	5.324	5.092	4.876	4.675
16	7.379	6.974	6.604	6.265	5.954	5.668	5.405	5.162	4.938	4.730
17	7.549	7.120	6.729	6.373	6.047	5.749	5.475	5.222	4.990	4.775
18	7.702	7.250	6.840	6.467	6.128	5.818	5.534	5.273	5.033	4.812
19	7.839	7.366	6.938	6.550	6.198	5.877	5.584	5.316	5.070	4.843
20	7.963	7.469	7.025	6.623	6.259	5.929	5.628	5.353	5.101	4.870

FORMULAE

PROBABILITY

$A \cup B = $ **A or B**.

$A \cap B = $ **A and B** (overlap).

$P(B \mid A) = $ probability of B, **given** A.

Rules of Addition

If A and B are mutually exclusive: $\quad P(A \cup B) = P(A) + P(B)$

If A and B are **not** mutually exclusive: $\quad P(A \cup B) = P(A) + P(B) - P(A \cap B)$

Rules of Multiplication

If A and B are *independent*: $\quad P(A \cap B) = P(A) * P(B)$

If A and B are **not** *independent*: $\quad P(A \cap B) = P(A) * P(B \mid A)$

$E(X) = \Sigma$ (probability * payoff)

DESCRIPTIVE STATISTICS

Arithmetic Mean

$$\bar{x} = \frac{\Sigma x}{n} \qquad \bar{x} = \frac{\Sigma fx}{\Sigma f} \quad \text{(frequency distribution)}$$

Standard Deviation

$$SD = \sqrt{\frac{\Sigma(x - \bar{x})^2}{n}} \qquad SD = \sqrt{\frac{\Sigma fx^2}{\Sigma f} - \bar{x}^2} \quad \text{(frequency distribution)}$$

INDEX NUMBERS

Price relative = $100 * P_1/P_0$

Quantity relative = $100 * Q_1/Q_0$

Price:

$$\frac{\Sigma w * \left[\dfrac{P_1}{P_0}\right]}{\Sigma w} \times 100$$

Quantity:

$$\frac{\Sigma w * \left[\dfrac{Q_1}{Q_0}\right]}{\Sigma w} \times 100$$

TIME SERIES

Additive Model   Series = Trend + Seasonal + Random

Multiplicative Model   Series = Trend * Seasonal * Random

FINANCIAL MATHEMATICS

Compound Interest (Values and Sums)

Future Value *S*, of a sum of *X*, invested for *n* periods, compounded at *r*% interest

$S = X[1 + r]^n$

Annuity

Present value of an annuity of £1 per annum receivable or payable for *n* years, commencing in one year, discounted at *r*% per annum:

$$PV = \frac{1}{r}\left(1 - \frac{1}{[1+r]^n}\right)$$

Perpetuity

Present value of £1 per annum, payable or receivable in perpetuity, commencing in one year, discounted at *r*% per annum:

$$PV = \frac{1}{r}$$

LEARNING CURVE

$Y_x = aX^b$

where:

Y_x = the cumulative average time per unit to produce *X* units;

a = the time required to produce the first unit of output;

X = the cumulative number of units;

b = the index of learning.

The exponent *b* is defined as the log of the learning curve improvement rate divided by log 2.

INVENTORY MANAGEMENT

Economic Order Quantity

$$EOQ = \sqrt{\frac{2C_oD}{C_h}}$$

where: C_o = cost of placing an order

C_h = cost of holding one unit in inventory for one year

D = annual demand

Section 1

SECTION A-TYPE QUESTIONS

PRICING AND PRODUCT DECISIONS

1   **BVX**

BVX manufactures three garden furniture products – chairs, benches and tables. The budgeted unit cost and resource requirements of each of these items is detailed below:

	Chair	Bench	Table
	$	$	$
Timber cost	5.00	15.00	10.00
Direct labour cost	4.00	10.00	8.00
Variable overhead cost	3.00	7.50	6.00
Fixed overhead cost	4.50	11.25	9.00
	16.50	43.75	33.00
Budgeted volumes per annum	4,000	2,000	1,500

These volumes are believed to equal the market demand for these products.

The fixed overhead costs are attributed to the three products on the basis of direct labour hours.

The labour rate is $4.00 per hour; the cost of the timber is $2.00 per square metre.

The products are made from a specialist timber. A memo from the purchasing manager advises you that because of a problem with the supplier, it is to be assumed that this specialist timber is limited in supply to 20,000 square metres per annum.

The sales director has already accepted an order for 500 chairs, 100 benches and 150 tables which if not supplied would incur a financial penalty of $2,000. These quantities are included in the market demand estimates above. The selling prices of the three products are:

  Chair $20.00   Bench $50.00   Table $40.00

Required:

(a)   **Determine the optimum production plan AND state the net profit that this should yield per annum.**   **(6 marks)**

(b)   **Calculate AND explain the maximum prices which should be paid per square metre in order to obtain extra supplies of the timber.**   **(4 marks)**

(Total: 10 marks)

2   THREE PRODUCTS

Three products – X, Y and Z – are made and sold by a company; information is given below:

		Product X	Product Y	Product Z
		$	$	$
Standard costs				
Direct materials		50	120	90
Variable overhead		12	7	16
Direct labour:	Rate per hour	Hours	Hours	Hours
	$			
Department A	5	14	8	15
Department B	6	4	3	5
Department C	4	8	4	15

Total fixed overhead for the year was budgeted at $300,000. The budget for the current financial year was based on the following sales:

Product	Sales in units	Selling price per unit
		$
X	7,500	210
Y	6,000	220
Z	6,000	300

However, the market for each of the products has improved and the Sales Director believes that, without a change in selling prices, the number of units sold could be increased for each product by the following percentages:

Product	Increase
X	20%
Y	25%
Z	33⅓%

When the Sales Director's views were presented to a management meeting the Production Director declared that, although it might be possible to sell more units of product, output could not be expanded because he was unable to recruit more staff for Department B (there being a severe shortage of the skills needed by this department).

Required:

(a)   to show in the form of a statement for management, the unit costs of each of the three products and the total profit expected for the current year based on the original sales figures   **(4 marks)**

(b)   to state the profit if the most profitable mixture of the products were made and sold, utilising the higher sales figures and the limitation on Department B.

(6 marks)

(Total: 10 marks)

3   LIFECYCLE AND LEARNING CURVE (NOV 11)

A company has developed a new product. Details are as follows:

Selling price and product life cycle

The product will have a life cycle of 10,000 units. It is estimated that the first 9,000 units will be sold for $124 each and then the product will enter the "decline" stage of its life cycle. It is difficult to forecast the selling price for the 1,000 units that will be sold during this stage.

Costs

Labour will be paid at $12 per hour. Other variable costs will be $38 per unit. Fixed costs will total $80,000 over the life cycle of the product. The labour rate and both of these costs will not change throughout the product's life cycle.

Learning curve

The first batch of 100 units will take 1,500 labour hours to produce. There will be an 85% learning curve that will continue until 6,400 units have been produced. Batches after this level will each take the same amount of time as the 64th batch. The batch size will always be 100 units.

Required:

Calculate

(a)   the cumulative average time per batch for the first 64 batches   (2 marks)

(b)   the time taken for the 64th batch   (3 marks)

(c)   the average selling price of the final 1,000 units that will allow the company to earn a total profit of $100,000 from the product.   (5 marks)

Note: The learning index for an 85% learning curve is –0.2345

Ignore the time value of money.   (Total: 10 marks)

4   CATERPILLAR

The Caterpillar China Company produces a range of five similar products – A, B, C, D and E. The following table shows the quantity of each of the required inputs necessary to produce one unit of each product, together with the weekly inputs available and the selling price per unit of each product.

Inputs	Product					Weekly inputs available
	A	B	C	D	E	
Raw material (kg)	6.00	6.50	6.10	6.10	6.40	35,000
Forming (hours)	1.00	0.75	1.25	1.00	1.00	6,000
Firing (hours)	3.00	4.50	6.00	6.00	4.50	30,000
Packing (hours)	0.50	0.50	0.50	0.75	1.00	4,000
Selling price ($)	40	42	44	48	52	

The costs of each input are as follows:

Materials	$2.10 per kg
Forming	$3.00 per hour
Firing	$1.30 per hour
Packing	$8.00 per hour

The output from the computer package produces the following final tableau of a simple solution to this problem.

Basic	A	B	C	D	E	X	S	T	U	Value
A	1	1.18	1.04	0.46	0	0.36	0	0	−2.29	3,357
S	0	−0.34	0.23	0.02	0	−0.18	1	0	0.14	321
T	0	1.37	2.97	2.28	0	−0.27	0	1	−2.79	9,482
E	0	−0.09	−0.02	0.52	1	−0.18	0	0	2.14	2,321
	0	1.26	1.06	0.51	0	2.02	0	0	8.81	105,791

Where A, B, C, D and E are the weekly production levels for the five products; X is the slack variable for raw materials; S, T, U are the respective slack variables for the number of hours of forming time, firing time and packing time.

Required:

Use this tableau to find the optimum weekly production plan for the Caterpillar China Company. Describe the implications of using this plan in terms of the unused resources and overall contribution to profit. **(10 marks)**

5   **NLM (NOV 08)** *Walk in the footsteps of a top tutor*

NLM uses a common process to manufacture three joint products: X, Y and Z. The costs of operating the common process total $75,400 each month. This includes $6,800 of apportioned head office costs. The remaining costs are specific to the common process and would be avoided if it were discontinued. Common costs are apportioned to the joint products on the basis of their respective output volumes.

The normal monthly output from the common process is:

X   4,000 litres   Y   5,000 litres   Z   4,500 litres

There are a number of manufacturers of products that are identical to products X, Y and Z and as a result there is a competitive market in which these products can be bought and sold at the following prices:

X $5.00 per litre   Y $4.50 per litre   Z $5.50 per litre

Currently NLM uses the output from the common process as input to three separate processes where X, Y and Z are converted into SX, SY and SZ. The specific costs of these further processes (which are avoidable if the further process is discontinued) are as follows:

X to SX $1.25 per litre plus $1,850 per month

Y to SY $1.80 per litre plus $800 per month

Z to SZ $1.55 per litre plus $2,400 per month

The market selling prices of the further processed products are:

SX $6.75 per litre

SY $7.50 per litre

SZ $7.20 per litre

Required:

(a)   Advise NLM as to which (if any) of the further processes should continue to be operated. State any relevant assumptions.   **(6 marks)**

(b)   Advise NLM whether they should continue to operate the common process. State any relevant assumptions.   **(4 marks)**

(Total: 10 marks)

6   WX PRICING (MAY 11)

WX is reviewing the selling price of one of its products. The current selling price of the product is $25 per unit and annual demand is forecast to be 150,000 units at this price. Market research indicates that the level of demand would be affected by any change in the selling price.

Detailed analysis from this research shows that for every $1 increase in selling price, annual demand would reduce by 25,000 units and that for every $1 decrease in selling price, annual demand would increase by 25,000 units.

A forecast of the annual costs that would be incurred by WX in respect of this product at differing activity levels is as follows:

Annual production (units)	100,000	160,000	200,000
	$000	$000	$000
Direct materials	200	320	400
Direct labour	600	960	1,200
Overhead	880	1,228	1,460

The cost behaviour patterns represented in the above forecast will apply for the whole range of output up to 300,000 units per annum of this product.

Required:

(a)   (i)   Calculate the total variable cost per unit.   **(2 marks)**

        (ii)   Calculate the selling price of the product that will maximise the company's profits.   **(4 marks)**

        Note: If Price (P) = a – bx then Marginal Revenue = a – 2bx

(b)   Explain TWO reasons why the company might decide NOT to use this optimum selling price.   **(4 marks)**

(Total: 10 marks)

7 HZ SELLING PRICE (SEPT 11)

HZ is reviewing the selling price of one of its products. The current selling price of the product is $45 per unit and annual demand is forecast to be 130,000 units at this price. Market research shows that the level of demand would be affected by any change in the selling price. Detailed analysis of this research shows that for every $1 increase in selling price, annual demand would reduce by 10,000 units and that for every $1 decrease in selling price, annual demand would increase by 10,000 units.

A forecast of the costs that would be incurred by HZ in respect of this product at differing activity levels is as follows:

Annual production and sales (units)	100,000	160,000	200,000
	$000	$000	$000
Direct materials	280	448	560
Direct labour	780	1,248	1,560
Variable overhead	815	1,304	1,630
Fixed overhead	360	360	360

The company seeks your help in determining the optimum selling price to maximise its profits.

Required:

(a) Calculate the optimum forecast annual profit from the product. **(6 marks)**

(b) Explain the effect on the optimal price and quantity sold of independent changes to:

    (i) the direct material cost per unit **(2 marks)**

    (ii) the annual fixed overhead cost. **(2 marks)**

(Total: 10 marks)

8 HS (NOV 07)

HS manufactures components for use in computers. The business operates in a highly competitive market where there are a large number of manufacturers of similar components. HS is considering its pricing strategy for the next 12 weeks for one of its components. The Managing Director seeks your advice to determine the selling price that will maximise the profit to be made during this period.

You have been given the following data:

Market demand

The current selling price of the component is $1,350 and at this price the average weekly demand over the last four weeks has been 8,000 components. An analysis of the market shows that, for every $50 increase in selling price, the demand reduces by 1,000 components per week. Equally, for every $50 reduction in selling price, the demand increases by 1,000 components per week.

Costs

The direct material cost of each component is $270. This price is part of a fixed price contract with the material suppliers and the contract does not expire for another year.

Production labour and conversion costs, together with other overhead costs and the corresponding output volumes, have been collected for the last four weeks and they are as follows:

Week	Output volume (units)	$000
1	9,400	7,000
2	7,600	5,688
3	8,500	6,334
4	7,300	5,446

No significant changes in cost behaviour are expected over the next 12 weeks.

Required:

(a) Calculate the optimum (profit-maximising) selling price of the component for the period.

Note: If Price = a – bq, then Marginal revenue = a – 2bq (6 marks)

(b) Identify and explain two reasons why it may be inappropriate for HS to use this theoretical pricing model in practice. (4 marks)

(Total: 10 marks)

9 **MULTI-PRODUCT BREAKEVEN ANALYSIS (SEPT 10)**

A company manufactures five products in one factory. The company uses a Just-in-Time (JIT) production system. The company's budgeted fixed costs for the next year are $300,000. The table below summarises the budgeted sales and contribution details for the five products for the next year.

Product	A	B	C	D	E
Unit selling price ($)	40	15	40	30	20
Total sales ($000)	400	180	1,400	900	200
Contribution/sales ratio (%)	45	30	25	20	(10)

The following diagram has been prepared to summarise the above budget figures:

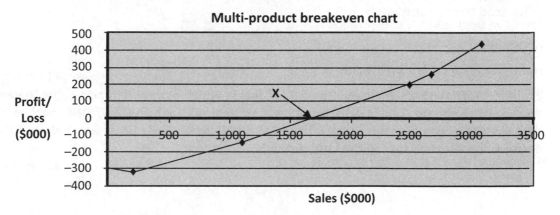

After the diagram had been prepared, the Marketing Director has said that Products A and E are complementary products. The budget assumes that there are no sales of Product A without also selling Product E and no sales of Product E without selling Product A.

Required:

(a)   (i)   Explain TWO reasons why the chart does not provide a useful summary of the budget data provided.   **(4 marks)**

       (ii)   Explain the meaning of point X on the chart.   **(2 marks)**

(b)   Calculate the breakeven revenue for the next year using the budgeted sales mix.

       All workings must be shown.   **(4 marks)**

                                                                          (Total: 10 marks)

10   Z MARKETING PACKAGE (MAY 13)

The owner, Z, of a business has been attending a course on scenario planning and decision making. As a result of that advice the owner has produced, by using cost volume and profit analysis, 12 scenarios for a new product that the business will launch in the near future. There are four possible marketing packages that could be used (A, B, C or D) and there are three possible market conditions (poor, average or good) that could be encountered. The Net Present Value of the cash flows resulting from each of the scenarios is shown in the table below.

	Marketing package			
Market conditions	**A** $000	**B** $000	**C** $000	**D** $000
Poor	180	230	220	190
Average	190	200	210	275
Good	550	260	210	500

Unfortunately Z missed the session on how to deal with risk and uncertainty. He has sent the above table to the tutor for the course and has asked for help. The tutor replied "I will send you some notes. Based on your table you will need the methods in the section on 'Uncertainty'. If you can estimate the probability of each type of market condition occurring you need 'Risk based methods'. However, whichever method you use, your decision will be influenced by your attitude."

Required:

Note: calculations are NOT required.

Explain FOUR methods that could help Z to decide which marketing package to choose. Your answer should include THREE methods to deal with uncertainty, ONE method to deal with risk, and an explanation of the "attitude" that would be associated with the decision maker using each of the four methods.

                                                                             (10 marks)

COST PLANNING AND ANALYSIS FOR COMPETITIVE ADVANTAGE

11   JIT (NOV 12)

CDE has recently won a contract to supply a component to a major car manufacturer that is about to launch a new range of vehicles. This is a great success for the design team of CDE as the component has many unique features and will be an important feature of some of the vehicles in the range.

CDE is currently building a specialised factory to produce the component. The factory will start production on 1 January 2013. There is an expected demand for 140,000 units of the component in 2013.

Forecast sales and production costs for 2013:

Quarter	1	2	3	4
Sales (units)	19,000	34,000	37,000	50,000
	$	$	$	$
Variable production cost per unit	60	60	65	70

Fixed production overheads for the factory are expected to be $2.8 million in 2013.

A decision has to be made about the production plan. The choices are:

Plan 1: Produce at a constant rate of 35,000 units per quarter

Inventory would be used to cover fluctuations in quarterly demand. Inventory holding costs will be $13 per unit and will be incurred quarterly based on the average inventory held in each of the four quarters.

Plan 2: Use a just-in-time (JIT) production system

The factory would be able to produce 36,000 units per quarter in 'normal' time and up to a further 20,000 units in 'overtime'. However, each unit produced in 'overtime' would incur additional costs equal to 40% of the forecast variable production cost per unit for that quarter.

Required:

(a)   Produce calculations using the above data to show which of the two plans would incur the lowest total cost in 2013.   **(6 marks)**

(b)   Explain TWO reasons why the decision about the production plan should not be based on your answer to part (a) alone.   **(4 marks)**

(Total: 10 marks)

12   JYT KAIZEN (MAY 11)

JYT manufactures and sells a range of products. It is not dominant in the market in which it operates and, as a result, it has to accept the market price for each of its products. The company is keen to ensure that it continues to compete and earn satisfactory profit at each stage throughout a product's life cycle.

Required:

Explain how JYT could use Target Costing AND Kaizen Costing to improve its future performance.

Your answer should include an explanation of the differences between Target Costing and Kaizen Costing.   **(10 marks)**

13   HT QUALITY (SEPT 10)

HT manufactures and sells consumer goods. The market in which it operates is highly competitive and HT is constantly designing new products in order to maintain its market share. The life cycle of products in the market is extremely short with all of the manufacturers constantly introducing new products or variations on existing products.

Consumers consider two main factors when buying these products: price and quality. HT uses a penetration pricing policy when launching its products and is always striving to improve its quality from product design stage through to customer care. As a result it has a 15% market share, and its largest competitor has a 6% market share with around 30 other companies sharing the remainder of the market.

Required:

(a)   **Compare and contrast:**

 • **Costs of quality conformance; and**

 • **Costs of quality non-conformance.**   **(3 marks)**

(b)   **Discuss the relationship between quality conformance costs and product selling prices in HT.**   **(4 marks)**

(c)   **Explain how Kaizen principles could be used by HT to extend the life of its products.**   **(3 marks)**

(Total: 10 marks)

14   CONFORMANCE (NOV 12)

A manufacturing company is reviewing its progress towards meeting its objective of having a reputation for producing high quality products. Extracts from the company's records for each of the years ended 30 September 2011 and 2012 are shown below.

	2012	*2011*
% of units rejected by customers	12%	20%
% of units rejected before delivery	12%	3%
Costs as % of revenue		
Raw material inspection	8%	3%
Direct material	18%	20%
Direct labour	13%	12%
Training	8%	4%
Preventative machine maintenance	8%	2%
Machine breakdown maintenance	5%	10%
Finished goods inspection	7%	1%

Required:

(a)   **Explain each of the four quality cost classifications using examples from the above data.**   **(4 marks)**

(b)   **Discuss, using the above data, the relationship between conformance costs and non-conformance costs and its importance for this company.**   **(6 marks)**

(Total: 10 marks)

15   KAIZEN AND STANDARD (SEPT 11)

In order to compete globally many companies have adopted Kaizen Costing. Consequently they are changing their performance measurement systems and are abandoning standard costing systems as they think traditional standard costing and variance analysis is of little use in the modern environment.

Required:

Discuss why Kaizen Costing could be more useful for performance measurement than standard costing and variance analysis in such companies.   **(10 marks)**

16   SW

SW is a member of the SWAL Group of companies. SW manufactures cleaning liquid using chemicals that it buys from a number of suppliers. In the past SW has used a periodic review inventory control system with maximum, minimum and re-order levels to control the purchase of the chemicals and the economic order quantity model to minimise its costs.

The Managing Director of SW is considering a change by introducing a Just in Time (JIT) system.

Required:

As Management Accountant, prepare a report to the Managing Director that explains how a JIT system differs from the system presently being used and the extent to which its introduction would require a review of SW's quality control procedures.

(10 marks)

17 PT MANUFACTURING (MAY 11)

PT manufactures and sells a number of products. All of its products have a life cycle of six months or less. PT uses a four stage life cycle model (Introduction; Growth; Maturity; and Decline) and measures the profits from its products at each stage of their life cycle.

PT has recently developed an innovative product. Since the product is unique it was decided that it would be launched with a market skimming pricing policy. However PT expects that other companies will try to enter the market very soon.

This product is generating significant unit profits during the Introduction stage of its life cycle. However there are concerns that the unit profits will reduce during the other stages of the product's life cycle.

Required:

For each of the (i) Growth; and (ii) Maturity stages of the new product's life cycle, explain the likely changes that will occur in the unit selling prices AND in the unit production costs, compared to the preceding stage. **(10 marks)**

18 PQ ELECTRONICS (MAY 10)

PQ manufactures and sells consumer electronics. It is constantly working to design the latest gadgets and "must-haves" which are unique in the market place at the time they are launched. The management of PQ are aware of the short product life cycles in this competitive market and consequently use a market skimming pricing strategy at the introduction stage.

Required:

Explain the changes that are likely to occur in the following items at the three later stages in the product life cycle of a typical PQ product.

(i)   Selling price

(ii)   Production costs

(iii) Selling and marketing costs **(10 marks)**

19 COST OF QUALITY REPORT (SEPT 12)

A company manufactures a single product. The selling price, production cost and contribution per unit for this product for 2013 have been predicted as follows:

		$ per unit
Selling price		90.00
Direct materials (components)	30.00	
Direct labour	35.00	
Variable overhead	10.00	75.00
		───
Contribution		15.00
		───

The company has forecast that demand for the product during 2013 will be 24,000 units. However to satisfy this level of demand, production of 35,294 units will be required because:

- 15% of the items delivered to customers (4,235 units) will be rejected as faulty and will require free replacement. The cost of delivering the replacement item is $5 per unit

- 20% of the items manufactured (7,059 units) will be discovered to be faulty before they are despatched to customers.

In addition, before production commences, 10% of the components that the company purchases are damaged while in storage.

As a consequence of all of the above, total quality costs for the year amount to $985,885. The company is now considering the following proposal:

(1) Spending $30,000 per annum on a quality inspector which would reduce the percentage of faulty items delivered to customers to 13%; and

(2) Spending $500,000 per annum on training courses for the production workers which management believes will reduce and sustain the level of faulty production to 10%.

Required:

(a) **Prepare a statement that shows the quality costs that the company would expect to incur if it accepted the above proposal. Your answer should clearly show the costs analysed using the four recognised quality cost headings.** **(7 marks)**

(b) **Recommend with reasons, whether or not the company should accept the proposal.** **(3 marks)**

(Total: 10 marks)

20 PRODUCT LIFECYCLE (SEPT 12)

A company has carried out extensive product research and as a result has just launched a new innovative product unlike anything else that is currently available on the market. The company has launched this product using a market skimming pricing policy.

The market in which it operates is highly competitive and historically success has been achieved by being the first to market with new products. Only a small number of companies have survived in the market and those that remain are constantly aiming to develop new products either by improving those already in the market or by extensive product research.

Required:

Explain, with reasons, the changes that the company may need to make to the unit selling price of the product as it moves through each of the four stages of its product life cycle.

(10 marks)

21   CUSTOMER LIFECYCLE COSTING (SEPT 11)

DTG is a management accounting consultancy that specialises in providing services to small businesses that do not have in-house expertise in management accounting techniques. Its clients vary in size and operate in many different sectors including manufacturing, retail and service industries. Although they are different, all clients require similar services most of which are provided by DTG's team of employed accountants and support staff. Occasionally DTG will engage the services of specialists on a one-off contract basis to help to solve the problem faced by a particular client.

Before accepting clients, DTG will meet with them to discuss their requirements and to agree the basis of their fees.

DTG has an ongoing relationship with many of its clients. This level of involvement within the client's business enables DTG to foresee potential problems for the client and offer further services. This works well for the clients and particularly well for DTG who gain a considerable number of new assignments in this way.

New clients tend to be initially for "one-off" assignments. Working with new clients requires time and effort to be invested to become familiar with the client's business and procedures. DTG hopes to form a relationship and attract more assignments and referrals from each client it works with.

Required:

Explain how Customer Life Cycle costing could be used by DTG.   **(10 marks)**

22   SF (NOV 11)

SF manufactures and sells a limited range of flat pack furniture. Due to the standardisation of its products, SF uses a standard costing system to monitor its performance. At the start of each financial year the company directors agree a set of standard costs for each of the company's products. Monthly variance reports are discussed at each monthly board meeting.

A few months ago the Production Director attended a conference on World Class Manufacturing and was very interested in a presentation on Kaizen Costing. The presenter illustrated how the use of Kaizen Costing had enabled her company to reduce its unit manufacturing costs by 20%.

Required:

(a)   **Explain the principles of Kaizen Costing.**   **(4 marks)**

(b)   **Discuss how Kaizen Costing conflicts with SF's current performance reporting procedures.**   **(6 marks)**

                                                                                    (Total: 10 marks)

23 LEARNING CURVES AND LABOUR VARIANCES (MAY 10)

The budget for the production cost of a new product was based on the following assumptions:

(i)   Time for the 1st batch of output = 10 hours

(ii)   Learning rate = 80%

(iii)   Learning will cease after 40 batches, and thereafter the time per batch will be the same as the time of the final batch during the learning period, i.e. the 40th batch

(iv)   Standard direct labour rate per hour = $12.00

An extract from the out-turn performance report based on the above budget is as follows:

	Budget	Actual	Variance
Output (batches)	60	50	10 adverse
Direct labour hours	163.53	93.65	69.88 favourable
Direct labour cost	$1,962	$1,146	$816 favourable

Further analysis has shown that, due to similarities between this product and another that was developed last year, the rate of learning that should have been expected was 70% and that the learning should have ceased after 30 batches. Other budget assumptions for the new product remain valid.

Required:

(a)   **Prepare a revised out-turn performance report for the new product that**

    (i)   **shows the flexed budgeted direct labour hours and direct labour cost based on the revised learning curve data, and**

    (ii)   **shows the variances that reconcile the actual results to your flexed budget in as much detail as possible.** **(7 marks)**

(b)   **Explain why your report is more useful to the production manager than the report shown above.** **(3 marks)**

Note: The learning index values for an 80% and a 70% learning curve are −0.3219 and −0.5146 respectively.

(Total: 10 marks)

24 LEARNING CURVES, PLANNING AND OPERATIONAL VARIANCES (SEPT 10)

 Walk in the footsteps of a top tutor

The following details show the direct labour requirements for the first six batches of a new product that were manufactured last month:

	Budget	Actual
Output (batches)	6	6
Labour hours	2,400	1,950
Total labour cost	$16,800	$13,650

The Management Accountant reported the following variances:

Total labour cost variance	$3,150 favourable
Labour rate variance	Nil
Labour efficiency variance	$3,150 favourable

The Production Manager has now said that he forgot to inform the Management Accountant that he expected a 90% learning curve to apply for at least the first 10 batches.

Required:

(a) **Calculate planning and operational variances that analyse the actual performance taking account of the anticipated learning effect.** **(6 marks)**

Note: The learning index for a 90% learning curve is –0.1520.

(b) **Explain the differences between standard costing and target costing.** **(4 marks)**

(Total: 10 marks)

25 BATCHES, LEARNING CURVES AND VARIANCES (MAR 11)

The standard direct labour cost of one batch of 100 units of a product is $50.40. This assumes a standard time of 4.2 hours, costing $12 per hour. The standard time of 4.2 direct labour hours is the average time expected per batch based on a product life of 12,800 units or 128 batches. The expected time for the first batch was 20 hours and an 80% learning curve is expected to apply throughout the product's life.

The company has now completed the production of 32 batches of the product and the total actual direct labour cost was $3,493. The following direct labour variances have also been calculated:

| Direct labour rate | $85 Adverse |
| Direct labour efficiency | $891 Adverse |

Further analysis has shown that the direct labour efficiency variance was caused solely by the actual rate of learning being different from that expected. However, the time taken for the first batch was 20 hours as expected.

Required:

(a) **Calculate the actual rate of learning that occurred.** **(6 marks)**

(b) **Assuming that the actual rate of learning and the actual labour rate continue throughout the life of the product, calculate the total direct labour cost that the company will incur during the life of the product.** **(4 marks)**

(Total: 10 marks)

26 LEARNING CURVES AND VARIANCES (NOV 10)

The following variances have been calculated in respect of a new product:

Direct labour efficiency variance	$14,700 Favourable
Direct labour rate variance	$5,250 Adverse

The variances were calculated using standard cost data which showed that each unit of the product was expected to take 8 hours to produce at a cost of $15 per hour. Actual output of the product was 560 units and actual time worked in the manufacture of the product totalled 3,500 hours at a cost of $57,750.

However, the production manager now realises that the standard time of 8 hours per unit was the time taken to produce the first unit and that a learning rate of 90% should have been anticipated for the first 600 units.

Required:

(a) Calculate planning and operating variances following the recognition of the learning curve effect. **(6 marks)**

(b) Explain the importance of learning curves in the context of target costing. **(4 marks)**

Note: The learning index for a 90% learning curve is –0.1520 **(Total: 10 marks)**

27 LEARNING CURVES AND SENSITIVITY (MAY 13)

A new product has a budgeted total profit of $75,000 from the first 64 units. The time taken to produce the first unit was 225 hours. The labour rate is $40 per hour. A 90% learning curve is expected to apply indefinitely.

Note: The learning index for a 90% learning curve is-0.152

Required:

Calculate the sensitivity of the budgeted total profit from the first 64 units to independent changes in:

(i) The labour rate

(ii) The learning rate. **(Total: 10 marks)**

28 LEARNING AND SENSITIVITY (SEPT 13)

The standard selling price and costs per unit of a new product for the first period are shown below:

		$
Selling price		750
Materials	6 kg at $50 per kg	300
Labour (see below)	20 hours at $10 per hour	200
Variable overheads	25 machine hours at $4 per machine hour	100
Fixed overheads (see below)		120

Labour hours

The labour hours are the average labour hours per unit based on the budgeted output for the period of 128 units and the assumption that a 90% learning curve will apply throughout the period. The learning index for a 90% learning curve is -0.152.

Fixed overheads

The fixed overheads are specific fixed overheads for this product and the absorption rate was based on the budgeted output for the period of 128 units.

Required:

(a) Calculate the sensitivity of the budgeted profit for the period for this product to a change in the price per kg of materials. **(2 marks)**

(b) Calculate the budgeted labour hours for the first unit of this product to be produced. **(4 marks)**

(c) Calculate the sensitivity of the budgeted profit for the period for this product to a change in the rate of learning. **(4 marks)**

Note: all workings must be shown. **(Total: 10 marks)**

29 TOTAL COST PLUS PRICING AND TARGET COSTING (MAY 12)

A company uses "total cost plus" pricing. Recent results show that profits are falling and that the company is losing market share in what is becoming a very competitive market.

Required:

(a) Explain TWO disadvantages of "total cost plus" pricing. **(4 marks)**

(b) Explain how target costing could be of benefit to the company. **(6 marks)**

(Total: 10 marks)

30 LEARNING CURVES AND GAIN SHARING ARRANGEMENTS (NOV 08)

(a) A manufacturing company has developed a new product. The time taken to manufacture the first unit was 24 minutes. It is expected that an 80% learning curve will apply for the first three months of production and that by the end of that period the total number of units produced will have reached 1,024. It is then expected that the time taken for each subsequent unit will be the same as the time taken for the 1,024th unit.

Required:

(i) Calculate the expected time taken for the 8th unit. **(3 marks)**

(ii) Explain two reasons why the time taken for the 1025th unit may be more than expected. **(2 marks)**

Note: The value of the 80% learning index is −0.3219

(b) Explain the importance of considering the learning curve when deciding on the terms for a gain sharing arrangement with employees. **(5 marks)**

(Total: 10 marks)

31 LEARNING CURVES AND TARGETS (MAR 12)

A company has developed a new product which it will launch next month. During the initial production phase the company expects to produce 6,400 units in batches of 100 units. The first batch to be produced is expected to require 25 hours of direct labour. The following details are expected to apply throughout the initial production phase:

Direct material cost per unit is expected to be $4; Direct labour is to be paid $10 per hour.

A 90% learning curve is expected to apply. Other variable costs are expected to be $2 per unit.

Note: The learning index for a 90% learning curve is –0.1520

Required:

(a) **Calculate the total variable cost of the 6,400 units of the new product.** **(4 marks)**

You have shown your calculation to the Finance Director who has now told you that the company needs to achieve a total variable cost target of $45,000 for the first 6,400 units in order to achieve its initial production phase profit target.

(b) **Calculate the rate of learning at which the initial production phase profit target would be achieved, assuming no other cost savings can be made.** **(6 marks)**

(Total: 10 marks)

32 LIFETIME, LIFECYCLE (MAY 12)

A company is developing a new product. During its expected life it is expected that 8,000 units of the product will be sold for $90 per unit.

The direct material and other non-labour related costs will be $45 per unit throughout the life of the product.

Production will be in batches of 1,000 units throughout the life of the product. The direct labour cost is expected to reduce due to the effects of learning for the first four batches produced. Thereafter the labour cost will remain at the same cost per batch as the 4th batch. The direct labour cost of the first batch of 1,000 units is expected to be $40,000 and a 90% learning effect is expected to occur.

There are no fixed costs that are specific to the product.

Required:

(a) **(i)** **Calculate the average direct labour cost per batch of the first four batches.**

(2 marks)

(ii) **Calculate the direct labour cost of the 4th batch.** **(2 marks)**

(iii) **Calculate the contribution earned from the product over its lifetime.**

(2 marks)

Note: The learning index for a 90% learning curve = –0.152

Due to the low lifetime product volume of 8,000 units the company now believes that learning may continue throughout its entire product life.

(b) **Calculate the rate of learning required (to the nearest whole percentage) to achieve a lifetime product contribution target of $150,000, assuming that a constant rate of learning applies throughout the product's life.** **(4 marks)**

(Total: 10 marks)

33 PR AND JIT (MAR 11)

PR currently uses a constant flow production system to manufacture components for the motor industry. The demand from the motor industry is higher in certain months of the year and lower in others. PR holds inventory so that it can supply the components as they are demanded. Increasingly, the costs to PR of holding inventory are having a significant effect on its profits and the management of PR are considering changing the production system to one that operates on a just-in-time (JIT) basis.

Required:

(a) Explain the concepts of a JIT production system. (4 marks)

(b) Explain TWO reasons why the profit of PR may NOT increase as a result of changing to a JIT production system. (6 marks)

(Total: 10 marks)

34 OVERTIME WORKING (MAY 12)

A company has predicted its sales demand for each of the four quarters of 2013 as follows:

Quarter	1	2	3	4
Sales volume (units)	100,000	110,000	190,000	140,000

The company has a normal production capacity of 135,000 units per quarter without needing to utilise any overtime working. However the capacity can be increased by up to 40% by working overtime.

It is current company policy to manufacture units using a constant level production system. This means that although the opening and closing levels of inventory for the year are zero units there are increases and decreases in the quarterly inventory levels. On this basis the selling price, variable production costs and contribution for 2013 are expected to be as follows:

		$ per unit
Selling price		90.00
Direct materials	30.00	
Direct labour	35.00	
Variable production overhead	10.00	75.00
		─────
Contribution		15.00
		─────

However, any overtime working will increase the unit direct labour cost by 50% and the unit variable production overhead cost by 30% for those units produced during overtime working.

In addition, the company incurs a storage cost of $4 per unit per quarter for each item that is held in inventory. These costs are not included in the production costs above.

The company is considering whether it should change to a just-in-time (JIT) production system, but is concerned that due to the fluctuating levels of its sales demand this may not be financially beneficial. If the company did change to a JIT production system:

- No inventory would be held.

- There would be no change in the behaviour of variable production costs.

Required:

(a) Calculate the cost of holding inventory (based on average inventory levels in each of the quarters) for each of the quarters and the year in total under the current production system. Assume that sales occur evenly during each quarter.   (4 marks)

(b) Calculate the financial impact of changing to a JIT production system.   (6 marks)

(Total: 10 marks)

35   LEARNING CURVES AND BREAKEVEN (SEPT 12)

A company is developing a new product. During its expected life it is forecast that 6,400 units of the product will be sold for $70 per unit.

The direct material and other non-labour related costs are expected to be $45 per unit throughout the life of the product.

Production is expected to be in batches of 100 units throughout the life of the product. The direct labour cost is expected to reduce due to the effects of learning throughout the life of the product. The total direct labour cost of the first batch of 100 units is expected to be $6,000 and an 80% learning effect is expected to occur.

Fixed costs specific to this product are expected to be $60,000 in total for the life of the product.

Note: The value of the learning index for an 80% learning curve is –0.3219

Required:

(a) Calculate the total direct labour cost of the first:

   (i)   800 units

   (ii)   1,600 units

   (iii)   3,200 units

   (iv)   6,400 units   (4 marks)

(b) Apply the results from part (a) to advise the company management of the approximate break-even level of sales of the product.   (3 marks)

(c) Explain the effect on the break-even level of sales if the rate of learning was 90%. (No calculations are required.)   (3 marks)

(Total: 10 marks)

36   NEW PRODUCT (NOV 12)

A company has developed a new product. The following information was prepared by the trainee accountant for presentation at the first performance review meeting for the new product.

Standard labour wage rate	$12 per labour hour
Standard labour hours per unit	25 hours
Output to date	32 units
Actual labour hours worked	460 hours
Labour efficiency variance	$4,080 favourable

The Management Accountant pointed out that this analysis ignored the learning curve and that 25 hours was the time taken for the first unit. The Management Accountant said that a better representation of the performance would be obtained by splitting the variance into planning and operating elements and calculated them to be as shown below:

Labour efficiency planning variance	$4,320 favourable
Labour efficiency operating variance	$240 adverse

Required:

(a)   Calculate the learning rate that the Management Accountant assumed when recalculating the variances.   **(6 marks)**

(b)   Explain TWO reasons why it is important for production planning and control purposes to identify the learning curve.   **(4 marks)**

(Total: 10 marks)

37   LEARNING CURVES AND BREAKEVEN (MAR 13)

A company has developed a new product that has a short life cycle. Information about the product is as follows:

Selling price and product life cycle

The product will have a life cycle of 4,000 units. It is estimated that the first 3,500 units will be sold for $215 each. The product will then enter the "decline" stage of its life cycle when the selling price will be reduced.

Production and costs

The product will be produced in batches of 100 units.

Labour will be paid at $24 per hour. Other variable costs will be $6,000 per batch. Fixed costs will total $130,000. These costs will apply throughout the product's life.

Learning curve

The first batch will take 500 labour hours to produce. There will be a 90% learning curve that will continue until 32 batches have been produced. Every batch produced above this level of output will take the same amount of labour time as the 32nd batch.

Note: The learning index for a 90% learning curve = -0.152

Required:

(a)   Calculate the time taken for the 32nd batch.   **(4 marks)**

(b)   Calculate the selling price of the final 500 units that will allow the company to earn a total profit of $150,000 from the product   **(6 marks)**

(Total: 10 marks)

38 XY COMPANY (MAY 10)

XY, a company that manufactures a range of timber products, is considering changing to a just-in-time (JIT) production system.

Currently XY employs staff who are contracted to work and be paid for a total of 3,937.75 hours per month. Their labour efficiency ratio is 96% and, as a result, they are able to produce 3,780 standard hours of output each month in normal working hours.

Overtime working is used to meet additional demand, though the management of XY try to avoid the need for this because it is paid at a 50% premium to the normal hourly rate of $10 per hour. Instead, XY plan production so that in months of lower demand inventory levels increase to enable sales demand to be met in other months. XY has determined that the cost of holding inventory is $6 per month for each standard hour of output that is held in inventory.

XY has forecast the demand for its products for the next six months as follows:

Month	Demand (standard hours)
1	3,100
2	3,700
3	4,000
4	3,300
5	3,600
6	4,980

You may assume that all production costs (other than labour) are either fixed or are not driven by labour hours worked, and that there is zero inventory at the start of month 1 and at the end of month 6. Assume also that production and sales occur evenly during each month at present, and that the minimum contracted hours will remain the same with the JIT system.

Required:

(a)   With the current production system,

   (I)   Calculate for each of the six months and the period in total, the total inventory holding costs.

   (ii)   Calculate the total production cost savings made by changing to a JIT production system. **(6 marks)**

(b)   Explain TWO other factors that should be considered by XY before changing to a JIT production system. **(4 marks)**

(Total: 10 marks)

39 XY ACCOUNTANCY SERVICES (NOV 10)

XY provides accountancy services and has three different categories of client: limited companies, self employed individuals, and employed individuals requiring taxation advice. XY currently charges its clients a fee by adding a 20% mark-up to total costs. Currently the costs are attributed to each client based on the hours spent on preparing accounts and providing advice.

XY is considering changing to an activity based costing system. The annual costs and the causes of these costs have been analysed as follows:

	$
Accounts preparation and advice	580,000
Requesting missing information	30,000
Issuing fee payment reminders	15,000
Holding client meetings	60,000
Travelling to clients	40,000

The following details relate to three of XY's clients and to XY as a whole:

	Client			XY
	A	B	C	
Hours spent on preparing accounts and providing advice	1,000	250	340	18,000
Requests for missing information	4	10	6	250
Payment reminders sent	2	8	10	400
Client meetings held	4	1	2	250
Miles travelled to meet clients	150	600	0	10,000

Required:

Prepare calculations to show the effect on fees charged to each of these three clients of changing to the new costing system. **(10 marks)**

40 FACTORY ABC (SEPT 13)

A factory uses a standard absorption costing system. The fixed production overhead absorption rate is based on labour hours. Extracts from the budgeted and actual results for the previous period are shown below:

	Budget	Actual
Output (units)	1,500	1,600
Fixed production overhead	$300,000	$310,000
Labour hours	600	580

Required:

(a) Calculate:

(i) The fixed production overhead expenditure variance

(ii) The fixed production overhead volume variance **(3 marks)**

The factory is thinking of introducing an activity based costing system. An analysis of the fixed production overheads for the previous period showed that included in the budgeted fixed production overheads of $300,000 was $72,000 for materials handling. Costs for materials handling are incurred when materials are shipped from the storage area to the processing plant. Further analysis revealed:

	Budget	Actual
Materials handling costs	$72,000	$69,000
Number of material shipments	90	85
Total quantity of materials shipped	360 tonne	348 tonne

Required:

(b)   Calculate using activity based costing principles:

     (i)   The materials handling shipment expenditure variance

     (ii)   The materials handling shipment efficiency variance   **(7 marks)**

(Total: 10 marks)

41   HIERARCHY OF ACTIVITIES (SEPT 13)

Required:

Discuss how activity based costing could improve the linkage between cost control and responsibility accounting at each of the four levels of the activity based costing hierarchy of activities.   **(10 marks)**

42   DCPA (SEPT 10)

ST is a distribution company which buys a product in bulk from manufacturers, repackages the product into smaller packs and then sells the packs to retail customers. ST's customers vary in size and consequently the size and frequency of their orders also varies. Some customers order large quantities from ST each time they place an order. Other customers order only a few packs each time.

The current accounting system of ST produces very basic management information that reports only the overall company profit. ST is therefore unaware of the costs of servicing individual customers. However, the company has now decided to investigate the use of Direct Customer Profitability Analysis (DCPA).

ST would like to see the results from a small sample of customers before it decides whether to fully introduce DCPA.

The information for two customers, and for the whole company, for the previous period was as follows:

	Customer B	Customer D	Company
Factory contribution ($000)	75	40.5	450
Number of:			
Packs sold (000)	50	27	300
Sales visits to customers	24	12	200
Orders placed by customers	75	20	700
Normal deliveries to customers	45	15	240
Urgent deliveries to customers	5	0	30

Activity costs:	$000s
Sales visits to customers	50
Processing orders placed by customers	70
Normal deliveries to customers	120
Urgent deliveries to customers	60

Required:

(a) **Prepare a Direct Customer Profitability Analysis for each of the two customers.**

(6 marks)

(b) **Explain how ST could use DCPA to increase its profits.** (4 marks)

(Total: 10 marks)

43 TREE FARM (MAY 13)

A tree farm supplies shrubs to two customers. Each shrub has a selling price of $60. It costs $25 to grow a shrub and get it to the point of sale. Additional costs incurred by the farm are $100 per order fulfilled and delivery costs of $500 per order delivered.

Details of two of the farm's customers (B and C) for the previous period are as follows:

	Customer B	Customer C
Shrubs purchased	960	650
Discount allowed	15%	20%
Orders fulfilled	8 (each for 120 shrubs)	10 (each for less than 100 shrubs)
Deliveries made	8	0

Customers are given a 15% discount on orders for 100 shrubs or more.

Customer C is given a 20% discount for collecting the shrubs using its own transport.

Required:

Evaluate the two customers. (Your answer should include customer profitability statements and appropriate measures.) (10 marks)

44 SOFTWARE DEVELOPMENT (MAY 09)

A software development company sells three software products: AXPL1, FDR2 and VBG3. The company's marketing department adds a 25% mark-up to product costs to calculate the selling prices of the company's products. The current selling prices are based on the product costs that were calculated using a traditional absorption costing system. The company has just installed an activity based costing system and consequently changed its working practices with the result that all costs are now treated as effectively variable. The marketing department has not yet been informed about the revised product costs.

The company has carried out some market research and there is a linear relationship between the price it charges for its software products and the resulting market share. The research shows that a change in price causes there to be a proportionate change in market share. A summary of the research shows that for every $2 increase in selling price there would be a 3% reduction in market share and for every $2 decrease in selling price there would be a 3% increase in market share. For example, if the selling price of AXPL1 were to be increased to $52 per unit its market share would reduce to 42%.

The following data relate to the three software products:

	AXPL1	FDR2	VBG3
Current unit selling price ($)	50.00	75.00	65.00
Current market share %	45%	15%	80%
Market size for the remaining life of the product (units)	2,500	3,000	4,000
Activity based cost per unit ($)	48.00	42.00	75.00

Required:

(a) **Explain, using the above information, why VBG3 currently has a high market share.**

(3 marks)

(b) **The marketing department is now considering using the new product costings to set the selling price by adding 25% mark-up to the unit Activity Based Cost.**

Calculate the impact on the remaining lifetime profits of each software product and the company as a result of the marketing department using this approach.

(7 marks)

45 PQ BUILDING (MARCH 13)

PQ is a building supplies retailer that operates a chain of shops throughout the country. The company has grown rapidly but profits have started to fall. The company has an excellent Inventory Procurement and Management System but the accounting systems are very poor. A management accountant has recently been appointed to help improve decision making within the company.

The company sells building supplies, ranging from bags of nails and screws to pre-packed kitchen units, to a wide range of customers including home owners and professional builders. The company offers a free delivery service on all orders totalling over $100.

Within each shop there are specialist sections that have skilled staff to offer help and advice to customers. Examples include:

- The "Design Station" which offers free advice on kitchen and bathroom installation and design.

- The "Cutting Bay" which cuts timber to customers' specific requirements. There is no charge for this service.

Other areas of the shop are "help yourself" where customers select their requirements from racked displays of products and then pay at the check-out points.

The recently appointed management accountant was shocked to discover that the company's pricing policy is to add a 100% mark-up to the bought in cost of all products. The management accountant has suggested that the mark-up should not be the same for all products because certain products and certain types of customer will be more costly to sell and service respectively. The management accountant has suggested that an activity based costing system should be introduced to allow Direct Product Profitability and Customer Profitability Analyses to take place.

Required:

(a) **Explain how the allocation and absorption of costs differs in activity based costing compared to traditional absorption costing.** **(4 marks)**

(b) **Explain how activity based costing could help to increase the profits of PQ.**

(6 marks)

(Total: 10 marks)

46 QW (NOV 10)

QW is a company that manufactures machine parts from sheet metal to specific customer order for industrial customers. QW is considering diversification into the production of metal ornaments. The ornaments would be produced at a constant rate throughout the year. It then plans to sell these ornaments from inventory through wholesalers and via direct mail to consumers.

Presently, each of the machine parts is specific to a customer's order. Consequently, the company does not hold an inventory of finished items but it does hold the equivalent of one day's production of sheet metal so as to reduce the risk of being unable to produce goods demanded by customers at short notice. There is a one day lead time for delivery of sheet metal to QW from its main supplier though additional supplies could be obtained at less competitive prices.

Demand for these industrial goods is such that delivery is required almost immediately after the receipt of the customer order. QW is aware that if it is unable to meet an order immediately the industrial customer would seek an alternative supplier, despite QW having a reputation for high quality machine parts.

The management of QW is not aware of the implications of the diversification for its production and inventory policies.

Required:

(a) **Compare and contrast QW's present production and inventory policy and practices with a traditional production system that uses constant production levels and holds inventory to meet peaks of demand.** (5 marks)

(b) **Discuss the importance of a Total Quality Management (TQM) system in a just-in-time (JIT) environment. Use QW to illustrate your discussion.** (5 marks)

(Total: 10 marks)

47 VALUE AND FUNCTIONAL ANALYSIS (MAY 06)

A firm of financial advisors has established itself by providing high quality, personalised, financial strategy advice. The firm promotes itself by sponsoring local events, advertising, client newsletters, having a flexible attitude towards the times and locations of meetings with clients and seeking new and innovative ideas to discuss with its clients.

The senior manager of the firm has recently noticed that the firm's profitability has declined, with fewer clients being interested in the firm's new investment ideas. Indeed, many clients have admitted to not reading the firm's newsletters.

The senior manager seeks your help in restoring the firm's profitability to its former level and believes that the techniques of value analysis and functional analysis may be appropriate.

Required:

(a) **Explain the meanings of, and the differences between, value analysis and functional analysis.** (4 marks)

(b) **Briefly explain the series of steps that you would take to implement value analysis for this organisation.** (6 marks)

(Total: 10 marks)

48 ZX AND TQM (MAR 11)

ZX is a new banking organisation which is about to open its first branches. ZX believes that it needs to offer potential customers a new banking experience if it is to win customers from other banks.

Whereas other banks have focused on interest rates and levels of bank charges, ZX believes that quality and availability of service is an important factor in the choice made by customers.

Required:

Explain how Total Quality Management (TQM) would enable ZX to gain competitive advantage in the banking sector. **(10 marks)**

49 TQM (MAY 09)

You have recently been appointed as a company's Assistant Management Accountant. The company has recently begun operating a just-in-time production system but is having problems in meeting the demands of its customers because of quality failures within its production function. Previously, the company used to hold sufficient levels of finished goods inventory so that quality problems did not lead to lost sales. However, it was costly to hold high inventories and, as a result, the company decided to adopt the just-in-time approach. The Production Director believes that higher expenditure on Compliance costs is necessary to avoid the costs of Non-compliance, but he is having difficulty convincing the Managing Director and seeks your help.

Required:

Prepare a report addressed to the Managing Director that

- **explains briefly the principles of Total Quality Management**

- **explains the four categories of quality costs**

- **and explains the relationship between Compliance and Non-compliance costs in the context of Total Quality Management.** **(10 marks)**

50 CAL (NOV 10)

CAL manufactures and sells solar panels for garden lights. Components are bought in and assembled into metal frames that are machine manufactured by CAL. There are a number of alternative suppliers of these solar panels. Some of CAL's competitors charge a lower price, but supply lower quality panels; whereas others supply higher quality panels than CAL but for a much higher price.

CAL is preparing its budgets for the coming year and has estimated that the market demand for its type of solar panels will be 100,000 units and that its share will be 20,000 units (i.e. 20% of the available market). The standard cost details of each solar panel are as follows:

		$ per unit
Selling price		60
Bought-in components (1 set)	15	
Assembly & machining cost	25	
Delivery cost	5	45
		—
Contribution		**15**

An analysis of CAL's recent performance revealed that 2% of the solar panels supplied to customers were returned for free replacement, because the customer found that they were faulty. Investigation of these returned items shows that the components had been damaged when they had been assembled into the metal frame. These returned panels cannot be repaired and have no scrap value. If the supply of faulty solar panels to customers could be eliminated then, due to improved customer perception, CAL's market share would increase to 25%.

Required:

(a)   Explain, with reference to CAL, quality conformance costs and quality non-conformance costs and the relationship between them.   **(4 marks)**

(b)   Assuming that CAL continues with its present systems and that the percentage of quality failings is as stated above:

   (i)   Calculate, based on the budgeted figures and sales returns rate, the total relevant costs of quality for the coming year.   **(4 marks)**

   (ii)   Calculate the maximum saving that could be made by implementing an inspection process for the solar panels, immediately before the goods are delivered.   **(2 marks)**

(Total: 10 marks)

51   ZZ GROOMING (MAR 13)

ZZ manufactures and sells electronic personal grooming and beauty products. The products are sold throughout the world and 90% of ZZ's total revenue comes from export sales. The production takes place in one factory. Materials are sourced from a variety of suppliers.

The company is keen to build a reputation for quality and gives a five year guarantee with all of its products. The Managing Director of ZZ recently issued a memo to all of the company's managers which stated "My objective for the forthcoming year is to reduce our quality costs in each of the primary activities in our value chain".

Required:

(a)   State the primary activities in the value chain of a manufacturing company.

(2 marks)

(b)   Explain, by giving examples, how each of the FOUR types of quality cost could be reduced. You should identify in which primary activity each one of your examples would occur in ZZ's value chain.   **(8 marks)**

(Total: 10 marks)

52 LCG (NOV 11)

LCG was established in 1998 and manufactures a range of garden tables and chairs which it makes from timber purchased from a number of suppliers.

The recently appointed Managing Director has expressed increasing concern about the trends in falling sales volumes, rising costs and hence declining profits over the last two years. There is general agreement amongst the managers of LCG that these trends are the result of the increased intense competition that has emerged over the last two years. LCG continues to have a reputation for high quality but this quality is now being matched by the competition.

The competitors are taking LCG's share of the market by selling equivalent products at lower prices. It is thought that in order to offer such low prices the production costs of the competitors must be lower than LCG's.

Required:

Discuss how LCG could improve its sales volumes, costs and profits by using (i) value analysis and (ii) functional cost analysis. **(10 marks)**

53 BUSINESS PROCESS RE-ENGINEERING (MAR 12)

MLC, which was established in 1998, manufactures a range of garden sheds and summerhouses using timber purchased from a number of suppliers.

The recently appointed managing director has expressed increasing concern about the falling sales volumes, rising costs and hence declining profits over the last two years.

Required:

Discuss how business process re-engineering could help to improve the profits of MLC.
(10 marks)

54 INBOUND CALL CENTRES (SEPT 13)

Many service organisations, for example banks, have outsourced their customer liaison and support service operations to "inbound call centres". Inbound call centres deal with product support or information enquiries from customers.

Required:

Explain, in the context of the modern business environment, the advantages and disadvantages of outsourcing customer liaison and product support to "inbound call centres". **(10 marks)**

BUDGETING AND MANAGEMENT CONTROL

55   ENGINEERING (NOV 12)

A newly formed engineering company has just completed its first three months of trading. The company manufactures only one type of product. The external accountant for the company has produced the following statement to present at a meeting to review performance for the first quarter.

Performance report for the quarter ending 31 October 2012

	Budget		Actual		Variance
Sales units		12,000		13,000	1,000
Production units		14,000		13,500	(500)
	$000	$000	$000	$000	$000
Sales		360		385	25
Direct materials	70		69		1
Direct labour	140		132		8
Variable production overhead	42		43		(1)
Fixed production overhead	84		85		(1)
Inventory adjustment	(48)		(12)		(36)
Cost of sales		288		317	(29)
Gross profit		72		68	(4)

The external accountant has stated that he values inventory at the budgeted total production cost per unit.

Required:

(a)   **Produce an amended statement for the quarter ending 31 October 2012 that is based on a flexed budget.**   **(6 marks)**

(b)   **Explain ONE benefit and ONE limitation of the statement you have produced.**
                                                                                  (4 marks)

                                                                  (Total: 10 marks)

56   DW TRANSPORT (NOV 10)

DW, a transport company, operates three depots. Each depot has a manager who reports directly to the Operations Director.

For many years the depot managers have been asked by the Operations Director to prepare a budget for their depot as part of the company's annual budgeting process. A new depot manager has been appointed to the Southern region and he has concerns about the validity of these annual budgets. He argues that they soon become out of date as operational circumstances change. At a recent manager's meeting he said, "They are restrictive. They do not permit the depot managers to make decisions in response to operational changes, or change working practices for next year until that year's budget has been approved."

Required:

(a)   **Explain the differences between the above annual budgeting system and a rolling budget system.**   **(4 marks)**

(b)   **Discuss how the Southern region depot manager could use a rolling budget system to address his concerns.**   **(6 marks)**

                                                                                                        (Total: 10 marks)

57   RESPONSIBILITY ACCOUNTING

Z Limited produces signs and labels for a number of businesses. Some of the signs are produced on vinyl and then fixed to vehicles and display panels whereas others are produced on metal and fixe to machinery and equipment to indicate how they are to be operated safely.

For some time the managers of Z Limited have complained that the responsibility accounting system is unfair. Managers are given targets that have been set by the Board of Directors and are expected to achieve the targets, regardless of the level of actual activity and any changes that may have occurred since the targets were set.

Required:

(a)   **Explain the meaning of responsibility accounting.**   **(3 marks)**

(b)   **Discuss the implications of the scenario described above and describe the changes that could be made to improve acceptance by managers of the responsibility accounting system.**   **(7 marks)**

                                                                                                        (Total: 10 marks)

58 CONTROLLABILITY (MAY 11)

SFG is a national hotel group that operates more than 100 hotels. The performance of the manager of each hotel is evaluated using financial measures.

Many of the hotel's managers are not happy. They believe that there can be conflict between good performance and achieving short-term profits. They are also unhappy that their profit reports include a share of head office costs and other costs that they cannot control.

Required:

(a) Explain why non-financial performance measures are important in the service sector. **(2 marks)**

(b) Recommend, with reasons, TWO non-financial performance measures that SFG could use to evaluate the performance of the hotel managers. **(4 marks)**

(c) Explain why, and how, non-controllable costs should be shown on the profit reports. **(4 marks)**

(Total: 10 marks)

59 SOLICITORS (MAY 10)

A firm of solicitors is using budgetary control during 2010. The senior partner estimated the demand for the year for each of the firm's four divisions: Civil, Criminal, Corporate, and Property. A separate partner is responsible for each division.

Each divisional partner then prepared a cost budget based on the senior partner's demand estimate for the division. These budgets were then submitted to the senior partner for his approval. He then amended them as he thought appropriate before issuing each divisional partner with the final budget for the division. He did not discuss these amendments with the respective divisional partners. Actual performance is then measured against the final budgets for each month and each divisional partner's performance is appraised by asking the divisional partner to explain the reasons for any variances that occur.

The Corporate partner has been asked to explain why her staff costs exceeded the budgeted costs for last month while the chargeable time was less than budgeted. Her reply is below:

"My own original estimate of staff costs was higher than the final budgeted costs shown on my divisional performance report. In my own cost budget I allowed for time to be spent developing new services for the firm's corporate clients and improving the clients' access to their own case files. This would improve the quality of our services to clients and therefore increase client satisfaction. The trouble with our present system is that it focuses on financial performance and ignores the other performance indicators found in modern performance management systems."

Required:

(a) Discuss the present budgeting system and its likely effect on divisional partner motivation. **(6 marks)**

(b) Explain two non-financial performance indicators (other than client satisfaction and service quality) that could be used by the firm. **(4 marks)**

(Total: 10 marks)

60   SD KAIZEN (MAR 12)

SD manufactures and sells a small range of timber products. The main differences between the products are their size and the type of timber used. SD prepares annual budgets and sets a standard cost for each different product at the start of each year. Variance reports are produced every month.

Recently, there have been significant differences between the actual costs and standard costs of the products manufactured.

SD recently introduced a system of Kaizen Costing which has resulted in changes to the methods used to manufacture the timber products.

Some of the directors have suggested that the use of standard costs as a means of monitoring performance is no longer appropriate and that the monthly variance report is meaningless.

Required:

(a)   **Explain the principles of Kaizen Costing.**   **(4 marks)**

(b)   **Discuss how SD can use standard costing and variance analysis to prepare meaningful reports when using Kaizen Costing.**   **(6 marks)**

(Total: 10 marks)

61   AIRLINE BSC (NOV 11)

An airline company has operated short haul passenger and cargo flights to various destinations from a busy airport for several years. Its competitive advantage has been the fact that it offers low ticket prices to passengers. It now faces increased competition on a number of its routes.

The company currently monitors its performance using financial measures. These financial measures have served it well in the past, but a new director has suggested that non-financial measures may also be used to provide a better indication of overall performance. She has suggested that the company should consider using the Balanced Scorecard.

Required:

(a)   **Explain the concepts of the Balanced Scorecard and how it could be used by the airline company.**   **(6 marks)**

(b)   **Explain TWO non-financial measures that the airline company could use to monitor its performance.**   **(4 marks)**

(Total: 10 marks)

62   COLLEGE (MAR 12)

A college currently measures its performance by comparing its actual costs against its budgeted costs for the year. Now that the college is facing increased competition from other colleges and private education providers, one of its professors has suggested that it needs to consider additional performance measures such as those indicated by the Balanced Scorecard.

Required:

(a)   Explain the concepts of the Balanced Scorecard and how this approach to performance measurement could be used by the college.   **(6 marks)**

(b)   Explain TWO non-financial measures (chosen from different perspectives of the balanced scorecard) that the college could use to measure its performance.

(4 marks)

(Total: 10 marks)

63   WX CONSULTANCY (NOV 11)

WX, a consultancy company, is preparing its budgets for the year to 31 December 2012. The directors of the company have stated that they would like to reduce the company's overdraft to zero by 30 June 2012 and to have a positive cash balance of $145,000 by the end of the year. In addition, the directors would like to achieve a 20% growth in sales revenue compared to 2011 and a pre-tax profit of $180,000 for the year.

Required:

Illustrate the differences between feedforward control and feedback control using the above information about WX's cash budget.   **(10 marks)**

64   FEEDBACK AND FEEDFORWARD (SEPT 13)

Required:

Compare and contrast feedforward and feedback controls by using a budgeting system to explain your points.   **(10 marks)**

65   TRANSPORT COMPANY (MAR 12)

A transport company is preparing its cost budgets for the coming year. It has been set both social objectives and cost targets by the government which it must achieve in order to receive a subsidy. Part of the subsidy is paid when acceptable budgets have been submitted to the government's transport office and the balance is payable at the end of the year provided the company has achieved its social objectives and cost targets.

The first draft of the cost budgets has been completed and submitted to the budget committee.

Required:

Explain to the Board of Directors how

(i)   feedforward control; and

(ii)   feedback control

should be used in the transport company. (You should use examples from the company's budgeting system in your answer.)   **(10 marks)**

66   ZERO BASED BUDGETING (MAY 13)

PP is a telecoms provider. It has been operating for five years and has experienced good results; profits have increased by an average of 15% each year. It is accepted within the company that this success has been the result of the continuous stream of new and varied 'cutting edge' products that PP offers. The Research and Development Division has enjoyed the freedom of working with the directive of "Be creative".

The Director of the Research and Development Division of PP is not happy. At a recent board meeting she said:

"The Research and Development Division is finding it extremely difficult to maintain its current levels of achievement. The Division is suffering from a lack of funds as a result of PP's budgeting system. We receive an uplift of 5% each year from the previous year's budget. This does not provide the necessary funds or freedom to be able to keep the company ahead of the competition. I would like to see incremental budgeting replaced by zero based budgeting in my division".

Required:

Discuss the potential disadvantages of implementing zero based budgeting for the allocation of funds to the Research and Development Division from the perspective of the Director of Research and Development. **(10 marks)**

67   CW RETAIL (SEPT 10)

CW is a retail company that operates five stores. Each store has a manager and there is also a General Manager who reports directly to the Board of directors of the company.

For many years the General Manager has set the budgets for each store and the store managers' performances have been measured against their respective budgets even though they did not actively participate in their preparation. If a store manager meets his budgeted target then he is financially rewarded for his performance.

The company has recently appointed a new Finance Director who has questioned this previous practice and suggested that each store manager should be involved in the preparation of their own budget. The General Manager is very concerned about this. She thinks that the store managers will overstate their costs and resource requirements in order to make it easier for them to achieve their budget targets.

Required:

(a)   **Explain the problems that could arise, for planning and decision making purposes within CW, if the store managers did overstate their budgeted costs and resource requirements.** **(4 marks)**

(b)   **Discuss the behavioural issues that could arise if excess costs and resources are removed from the store managers' budgets.** **(6 marks)**

(Total: 10 marks)

68   BUDGETING IN COLLEGE (MAR 11)

A college is preparing its budget for 2012. In previous years the director of the college has prepared the college budget without the participation of senior staff and presented it to the college board for approval.

Last year the college board criticised the director over the lack of participation of his senior staff in the preparation of the budget for 2011 and requested that for the 2012 budget the senior staff were to be involved.

Required:

Discuss the potential advantages and disadvantages to the college of involving the senior staff in the budget preparation process.   **(10 marks)**

69   KL RAIL TRANSPORT (NOV 12)

KL is a transport company that has recently won a five-year government contract to provide rail transport services. The company appointed a new Director to take responsibility for the government contract. She has worked in various positions in other rail transport companies for a number of years. She has put together a team of managers by recruiting some of her former colleagues and some of KL's current managers.

The contract stipulates that the company should prepare detailed budgets for its first year of operations to show how it intends to meet the various operating targets that are stated in the contract. The new Director is undecided about whether she should prepare the budgets herself or whether she should involve her management team, including the newly recruited managers, in the process.

Required:

Produce a report, addressed to the new Director, that discusses participative budgeting.

Note: your report must

- **explain TWO potential benefits and TWO potential disadvantages of involving the new and existing managers in the budget setting process.**

- **provide a recommendation to the new Director.**   **(10 marks)**

70 SUMMARY STATEMENT (MAY 12)

A company has prepared the following summary from its functional budgets for the year ended 30th September 2013.

	$000	$000
Sales (100,000 units)		1,500
Opening inventory (zero units)	nil	
Production costs (115,000 units):		
Direct materials	460	
Direct labour	575	
Variable overhead	115	
Fixed overhead	230	
	1,380	
Closing inventory (15,000 units)	180	
Cost of sales		1,200
Gross profit		300
Other overhead costs		200
Net profit		100

The directors of the company have now met to review the above statement. They have decided to revise the budget as follows:

- Due to competition, reduce the selling price by $5 per unit and despite the reduction in selling price the demand for the product will reduce to 90,000 units.

- Increase some of the unit production costs: direct labour by 10% and variable overhead by 5%. No change is expected to any other costs.

- Reduce production to 100,000 units.

Required:

(a) **Prepare a summary statement (in the same format as that shown above) which clearly shows the effect of all of the changes proposed by the directors of the company.** **(6 marks)**

(b) **Discuss the motivational factors in involving functional managers in the setting of functional budgets.** **(4 marks)**

(Total: 10 marks)

71 RECONCILING (MAR 13)

XXX uses a standard marginal costing system. Data relating to Y, the only product that it manufactures are as follows:

	Standard cost per unit of Y
Materials	6 kg @ $10 per kg
Labour	5 hours @ $9 per hour
Variable overhead	6 machine hours @ $5 per machine hour
Total variable production cost	

Based on the above standard cost data the following out-turn performance report was produced for February:

	Budget	Actual
Output (units)	1,100	1,100
	$	$
Materials	66,000	69,240
Labour	49,500	57,820
Variable overheads	33,000	35,000
Total variable costs	148,500	162,060

The Production Director has criticised the above report because "It does not give me the information I need to be able to make informed decisions. It tells me that the costs were higher but I need to be able to identify areas of responsibility".

You have been asked to provide a statement that is better suited to the needs of the Production Director. You have obtained the following information:

Materials: 5,770 kg were purchased and used.

Labour: The standard rate of $9 per hour had not been updated to incorporate a 5% pay rise. The 5,900 hours that were paid included 460 hours of idle time.

Variable overhead: 6,400 machine hours were used.

Required:

Prepare a statement that reconciles the budget variable production cost with the actual variable production cost. Your statement should show the variances in as much detail as possible. (10 marks)

72 LINKS (SEPT 12)

Required:

(a) Explain the links between budgets, standard costs and flexible budgeting. (6 marks)

(b) Discuss the importance of your answer to (a) for management control. (4 marks)

(Total: 10 marks)

73   ZJET BALANCED SCORECARD (SEPT 11)

ZJET is an airline company that operates both domestically and internationally using a fleet of 20 aircraft. Passengers book flights using the internet or by telephone and pay for their flights at the time of booking using a debit or credit card.

The airline has also entered into profit sharing arrangements with hotels and local car hire companies that allow rooms and cars to be booked by the airline's passengers through the airline's web site.

ZJET currently measures its performance using financial ratios. The new Managing Director has suggested that other measures are equally important as financial measures and has suggested using the Balanced Scorecard.

Required:

(a)   **Discuss how the Balanced Scorecard differs from traditional financial performance measurement.**   **(4 marks)**

(b)   **Explain THREE non-financial performance measures (ONE from EACH of THREE different perspectives of the Balanced Scorecard) that ZJET could use as part of its performance measurement process.**   **(6 marks)**

(Total: 10 marks)

74   PATHOLOGY LAB (MAR 13)

The Pathology Laboratory service of the County Hospital provides diagnostic services to support the care provided by the County Hospital, local General Practitioners, other hospitals and healthcare providers. The importance of the work done by the Pathology Laboratory was summarised by the Head of the laboratory:

"Over 70% of diagnostic and treatment decisions made by doctors are based on medical laboratory test results. Without our work, doctors would not be able to confirm their diagnosis. Laboratory results give us the ability to identify diseases in their earliest stages so that we have a better chance of treating people effectively. The types of tests performed by our highly-trained staff encompass the entire spectrum of human disease, from routine diagnostic services to clinical laboratories that specialise in bone marrow transplants. The laboratories provide over four million tests each year, providing doctors with the information needed for diagnosis and treatment of all kinds of condition. Our vision is to continually improve the efficiency of the laboratory to ensure the best economic approach to patient care."

The management team of the County Hospital has decided that the use of the balanced scorecard should be cascaded down to departmental level. Consequently, departmental managers have been given the task of designing a balanced scorecard for their departments.

Required:

Recommend an objective and a suitable performance measure for each of three non-financial perspectives of a balanced scorecard that the Pathology Laboratory could use.

Note: in your answer you should state three perspectives and then recommend an objective and a performance measure for each one of your three perspectives.   **(10 marks)**

75 PLAYERS (MAY 11)

A company produces and sells DVD players and Blu-ray players. Extracts from the budget for April are shown in the following table:

	Sales (players)	Selling price (per player)	Standard cost (per player)
DVD	3,000	$75	$50
Blu-ray	1,000	$200	$105

The Managing Director has sent you a copy of an e-mail she received from the Sales Manager. The content of the e-mail was as follows:

'We have had an excellent month. There was an adverse sales price variance on the DVDs of $18,000 but I compensated for that by raising the price of Blu-ray players. Unit sales of DVD players were as expected but sales of the Blu-rays were exceptional and gave a total sales volume profit variance of $19,000. I think I deserve a bonus!'

The Managing Director has asked for your opinion on these figures. You obtained the following information:

Actual results for April were:

	Sales (players)	Selling price (per player)
DVD	3,000	$69
Blu-ray	1,200	$215

The total market demand for DVD players was as budgeted but as a result of distributors reducing the price of Blu-ray discs the total market for Blu-ray players grew by 50% in April.

The company had sufficient capacity to meet the revised market demand for 1,500 units of its Blu-ray players and therefore maintained its market share.

Required:

(a) Calculate the following operational variances based on the revised market details:

    (i) The total sales mix profit margin variance. **(2 marks)**

    (ii) The total sales volume profit variance. **(2 marks)**

(b) Explain, using the above scenario, the importance of calculating planning and operational variances for responsibility centres. **(6 marks)**

(Total: 10 marks)

76   KHL RECONCILIATION (MAR 11)

KHL manufactures a single product and operates a budgetary control system that reports performance using variances on a monthly basis. The company has an agreement with a local supplier and calls off raw materials as and when required. Consequently there is no inventory of raw materials.

The following details have been extracted from the budget working papers for 2011:

	Annual Activity (units)		
	50,000	70,000	90,000
	$000	$000	$000
Sales revenue	3,200	4,480	5,760
Direct materials (3 kgs per unit)	600	840	1,080
Direct labour (2 hours per unit)	1,000	1,400	1,800
Variable overhead (2 hours per unit)	400	560	720
Fixed overhead (2 hours per unit)*	600	600	600

*The fixed overhead absorption rate of $5 per hour was based on an annual budget of 60,000 units of the product being produced at a constant monthly rate throughout the year, with the fixed overhead cost being incurred in equal monthly amounts.

The following actual performance relates to February 2011:

	$	$
Sales revenue (5,700 units)		330,600
Direct materials (18,600 kgs)	70,680	
Direct labour (11,500 hours)	128,800	
Variable overhead (11,500 hours)	47,150	
Fixed overhead absorbed	60,000	
	306,630	
Finished goods inventory adjustment	– 15,000	291,630
Gross profit		38,970
Fixed overhead over-absorption		3,000
Profit		41,970

For February 2011 budgeted sales were 6,000 units, the selling price variance was $34,200 Adverse and the sales volume profit variance was $4,200 Adverse. The actual fixed overhead incurred was $57,000.

Budgeted profit for February 2011 was $84,000.

Required:

Prepare a statement for February 2011 that reconciles the budgeted profit of $84,000 with the actual profit of $41,970. You should show the variances in as much detail as possible given the data provided.   (10 marks)

77   GRV MIX AND YIELD (SEPT 11)

GRV is a chemical processing company that produces sprays used by farmers to protect their crops. One of these sprays is made by mixing three chemicals. The standard material cost details for 1 litre of this spray is as follows:

	$
0.4 litres of chemical A @ $30 per litre	12.00
0.3 litres of chemical B @ $20 per litre	6.00
0.5 litres of chemical C @ $15 per litre	− 7.50
Standard material cost of 1 litre of spray	25.50

During August GRV produced 1,000 litres of this spray using the following chemicals:

600 litres of chemical A costing $18,000

250 litres of chemical B costing $8,000

500 litres of chemical C costing $8,500

You are the Management Accountant of GRV and the Production Manager has sent you the following e-mail:

I was advised by our purchasing department that the worldwide price of chemical B had risen by 50%. As a result, I used an increased proportion of chemical A than is prescribed in the standard mix so that our costs were less affected by this price change.

Required:

(a)   **Calculate the following operational variances:**

    (i)   **direct material mix and**   **(3 marks)**

    (ii)   **direct material yield**   **(2 marks)**

(b)   **Discuss the decision taken by the Production Manager.**   **(5 marks)**

(Total: 10 marks)

78   BEYOND BUDGETING

Some critics of traditional budgeting advocate techniques that are 'beyond budgeting'.

Required:

Describe their criticisms of traditional budgeting and outline what they suggest should be the features of an appropriate system of planning and control.   **(10 marks)**

79   CULTURAL FRAMEWORK (MAY 13)

The modern dynamic business environment has been described as a "buyer's market" in which companies must react to the rapidly changing characteristics of the market and the needs of customers. Many managers have criticised traditional forms of budgeting for being too restrictive and for being of little use for performance management and control.

Required:

Explain how the principles of "Beyond Budgeting" promote a cultural framework that is suitable for the modern dynamic business environment.   **(10 marks)**

CONTROL AND PERFORMANCE MEASUREMENT OF RESPONSIBILITY CENTRES

80   LMN (MAY 10)

LMN comprises three trading divisions plus a Head Office. There is a director for each trading division and, in addition, there is a Managing Director who is based in Head Office. Divisional directors are empowered to make decisions concerning the day to day operations of their division and investment decisions requiring an initial investment up to $100,000. Investment decisions involving greater initial expenditure must be authorised by the Managing Director. Inter-divisional trading occurs between all of the trading divisions. The transfer prices are determined by Head Office. Head Office provides services and facilities to each of the trading divisions.

At the end of each month, the actual costs of Head Office are apportioned to the trading divisions. Each Head Office cost is apportioned to the trading divisions using an appropriate basis. The bases used are: number of employees; value of sales; capital invested; and standard hours of service delivered.

The Head Office costs, together with the costs and revenues generated at divisional level, are summarised in a divisional performance statement each month. The divisional directors are not happy with the present performance statement and how it is used to appraise their performance.

Required:

(a)   **Explain, using examples from the scenario, three issues that LMN should consider when designing a new divisional performance statement.**   **(6 marks)**

LMN is thinking of introducing Activity Based Costing at its Head Office to help with the apportionment of all its costs to the divisions.

(b)   **Discuss the advantages of applying Activity Based Costing to apportion all of the Head Office costs.**   **(4 marks)**

(Total: 10 marks)

81   RETURN ON INVESTMENT

Our Timbers is a market leader in the supply of timber-based products to the construction industry. The company has two divisions, namely the RP division which manufactures products used in the construction of residential properties and the IP division which manufactures products used in construction of industrial properties.

The following information is available in respect of the three year period ended 31 December 20X3:

(1)   (i)   Net assets as at 31 December were as follows:

	20X3	20X2	20X1
	$000	$000	$000
Non-current assets (net book value)	75,600	64,800	54,000
Net current assets	64,400	55,200	56,000
Capital employed	140,000	120,000	110,000
Non-current assets acquired in year	19,200	18,000	

Note: No disposals of non-current assets took place during the above periods.

(ii)   The total capital employed of Our Timbers was invested in the divisions during each year as follows:

Division	% of total capital employed
RP	40
IP	60

(iii)   Depreciation is charged at 10% per annum on a reducing balance basis.

(2)   Operating cash flows were as follows:

Division	20X3 $m	20X2 $m
RP	14.4	13.1
IP	20.0	18.0

(3)   Each division has a target return on investment (ROI) of 22.5% on average capital employed throughout each year. Divisional managers are eligible to receive an annual bonus amounting to 10% of annual salary if the target rate of return is achieved.

Required:

(i)   **Calculate the return on investment (ROI) (using average capital employed) achieved by each of the divisions during the years ended 31 December 20X2 and 31 December 20X3.**   **(6 marks)**

(ii)   **Comment briefly on how divisional managers might respond to the results achieved and ONE potential problem that might be experienced by Our Timbers as a result of using ROI to appraise the performance of the divisions. Recommend ONE alternative performance measure that could be used to address this problem.**

(4 marks)

(Total: 10 marks)

82   DESIGNING BONUS SCHEMES (MAY 07)

G Group consists of several autonomous divisions. Two of the divisions supply components and services to other divisions within the group as well as to external clients. The management of G Group is considering the introduction of a bonus scheme for managers that will be based on the profit generated by each division.

Briefly explain the factors that should be considered by the management of G Group when designing the bonus scheme for divisional managers.   **(10 marks)**

Section 2

SECTION B-TYPE QUESTIONS

PRICING AND PRODUCT DECISIONS

83   ENGINEERING PROJECT (MAY 09)   *Walk in the footsteps of a top tutor*

Top tutor tips

(1) For tips on approaching the question, work through the boxed notes in order.

Once each requirement has been completed review the answer detail. Use this approach to reading and answering the question when tackling other questions.

A company has been asked to provide a quotation for an engineering project that will take one year to complete. An analysis of the project has already been completed and the following resource requirements have been identified:

(1)   A specialised machine will be required for a total of 10 weeks. Two of these weeks are at the start of the project and three of them are at the end. The machine could be hired in from a reputable supplier, who would guarantee its availability when it is required, for $4,000 per week. Alternatively it could be purchased at a cost of $250,000. If it were purchased it could be sold in one year's time for $150,000. If the machine were purchased it could be hired out to other companies for $2,500 per week and it is believed that it would be hired out for a total of 30 weeks.

(2) Faced with an alternative, the lowest cost option should be picked.

(2)   The machinery has a running cost of $720 per week. This cost is incurred by the user of the machine.

(3) Remember the rule of thumb for relevant costs – to be relevant, a cost must be future, cash and incremental.

(3)   It is company policy to depreciate non-current assets by 25% per year on a reducing balance basis.

(4) Depreciation is never relevant, because it is not cash.

(4)   Skilled labour would be required for a total of 9,000 hours during the year. The labour required could be recruited at an hourly rate of $12. Alternatively some of the employees currently working on other projects within the company could be transferred to this project. Their hourly rate is $10 per hour. If these existing employees were to be transferred to this project then they would need to be replaced on their existing project work. Replacements for their existing project work would cost $11 per hour.

(5) Alternatives to choose from here again; but the current hourly rate of $10 is irrelevant, as it would be paid anyway.

(5)   Unskilled labour would be required for a total of 12,000 hours during the year. These employees would need to be recruited on a one year contract at a cost of $8 per hour.

(6) Cash, incremental, future. Our three conditions are fulfilled.

(6)   The project would need to be supervised and it is estimated that there would be a total of 500 hours of supervision required during the year. One of the existing supervisors could undertake this work, but if he did so he would have to work a total of 300 hours overtime during the year to carry out the supervision on this project as well as his existing duties. The supervisor earns a salary of $50,000 per year for working 2,000 hours and is not paid for overtime work. If this project goes ahead the supervisor will be paid a bonus of $500, which would not be paid if the project is not undertaken.

*(7) What is the **only** incremental cost here, if overtime is not paid extra?*

(7) The direct materials required for the project are as follows:

Material A

The total amount required for the project would have to be purchased at a cost of $15,000.

(8) Cash, incremental, future. Our three conditions are fulfilled.

Material B

The total amount required would be 10,000 square metres. The company purchased 25,000 square metres of this material for a project two years ago at a total cost of $100,000. The earlier project used 20,000 square metres of the material and the remainder is currently held in inventory. The company does not foresee any other use for this material in the future and could sell it for $2 per square metre. The current purchase price of the material is $5 per square metre.

(9) Two different contexts will lead to two different paths to establish the cost of materials. Remember the diagram from your Study Notes!

(8) The company has already incurred expenditure of $25,000 in analysing the resource requirements of the project.

*(10) 'already incurred' = here is a **sunk** cost.*

(9) It is company policy to attribute overhead costs to projects using an absorption rate of 40% of prime costs.

(11) Unless they are project-specific (i.e. incremental), overheads are not relevant.

(10) It is company policy to add a 25% profit mark-up to total costs when setting its prices.

*(12) Remember the question requirement, that asked for relevant **costs** – a profit mark-up is not a cost.*

Required:

(13) Start by reading each requirement and allocating time (1.8 mins per mark). Now read back through the question. Make notes or annotate the question whilst reading.

(a) **Prepare a statement that shows the relevant cost of the project. For each of the resources indicated in notes (1) to (10) you must clearly explain the reason for the cost value that you have used.**

Ignore the time value of money and taxation. (20 marks)

(14) Now answer part (a). This should take you 20 × 1.8 marks = 36 minutes.

(b) **Assume that the company used your calculations as the basis of the quotation and then added $125,000 for profit. Also assume that all costs incurred were the same as forecast.**

Explain why the financial profit reports at the end of the year would not show a profit of $125,000 for the engineering project. (5 marks)

(15) The rest of your available time should be spent answering this part of the requirement.

(Total: 25 marks)

84 THREE SEASONS HOTEL (MAY 11)

The management of a hotel is planning for the next year. The hotel has 100 bedrooms. The price of a room night includes breakfast for the guests. Other services (a snack service and a bar and restaurant) are available but are not included in the price of the room night. These additional services are provided to hotel guests only.

For planning purposes the hotel divides the year (based on 360 days) into three seasons: peak, mid and low.

Details of the hotel and its services and forecasts for the next year are given below.

(1) **Seasons, room charges, room occupancy, guests per room and room revenue**

The hotel charges a price per room per night (including breakfast) irrespective of the number of guests per room. The price charged is different in each of the seasons.

Season	Peak	Mid	Low
Number of days	90	120	150
Price charged per room per night ($)	100.00	80.00	55.00
Hotel room occupancy %	95	75	50
Average number of guests per room	1.8	1.5	1.2
Total room revenue ($)	855,000	720,000	412,500

(2) **Guest related costs**

The hotel incurs some costs, including providing breakfast, that are directly related to the number of guests in the hotel. These are $12 per guest per night in all seasons.

(3) **Room related costs**

The hotel incurs some costs that are directly related to the number of rooms occupied. These include cleaning and laundry costs of $5 per occupied room per night regardless of season. There are also power and lighting costs of $3 in the peak season, $4 in the mid season and $6 in the low season per occupied room per night.

(4) **Hot snacks**

The hotel offers a 24 hour hot snacks service to the guests. Past records show that this service has been used by 30% of its guests in the mid and low seasons but only 10% in the peak season. It is forecast that the average spend per guest per night will be $10. The hotel earns a 30% gross contribution from this income.

The hotel employs a cook on a salary of $20,000 per year to provide this service. All of the costs for the hot snacks service, except for the cook's salary, are variable. The cook could be made redundant with no redundancy costs.

(5) **Restaurant and bar**

Past records show that the usage of the restaurant and bar is seasonal. The restaurant and bar are particularly popular with the hotel's business guests. The forecast usage is shown below.

Season	Daily demand
Peak	30% of hotel guests spend an average of $15 each
Mid	50% of hotel guests spend an average of $20 each
Low	70% of hotel guests spend an average of $30 each

The hotel earns a 25% gross contribution from this income and employs two chefs on a combined salary of $54,000 per year to provide this facility. All of the costs in the restaurant and bar, except for the salaries of the chefs, are variable.

The two chefs could be made redundant with no redundancy costs.

(8) **General hotel costs**

These include the costs of reception staff, the heating and lighting of the common areas and other facility related costs. The forecast costs for next year are:

Peak season	$300,000
Mid season	$400,000
Low season	$500,000

These costs could be reduced by 75% if the hotel were to close temporarily for one or more seasons of the year.

There are also some costs that are incurred by the hotel and can only be avoided by its permanent closure. These are estimated to $200,000 for next year.

Required:

(a)   Prepare, in an appropriate format, a columnar statement that will help the managers of the hotel to plan for next year. Your statement should show the hotel's activities by season and in total.   **(18 marks)**

(b)   (i)   Identify, based on your statement, the actions that the managers could take to maximise the profit of the hotel for next year.   **(3 marks)**

(ii)   Explain TWO factors that the managers should consider before implementing the actions you identified in (b)(i).   **(4 marks)**

(Total: 25 marks)

85   CHOICE OF CONTRACTS

A company in the civil engineering industry with headquarters located 22 miles from London undertakes contracts anywhere in the United Kingdom.

The company has had its tender for a job in North-East England accepted at £288,000 and work is due to begin in March 20X3. However, the company has also been asked to undertake a contract on the South-Coast of England. The price offered for this contract is £352,000. Both of the contracts cannot be taken simultaneously because of constraints on staff site management personnel and on plant available. An escape clause enables the company to withdraw from the contract in the North-East, provided notice is given before the end of November and an agreed penalty of £28,000 is paid.

The following estimates have been submitted by the company's quantity surveyor:

Cost estimates

	North-East £	South-Coast £
Materials:		
In inventory at original cost, Material X	21,600	
In inventory at original cost, Material Y		24,800
Firm orders placed at original cost, Material X	30,400	
Not yet ordered – current cost, Material X	60,000	
Not yet ordered – current cost, Material Z		71,200
Labour – hired locally	86,000	110,000
Site management	34,000	34,000
Staff accommodation and travel for site management	6,800	5,600
Plant on site – depreciation	9,600	12,800
Interest on capital, 8%	5,120	6,400
Total local contract costs	253,520	264,800
Headquarters costs allocated at rate of 5% on total		
Contract costs	12,676	3,240
	266,196	278,040
Contract price	288,000	352,000
Estimated profit	21,804	73,960

Notes:

(1)   X, Y and Z are three building materials. Material X is not in common use and would not realise much money if re-sold; however, it could be used on other contracts but only as a substitute for another material currently quoted at 10% less than the original cost of X. The price of Y, a material in common use, has doubled since it was purchased; its net realisable value if re-sold would be its new price less 15% to cover disposal costs. Alternatively it could be kept for use on other contracts in the following financial year.

(2)   With the construction industry not yet recovered from the recent recession, the company is confident that manual labour, both skilled and unskilled, could be hired locally on a sub-contracting basis to meet the needs of each of the contracts.

(3)   The plant which would be needed for the south coast contract has been owned for some years and £12,800 is the year's depreciation on a straight-line basis. If the north-east contract is undertaken, less plant will be required but the surplus plant will be hired out for the period of the contract at a rental of £6,000.

(4)   It is the company's policy to charge all contracts with notional interest at 8% on estimated working capital involved in contracts. Progress payments would be receivable from the contractee.

(5)   Salaries and general costs of operating the small headquarters amount to about £108,000 each year. There are usually ten contracts being supervised at the same time.

(6)   Each of the two contracts is expected to last from March 20X3 to February 20X4 which, coincidentally, is the company's financial year.

(7)   Site management is treated as a fixed cost.

You are required, as the management accountant to the company:

(a)   **to present comparative statements to show the net benefit to the company of undertaking the more advantageous of the two contracts**   **(12 marks)**

(b)   **to explain the reasoning behind the inclusion in (or omission from) your comparative financial statements, of each item given in the cost estimates and the notes relating thereto.**   **(13 marks)**

(Total: 25 marks)

86   JRL (MAR 12)

JRL manufactures two products from different combinations of the same resources. Unit selling prices and unit cost details for each product are as follows:

Product	J	L
	$/unit	$/unit
Selling price	115	120
Direct material A ($10 per kg)	20	10
Direct material B ($6 per kg)	12	24
Skilled labour ($14 per hour)	28	21
Variable overhead ($4 per machine hour)	14	18
Fixed overhead*	28	36
Profit	13	11

*Fixed overhead is absorbed using an absorption rate per machine hour. It is an unavoidable central overhead cost that is not affected by the mix or volume of products produced.

The maximum weekly demand for products J and L is 400 units and 450 units respectively and this is the normal weekly production volume achieved by JRL. However, for the next four weeks the achievable production level will be reduced due to a shortage of available resources.

The resources that are expected to be available are as follows:

Direct material A	900 kg
Direct material B	1,750 kg
Skilled labour	1,250 hours
Machine time	2,400 machine hours

Required:

(a)   **Identify, using graphical linear programming, the weekly production schedule for products J and L that will maximise the profits of JRL during the next four weeks.**

(15 marks)

(b)   **The optimal solution to part (a) shows that the shadow prices of skilled labour and direct material A are as follows:**

   Skilled labour $Nil

   Direct material A $11.70

   Explain the relevance of these values to the management of JRL.   (6 marks)

(c)   **Explain, using the graph you have drawn in part (a), how you would calculate by how much the selling price of Product J could increase before the optimal solution would change.   (4 marks)**

(Total: 25 marks)

87   THS (MAR 13)

THS produces two products from different combinations of the same resources. Details of the products are shown below:

	E	R
	per unit	*per unit*
Selling price	$99	$159
Material A ($2 per kg)	3 kgs	2 kgs
Material B ($6 per kg)	4 kgs	3 kgs
Machining ($7 per hour)	2 hours	3 hours
Skilled labour ($10 per hour)	2 hours	5 hours
Maximum monthly demand (units)	unlimited	1,500

THS is preparing the production plan for next month. The maximum resource availability for the month is:

Material A	5,000 kgs
Material B	5,400 kgs
Machining	3,000 hours
Skilled labour	4,500 hours

Required:

(a)   Identify, using graphical linear programming, the optimal production plan for products E and R to maximise THS's profit in the month.   (13 marks)

The Production Manager has now been able to source extra resources:

An employment agency would supply skilled labour for a monthly fee of $1,000 and $14 per hour worked.

A machine that has the same variable running costs per hour as the current machinery can be leased. The leased machine would be able to run for 2,000 hours per month.

Required:

(b)   Calculate the maximum amount that should be paid next month to lease the machine. (Note: you should assume that a contract has already been signed with the employment agency.)   (8 marks)

(c)   Explain TWO major factors that should be considered before deciding to lease the machine. (Note: you should assume that the data supplied is totally accurate.)

(4 marks)

(Total: 25 marks)

88   CD COMPANY

The opportunities afforded by the European Union have created a pleasant problem for CD Company, which is considering concentrating its production on one of two products – 'Robroy' or 'Trigger' – both of which are currently made and sold. With the possible expansion in sales, either product can be sold in quantities which exceed the capacity of the present production facilities. Therefore, the use of sub-contractors is being considered.

Sub-contractor Jason can produce up to a maximum of 10,000 units of Robroy or 8,000 units of Trigger in a year **for the type of work done by Department 1**. Jason's prices would be $110 for Robroy and $170 for Trigger, both prices being inclusive of the raw materials.

Sub-contractor Nadira can produce up to a maximum of 6,400 units of Robroy or 4,000 units of Trigger in a year **for the type of work done by Department 2**. Nadira's prices would be $120 for Robroy and $154 for Trigger, both prices being inclusive of the raw materials.

A market research study has shown that for more than 20,000 units of Robroy to be sold in a year, the price of the total quantity sold would need to be reduced to $270 each. If more than 16,000 units of Trigger are to be sold in a year, the price of the total quantity sold would need to be reduced to $390 each.

CD Company has stated that its standard selling prices and standard prime costs for each product for the forthcoming year are:

	Robroy		Trigger	
	Hours	$	Hours	$
Selling prices		300		430
Costs – Department 1:				
Direct materials		45		75
Direct wages	5	40	7.5	60
Costs – Department 2:				
Direct materials		15		20
Direct wages	7.5	75	10	100

Production overheads are to be absorbed on a direct labour hour basis and the budgeted overheads for the forthcoming year are:

	Department 1	Department 2
Fixed	$400,000	$800,000
Variable – per direct labour hour	$2.00	$2.40
Budgeted maximum labour hours available	100,000	160,000

Required:

(a)   **State, with supporting calculations and estimated profit figures, whether CD Company should concentrate its resources on Robroy or Trigger if:**

    (i)   **it does not use sub-contractors**   (9 marks)

    (ii) **it does use sub-contractors and restricts its sales to either 22,000 units of Robroy or 18,000 units of Trigger.**   (9 marks)

(b)   **Describe briefly one possible problem arising for each of the following situations:**

    (i)   **if your conclusion in (a) (i) above is followed**

    (ii) **if your conclusion in (a) (ii) above is followed.**   (2 marks)

(c)   **Comment briefly on the usefulness of marginal costing for decision making.**
                                                                        (5 marks)

                                                                        (Total: 25 marks)

89 WTL DECISION (SEP 11)

WTL manufactures and sells four products: W, X, Y, and Z from a single factory. Each of the products is manufactured in batches of 100 units using a just-in- time manufacturing process and consequently there is no inventory of any product.

This batch size of 100 units cannot be altered without significant cost implications. Although the products are manufactured in batches of 100 units, they are sold as single units at the market price. WTL has a significant number of competitors and is forced to accept the market price for each of its products.

It is currently reviewing the profit it makes from each product, and for the business as a whole, and has produced the following statement for the latest period:

Product	W	X	Y	Z	Total
Number of:					
units sold	100,000	130,000	80,000	150,000	
Machine hours	200,000	195,000	80,000	300,000	775,000
Direct labour hours	50,000	130,000	80,000	75,000	335,000
	$	$	$	$	$
Sales	1,300,000	2,260,000	2,120,000	1,600,000	7,280,000
Direct materials	300,000	910,000	940,000	500,000	2,650,000
Direct labour	400,000	1,040,000	640,000	600,000	2,680,000
Overhead costs	400,000	390,000	160,000	600,000	1,550,000
Profit /(Loss)	200,000	(80,000)	380,000	(100,000)	400,000

WTL is concerned that two of its products are loss making and has carried out an analysis of its products and costs. This analysis shows:

(1) The sales of each product are completely independent of each other.

(2) The overhead costs have been absorbed into the above product costs using an absorption rate of $2 per machine hour.

(3) Further analysis of the overhead cost shows that some of it is caused by the number of machine hours used, some is caused by the number of batches produced and some of the costs are product specific fixed overheads that would be avoided if the product were discontinued. Other general fixed overhead costs would be avoided only by the closure of the factory. Details of this analysis are as follows:

	$000	$000
Machine hour related		310
Batch related		230
Product specific fixed overhead:		
Product W	500	
Product X	50	
Product Y	100	
Product Z	50	700
General fixed overhead		310
		1,550

Required:

(a) Prepare a columnar statement that is more useful for decision making than the profit statement prepared by WTL. Your statement should also show the current total profit for the business. **(8 marks)**

(b) Prepare a report to the Board of WTL that:

    (i) Explains why your statement is suitable for decision making **(4 marks)**

    (ii) Advises WTL which, if any, of its four products should be discontinued in order to maximise its company profits. **(4 marks)**

(c) Calculate the break even volume (in batches) for Product W. **(4 marks)**

(d) Explain how WTL could use Value Analysis to improve its profits. **(5 marks)**

(Total: 25 marks)

90 WZ MANUFACTURING (MAR 11)

WZ is a manufacturing company with two factories. The company's West factory currently produces a number of products. Four of these products use differing quantities of the same resources. Details of these four products and their resource requirements are as follows:

Product	J	K	L	M
	$/unit	$/unit	$/unit	$/unit
Selling price	56	40	78	96
Direct labour ($8 per hour)	20	16	24	20
Direct material A ($3 per litre)	6	3	0	9
Direct material B ($5 per kg)	10	0	15	20
Variable overhead (see note 1)				
Labour related	1.25	1	1.50	1.25
Machine related	1.25	2	0.75	1
Total variable cost	38.50	22	41.25	51.25
Other data:				
Machine hours per unit	5	8	3	4
Maximum demand per week	1,000	3,500	2,800	4,500

Notes:

(1) An analysis of the variable overhead shows that some of it is caused by the number of labour hours and the remainder is caused by the number of machine hours.

(2) Currently WZ purchases a component P from an external supplier for $35 per component. A single unit of this component is used in producing N the company's only other product. Product N is produced in WZ's other factory and does not use any of the resources identified above. Product N currently yields a positive contribution. WZ could manufacture the component in its West factory, but to do so would require: 1 hour of direct labour, 0.5 machine hours, and 2 kgs of direct material B. WZ purchases 500 components per week. WZ could not produce the component in its other factory.

(3) The purchasing director has recently advised you that the availability of direct materials A and B is to be restricted to 21,000 litres and 24,000 kgs per week respectively. This restriction is unlikely to change for at least 10 weeks. No restrictions are expected on any other resources.

(4)   WZ does not hold inventory of either finished goods or raw materials.

(5)   WZ has already signed a contract, which must be fulfilled, to deliver the following units of its products each week for the next 10 weeks:

Product	Contract units
J	100
K	200
L	150
M	250

These quantities are in addition to the maximum demand identified above.

Required:

(a)   **Calculate whether WZ should continue to purchase the component P or whether it should manufacture it internally during the next 10 weeks.** **(11 marks)**

(b)   **Prepare a statement to show the optimum weekly usage of the West factory's available resources.**

   Note: You are NOT required to use linear programming. **(3 marks)**

(c)   (i)   **Assuming no other changes, calculate the purchase price of the component P at which your advice in part (a) above would change.** **(4 marks)**

   (ii)   **Explain TWO non-financial factors that should be considered before deciding whether or not to manufacture the component internally.** **(4 marks)**

(d)   **If you were to solve part (b) above using linear programming state the following:**

   The objective function; The inequality for the material A constraint; The inequality for the material B constraint **(3 marks)**

(Total: 25 marks)

91   EXE

You have received a request from EXE to provide a quotation for the manufacture of a specialised piece of equipment. This would be a one-off order, in excess of normal budgeted production. The following cost estimate has already been prepared:

		Note	$
Direct materials:			
Steel	$10m^2$ @ $5.00 per m^2	(1)	50
Brass fittings		(2)	20
Direct labour:			
Skilled	25 hours @ $8.00 per hour	(3)	200
Semi-skilled	10 hours @ $5.00 per hour	(4)	50
Overhead	35 hours @ $10.00 per hour	(5)	350
Estimating time		(6)	100
			———
Production cost			770
Administration overhead @ 20% of production cost		(7)	154
			———
			924
Profit @ 25% of total cost		(8)	231
			———
Selling price			1,155
			———

Notes:

(1) The steel is regularly used, and has a current inventory value of $5.00 per square metre. There are currently 100 square metres in inventory. The steel is readily available at a price of $5.50 per square metre.

(2) The brass fittings would have to be bought specifically for this job: a supplier has quoted the price of $20 for the fittings required.

(3) The skilled labour is currently employed by your company and paid at a rate of $8.00 per hour. If this job were undertaken it would be necessary either to work 25 hours' overtime, which would be paid at time plus one half, OR in order to carry out the work in normal time, reduce production of another product that earns a contribution of $13.00 per hour.

(4) The semi-skilled labour currently has sufficient paid idle time to be able to complete this work.

(5) The overhead absorption rate includes power costs which are directly related to machine usage. If this job were undertaken, it is estimated that the machine time required would be ten hours. The machines incur power costs of $0.75 per hour. There are no other overhead costs that can be specifically identified with this job.

(6) The cost of the estimating time is that attributed to the four hours taken by the engineers to analyse the drawings and determine the cost estimate given above.

(7) It is company policy to add 20% to the production cost as an allowance for administration costs associated with the jobs accepted.

(8) This is the standard profit added by your company as part of its pricing policy.

Required:

(a) **Prepare, on a relevant cost basis, the lowest cost estimate that could be used as the basis for a quotation. Explain briefly your reasons for using EACH of the values in your estimate.** **(12 marks)**

(b) Now that the cost estimate has been prepared, the engineers have considered the skilled labour rate and hourly power costs that have been used. They have now realised that the following alternative values may occur and they have estimated the probabilities of each value:

Skilled labour		Power costs	
$/hour	Probability	$/hour	Probability
10	0.3	0.90	0.25
8	0.6	0.75	0.55
7	0.1	0.65	0.20

The following two-way data table shows the effects of these possible changes on the lowest cost estimate (all values in $):

Skilled labour rate (per hour)	Power costs (per hour)		
	0.90	0.75	0.65
10	+ 76.50	+ 75.00	+ 74.00
8	+ 1.50	0.00	− 1.00
7	− 36.00	− 37.50	− 38.50

Required:

Demonstrate and explain how the two-way data table may be used to assist the company in making a decision concerning the contract. (13 marks)

(Total: 25 marks)

92 ELECTRICAL APPLIANCES (SEP 10)

A manufacturer of electrical appliances is continually reviewing its product range and enhancing its existing products by developing new models to satisfy the demands of its customers. The company intends to always have products at each stage of the product life cycle to ensure the company's continued presence in the market.

Currently the company is reviewing three products:

Product K was introduced to the market some time ago and is now about to enter the maturity stage of its life cycle. The maturity stage is expected to last for ten weeks. Each unit has a variable cost of $38 and takes 1 standard hour to produce. The Managing Director is unsure which of four possible prices the company should charge during the next ten weeks. The following table shows the results of some market research into the level of weekly demand at alternative prices:

Selling price per unit	$100	$85	$80	$75
Weekly demand (units)	600	800	1,200	1,400

Product L was introduced to the market two months ago using a penetration pricing policy and is now about to enter its growth stage. This stage is expected to last for 20 weeks. Each unit has a variable cost of $45 and takes 1.25 standard hours to produce. Market research has indicated that there is a linear relationship between its selling price and the number of units demanded, of the form $P = a − bx$. At a selling price of $100 per unit demand is expected to be 1,000 units per week. For every $10 increase in selling price the weekly demand will reduce by 200 units and for every $10 decrease in selling price the weekly demand will increase by 200 units.

Product M is currently being tested and is to be launched in ten weeks' time. This is an innovative product which the company believes will change the entire market. The company has decided to use a market skimming approach to pricing this product during its introduction stage.

The company currently has a production facility which has a capacity of 2,000 standard hours per week. This facility is being expanded but the extra capacity will not be available for ten weeks.

Required:

(a) (i)   Calculate which of the four selling prices should be charged for product K, in order to maximise its contribution during its maturity stage **(3 marks)**

and as a result, in order to utilise all of the spare capacity from your answer to (i) above,

(ii) Calculate the selling price of product L during its growth stage. **(6 marks)**

(b) Compare and contrast penetration and skimming pricing strategies during the introduction stage, using product M to illustrate your answer. **(6 marks)**

(c) Explain with reasons, for each of the remaining stages of M's product life cycle, the changes that would be expected in the

(i)   average unit production cost

(ii) unit selling price **(10 marks)**

(Total: 25 marks)

93   PRICING STRATEGIES (NOV 08)

(a) A manufacturing company is considering its pricing policy for next year. It has already carried out some market research into the expected levels of demand for one of its products at different selling prices, with the following results:

Selling price per unit	Annual demand (units)
$100	50,000
$120	45,000
$130	40,000
$150	25,000
$160	10,000
$170	5,000

This product is manufactured in batches of 100 units, and analysis has shown that the total production cost depends on the number of units as well as the number of batches produced each year. This analysis has produced the following formula for total cost:

$Z = 70x + 80y + \$240,000$

Where   Z represents the total production cost

x represents the number of units produced; and

y represents the number of batches of production.

Required:

(i)   Prepare calculations to identify which of the above six selling prices per unit will result in the highest annual profit from this product. **(7 marks)**

(ii) Explain why your chosen selling price might not result in the highest possible annual profit from this product. **(3 marks)**

(b)   The company is also launching a new product to the market next year and is currently considering its pricing strategy for this new product. The product will be unlike any other product that is currently available and will considerably improve the efficiency with which garages can service motor vehicles. This unique position in the market place is expected to remain for only six months before one of the company's competitors develops a similar product.

The prototype required a substantial amount of time to develop and as a result the company is keen to recover its considerable research and development costs as soon as possible. The company has now developed its manufacturing process for this product and as a result the time taken to produce each unit is much less than was required for the first few units. This time reduction is expected to continue for a short period of time once mass production has started, but from then a constant time requirement per unit is anticipated.

Required:

(i)   **Explain the alternative pricing strategies that may be adopted when launching a new product.**   **(6 marks)**

(ii) **Recommend a pricing strategy to the company for its new product and explain how the adoption of your chosen strategy would affect the sales revenue, costs and profits of this product over its life cycle.**   **(9 marks)**

(Total: 25 marks)

94   WRX (MAY 12)

WRX manufactures three products using different quantities of the same resources. Details of these products are as follows:

Product	W	R	X
	$/unit	$/unit	$/unit
Market selling price	90	126	150
Direct labour ($7/hour)	14	28	35
Material A ($3/kg)	15	12	21
Material B ($6/kg)	24	36	30
Variable overhead ($4/hour)	8	16	20
Fixed overhead	12	7	12
	73	99	118
Profit	17	27	32

The management of WRX has predicted the demand for these products for July as follows:

Product W   500 units

Product R   800 units

Product X   1,600 units

These demand estimates do NOT include an order from a major customer to supply 400 units per month of each of the three products, at a discount of $10 per unit from the market selling price.

During July the management of WRX anticipate that there will be a shortage of material B, and that only 17,500 kgs will be available.

It is not possible for WRX to hold inventory of any raw materials, work in progress or finished products.

Required:

(a) **Prepare calculations to show the optimum product mix to maximise WRX's profit for July, assuming that the order with the major customer is supplied in full.**

(7 marks)

WRX has now realised that the contract with the major customer does not have to be met in full for any of the three products. The customer will accept whatever WRX is prepared to supply at the contracted prices but they will charge a financial penalty if WRX does not supply them in full in July.

(b) **Calculate the lowest value of the financial penalty that the major customer would need to insert in the contract to ensure that WRX meets its order in full in July.**

(8 marks)

(c) Now that you have presented your answers to (a) and (b) above to the management team of WRX, the production manager has advised that, due to holidays, the number of direct labour hours available will be reduced to a total of 9,800 hours in July.

A decision has been made that WRX will fulfil its order with the major customer in full in July, and it has been agreed that a linear programming model will be used to determine the optimum usage of the resources that will be available after setting aside those required for the major customer's order.

Required:

(i) **Identify the objective function and the constraints to be used in the linear programming model to determine the optimum usage of the remaining resources to maximise the company's profits for July.** (6 marks)

(ii) **The optimal solution has been determined as:**

W   500 units

R   0 units

X   880 units

Explain which of the constraints you stated in (c)(i) are binding on the solution. (You are not required to draw a graph.) (4 marks)

(Total: 25 marks)

95   RAB CONSULTING

RAB Consulting specialises in two type of consultancy project.

Each Type A project requires 20 hours of work from qualified researchers and 8 hours of work from junior researchers.

Each Type B project requires 12 hours of work from qualified researchers and 15 hours of work from junior researchers.

Researchers are paid on an hourly basis at the following rates:

Qualified researchers	$30/hour
Junior researchers	$14/hour

Other data relating to the projects:

Project type	A	B
	$	$
Revenue per project	1,700	1,500
Direct project expenses	408	310
Administration*	280	270

*Administration costs are attributed to projects using rate per project hour. Total administration costs are $28,000 per four-week period.

During the four-week period ending on 30 June 2000, owing to holidays and other staffing difficulties the number of working hours available are:

Qualified researchers	1,344
Junior researchers	1,120

An agreement has already been made for 20 Type A projects with XYZ group. RAB Consulting must start and complete these projects in four-week period ending 30 June 2000. A maximum of 60 Type B projects may be undertaken during the four-week period ending 30 June 2000.

RAB Consulting is preparing its detailed budget for the four-week period ending 30 June 2000 and needs to identify the most profitable use of the resources it has available.

Required:

(a)   (i)   Calculate the contribution from each type of project.   **(4 marks)**

        (ii)   Formulate the linear programming model for the four-week period ending 30 June 2000.   **(4 marks)**

        (iii)   Calculate, using a graph, the mix of projects that will maximise profit for RAB Consulting for the four-week period ending 30 June 2000.   **(9 marks)**

        Note: Projects are not divisible.

(b)   Calculate the profit that RAB Consulting would earn from the optimal plan.

                    (3 marks)

(c)   Explain the importance of identifying scarce resources when preparing budgets and the use of linear programming to determine the optimum use of resources.

                    (5 marks)

                    (Total: 25 marks)

96 RT LINEAR (MAY 10)

RT produces two products from different quantities of the same resources using a just-in-time (JIT) production system. The selling price and resource requirements of each of the products are shown below:

	R	T
Unit selling price ($)	130	160
Resources per unit:		
Direct labour ($8 per hour)	3 hours	5 hours
Material A ($3 per kg)	5 kgs	4 kgs
Material B ($7 per litre)	2 litres	1 litre
Machine hours ($10 per hour)	3 hours	4 hours

Market research shows that the maximum demand for products R and T during June 2010 is 500 units and 800 units respectively. This does not include an order that RT has agreed with a commercial customer for the supply of 250 units of R and 350 units of T at selling prices of $100 and $135 per unit respectively. Although the customer will accept part of the order, failure by RT to deliver the order in full by the end of June will cause RT to incur a $10,000 financial penalty.

At a recent meeting of the purchasing and production managers to discuss the production plans of RT for June, the following resource restrictions for June were identified:

Direct labour hours	7,500 hours
Material A	8,500 kgs
Material B	3,000 litres
Machine hours	7,500 hours

Required:

(a) Assuming that RT completes the order with the commercial customer, prepare calculations to show, from a financial perspective, the optimum production plan for June 2010 and the contribution that would result from adopting this plan.

(6 marks)

(b) Prepare calculations to show, from a financial perspective, whether RT should complete the order from the commercial customer (3 marks)

You have now presented your optimum production plan to the purchasing and production managers of RT. During your presentation it became clear that the predicted resource restrictions were rather optimistic. In fact the managers agreed that the availability of all of the resources could be as much as 10% lower than their original predictions.

(c) Assuming that RT completes the order with the commercial customer, and using graphical linear programming, prepare a graph to show the optimum production plan for RT for June 2010 on the basis that the availability of all resources is 10% lower than originally predicted. (11 marks)

(d) Discuss how the graph in your solution to (c) above can be used to help to determine the optimum production plan for June 2010 if the actual resource availability lies somewhere between the managers' optimistic and pessimistic predictions. (5 marks)

(Total: 25 marks)

97   COMPANY WX (NOV 12)

Scenario for parts (a) and (b)

Company WX manufactures a number of finished products and two components. Three finished products (P1, P2, and P3) and two components (C1 and C2) are made using the same resources (but in different quantities). The components are used internally by the company when producing other products but they are not used in the manufacture of P1, P2 or P3.

Budgeted data for December for P1, P2, P3, C1 and C2 are as follows:

	P1	P2	P3	C1	C2
Units demanded	500	400	600	250	150
	$/unit	$/unit	$/unit	$/unit	$/unit
Selling price	155	125	175	–	–
Direct labour ($10/hour)	25	15	30	10	15
Direct material ($50/kg)	10	20	20	5	10
Variable production overhead ($40/machine hour)	10	15	20	10	20
Fixed production overhead ($20/labour hour)	50	30	60	20	30
Gross profit	60	45	45	–	–

Further information for December:

Direct labour: 4,300 hours are available.

Direct material: 420 kgs are available.

Machine hours: no restrictions apply.

Components: C1 and C2 are readily available from external suppliers for $50 and $80 per unit respectively. The external suppliers are reliable and the quality of the components is similar to that of those manufactured by the company.

Required:

(a)   Produce calculations to determine the optimal production plan for P1, P2, P3, C1 and C2 during December.

Note: it is not possible to produce partly finished units or to hold inventory of any of these products or components.   **(10 marks)**

(b)   There is a possibility that more of the direct material may become available during December. The shadow price per kg of the direct material has been calculated to be $200, $187.50 and $175 depending on how much extra becomes available.

Required:

Explain the shadow prices of $200, $187.50 and $175 for the direct material. Your answer should show the changes to the resource usage and the production plan for each of the shadow prices.   **(6 marks)**

Scenario for parts (c) and (d)

Company YZ manufactures products L, M and N. These products are always sold in the ratio 9L:6M:5N. The budgeted sales volume for December is a total of 14,000 units. The budgeted sales volumes, selling price per unit and variable cost per unit for each of the products are shown below:

	L	M	N
Sales budget (units)	6,300	4,200	3,500
	$	$	$
Selling price per unit	300	600	230
Variable cost per unit	100	300	50

The budgeted fixed costs of the company for December are $2.7 million.

Required:

(c)   Calculate the number of units of each product that must be sold for Company YZ to break even in December given the current sales mix ratio.   **(4 marks)**

(d)   The Sales Manager has now said that to be able to sell 6,300 units of product L in December it will be necessary to reduce the selling price of product L.

Calculate the sensitivity of Company YZ's total budgeted profit for December to a change in the selling price per unit of product L.   **(5 marks)**

(Total: 25 marks)

98   DFG (NOV 07)

DFG manufactures two products from different combinations of the same resources. Unit selling prices and unit cost details for each product are as follows:

Product	D	G
	$/unit	$/unit
Selling price	115	120
Direct material A ($5 per kg)	20	10
Direct material B ($3 per kg)	12	24
Skilled labour ($7 per hour)	28	21
Variable overhead ($2 per machine hour)	14	18
Fixed overhead*	28	36
Profit	13	11

*Fixed overhead is absorbed using an absorption rate per machine hour. It is an unavoidable central overhead cost that is not affected by the mix or volume of products produced.

The maximum weekly demand for products D and G is 400 units and 450 units respectively and this is the normal weekly production volume achieved by DFG. However, for the next four weeks, the achievable production level will be reduced due to a shortage of available resources. The resources that are expected to be available are as follows:

Direct material A	1,800 kg
Direct material B	3,500 kg
Skilled labour	2,500 hours
Machine time	6,500 machine hours

Required:

(a) **Using graphical linear programming identify the weekly production schedule for products D and G that maximises the profits of DFG during the next four weeks.**

(15 marks)

(b) **The optimal solution to part (a) shows that the shadow prices of skilled labour and direct material A are as follows:**

Skilled labour	**$Nil**
Direct material A	**$5.82**

Explain the relevance of these values to the management of DFG. (6 marks)

(c) **Using the graph you have drawn in part (a), explain how you would calculate by how much the selling price of product D could rise before the optimal solution would change.**

Note: Assume that demand is not affected by the selling price. You are not required to perform any calculations. (4 marks)

(Total: 25 marks)

99 LM (NOV 10)

LM produces two products from different quantities of the same resources using a just-in-time (JIT) production system. The selling price and resource requirements of each of these two products are as follows:

Product	L	M
Unit selling price ($)	70	90
Variable costs per unit:		
Direct labour ($7 per hour)	28	14
Direct material ($5 per kg)	10	45
Machine hours ($10 per hour)	10	20
Fixed overheads absorbed	12	6
Profit per unit	10	5

Fixed overheads are absorbed at the rate of $3 per direct labour hour.

Market research shows that the maximum demand for products L and M during December 2010 will be 400 units and 700 units respectively.

At a recent meeting of the purchasing and production managers to discuss the company's production plans for December 2010, the following resource availability for December 2010 was identified:

Direct labour	3,500 hours
Direct material	6,000 kg
Machine hours	2,000 hours

Required:

(a) **Prepare calculations to show, from a financial perspective, the optimum production plan for December 2010 and the contribution that would result from adopting your plan.** **(6 marks)**

You have now presented your optimum plan to the purchasing and production managers of LM. During the presentation, the following additional information became available:

(i) The company has agreed to an order for 250 units of product M for a selling price of $90 per unit from a new overseas customer. This order is in addition to the maximum demand that was previously predicted and must be produced and delivered in December 2010.

(ii) The originally predicted resource restrictions were optimistic. The managers now agree that the availability of all resources will be 20% lower than their original predictions.

Required:

Construct the revised resource constraints and the objective function to be used to identify, given the additional information above, the revised optimum production plan for December 2010. **(6 marks)**

(b) The resource constraints and objective function requested in part (b) above have now been processed in a simplex linear programming model and the following solution has been printed:

Product L	400	Product L other value	0
Product M	194	Product M other value	**506**
Direct labour	312		
Direct material ($)	**1.22**		
Machine hours	**312**		
Contribution ($)	**10,934.00**		

Required:

Analyse the meaning of each of the above eight values in the solution to the problem.

Your answer should include a proof of the five individual values highlighted in bold. **(13 marks)**

(Total: 25 marks)

100   D, E AND F (MAY 13)

A company manufactures three products D, E and F which use the same resources (but in different amounts). In addition to these resources each unit of Product F uses a component which the company currently purchases from an external supplier for $80. The demand for the products in Month 1 and the details per unit of the three products are as shown below:

	D	E	F
Demand (units)	2,400	2,200	3,000
	$	$	$
Selling price	112	136	153
Component			80
Direct materials ($4 per kg)	12	16	12
Skilled labour ($16 per hour)	16	24	8
Unskilled labour ($12 per hour)	18	12	9
Variable overhead ($3 per machine hour)	12	12	9

The fixed costs of the company are $150,000 per month.

The company has reverse engineered the component and has realised that it could make the component in-house. The cost of making a component is shown below:

	$
Direct materials ($4 per kg)	12
Skilled labour ($16 per hour)	16
Unskilled labour ($12 per hour)	3
Variable overhead ($3 per machine hour)	6

There would be no incremental fixed costs incurred as a result of making the component in-house. In Month 1 the maximum availability of skilled labour is 5,400 hours but all other resources are readily available. The company bases all short term decisions on profit maximisation.

Required:

(a)   Calculate the optimum production plan for Month 1 and the resulting profit. (Note: **The company would either buy the component or make it in-house; it would not do a mixture of the two options.)**   **(11 marks)**

For legal reasons it will not be possible to produce Product F in Month 2. Demand for products D and E will be 3,000 units each in Month 2. No inventories can be held.

The availability of resources in Month 2 is as follows:

Direct materials	16,000	kg
Skilled labour	5,400	hours
Unskilled labour	5,000	hours
Machine hours	19,600	hours

Required:

(b) (i) Identify the objective function and the constraints to be used in a linear programming model to determine the optimum production plan for Month 2.

(4 marks)

(ii) The solution to the linear programming model shows that the only binding constraints in Month 2 are those for skilled labour and unskilled labour. Produce, using simultaneous equations, the optimum production plan and resulting profit for Month 2. (You are NOT required to draw or sketch a graph.)

(4 marks)

(c) It has now been decided that Product F will be redesigned. A team will be formed with representatives from various departments in the company to undertake a value analysis exercise on Product F.

Required:

Describe the stages involved in a Value Analysis exercise.

(6 marks)

(Total: 25 marks)

101 X, Y AND Z PRODUCTION PLANNING (SEP 13)

A company produces three products (X, Y and Z) from the same resources (but in different quantities). Extracts from the original budget for Month 11 are shown below:

	X	Y	Z
Selling price ($ per unit)	24	41	42
Total cost ($ per unit)	20	20	35
Labour hours per unit	0.5	1.5	1.5
Machine hours per unit	1	2	0.75
Production and sales (units)	10,000	6,000	10,000

Variable costs are 40% of the total cost of each unit.

Fixed costs are absorbed at the rate of 150% of variable costs based on the budgeted production quantities as shown above.

It has now become known that during Month 11 essential maintenance work will have to be carried out. This will limit the availability of resources to:

Labour hours: 12,500 hours

Machine hours: 30,000 hours

Required:

(a) **Produce, using marginal costing principles, a columnar statement that shows the profit maximising production plan for Month 11 and the resulting profit or loss.**

(9 marks)

(b) **Calculate the three shadow prices for labour hours. Your answer must state the range of labour hours that each shadow price covers.**

(5 marks)

Marketing intelligence has now revealed that a new competitor is about to enter the market in Month 11 with a product that is much better than Product Y. It has therefore been decided that production of Product Y will stop immediately. The competitor will also sell products that will have an impact on the demand for Products X and Z.

Further work by the Marketing Department has revealed the relationships between the selling price and the monthly demand for Product X, and also for Product Z, as shown in the table below. There is no relationship between Product X and Product Z other than they use the same resources. The products must be produced separately, each in batches of 1,000 units.

	Selling price ($)	
Demand (units)	Product X	Product Z
2,000	28	66
4,000	27	60
6,000	26	54
8,000	25	48
10,000	24	42
12,000	23	36
14,000	22	30
16,000	21	24

The table should be interpreted as follows:

If the selling price of Product X was set at $28 then up to 2,000 units could be sold. To sell more than 2,000 units it would be necessary to reduce the price. For example, if the price was reduced to $25 per unit up to 8,000 units could be sold. The only selling prices that would be used are those shown in the table.

Required:

(b) **Calculate:**

    (i) **The revised optimum production plan for Products X and Z.** (9 marks)

    (ii) **The total contribution that the plan in (c)(i) would earn.** (2 marks)

(Total: 25 marks)

102 CDF (SEP 12)

CDF is a manufacturing company within the DF group. CDF has been asked to provide a quotation for a contract for a new customer and is aware that this could lead to further orders. As a consequence, CDF will produce the quotation by using relevant costing instead of its usual method of full cost plus pricing.

The following information has been obtained in relation to the contract:

Material D

40 tonnes of material D would be required. This material is in regular use by CDF and has a current purchase price of $38 per tonne. Currently, there are 5 tonnes in inventory which cost $35 per tonne. The resale value of the material in inventory is $24 per tonne.

Components

4,000 components would be required. These could be bought externally for $15 each or alternatively they could be supplied by RDF, another company within the DF manufacturing group. The variable cost of the component if it were manufactured by RDF would be $8 per unit, and RDF adds 30% to its variable cost to contribute to its fixed costs plus a further 20% to this total cost in order to set its internal transfer price. RDF has sufficient capacity to produce 2,500 components without affecting its ability to satisfy its own external customers. However in order to make the extra 1,500 components required by CDF, RDF would have to forgo other external sales of $50,000 which have a contribution to sales ratio of 40%.

Labour hours

850 direct labour hours would be required. All direct labour within CDF is paid on an hourly basis with no guaranteed wage agreement. The grade of labour required is currently paid $10 per hour, but department W is already working at 100% capacity. Possible ways of overcoming this problem are:

- Use workers in department Z, because it has sufficient capacity. These workers are paid $15 per hour.

- Arrange for sub-contract workers to undertake some of the other work that is performed in department W. The sub-contract workers would cost $13 per hour.

Specialist machine

The contract would require a specialist machine. The machine could be hired for $15,000 or it could be bought for $50,000. At the end of the contract if the machine were bought, it could be sold for $30,000. Alternatively it could be modified at a cost of $5,000 and then used on other contracts instead of buying another essential machine that would cost $45,000.

The operating costs of the machine are payable by CDF whether it hires or buys the machine. These costs would total $12,000 in respect of the new contract.

Supervisor

The contract would be supervised by an existing manager who is paid an annual salary of $50,000 and has sufficient capacity to carry out this supervision. The manager would receive a bonus of $500 for the additional work.

Development time

15 hours of development time at a cost of $3,000 have already been worked in determining the resource requirements of the contract.

Fixed overhead absorption rate

CDF uses an absorption rate of $20 per direct labour hour to recover its general fixed overhead costs. This includes $5 per hour for depreciation.

Required:

(a) Calculate the relevant cost of the contract to CDF. You must present your answer in a schedule that clearly shows the relevant cost value for each of the items identified above. You should also explain each relevant cost value you have included in your schedule and why any values you have excluded are not relevant.

Ignore taxation and the time value of money. **(19 marks)**

(b) Discuss TWO problems that can arise as a result of setting prices using relevant costing. **(6 marks)**

(Total: 25 marks)

COST PLANNING AND ANALYSIS FOR COMPETITIVE ADVANTAGE

103 VWXYZ COMPANY

Background

The VWXYZ Company produces a variety of high-quality garden furniture and associated items, mostly in wood and wrought iron. Among its products are speciality garden seats, sheds, gates, summer pavilions, outdoor tables and chairs, barbecue equipment etc. VWXYZ currently sells mostly to the trade but there is a flourishing retail outlet on the same site as the factory at Guildford.

Product field

Some financial details of broad product categories for the last year are given below:

Product	Sales revenue	Variable costs	Contribution
	$000	$000	$000
Tables and chairs	340	328	12
Sheds	200	154	46
Barbecue equipment	140	120	20
Garden seats	120	103	17
Pavilions	70	41	29
Gates	50	37	13
Lawnmowers	30	22	8
Tools, toys, etc	15	14	1
Café	5	2	3

Required:

(a)   Using the financial data of products, carry out a Pareto analysis (80/20 rule), including a suitable diagram, of (i) sales and (ii) contribution.   (15 marks)

(b)   State your findings in a brief management report.   (10 marks)

(Total: 25 marks)

104 LM HOSPITAL

LM Hospital is a private hospital, whose management is considering the adoption of an activity-based costing (ABC) system for the year 20X1/X2. The main reason for its introduction would be to provide more accurate information for pricing purposes. With the adoption of new medical technology, the amount of time that some patients stay in hospital has decreased considerably, and the management feels that the current pricing strategy may no longer reflect the different costs incurred.

Prices are currently calculated by determining the direct costs for the particular type of operation and adding a mark-up of 135%. With the proposed ABC system, the management expects to use a mark-up for pricing purposes of 15% on cost. This percentage will be based on all costs except facility sustaining costs. It has been decided that the hospital support activities should be grouped into three categories – admissions and record keeping, caring for patients, and facility sustaining.

The hospital has four operating theatres that are used for 9 hours a day for 300 days a year. It is expected that 7,200 operations will be performed during the coming year. The hospital has 15 consultant surgeons engaged in operating theatre work and consultancy. It is estimated that each consultant surgeon will work at the hospital for 2,000 hours in 20X1/X2.

Expected costs for 20X1/X2:

	$
Nursing services and administration	9,936,000
Linen and laundry	920,000
Kitchen and food costs (3 meals a day)	2,256,000
Consultant surgeons' fees	5,250,000
Insurance of building and general equipment	60,000
Depreciation of buildings and general equipment	520,000
Operating theatre	4,050,000
Pre-operation costs	1,260,000
Medical supplies – used in the hospital wards	1,100,000
Pathology laboratory (where blood tests, etc are carried out)	920,000
Updating patient records	590,000
Patient/bed scheduling	100,000
Invoicing and collections	160,000
Housekeeping activities, including ward maintenance, window cleaning, etc	760,000

Other information for 20X1/X2

Nursing hours	480,000
Number of pathology laboratory tests	8,000
Patient days	44,000
Number of patients	9,600

Information relating to specific operations for 20X1/X2:

	ENT (Ear, nose and throat)	Cataract
Time of stay in hospital	4 days	1 day
Operation time	2 hours	0.5
Consultant surgeon's time (which includes time in the operating theatre)	3 hours	0.85 hour

Required:

(a) Before making the final decision on the costing/pricing system, management has selected two types of operation for review: an ear, nose and throat (ENT) operation and a cataract operation.

   (i) Calculate the prices that would be charged under each method for the two types of operation. (Your answer should include an explanation and calculations of the cost drivers you have used.)   **(10 marks)**

   (ii) Comment on the results of your calculations and the implications for the proposed pricing policy.   **(5 marks)**

(b) Critically assess the method you have used to calculate the ABC prices by selecting two items/categories above which you feel should have been dealt with in a different way.   **(5 marks)**

(c) Explain whether the concept of throughput accounting could be used in a hospital.
                          (5 marks)

                          (Total: 25 marks)

105 S & P PRODUCTS COMPANY

S & P Products Company purchases a range of good quality gift and household products from around the world; it then sells these products through 'mail order' or retail outlets. The company receives 'mail orders' by post, telephone and Internet. Retail outlets are either department stores or S & P Products Company's own small shops. The company started to set up its own shops after a recession in the early 1990s and regards them as the flagship of its business; sales revenue has gradually built up over the last 10 years. There are now 50 department stores and 10 shops.

The company has made good profits over the last few years but recently trading has been difficult. As a consequence, the management team has decided that a fundamental reappraisal of the business is now necessary if the company is to continue trading.

Meanwhile the budgeting process for the coming year is proceeding. S & P Products Company uses an activity-based costing (ABC) system and the following estimated cost information for the coming year is available:

Retail outlet costs:

Activity	Cost driver	Rate per cost driver	Number each year for:	
		$	Dept store	Own shop
Telephone queries and requests to S & P	Calls	15	40	350
Sales visits to shops and stores by S & P sales staff	Visits	250	2	4
Shop orders	Orders	20	25	150
Packaging	Deliveries	100	28	150
Delivery to shops	Deliveries	150	28	150

Staffing, rental and service costs for each of S & P Products Company's own shops are on average $300,000 a year.

Mail order costs:

		Rate per cost driver		
Activity	Cost driver	Post	Telephone	Internet
		$	$	$
Processing 'mail orders'	Orders	5	6	3
Dealing with 'mail order' queries	Orders	4	4	1
		Number of packages per order		
Packaging and deliveries for 'mail orders' – cost per packaging $10	Packages	2	2	1

The total number of orders through the whole 'mail order' business for the coming year is expected to be 80,000. The maintenance of the Internet link is estimated to cost $80,000 for the coming year.

The following additional information for the coming year has been prepared:

	Department store	Own shop	Post	Telephone	Internet
Sales revenue per outlet	$50,000	$1,000,000			
Sales revenue per order			$150	$300	$100
Gross margin: mark-up on purchase cost	30%	40%	40%	40%	40%
Number of outlets	50	10			
Percentage of 'mail orders'			30%	60%	10%

Expected Head Office and warehousing costs for the coming year:

	$
Warehouse	2,750,000
IT	550,000
Administration	750,000
Personnel	300,000
	————
	4,350,000
	————

Required:

(a) **(i)** **Prepare calculations that will show the expected profitability of the different types of sales outlet for the coming year.** **(13 marks)**

(ii) **Comment briefly on the results of the figures you have prepared.** **(3 marks)**

(b) **In relation to the company's fundamental reappraisal of its business,**

(i) **discuss how helpful the information you have prepared in (a) is for this purpose and how it might be revised or expanded so that it is of more assistance** **(6 marks)**

(ii) **advise what other information is needed in order to make a more informed judgement.** **(3 marks)**

(Total: 25 marks)

106   RS COMPANY

RS Company is a retail organisation. It has 15 supermarkets, all of which are the same size. Goods are transported to RS Company's central warehouse by suppliers' vehicles, and are stored at the warehouse until needed at the supermarkets – at which point they are transported by RS Company's lorries.

RS Company's costs are:

	$000
Warehouse costs, per week	
Labour costs	220
Refrigeration costs	160
Other direct product costs	340
	———
	720
	———

	$000
Head-office costs, per week	
Labour costs	80
Other costs	76
	———
	156
	———

	$000
Supermarket costs, per shop per week	
Labour costs	16
Refrigeration costs	24
Other direct product costs	28
	———
	68
	———

	$
Transport costs per trip	
Standard vehicles	3,750
Refrigerated vehicles	4,950

The company has always used retail sales revenue less bought-in price to calculate the relative profitability of the different products. However, the chief executive is not happy with this method and has asked for three products – baked beans, ice cream and South African white wine – to be costed on a direct product profit basis.

The accountant has determined the following information for the supermarket chain:

	Baked beans	Ice cream	White wine
No. of cases per cubic meter (m^3)	28	24	42
No. of items per case	80	18	12
Sales per week – items	15,000	2,000	500
Time in warehouse – weeks	1	2	4
Time in supermarket – weeks	1	2	2
Retail selling price per item	$0.32	$1.60	$3.45
Bought-in price per item	$0.24	$0.95	$2.85

Additional information:

Total volume of all goods sold per week	20,000 m^3
Total volume for refrigerated goods sold per week	5,000 m^3
Carrying volume of each vehicle	90 m^3
Total sales revenue per week	$5 m
Total sales revenue of refrigerated goods per week	$650,000

Required:

(a) Calculated the profit per item using the direct product profitability method.

(13 marks)

(b) Discuss the differences in profitability between the company's current methods and the results of your calculations in (a), and suggest ways in which profitability could be improved. (7 marks)

(c) Explain how the direct product profit method differs from traditional overhead absorption. (5 marks)

(Total: 25 marks)

107 X COMPANY

X Company manufactures and distributes three types of car (the C1, C2 and C3). Each type of car has its own production line. The company is worried by extremely difficult market conditions and forecasts losses for the forthcoming year.

Current operations

The budgeted details for next year are as follows:

	C1	C2	C3
	$	$	$
Direct materials	2,520	2,924	3,960
Direct labour	1,120	1,292	1,980
Total direct cost per car	3,640	4,216	5,940
Budgeted production (cars)	75,000	75,000	75,000
Number of production runs	1,000	1,000	1,500
Number of orders executed	4,000	5,000	5,600
Machine hours	1,080,000	1,800,000	1,680,000

Annual overheads

	Fixed	Variable
	$000	$
Set ups	42,660	13,000 per production run
Materials handling	52,890	4,000 per order executed
Inspection	59,880	18,000 per production run
Machining	144,540	40 per machine hour
Distribution and warehousing	42,900	3,000 per order executed

Proposed JIT system

Management has hired a consultant to advise them on how to reduce costs. The consultant has suggested that the company adopts a just-in-time (JIT) manufacturing system. The introduction of the JIT system would have the following impact on costs (fixed and variable):

Direct labour	Increase by 20%
Set ups	Decrease by 30%
Materials handling	Decrease by 30%
Inspection	Decrease by 30%
Machining	Decrease by 15%
Distribution and warehousing	Eliminated

Required:

(a) **Based on the budgeted production levels, calculate the total annual savings that would be achieved by introducing the JIT system.** (4 marks)

The following table shows the price/demand relationship for each type of car per annum:

C1		C2		C3	
Price $	Demand	Price $	Demand	Price $	Demand
5,000	75,000	5,750	75,000	6,500	75,000
5,750	65,000	6,250	60,000	6,750	60,000
6,000	50,000	6,500	45,000	7,750	45,000
6,500	35,000	7,500	35,000	8,000	30,000

(b) **Assuming that X Company adopts the JIT system and that the revised variable overhead cost per car remains constant (as per the proposed JIT system budget), calculate the profit-maximising price and output level for each type of car.**
(10 marks)

Investigations have revealed that some of the fixed costs are directly attributable to the individual production lines and could be avoided if a line is closed down for the year. The specific fixed costs for each of the production lines, expressed as a percentage of the total fixed costs, are:

C1   4%

C2   5%

C3   8%

(c)   Determine the optimum production plan for the forthcoming year (based on the JIT cost structure and the prices and output levels you recommended in answer to requirement (b)).   (4 marks)

(d)   Write a report to the management of X Company which explains the conditions that are necessary for the successful implementation of a JIT manufacturing system.   (7 marks)

(Total: 25 marks)

108   GAIN SHARING (MAY 07)

X operates in an economy that has almost zero inflation. Management ignores inflation when evaluating investment projects because it is so low as to be considered insignificant. X is evaluating a number of similar, alternative investments. The company uses an after-tax cost of capital of 6% and has already completed the evaluation of two investments. The third investment is a new product that would be produced on a just-in-time basis and which is expected to have a life of three years. This investment requires an immediate cash outflow of $200,000, which does not qualify for tax depreciation. The expected residual value at the end of the project's life is $50,000.

A draft financial statement showing the values that are specific to this third investment for the three years is as follows:

	Year 1	Year 2	Year 3
	$	$	$
Sales	230,000	350,000	270,000
Production costs:			
Materials	54,000	102,000	66,000
Labour	60,000	80,000	70,000
Other*	80,000	90,000	80,000
Profit	36,000	78,000	54,000
Closing receivables	20,000	30,000	25,000
Closing payables	6,000	9,000	8,000

*Other production costs shown above include depreciation calculated using the straight line method.

The company is liable to pay corporation tax at a rate of 30% of its profits. One half of this is payable in the same year as the profit is earned, the remainder is payable in the following year.

Required:

(a)   Calculate the net present value of the above investment proposal.   **(10 marks)**

(b)   Explain how the above investment project would be appraised if there were to be a change in the rate of inflation so that it became too significant to be ignored.

                                                                                                                (5 marks)

The evaluations of the other two investments are shown below:

Investment	Initial investment	Net present value
	$	$
W	300,000	75,000
Y	100,000	27,000

The company only has $400,000 of funds available. All of the investment proposals are non-divisible. None of the investments may be repeated.

Required:

(c)   **Recommend, with supporting calculations, which of the three investment proposals should be accepted.**   **(3 marks)**

(d)   (i)   **Briefly explain gain-sharing arrangements.**   **(3 marks)**

        (ii)   **Explain the reasons why X might not want to overcome its investment funding limitations by using a gain-sharing arrangement.**   **(4 marks)**

                                                                                                        (Total: 25 marks)

109   AVX (MAY 06)

AVX plc assembles circuit boards for use by high technology audio-video companies. Owing to the rapidly advancing technology in this field, AVX plc is constantly being challenged to learn new techniques.

AVX plc uses standard costing to control its costs against targets set by senior managers. The standard labour cost per batch of one particular type of circuit board (CB45) is set out below:

                                                                                        $
Direct labour – 50 hours @ $10 /hour   500

The following labour efficiency variances arose during the first six months of the assembly of CB45:

Month	Number of batches assembled and sold	Labour efficiency variance ($)
November	1	Nil
December	1	170.00 Favourable
January	2	452.20 Favourable
February	4	1,089.30 Favourable
March	8	1,711.50 Favourable
April	16	3,423.00 Favourable

An investigation has confirmed that all of the costs were as expected except that there was a learning effect in respect of the direct labour that had not been anticipated when the standard cost was set.

Required:

(a) (i) Calculate the monthly rates of learning that applied during the six months.

(ii) Identify when the learning period ended and briefly discuss the implications of your findings for AVX plc. **(10 marks)**

AVX plc initially priced each batch of CB45 circuit boards on the basis of its standard cost of $960 plus a mark-up of 25%. Recently the company has noticed that, due to increasing competition, it is having difficulty maintaining its sales volume at this price.

The Finance Director has agreed that the long-run unit variable cost of the CB45 circuit board is $672.72 per batch. She has suggested that the price charged should be based on an analysis of market demand. She has discovered that, at a price of $1,200, the demand is 16 batches per month; for every $20 reduction in selling price there is an increase in demand of 1 batch of CB45 circuit board; and for every $20 increase in selling price there is a reduction in demand of 1 batch.

Required:

(b) Calculate the profit-maximising selling price per batch using the data supplied by the Finance Director. **(8 marks)**

Note: If Price (P) = a–bx, then Marginal Revenue (MR) = a–2bx.

The Technical Director cannot understand why there is a need to change the selling price. He argues that this is a highly advanced technological product and that AVX plc should not reduce its price as this reflects badly on the company. If anything is at fault, he argues, it is the use of standard costing and he has asked whether target costing should be used instead.

Required:

(c) (i) Explain the difference between standard costs and target costs.

(ii) Explain the possible reasons why AVX plc needs to re-consider its pricing policy now that the CB45 circuit board has been available in the market for six months. **(7 marks)**

(Total: 25 marks)

110 RETAIL OUTLET (NOV 07)

A small retail outlet sells four main groups of products: basic foods (milk, bread, etc); newspapers and magazines; frozen foods; and canned foods. A budgeted weekly profit statement is shown below:

	Basic foods	Newspapers and magazines	Frozen foods	Canned foods
	$	$	$	$
Sales revenue	800	1,000	1,500	2,400
Cost of sales	600	700	550	1,200
Gross margin	200	300	950	1,200
Power for freezers*			100	
Overheads**	100	100	200	400
Net margin	100	200	650	800

*The freezers would be emptied and switched off as necessary during redecoration.

**Overhead costs comprise general costs of heating and lighting, rent and rates, and other general overhead costs. These costs are attributed to products in proportion to the floor area occupied by each product group which is as follows:

	Basic foods	Newspapers and magazines	Frozen foods	Canned foods
Floor area (m²)	50	50	100	200

For each product group, analysis has shown that the sales revenue achieved changes in direct proportion to the floor space allocated to the product.

The owner of the retail outlet has decided that the premises need to be redecorated but is undecided as to which of the following two options would be the most profitable.

Option 1:

Close the retail outlet completely for four weeks while the redecoration takes place.

The company that is to complete the redecoration would charge $2,500 under this option. It is expected that, following the re-opening of the retail outlet, there would be a loss of sales for the next 12 weeks because customers would have had to find alternative suppliers for their goods. The reduction in sales due to lost customers has been estimated to be 30% of the budgeted sales during the first four weeks of reopening; 20% during the next four weeks; and 10% during the third four weeks. In addition, in order to encourage customers to return to the retail outlet, there would be a 10% price reduction on all basic foods and canned foods for the entire 12-week period.

Option 2:

Continue to open the retail outlet while the redecoration takes place but with a reduced amount of floor area.

The useable floor area would be reduced to 40% of that originally available. After three weeks, the retail outlet would be closed for 0.5 weeks while the goods are moved to the newly redecorated area. The retail outlet would then continue to operate using 40% of its original floor area for a further three weeks before the work was fully completed. The company that is to complete the redecoration would charge $3,500 under this option and, in addition, there would be product movement costs of $1,000. The owner has determined that, in order to avoid losing customers, there should be no reduction in the amount of floor area given to basic foods and newspapers and magazines throughout this period. The floor area to be used by frozen foods and canned foods should be determined on the basis of their profitability per unit of area. However, the frozen foods are presently kept in four freezers, and therefore any reductions in floor area must be determined by complete freezer units. It may be assumed that each freezer unit incurs equal amounts of power costs.

Required:

(a)   **Advise the owner of the retail outlet which option to choose in order to minimise the losses that will occur as a result of the decision. All workings must be shown.**

(15 marks)

(b)   **Explain how activity-based costing may be used in a retail environment to improve the decision making and profitability of the business.** **(10 marks)**

(Total: 25 marks)

BUDGETING AND MANAGEMENT CONTROL

111 AHW

AHW is a food processing company that produces high-quality, part-cooked meals for the retail market. The five different types of meal that the company produces (Products A to E) are made by subjecting ingredients to a series of processing activities. The meals are different, and therefore need differing amounts of processing activities.

Budget and actual information for October 20X2 is shown below:

Budgeted data

	Product A	Product B	Product C	Product D	Product E
Number of batches	20	30	15	40	25
Processing activities per batch:					
Processing activity W	4	5	2	3	1
Processing activity X	3	2	5	1	4
Processing activity Y	3	3	2	4	2
Processing activity Z	4	6	8	2	3

Budgeted costs of processing activities:

	$000
Processing activity W	160
Processing activity X	130
Processing activity Y	80
Processing activity Z	200

All costs are expected to be variable in relation to the number of processing activities.

Actual data

Actual output during October 20X2 was as follows:

	Product A	Product B	Product C	Product D	Product E
Number of batches	18	33	16	35	28

Actual processing costs incurred during October 20X2 were:

	$000
Processing activity W	158
Processing activity X	139
Processing activity Y	73
Processing activity Z	206

Required:

(a) **Prepare a budgetary control statement (to the nearest $000) that shows the original budget costs, flexible budget costs, the actual costs, and the total variances of each processing activity for October 20X2.**   **(15 marks)**

Your control statement has been issued to the Managers responsible for each processing activity and the Finance Director has asked each of them to explain the reasons for the variances shown in your statement. The Managers are not happy about this as they were not involved in setting the budgets and think that they should not be held responsible for achieving targets that were imposed upon them.

Required:

(b)   **List three reasons why it might be preferable for Managers not to be involved in setting their own budgets.**   **(3 marks)**

(c)   (i)   **Explain the difference between fixed and flexible budgets and how each may be used to control production costs and non-production costs (such as marketing costs) within AHW plc.**   **(4 marks)**

      (ii) **Give two examples of costs that are more appropriately controlled using a fixed budget, and explain why a flexible budget is less appropriate for the control of these costs.**   **(3 marks)**

                                                                (Total: 25 marks)

112   PRODUCTS R, S AND T

X manufactures three products in a modern manufacturing plant, using cell operations.

Budgeted output for April was:

Product R   1,800 units in 36 batches

Product S   1,000 units in 10 batches

Product T   1,000 units in 40 batches

The product details are as follows:

	Product R	Product S	Product T
Standard labour hours per batch	25	30	12
Batch size (units)	50	100	25
Machine set-ups per batch	3	?	5
Power (kj) per batch	1.4	1.7	0.8
Purchase orders per batch	5	3	7
Machine hours per batch	10	7.5	12.5

During April the actual output was:

Product R   1,500 units in 30 batches

Product S   1,200 units in 12 batches

Product T   1,000 units in 40 batches

The following production overhead budgetary control statement has been prepared for April on the basis that the variable production overhead varies in relation to standard labour hours produced.

Production overhead budgetary control report April

	Original budget	Flexed budget	Actual	Variances
Output (standard hours produced)	1,800	1,710	1,710	
	$000	$000	$000	$000
Power	1,250	1,220	1,295	75 (A)
Stores	1,850	1,800	1,915	115 (A)
Maintenance	2,100	2,020	2,100	80 (A)
Machinery cleaning	800	760	870	110 (A)
Indirect labour	1,460	1,387	1,510	123 (A)
	7,460	7,187	7,690	503 (A)

After the above report had been produced, investigations revealed that every one of the individual costs could be classified as wholly variable in relation to the appropriate cost drivers.

Required:

(a)   List the factors that should be considered when selecting a cost driver.   (3 marks)

(b)   (i)   Calculate the budgeted cost per driver for each of the overhead costs.

(8 marks)

(ii)   Prepare a production overhead budgetary control report for April using an activity based approach.   (10 marks)

(c)   Comment on the validity of an activity based approach to budgetary control for an organisation such as X plc.   (4 marks)

(Total: 25 marks)

113   KEY METRICS

The following statements have been extracted from a company's master budget for the forthcoming period.

Income statement for the year ended 30 April 20X6

	$000
Revenue	4,885
Cost of sales	4,315
Gross profit	570
Selling/distribution/administration costs	275
Profit	295

Balance sheet as at 30 April 20X6

	$000	$000
Non-current assets		1,280
Current assets		
Inventory	335	
Trade receivables	320	
Bank	145	
	800	
		2,080
Capital and reserves		1,380
Non-current liabilities		370
Trade payables		280
Other short-term liabilities		50
		2,080

The directors intend to appraise the budget using the following key metrics.

		Target for relevant metric
(i)	Return on capital employed	19.0%
(ii)	Profit/sales ratio	6.0%
(iii)	Net asset turnover	3.2 times
(iv)	Non-current asset turnover	4.5 times
(v)	Current ratio	2.1 times
(vi)	Quick or acid test ratio	1.4 times

Required:

(a) Calculate the six key metrics and state whether or not they will be acceptable to the directors. **(10 marks)**

(b) For each key metric which would not be acceptable, suggest any actions that might be taken to help to achieve the company target. **(10 marks)**

(c) Explain the meaning of the term 'critical success factors' in a business giving examples of such factors. **(5 marks)**

(Total: 25 marks)

114   M PLC (MAY 06) *Walk in the footsteps of a top tutor*

M plc designs, manufactures and assembles furniture. The furniture is for home use and therefore varies considerably in size, complexity and value. One of the departments in the company is the Assembly Department. This department is labour intensive; the workers travel to various locations to assemble and fit the furniture using the packs of finished timbers that have been sent to them.

Budgets are set centrally and are given to the managers of the various departments who then have the responsibility of achieving their respective targets. Actual costs are compared against the budgets and the managers are then asked to comment on the budgetary control statement. The statement for April for the Assembly Department is shown below.

	Budget	Actual	Variance	
Assembly labour hours	6,400	7,140		
	$	$	$	
Assembly labour	51,970	58,227	6,257	Adverse
Furniture packs	224,000	205,000	19,000	Favourable
Other materials	23,040	24,100	1,060	Adverse
Overheads	62,060	112,340	50,280	Adverse
Total	361,070	399,667	38,597	Adverse

Note: The costs shown are for assembling and fitting the furniture (they do not include time spent travelling to jobs and the related costs). The hours worked by the manager are not included in the figure given for the assembly labour hours.

The manager of the Assembly Department is new to the job and has very little previous experience of working with budgets but he does have many years' experience as a supervisor in assembly departments. Based on that experience he was sure that the department had performed well. He has asked for your help in replying to a memo he has just received asking him to 'explain the serious overspending in his department'. He has sent you some additional information about the budget:

(1)   The budgeted and actual assembly labour costs include the fixed salary of $2,050 for the manager of the Assembly Department. All of the other labour is paid for the hours they work.

(2)   The cost of furniture packs and other materials is assumed by the central finance office of M plc to vary in proportion to the number of assembly labour hours worked.

(3)   The budgeted overhead costs are made up of three elements: a fixed cost of $9,000 for services from central headquarters; a stepped fixed cost which changes when the assembly hours exceed 7,000 hours; and some variable overheads. The variable overheads are assumed to vary in proportion to the number of assembly labour hours. Working papers for the budget showed the impact on the overhead costs of differing amounts of assembly labour hours:

Assembly labour hours	5,000	7,500	10,000
Overhead costs	$54,500	$76,500	$90,000

The actual fixed costs for April were as budgeted.

Required:

(a) Prepare, using the additional information that the manager of the Assembly Department has given you, a budgetary control statement that would be more helpful to him. **(10 marks)**

(b) (i) Discuss the differences between the format of the statement that you have produced and that supplied by M plc. **(5 marks)**

(ii) Discuss the assumption made by the central office of M plc that costs vary in proportion to assembly labour hours. **(4 marks)**

(c) Discuss whether M plc should change to a system of participative budgeting. **(6 marks)**

(Total: 25 marks)

CONTROL AND PERFORMANCE MEASUREMENT OF RESPONSIBILITY CENTRES

115 SPORTS EQUIPMENT (MAY 09)

A multi-national sports equipment manufacturer has a number of autonomous divisions throughout the world. Two of the divisions are in America, one on the west coast and one on the east coast. The west coast division manufactures cycle frames and assembles them into complete cycles using bought-in components. The east coast division produces wheels that are very similar to the wheel sets that are used by the Frames Division but it currently only sells them to external customers. Details of the two divisions are given below.

Frames Division (west coast)

The Frames Division buys the wheels that it needs from a local supplier. It has negotiated a price of $870 per set (there are two wheels in a set). This price includes a bulk purchase discount which is awarded if the division purchases 15,000 sets per year. The production budget shows that 15,000 sets will be needed next year.

Wheels Division (east coast)

The Wheels Division has a capacity of 35,000 sets per year. Details of the budget for the forthcoming year are as follows:

Sales	30,000 sets
Per set	$
Selling price	950
Variable costs	650

The fixed costs of the division at the budgeted output of 30,000 sets are $8m per year but they would rise to $9m if output exceeds 31,000 sets.

Note: The maximum external demand is 30,000 sets per year and there are no other uses for the current spare capacity.

Group directive

The Managing Director of the group has reviewed the budgets of the divisions and has decided that in order to improve the profitability of the group the Wheels Division should supply wheel sets to the Frames Division. She is also thinking of linking the salaries of the divisional managers to the performance of their divisions but is unsure which performance measure to use. Two measures that she is considering are 'profit' and the 'return on assets consumed' (where the annual fixed costs would be used as the 'assets consumed').

The Manager of the Wheels Division has offered to supply wheel sets to the Frames Division at a price of $900 per set. He has offered this price because it would earn the same contribution per set that is earned on external sales (this is after adjusting for distribution and packaging costs).

Required:

(a) Assume that the 15,000 wheel sets are supplied by the Wheels Division at a transfer price of $900 per set.

Calculate the impact on the profits of each of the divisions and the group. (4 marks)

(b) Calculate the minimum price at which the Manager of the Wheels Division would be willing to transfer the 15,000 sets to the Frames Division if his performance is to be measured against maintaining:

(i) the profit of the division (currently $1m)

(ii) the return on assets consumed by the division (currently 12.5%). (8 marks)

(c) Produce a report to the Managing Director of the group that:

(i) explains the problems that may arise from the directive and the introduction of performance measures (8 marks)

(ii) explains how the problems could be resolved. (5 marks)

Note: You should use your answers to parts (a) and (b) and other relevant calculations, where (a) and (b) and other relevant calculations, where appropriate, to illustrate points in your report.

(Total: 25 marks)

116 KDS

KDS is an engineering company which is organised for management purposes in the form of several autonomous divisions. The performance of each division is currently measured by calculation of its return on capital employed (ROCE).

KDS existing accounting policy is to calculate ROCE by dividing the net assets of each division at the end of the year into the operating profit generated by the division during the year. Cash is excluded from net assets since all divisions share a bank account controlled by KDS's head office. Depreciation is on a straight-line basis.

The divisional management teams are paid a performance-related bonus conditional upon achievement of a 15% ROCE target.

On 20 December 20X5 the divisional managers were provided with performance forecasts for 20X5 which included the following:

Forecast	Net assets at 31 December 20X5	20X5 operating profit	ROCE
	$	$	
Division K	4,400,000	649,000	14.75%
Division D	480,000	120,000	25.00%

Subsequently, the manager of Division K invited members of her management team to offer advice. The responses she received included the following:

From the divisional administrator:

'We can achieve our 20X5 target by deferring payment of a $90,000 trade debt payable on 20 December until 1 January. I should add that we will thereby immediately incur a $2,000 late payment penalty.'

From the works manager:

'We should replace a number of our oldest machine tools (which have nil book value) at a cost of $320,000. The new equipment will have a life of eight years and generate cost savings of $76,000 per year. The new equipment can be on site and operational by 31 December 20X5.'

From the financial controller:

'The existing method of performance appraisal is unfair. We should ask head office to adopt residual income (RI) as the key performance indicator, using the company's average 12% cost of money for a finance charge.'

Required:

(a) **Compare and appraise the proposals of the divisional administrator and the works manager, having regard to the achievement of the ROCE performance target in 20X5 and to any longer term factors you think relevant.** **(9 marks)**

(b) **Explain the extent to which you agree or disagree with the financial controller's proposal.** **(9 marks)**

(c) **Explain how non-financial performance measures could be used to assess the performance of divisions K and D.** **(7 marks)**

(Total: 25 marks)

117 CNJ (MAR 13)

CNJ operates a chain of fitness clubs. The clubs are structured into two divisions, the Eastern division and the Western division. Each division has a Managing Director who is responsible for revenue, cost and investment decisions at their clubs. A bonus is awarded each year to the Managing Director that generates the higher Return on Capital Employed (ROCE).

The following summary information shows the results of the divisions for the past two years:

Year ending 31st December	2012		2011	
	Eastern	Western	Eastern	Western
	$000	$000	$000	$000
Revenue	1,800	2,480	1,900	2,250
Staff costs	1,150	1,430	1,180	1,310
Other operating costs	460	675	500	620
Operating profit	190	375	220	320
Capital employed	500	900	750	1,200
Average number of members	6,790	9,300	7,150	8,420

Notes:

1   Revenue is comprised largely of income from membership fees.

2   CNJ uses net book value of non-current assets as the capital employed. The capital employed figures in the above table are the net book value of the non-current assets of each division at the end of the year.

3   Non-current assets are depreciated on a straight line basis over a period of five years and are assumed to have no residual value. There were no additions or disposals of non-current assets during the years 2011 and 2012.

4   Both divisions have a cost of capital of 15%.

5   Ignore taxation and inflation.

Required:

(a)   Discuss the relative performance of the two divisions using Return on Capital Employed and other performance measures that you think are appropriate.

(15 marks)

Investigations by CNJ'S audit team have revealed that at the end of 2011 the Managing Director of the Western Division rejected the opportunity to acquire a new building and equipment to set up a new fitness club at a total cost of $800,000. The building could have been purchased for $350,000 and for the purpose of this evaluation it is assumed that it would have held that value for five years and that no depreciation would have been charged on the building. The new equipment would have cost $450,000 and would have been depreciated in accordance with CNJ's policy over five years. The investment would have taken place on 1 January 2012.

The forecast annual profit and number of members for the proposed new club were as follows:

	$000	
Revenue	675	
Staff costs	371	
Other operating costs	160	(including depreciation of the equipment)
Operating profit	144	
Average number of members	2,200	

It is CNJ's policy that investments of this type should be appraised over five years using net present value.

Required:

(b)   (i)   Calculate the net present value of the investment. Ignore taxation and inflation.   (4 marks)

(ii)   Explain, using appropriate calculations based on the Western Division and the rejected investment, the limitations of ROCE as a divisional performance measure.

Note: you can assume that the actual figures for the Western Division for 2012 were the same as those budgeted. Therefore when the decision about the new club was being made the Managing Director based the decision on the figures for the investment and the 2012 results for the Western Division.   (6 marks)

(Total: 25 marks)

118 DIVISION A

Division A, which is a part of the ACF Group, manufactures only one type of product, a Bit, which it sells to external customers and also to division C, another member of the group. ACF Group's policy is that divisions have the freedom to set transfer prices and choose their suppliers.

The ACF Group uses residual income (RI) to assess divisional performance and each year it sets each division a target RI. The group's cost of capital is 12% a year.

Division A

Budgeted information for the coming year is:

Maximum capacity	150,000 Bits
External sales	110,000 Bits
External selling price	$35 per Bit
Variable cost	$22 per Bit
Fixed costs	$1,080,000
Capital employed	$3,200,000
Target residual income	$180,000

Division C

Division C has found two other companies willing to supply Bits:

X could supply at $28 per Bit, but only for annual orders in excess of 50,000 Bits. Z could supply at $33 per Bit for any quantity ordered.

Required:

(a)   Division C provisionally requests a quotation for 60,000 Bits from division A for the coming year.

    (i)   Calculate the transfer price per Bit that division A should quote in order to meet its residual income target. **(5 marks)**

    (ii)   Calculate the two prices division A would have to quote to division C, if it became group policy to quote transfer prices based on opportunity costs. **(4 marks)**

(b)   Evaluate and discuss the impact of the group's current and proposed policies on the profits of divisions A and C, and on group profit. Illustrate your answer with calculations. **(8 marks)**

(c)   Assume that divisions A and C are based in different countries and consequently pay taxes at different rates: division A at 55% and division C at 25%. Division A has now quoted a transfer price of $30 per Bit for 60,000 Bits.

Calculate whether it is better for the group if division C purchases 60,000 Bits from division A or from supplier X. **(8 marks)**

(Total: 25 marks)

119 DE TRANSFER (MAY 11)

The DE Company has two divisions. The following statement shows the performance of each division for the year ended 30 April 2011:

	D	E
	$000	$000
Sales	500,200	201,600
Variable cost	380,400	140,000
Contribution	119,800	61,600
Fixed costs	30,000	20,000
Operating profit	89,800	41,600

Division E manufactures just one type of component. It sells the components to external customers and also to Division D. During the year to 30 April 2011, Division E operated at its full capacity of 140,000 units. The transfer of 70,000 units to Division D satisfied that division's total demand for that type of component. However the external demand was not satisfied. A further 42,000 components could have been sold to external customers by Division E at the current price of $1,550.

The current policy of the DE Company is that internal sales should be transferred at their opportunity cost. Consequently during the year, some components were transferred to Division D at the market price and some were transferred at variable cost.

Required:

(a) **Prepare an analysis of the sales made by Division E that shows clearly, in units and in $, the internal and external sales made during the year.** **(3 marks)**

(b) **Discuss the effect of possible changes in external demand on the profits of Division E, assuming the current transfer pricing policy continues.** **(6 marks)**

Division E is considering investing in new equipment which would reduce its unit variable costs by 20% and increase its capacity by 10% for each of the next five years. The capital cost of the investment is $120m and the equipment would have no value after five years. The DE company and its divisional managers evaluate investments using net present value (NPV) with an 8% cost of capital.

External annual demand for the next five years will continue to be 112,000 components at $1,550 each but the DE Company will insist that the internal annual demand for 70,000 components must be satisfied.

Required:

Assuming that the current transfer pricing policy continues:

(c) (i) **Evaluate the investment from the perspective of the manager of Division E.** **(6 marks)**

(ii) **Evaluate the investment from the perspective of the DE Company.** **(4 marks)**

Note: Ignore inflation and taxation.

(d) **Explain TWO factors that should be considered when designing divisional performance measures.** **(6 marks)**

(Total: 25 marks)

120 SWZ (NOV 10)

SWZ is a manufacturing company that has many trading divisions. Return on Investment (ROI) is the main measure of each division's performance. Each divisional manager's salary is linked only to their division's ROI.

The following information summarises the financial performance of the S division of SWZ over the last three years:

Year ending 31 October	2008	2009	2010
	$000	$000	$000
Turnover	400	400	400
Cost of sales	240	240	240
Gross profit	160	160	160
Other operating costs	120	104	98
Pre-tax operating profit	40	56	62
Capital invested as at the end of the year	400	320	256

Other operating costs include asset depreciation calculated at the rate of 20% per annum on a reducing balance basis.

The figures shown in the above table for the capital invested as at the end of the year is the net book value of the division's fixed assets.

All of the above values have been adjusted to remove the effects of inflation. There have been no additions or disposals of fixed assets within the S division during this period.

Required:

(a)   Discuss the performance of the S division over the three year period.   (9 marks)

The manager of the S division is now considering investing in a replacement machine. The machine that would be replaced would be sold for its net book value which was $40,000 at 31 October 2010 and the new machine would cost $100,000. The new machine would have an expected life of five years and would be depreciated using the same depreciation rates as the existing machinery. The new machine would reduce the division's cost of sales by 10%. At the end of five years it would be sold for its net book value.

The divisional cost of capital is 8% per annum. The company has evaluated the investment and correctly determined that it has a positive Net Present Value (NPV) of $24,536.

Required:

(b)   Prepare calculations to show why the manager of the S division is unlikely to go ahead with the investment.

   Ignore taxation.   (11 marks)

(c)   Prepare calculations to show how the use of Residual Income (RI) as the performance measure would have led to a goal congruent decision by the manager of the S division in relation to the purchase of the replacement machine.

   Ignore taxation.   (5 marks)

   (Total: 25 marks)

121 H PERFUMES (MAY 10)

H manufactures perfumes and cosmetics by mixing various ingredients in different processes, before the items are packaged and sold to wholesalers. H uses a divisional structure with each process being regarded as a separate division with its own manager who is set performance targets at the start of each financial year which begins on 1 January. Performance is measured using Return on Investment (ROI) based on net book value of capital equipment at the start of the year. The company depreciates its capital equipment at the rate of 20% per annum on a reducing balance basis. The annual depreciation is calculated at the start of the financial year and one-twelfth of this annual amount is included as monthly depreciation in the fixed overhead costs of each process. Output transferred from one process to another is valued using transfer prices based on the total budgeted costs of the process plus a mark-up of 15%.

Process B

This is the first process. Raw materials are blended to produce three different outputs, two of which are transferred to Processes C and D respectively. The third output is accounted for as a by-product and sold in the external market without further processing. The equipment used to operate this process originally cost $800,000 on 1 January 2005.

The process B account for April 2010 was as follows:

	Litres	$		Litres	$
Opening WIP	NIL	NIL	Normal loss	3,000	3,000
Material W	10,000	25,000	By-product	5,000	5,000
Material X	5,000	10,000	Output to C	9,000	82,800
Material Y	12,000	24,000	Output to D	10,000	92,000
Direct labour		30,000	Closing WIP	NIL	NIL
Overhead		75,000			
Profit and loss		18,800			
Totals	27,000	182,800	Totals	27,000	182,800

The material costs are variable per unit of input and direct labour costs are fixed in the short term because employees' contracts provide them with a six month notice period. Overhead costs include a share of Head Office costs, and of the remaining overhead costs some vary with the input volume of the process. The level of activity in April 2010 was typical of the monthly volumes processed by the company.

Process C

This process receives input from Process B to which is added further materials to produce a finished product that is sold in the external market at the budgeted selling price of $20 per litre. The equipment used to operate this process originally cost $500,000 on 1 January 2008.

The Process C account for April 2010 was as follows:

	Litres	$		Litres	$
Opening WIP	1,000	11,200	Normal loss	3,000	1,500
Input from B	9,000	82,800	Abnormal loss	1,500	750
Material Z	3,000	15,000	Output	7,500	150,000
Direct labour	20,000		Closing WIP	1,000	11,200
Overhead		50,000			
			Profit and loss		15,550
Totals	13,000	179,000	Totals	13,000	179,000

The material costs are variable per unit of input and direct labour costs are fixed in the short term because employees' contracts provide them with a six month notice period. Overhead costs include a share of Head Office costs, and of the remaining overhead costs some vary with the input volume of the process. The level of activity that occurred in April 2010 was typical of the monthly volumes processed by the company, and the opening and closing work in process are identical in every respect. The process is regarded as an investment centre and completed output and losses are valued at their selling prices. The manager of Process C is concerned at the level of output achieved from the input volume and is considering investing in new equipment that should eliminate the abnormal loss. This would involve investing $1,000,000 in new processing equipment on 1 January 2011; the existing equipment would be sold on the same date at a price equal to its net book value.

Process D

This process receives input from Process B which is further processed to produce a finished product that is sold in the external market at the budgeted selling price of $16 per litre. The equipment used to operate this process originally cost $300,000 on 1 January 2000.

The Process D account for April 2010 was as follows:

	Litres	$		Litres	$
Opening WIP	1,000	5,500	Normal loss	1,000	3,000
Input from B	10,000	92,000	Output	9,000	144,000
Direct labour		30,000	Closing WIP	1,000	5,500
Overhead		30,000	Profit and loss		5,000
Totals	11,000	157,500	Totals	11,000	157,500

Direct labour costs are fixed in the short term because employees' contracts provide them with a six month notice period. Overhead costs include a share of Head Office costs, and of the remaining overhead costs some vary with the input volume of the process. The level of activity in April 2010 was typical of the monthly volumes processed by the company, and the opening and closing work in process are identical in every respect. The process is regarded as an investment centre and completed output and losses are valued at their selling prices. The manager of Process D believes that the transfer price from Process B is unfair because the equivalent material could be purchased in the open market at a cost of $7.50 per litre.

Required:

(a) (i) Calculate the annualised Return on Investment (ROI) achieved by each of the process divisions during April 2010. (4 marks)

(ii) Discuss the suitability of this performance measure in the context of the data provided for each process division. (4 marks)

(b) (i) Calculate the effect on the annualised Return on Investment in 2011 of Process Division C investing in new capital equipment. (4 marks)

(ii) Discuss the conflict that may arise between the use of NPV and ROI in this investment decision. (4 marks)

(c) Discuss the transfer pricing policy being used by H from the viewpoints of the managers of Process Division B and Process Division D. (9 marks)

(Total: 25 marks)

122 ALPHA GROUP (SEP 10)

The Alpha group comprises two companies, X Limited and Y Limited both of which are resident in a country where company profits are subject to taxation at 30%.

X Limited

X Limited has two trading divisions:

Consultancy division – provides consultancy services to the engineering sector.

Production division – assembles machinery which it sells to a number of industry sectors. Many of the components used in these machines are purchased from Y Limited.

Y Limited

Y Limited manufactures components from raw materials many of which are imported. The components are sold globally. Some of the components are sold to X Limited.

Financial results

The financial results of the two companies for the year ended 30 September 2010 are as follows:

	X Limited		Y Limited
	Consultancy division	*Production division*	
	$000	$000	$000
External sales	710	1,260	400
Sales to X Limited			350
			750
Cost of sales	240	900*	250
Administration costs	260	220	130
Operating profit	210	140	370
Capital employed	800	2,000	4,000

* includes the cost of components purchased from Y Limited

Required:

(a) Discuss the performance of each division of X Limited and of Y Limited using the following three ratios:

(i) Return on Capital Employed (ROCE)

(ii) Operating Profit Margin

(iii) Asset Turnover **(9 marks)**

Transfer prices

The current policy of the group is to allow the managers of each company or division to negotiate with each other concerning the transfer prices.

The manager of Y Limited charges the same price internally for its components that it charges to its external customers. The manager of Y argues that this is fair because if the internal sales were not made he could increase his external sales. An analysis of the market demand shows that currently Y Limited satisfies only 80% of the external demand for its components.

The manager of the Production division of X Limited believes that the price being charged by Y Limited for the components is too high and is restricting X Limited's ability to win orders. Recently X Limited failed to win a potentially profitable order which it priced using its normal gross profit mark-up. The competitor who won the order set a price that was less than 10% lower than X Limited's price.

An analysis of the cost structure of Y Limited indicates that 40% of the cost of sales is fixed costs and the remaining costs vary with the value of sales.

Required:

(b) **(i)** **Discuss how the present transfer pricing policy is affecting the overall performance of the group.** **(5 marks)**

(ii) **Explain, including appropriate calculations, the transfer price or prices at which the components should be supplied by Y Limited to X Limited.**

(8 marks)

(c) The group Managing Director is considering relocating Y Limited to a country that has a much lower rate of company taxation than that in its current location.

Required:

Explain the potential tax consequences of the internal transfer pricing policy if Y Limited were to relocate. **(3 marks)**

(Total: 25 marks)

123 PZ GROUP (MAR 11)

The PZ Group comprises two companies: P Limited and Z Limited. Both companies manufacture similar items and are located in different regions of the same country. Return on Capital Employed (ROCE) is used as the group's performance measure and is also used to determine divisional managers' bonuses. The results of the two companies and of the group for the year ended 31st December 2010 and the balance sheets at that date are as follows:

	P Limited	Z Limited	PZ Group
Revenue	200,000	220,000	400,000
Cost of sales	170,000	160,000	310,000
Gross profit	30,000	60,000	90,000
Administration costs	10,000	30,000	40,000
Interest payable	10,000	———	10,000
Pre-tax profit	10,000	30,000	40,000
Non-current assets:			
Original cost	1,000,000	1,500,000	2,500,000
Accumulated depreciation	590,400	1,106,784	1,697,184
Net book value	409,600	393,216	802,816
Net current assets	50,000	60,000	110,000
	459,600	453,216	912,816
Non-current borrowings	150,000		150,000
Shareholders' funds	309,600	453,216	762,816
Capital employed	459,600	453,216	912,816

Notes:

(1)   During the year Z Limited sold goods to P Limited that had cost Z Limited $10,000. The transactions relating to this sale have been eliminated from the PZ Group results stated above.

(2)   Both companies use the group depreciation policy of 20% per annum on a reducing balance basis for their non-current assets. Neither company made any additions or disposals of non-current assets during the year.

Required:

(a)   Calculate the Return on Capital Employed (ROCE) ratios for each of the two companies for the year and analyse these into their secondary ratio components of:

    (i)   Pre-tax profit %

    (ii)   Asset Turnover   **(3 marks)**

(b)   (i)   Calculate Z's gross profit margin on its internal sales and compare this to the gross profit margin on its external sales.   **(4 marks)**

    (ii)   Discuss the performance of the two companies EXCLUDING the effects of the intra group transactions.   **(11 marks)**

Due to operational difficulties, the directors of the PZ Group are to impose a transfer pricing policy.

(c)   Explain THREE factors that they should consider when setting the transfer pricing policy.   **(7 marks)**

(Total: 25 marks)

124   TY NPV (SEP 11)

TY comprises two trading divisions. Both divisions use the same accounting policies. The following statement shows the performance of each division for the year ended 31 August:

Division	T	Y
	$000	$000
Sales	3,600,000	3,840,000
Variable cost	1,440,000	1,536,000
Contribution	2,160,000	2,304,000
Fixed costs	1,830,000	1,950,000
Operating profit	330,000	354,000
Capital employed	3,167,500	5,500,000

Division Y manufactures a single component which it sells to Division T and to external customers. During the year to 31 August Division Y operated at 80% capacity and produced 200,000 components. 25% of the components were sold to Division T at a transfer price of $15,360 per component. Division T manufactures a single product. It uses one of the components that it buys from Division Y in each unit of its finished product, which it sells to an external market.

Investment by Division T

Division T is currently operating at its full capacity of 50,000 units per year and is considering investing in new equipment which would increase its present capacity by 25%. The machine has a useful life of three years. This would enable Division T to expand its business into new markets. However, to achieve this it would have to sell these additional units of its product at a discounted price of $60,000 per unit. The capital cost of the investment is $1.35bn and the equipment can be sold for $400m at the end of three years.

Division T believes that there would be no changes to its cost structure as a result of the expansion and that it would be able to sell all of the products that it could produce from the extra capacity. It is company policy of TY that all divisions use a 10% cost of capital to evaluate investments.

Required:

(a) **Prepare an analysis of the sales made by Division Y for the year ended 31 August to show the contribution earned from external sales and from internal sales. (3 marks)**

(b) **Assuming that the current transfer pricing policy continues:**

   (i) **Evaluate, using NPV, the investment in the new equipment from the perspective of Division T** **(8 marks)**

   (ii) **Evaluate, using NPV, the investment in the new equipment from the perspective of TY.**

   Ignore taxation and inflation. **(4 marks)**

(c) **Discuss the appropriateness of the current transfer pricing policy from the perspective of EACH of the divisional managers AND the company as a whole.**
(10 marks)

(Total: 25 marks)

125 RFT (NOV 11)

RFT, an engineering company, has been asked to provide a quotation for a contract to build a new engine. The potential customer is not a current customer of RFT, but the directors of RFT are keen to try and win the contract as they believe that this may lead to more contracts in the future. As a result they intend pricing the contract using relevant costs.

The following information has been obtained from a two-hour meeting that the Production Director of RFT had with the potential customer. The Production Director is paid an annual salary equivalent to $1,200 per 8-hour day.

110 square metres of material A will be required. This is a material that is regularly used by RFT and there are 200 square metres currently in inventory. These were bought at a cost of $12 per square metre. They have a resale value of $10.50 per square metre and their current replacement cost is $12.50 per square metre.

30 litres of material B will be required. This material will have to be purchased for the contract because it is not otherwise used by RFT. The minimum order quantity from the supplier is 40 litres at a cost of $9 per litre. RFT does not expect to have any use for any of this material that remains after this contract is completed.

60 components will be required. These will be purchased from HY. The purchase price is $50 per component.

A total of 235 direct labour hours will be required. The current wage rate for the appropriate grade of direct labour is $11 per hour. Currently RFT has 75 direct labour hours of spare capacity at this grade that is being paid under a guaranteed wage agreement. The additional hours would need to be obtained by either (i) overtime at a total cost of $14 per hour; or (ii) recruiting temporary staff at a cost of $12 per hour. However, if temporary staff are used they will not be as experienced as RFT's existing workers and will require 10 hours supervision by an existing supervisor who would be paid overtime at a cost of $18 per hour for this work.

25 machine hours will be required. The machine to be used is already leased for a weekly leasing cost of $600. It has a capacity of 40 hours per week. The machine has sufficient available capacity for the contract to be completed. The variable running cost of the machine is $7 per hour.

The company absorbs its fixed overhead costs using an absorption rate of $20 per direct labour hour.

Required:

(a) Calculate the relevant cost of building the new engine.

You should present your answer in a schedule that clearly shows the relevant cost value for each of the items identified above. You should also explain each relevant cost value you have included in your schedule and why the values you have excluded are not relevant. **(13 marks)**

(b) HY, the company that is to supply RFT with the components that are required for this contract, is another company in the same group as RFT. Each component is being transferred to RFT taking account of HY's opportunity cost of the component. The variable cost that will be incurred by HY is $28 per component.

Discuss the factors that would be considered by HY to determine the opportunity cost of the component. **(5 marks)**

(c) When there is no external market for the item being supplied between divisions of a company the transfer price is often based on the supplying division's cost.

(i) Illustrate, using a numerical example, the performance measurement problem that can arise when using a transfer price based on actual cost. **(3 marks)**

(ii) Explain how using standard costs rather than actual costs as the basis of the transfer price would solve the problem identified in (i) above. **(4 marks)**

(Total: 25 marks)

126   THE OB GROUP (NOV 12)

Scenario for part (a)

The OB group has two divisions: the Optics Division and the Body Division. The Optics Division produces optical devices, including lenses for cameras. The lenses can be sold directly to external customers or they can be transferred to the Body Division where they are sold with a camera body as a complete camera.

Optics Division

The relationship between the selling price of a lens and the quantity demanded by external customers is such that at a price of $6,000 there will be no demand but demand will increase by 600 lenses for every $300 decrease in the price. The variable cost of producing a lens is $1,200. The fixed costs of the division are $12 million each year. The Optics Division has the capacity to satisfy the maximum possible demand if required.

Body Division

After the lens has been included with a body to make a complete camera the relationship between selling price and demand is such that at a price of $8,000 there will be no demand for the complete camera but demand will increase by 300 complete cameras for every $100 decrease in the price. The Body Division has annual fixed costs of $15 million and has the capacity to satisfy the maximum possible demand if required. The total variable costs of a camera body and packaging it with a lens are $1,750 (this does not include the cost of a lens).

Note: If P = a − bx then Marginal Revenue (MR) will be given by MR = a − 2bx.

Required:

(a)   **Calculate the total revenue that would be generated by the complete cameras if:**

(i)   **the Manager of the Optics Division set the transfer price of a lens equal to the selling price which would be set to maximise profits from the sale of lenses to external customers**

(ii)   **the transfer price of a lens was set to maximise the profits of the OB group from the sale of complete cameras.**   **(10 marks)**

Scenario for parts (b) and (c)

The FF group is a divisionalised company that specialises in the production of processed fish. Each division is a profit centre. The Smoke Division (SD) produces smoked fish. The Packaging Division (PD) manufactures boxes for packaging products.

Smoke Division (SD)

The Manager of SD has just won a fixed price contract to supply 500,000 units of smoked fish to a chain of supermarkets. This will fully utilise the capacity of SD for the next year. Budget details for the next year are:

Variable cost per unit	$12.00 (excluding the box)
Fixed costs	$6.0 million
Revenue	$13.5 million
Output	500,000 units of smoked fish

Each unit of smoked fish requires one box.

Packaging Division (PD)

The Packaging Division has agreed to supply 500,000 boxes to SD at the same price that it sells boxes to external customers. Budget details for PD (including the order from SD) for the next year are:

Variable production cost	$1.40 per box
Fixed costs	$2.4 million
Output	4.48 million boxes
Capacity	4.50 million boxes

Company policy

It has been announced today that FF will be introducing a new performance appraisal system. The Divisional Managers will only be paid a bonus if the profit of their division is at least 12% of assets consumed during the next year. The value of the assets consumed is assumed to be the same as the fixed costs.

Required:

(b)   Calculate, following the change to the company policy:

    (i)   the minimum price per box that PD would be willing to charge   **(3 marks)**

    (ii)   the maximum price per box that SD would be willing to pay.   **(4 marks)**

(c)   The Manager of SD is unhappy about paying the same price per box as an external customer and thinks that transfer prices should be set using an opportunity cost-based approach.

Discuss the view that transfer prices should be set using opportunity cost. You should use the data from the FF group to illustrate your answer.   **(8 marks)**

                                           (Total: 25 marks)

127   SHG (NOV 11)

SHG manufactures and installs heating systems for commercial customers. SHG commenced trading in 1990. At first, all operations were confined to the northern region but since 2006 SHG has expanded its operations into the southern region. In May 2009 the directors of SHG decided to adopt a divisionalised structure in order to facilitate better management control of SHG's operations. SHG created two divisions, the Northern division and the Southern division.

The following information is available:

1   Net assets of SHG as at 31 May were as follows:

	2011		2010		2009	
Division	Northern	Southern	Northern	Southern	Northern	Southern
	$m	$m	$m	$m	$m	$m
Non-current assets (net book value)	78.75	146.25	72.45	134.55	70.00	130.00
Net current assets	47.25	87.75	46.55	86.45	42.00	78.00
Net assets	126.00	234.00	119.00	221.00	112.00	208.00
Non-current assets acquired in year	15.05	27.95	10.50	19.50		

Notes:

There were no disposals of non-current assets during the above periods.

Depreciation is charged at 10% per annum on a reducing balance basis in respect of all non-current assets held at the end of the year.

2   For the years ended 31 May 2010 and 2011, turnover and operating cashflows were as follows:

Division	2011 $m	2010 $m
Turnover:		
Northern	168	148
Southern	240	220
Operating cash flows:		
Northern	42	37
Southern	60	55

3   Each division has a target return on capital employed (ROCE) of 20% on average capital employed throughout each year. The managers of both divisions are entitled to receive an annual bonus under a management incentive scheme if the target rate of ROCE is achieved for their division.

Note: Ignore Taxation and Inflation.

Required:

(a)   (i)   **Calculate the Return on Capital Employed (ROCE) (using average capital employed) achieved by each division during the years ended 31 May 2010 and 31 May 2011.**   **(7 marks)**

      (ii)   **Calculate (1) the asset turnover and (2) the profit/sales % achieved by each division during the years ended 31 May 2010 and 31 May 2011.**   **(4 marks)**

      (iii) **Discuss the relative performances of the two divisions.**   **(4 marks)**

(b)   SHG realises that its present performance reporting system does not highlight quality costs. The reports contain the information below, but the directors require this to be reported in an appropriate format.

      The following information is available in respect of the year ended 31 May 2011:

      1   *Production data:*

Units requiring rework	1,500
Units requiring warranty repair service	1,800
Design engineering hours	66,000
Inspection hours (manufacturing)	216,000

      2   *Cost data:*

	$
Design engineering cost per hour	75
Inspection cost per hour (manufacturing)	40
Rework cost per heating system unit reworked (manufacturing)	3,000
Customer support cost per repaired unit (marketing)	200
Transportation costs per repaired unit (distribution)	240
Warranty repair costs per repaired unit	3,200

3   Staff training costs amounted to $150,000 and additional product testing costs were $49,000.

4   The marketing director has estimated that sales of 1,400 units were lost as a result of bad publicity in trade journals. The average contribution per heating system unit is estimated at $6,000.

Required:

Prepare a cost of quality report for SHG that shows its costs of quality (using appropriate headings) for the year ended 31 May 2011. **(10 marks)**

(Total: 25 marks)

128 HTL (MAR 12)

HTL owns three hotels in different regions of the same country. The company uses the same accounting policies and cost of capital of 10% per annum for all the hotels that it owns. All rooms are sold on a "bed and breakfast" basis. The hotels are open for 365 days per year. The restaurants provide breakfasts to hotel guests only. At all other times the restaurants are available to hotel guests and the general public. Details for each hotel for the year ended 31 December 2011 are as follows:

Hotel	Northern	Southern	Eastern
Number of bedrooms available	120	250	135
% bedroom occupancy	80%	75%	60%
Regional bedroom market share %	15%	16%	5%
Restaurant capacity per day (meals)	100	120	85
Restaurant utilisation	60%	40%	60%
	$000	$000	$000
Revenue:			
Bedroom with breakfast	3,328	8,500	2,365
Restaurant	876	776	837
Total	4,204	9,276	3,202
Profit before tax	832	1,100	576
Net assets at 31 December	4,200	7,400	4,400

An analysis of the costs incurred by each of the hotels for the year ended 31 December 2011 is as follows:

Hotel	Northern	Southern	Eastern
	$000	$000	$000
Bed and breakfast related	2,847	7,231	2,082
Restaurant related	525	945	544
Total	3,372	8,176	2,626

It has also been noted that the restaurant related costs, capacity and utilisation information does not include breakfasts.

Some of the following performance indicators have already been calculated:

Hotel	Northern	Southern	Eastern
Return on net assets	20%	15%	???
Residual income ($000)	412	???	136

Required:

(a) **Discuss the relative performance of the three hotels.**

Note: Your answer should include:

- **a review of the relative profits of the rooms and restaurants in each hotel; and**

- **calculations of the Return on Net Assets, Residual Income and other performance measures that you think are appropriate.**   **(18 marks)**

(b) The Northern Hotel manager has investment decision authority. The manager is considering investing $800,000 in the construction of a leisure facility at the hotel. The hotel has permission to build the leisure facility, but will have to accept the terms of an agreement with the local community before beginning its construction. The facility is expected to generate additional annual profit for the hotel over the next five years as follows:

	$000
2012	110
2013	120
2014	155
2015	145
2016	130

At the end of 2016 the facility will have to be sold to the local community for $550,000. If the facility is built, it will be depreciated on a straight line basis over the 5 year period (i.e. $50,000 per annum).

The investment has a positive net present value of $225,000 when discounted at the group's cost of capital.

The manager of the hotel receives an annual bonus if the hotel's Return on Net Assets is maintained or improved. As stated in part (a) this was 20% for 2011 based on net assets at the end of the year.

Required:

Discuss the effect of this investment on the future performance of the Northern Hotel and whether, in the light of this, the hotel manager is likely to proceed with the investment.   **(7 marks)**

(Total: 25 marks)

129   GHYD (MAY 12)

The GHYD company comprises two divisions: GH and YD. GH manufactures components using a specialised machine. It sells the same components both externally and to YD. The variable costs of producing the component are as follows:

	$/unit
Direct materials	25.00
Direct labour	35.00
Variable overhead	10.00
	70.00

GH currently sells its components to the external market for $125 per unit. GH also sells 4,000 components per month to YD. These are transferred at the same price as the external selling price.

YD uses two of these components in each unit of its CX product. The current selling price of the CX product is $375 per unit and at this selling price the demand for the CX is 2,000 units per month.

The variable costs of producing a unit of CX are as follows:

	$/unit
Direct materials	35.00
Components transferred from GH @ $125 each	250.00
Direct labour	15.00
Variable overhead	10.00

At this level of activity, the total monthly contribution earned by YD from the sale of the CX product is $130,000.

An analysis of the demand for the CX product indicates that for every $25 increase in its selling price the monthly demand would reduce by 500 units, and that for every $25 decrease in its selling price demand would increase by 500 units.

Note: If P = a − bx then MR = a − 2bx

Required:

(a) (i)   Calculate the selling price per unit of CX that would maximise the profits generated by that product for the YD division.   **(4 marks)**

(ii)   Calculate, based on the selling price you calculated in (a)(i) above, the monthly contribution that CX would generate for:

• **GHYD as a whole**

• **GH division**

• **YD division**

Note: Your answer should show three separate amounts.   **(6 marks)**

(b) GHYD has now reviewed its transfer pricing policy and decided that all transfer prices should be set so as to lead to optimal decision making for the company as a whole. Assuming that the transfer price for the component is changed to reflect this new policy:

   (i) Calculate the selling price per unit of CX that would maximise the profits earned by CX for the company as a whole. *Note:* You should assume that there is sufficient capacity within the company. **(4 marks)**

   (ii) Calculate, based on the selling price you calculated in (b)(i) above, the monthly contribution that CX would generate for:

   - GHYD as a whole

   - GH division

   - YD division

   Note: Your answer should show three separate amounts. **(3 marks)**

(c) Discuss, using your answers to (a) and (b) above, the impact that alternative transfer prices have on the divisional profits of GH and YD and on the company as a whole. **(8 marks)**

(Total: 25 marks)

130 HPS TRANSFER PRICING (SEP 13)

HPR harvests, processes and roasts coffee beans. The company has two divisions:

Division P is located in Country Y. It harvests and processes coffee beans. The processed coffee beans are sold to Division R and external customers.

Division R is located in Country Z. It roasts processed coffee beans and then sells them to external customers.

Countries Y and Z use the same currency but have different taxation rates.

The budgeted information for the next year is as follows:

Division P

Capacity	1,000 tonnes
External demand for processed coffee beans	800 tonnes
Demand from Division R for processed coffee beans	625 tonnes
External market selling price for processed coffee beans	$11,000 per tonne
Variable costs	$7,000 per tonne
Annual fixed costs	$1,500,000

Division R

Sales of roasted coffee beans	500 tonnes
Market selling price for roasted coffee beans	$20,000 per tonne

The production of 1 tonne of roasted coffee beans requires an input of 1.25 tonnes of processed coffee beans. The cost of roasting is $2,000 per tonne of input plus annual fixed costs of $1,000,000.

Transfer pricing policy of HPR

Division P must satisfy the demand from Division R for processed coffee beans before selling any to external customers.

The transfer price for the processed coffee beans is variable cost plus 10% per tonne.

Taxation

The rate of taxation on company profits is 45% in Country Y and 25% in Country Z.

Required:

(a) (i) **Produce statements that show the budgeted profit after tax for the next year for each of the two divisions. Your profit statements should show sales and costs split into external sales and internal transfers where appropriate.**

(8 marks)

(ii) **Discuss the potential tax consequences of HPR's current transfer pricing policy.** (6 marks)

(b) **Produce statements that show the budgeted contributions that would be earned by each of the two divisions if HPR's head office changed its policy to state that transfers must be made at opportunity cost. Your statements should show sales and costs split into external sales and internal transfers where appropriate.**

(6 marks)

(c) **Explain TWO behavioural issues that could arise as a result of the head office of HPR imposing transfer prices instead of allowing the divisional managers to set the prices.** (5 marks)

(Total: 25 marks)

131   S AND R DIVISIONS (MAY 13)

S Division and R Division are two divisions in the SR group of companies. S Division manufactures one type of component which it sells to external customers and also to R Division.

Details of S Division are as follows:

Market price per component	$200
Variable cost per component	$105
Fixed costs	$1,375,000 per period
Demand from R Division	20,000 components per period
Capacity	35,000 components per period

R Division assembles one type of product which it sells to external customers. Each unit of that product requires two of the components that are manufactured by S Division.

Details of R Division are as follows:

Selling price per unit	$800
Variable cost per unit:	
Two components from S	2 @ transfer price
Other variable costs	$250
Fixed costs	$900,000 per period
Demand	10,000 units per period
Capacity	10,000 units per period

Group transfer pricing policy

Transfers must be at opportunity cost.

R must buy the components from S.

S must satisfy demand from R before making external sales.

Required:

(a) **Calculate the profit for each division if the external demand per period for the components that are made by S Division is:**

    (i)   **15,000 components**

    (ii)   **19,000 components**

    (iii) **35,000 components** (12 marks)

(b) **Calculate the financial impact on the Group if R Division ignored the transfer pricing policy and purchased all of the 20,000 components that it needs from an external supplier for $170 each. Your answer must consider the impact at each of the three levels of demand (15,000, 19,000 and 35,000 components) from external customers for the component manufactured by S Division.** (6 marks)

(c) The Organisation for Economic Co-operation and Development (OECD) produced guidelines with the aim of standardising national approaches to transfer pricing. The guidelines state that where necessary transfer prices should be adjusted using an "arm's length" price.

    Required:

    Explain:

    (i)   **An "arm's length" price**

    (ii)   **The THREE methods that tax authorities can use to determine an "arm's length" price.** (7 marks)

(Total: 25 marks)

132 HJ AND KL (SEP 12)

HJ and KL are two companies that operate in the same industry sector. Details for the two companies for the year ended 31 December 2011 are as follows:

	HJ	*KL*
	$000	$000
Revenue	1,600	990
Cost of sales:		
Variable production costs	400	400
Fixed production costs (including depreciation see Note 3)	800	390
	1,200	790
Gross profit	400	200
Administration costs (fixed)	120	80
Operating profit	280	120
Non-current assets:		
Cost	2,000	1,800
Depreciation (see below)	400	1,230
	1,600	570
Net current assets	200	150
Capital employed	1,800	720
Performance measures		
Return on Capital Employed (ROCE)	15.56%	16.67%
Operating profit margin	17.50%	12.12%
Asset turnover	0.89	1.38

Notes:

1   Assume that the non-current assets of both companies are all used in their manufacturing processes.

2   The two companies use different depreciation policies: HJ depreciates its non-current assets using straight-line depreciation at the rate of 20% of cost with no residual value; whereas KL uses the reducing balance method of depreciation at the rate of 25% per annum.

3   Included in the fixed costs of the year ended 31 December 2011 is depreciation of $400,000 for HJ and $190,000 for KL.

4   Each company purchased all of its non-current assets in the month the company was formed. Neither company has purchased or disposed of any non-current assets since their original purchase.

5   HJ has undertaken a benchmarking exercise. The Managing Director (MD) of HJ has been asked to explain the company's results compared to those of KL. The MD says the differences are because of HJ's depreciation policy and the age of the company's assets.

Required:

(a) Calculate the THREE revised performance ratios of HJ after adjusting its results to align the age of its assets and its depreciation policy with that of KL. **(9 marks)**

(b) Calculate, for KL only, the break-even sales value in 2013 assuming that there are no changes to its cost and selling price structure or to its mix of sales, there are no purchases or disposals of non-current assets and that the existing depreciation policy continues to be applied. **(4 marks)**

The directors of KL are now considering replacing its non-current assets with new equipment that will be fully operational from 1 January 2013. The manufacturer of the new equipment has offered to accept the company's old equipment as a trade in at its net book value at 31 December 2012 of $427,500. If this offer is not accepted KL does not expect to be able to dispose of the old equipment for ANY value at any time in the future.

The new equipment:

• Has a cost of $1.2 million before any trade in value is deducted

• Increases the fixed production cost (excluding depreciation) by 30% per annum

• Reduces the variable production cost per unit by 20%

• Has a life of five years, a residual value after five years of $285,000 and is to be depreciated using the same depreciation method that is currently being used for the existing equipment.

Assume that

• There is no change to the unit selling price or demand for KL's product

• KL's cost of capital for this type of investment is 10% per annum.

Required:

(c) (i) Recommend, based on Net Present Value, whether or not KL should replace its existing non-current assets.

Ignore taxation and inflation. **(6 marks)**

(ii) Discuss the effect on the break-even sales value in 2013 of investing in the new equipment. Your answer should be supported by appropriate calculations. **(6 marks)**

(Total: 25 marks)

Section 3

ANSWERS TO SECTION A-TYPE QUESTIONS

PRICING AND PRODUCT DECISIONS

1 BVX

(a)

	Chair	Bench	Table	Total
Contribution/unit	$8.00	$17.50	$16.00	
Timber/unit (m²)	2.5	7.5	5	
Contribution/m²	$3.20	$2.33	$3.20	
Ranking	1st	3rd	1st	
Minimum units to avoid penalty	500	100	150	
Timber required for minimum units (m²)	1,250	750	750	2,750
Number of units to maximum demand/ production resources	3,500	233	1,350	
Timber used for production above minimum units	8,750	1,747.5	6,750	17,247.5
Timber used				10,007.5
Timber available				20,000
Total number of units to be produced	4,000	333	1,500	

Contribution from:		$
Chairs	4,000 × $8.00	32,000.00
Benches	333 × $17.50	5,827.50
Tables	1,500 × $16.00	24,000.00
		61,827.50
Fixed costs		54,000.00
Profit		7,827.50

Since the optimum plan includes production of sufficient quantities of each item to meet the order comprising the minimum demand, and production of the most profitable items already meets the maximum demand, there is no need to consider the financial penalty.

(b) The maximum price which should be paid for the timber, a scarce resource, is also known as its shadow price.

The shadow price is the price at which the purchaser makes a nil contribution from its use. Therefore to answer the question it is necessary to consider the use of any additional timber acquired.

The present situation is that demand for chairs and tables is fully satisfied from the existing resources, but there is some unsatisfied demand for benches. Thus any additional timber would be used to manufacture more benches.

Based on the current input cost of $2.00 per m^2 each m^2 of timber earns a contribution of $2.33. Thus the maximum price to be paid is the sum of these values i.e. $4.33 per m^2.

However, there is no benefit in obtaining more timber than can be used to satisfy the total demand for benches, so this shadow price of $4.33 per m^2 only applies for up to 12,500 m^2 of timber. Thereafter there is no use for the timber, so its shadow price is nil.

2 THREE PRODUCTS

(a)

	Product X	Product Y	Product Z	Total
Unit costs	$	$	$	$
Direct materials	50	120	90	
Direct labour: A	70	40	75	
B	24	18	30	
C	32	16	60	
Variable overhead	12	7	16	
	188	201	271	
Selling price	210	220	300	
Contribution per unit	22	19	29	
Sales volume (units)	7,500	6,000	6,000	
Total contribution ($)	165,000	114,000	174,000	453,000
Less fixed costs				300,000
Profit				153,000

(b)

	X	Y	Z
Contribution/unit	$22	$19	$29
Department B hours/unit	4	3	5
Contribution/hr	$5.50	$6.33	$5.80
Ranking	(3)	(1)	(2)

Maximum Dept B hours

= (7,500 × 4) + (6,000 × 3) + (6,000 × 5)

= 78,000 hours

The maximum sales level, with the increase is:

X 9,000

Y 7,500

Z 8,000

∴ Manufacture: Max 7,500 units of Y using   22,500 hours

Max 8,000 units of Z using   40,000 hours

Balance 3,875 units of X using   15,500 hours (W1)

————

78,000

————

This yields a contribution of:

	$
X: 3,875 × $22 =	85,250
Y: 7,500 × $19 =	142,500
Z: 8,000 × $29 =	232,000
	————
	459,750
Less fixed costs	300,000
	————
Profit	159,750
	————

Workings:

(W1) This is the balancing number of department B hours available.

3   LIFECYCLE AND LEARNING CURVE (NOV 11)

(a) The average time for 64 batches (i.e. 6,400 units) is $Y = ax^b$

$$Y = 1500 \times 64^{-0.2345}$$

$$Y = 565.64 \text{ hours}$$

(b) The total time for 64 batches is 64 × 565.64 hours, which is a total of 36,200.96 hours

The average time for 63 batches is $Y = ax^b = 1,500 \times 63^{-0.2345}$

$$Y = 567.735 \text{ hours.}$$

This represents a total of 35,767.31 hours. Thus the time for the 64th and subsequent batches is 433.65 hours.

(c)

		$
Revenue from 9,000 units (9,000 units @ $124)		1,116,000
Costs of 10,000 units:		
Variable costs:		
Non-labour (10,000 units @ $38)	380,000	
Direct labour (see below)	621,748	
	1,001,748	
Fixed costs	80,000	1,081,748
		34,252
Profit target		100,000
Revenue required from final 1,000 units		65,748

Direct labour cost:

Total time = 36,200.96 hours + (36 batches × 433.65 hours) = 51,812.36 hours

The direct labour rate is $12 per hour so this gives a cost of $621,748.32

The 1,000 units being sold in the decline stage need to be sold at an average selling price of $65.75 ($65,748/1000) in order to meet the profit target of $100,000.

4   CATERPILLAR

The maximum contribution is $105,791.

This will be earned by manufacturing 3,357 units of Product A and 2,321 units of Product E. Products B, C and D will not be produced at all.

This plan will fully utilise the 35,000 kg of raw material (slack is zero). If one more kg of raw material were to become available, then contribution would increase by $2.02. This is the shadow price of this scarce resource.

The 4,000 machine hours in the packing department are also fully utilised. If one more hour of time becomes available in this department, then contribution will increase by $8.81.

The production plan will not use all the available hours in the forming department. There will be 321 hours unused in this department at the end of the period. This is called the slack of the resource. Similarly, there will be 9,482 hours left over in the firing department.

If it becomes necessary to make one unit of Product B, then contribution will fall by $1.26.

If it becomes necessary to make one unit of Product C, then contribution will fall by $1.06.

If it becomes necessary to make one unit of Product D, then contribution will fall by $0.51.

5   NLM (NOV 08) *Walk in the footsteps of a top tutor*

Key answer tips

This an example of a question for which obtaining maximum marks depends not just on carrying out the calculations correctly, but on demonstrating that you are aware of the other factors which affect the decision such as marketing. The complementarities of products is always a good marketing consideration to include in an answer.

Step 1

Read the requirements, and split your time between (a) and (b) according to the mark allocation. Then, read the question.

Step 2

Get the easy marks out of the way first, and state a few assumptions.

(a)   Assuming that:

- The 'normal output' is representative of all months

- No losses are occurring in the common process or the three further processes

- All monthly output can be sold at the prices given

- The $6,800 apportioned head office costs are not relevant – we assume that they are not affected by our decision to process further.

Step 3

State the decision rule. The further process should only be continued if the extra benefit it brings exceeds the extra cost. This is the best technique, and most concise approach – establishing that further processing is worthwhile if the further processing cost is less than the incremental revenue, i.e. if it translates into an increase or decrease in profits for each of the SX, SY and SZ processes.

On financial grounds, further processing is worthwhile if the further processing cost is less than the incremental revenue.

Evaluation of further processing

(based on our current monthly process):

Product	Incremental revenue $	Incremental cost $	Increase/ (decrease) in profit
SX	4,000 × ($6.75 – $5.00) = $7,000	(4,000 × $1.25) + $1,850 = $6,850	$150
SY	5,000 × ($7.50 – $4.50) = $15,000	(5,000 × $1.80) + $800 = $9,800	$5,200
SZ	4,500 × ($7.20 – $5.50) = $7,650	(4,500 × $1.55) + $2,400 = $9,375	$(1,725)

Step 4

Decision time! Often, a good way to gain marks is to (1) state the obvious ('discontinue Z') and (2) think of the bigger picture ('impact on other two products'). However, only a handful of marks are available here and time is of the essence – do not produce a whole essay on the complementarity of products!

Taking each product individually, it can be seen that products X and Y should be converted and processed further, as the incremental revenue exceeds the incremental cost of further processing.

Considered in isolation, product Z should not be converted, as its incremental revenues do not cover its incremental costs. However, there may be other reasons for producing all three products in order to sell the two most profitable products X and Y. Some customers may expect to buy them together.

(b)

Step 5

Bag in the assumptions marks early again.

Assuming that:

- The 'normal output' is representative of all months

- No losses are occurring in the common process

- All monthly output can be sold at the prices given

Product	Selling price/litre $	Monthly output litres	Sales value $
X	$5.00	4,000	$20,000
Y	$4.50	5,000	$22,500
Z	$3.50	4,500	$24,750
			$67,250

Sales revenue after common process	$67,250
Total costs of common process	($68,600)
Loss per 'normal' month	**($1,350)**
Benefit from further processing X (as per (a))	$150
Benefit from further processing Y (as per (a))	$$5,200
Total	$4,000

Step 6

*Don't forget to conclude. Pay particular attention to the conclusion that the common process should be operated **as long as X and Y are processed further**.*

NLM should continue to operate the common process. It is financially viable, as long as X and Y are processed further.

6   WX PRICING (MAY 11)

(a)

Examiner's comments: It was surprising, even disappointing, to find that many candidates were not able to apply the 'high – low' technique to calculate the total variable cost of the unit. This is one of the most basic, but important, tools that should be in the armoury of all management accounting students, and should have been knowledge brought forward from the foundation stage.

(i)   The optimum selling price occurs where marginal cost = marginal revenue.

Marginal cost is assumed to be the same as variable cost. From the data it can be determined that the costs of direct materials and direct labour are wholly variable and total $8 per unit. [($200,000 + $600,000)/100,000]

The overhead costs appear to be semi-variable and will be analysed using the High Low method:

	Units	$000
High	200,000	1,460
Low	100,000	880
Difference	100,000	580

Thus the variable overhead cost per unit is $580,000/100,000 = $5.80.

The total variable cost per unit is therefore $13.80

(ii)

> **Examiner's comments:** This part was generally answered well, but a significant number of candidates made an error when calculating the selling price that would maximise the company's profit, and put forward an answer that could not be possible in the context of the question. Candidates are advised to 'sensibilise' their answers, and if the error cannot be found clearly indicate to the marker that you are aware that the answer is incorrect.

The price at which there is zero demand can be calculated to be $25 + ((150,000/25,000) \times \$1)) = \$31$

There is a change in demand of 25,000 units for every \$1 change in selling price so the equation of the selling price is:

$\$31 - 0.00004x$

And thus the equation for marginal revenue is:

$\$31 - 0.00008x$

Equating marginal cost and marginal revenue gives:

$13.80 = 31 - 0.00008x$

$-17.20 = -0.00008x$

$-17.2/-0.00008 = x = 215,000$

If $x = 215,000$ then the optimum selling price is:

$\$31 - (0.00004 \times 215,000) = \$22.40$

(b) There are many reasons why this price may not be used (candidates are expected to explain two).

- There may be inaccuracies in the demand forecasts at different prices because the model assumes that demand is driven solely by price. In fact there are many different factors that influence demand; these include advertising, competitor actions and changing fashions/tastes.

- The model also assumes that the relationship between price and demand is static whereas in reality it is regularly changing.

- There may be inaccuracies in the determination of the marginal cost, the assumption that marginal cost equals variable cost may itself be invalid, but even if this is acceptable then the assumption that all variable costs vary with volume is unrealistic. Some of these costs may be driven by factors other than volume. Again there is an assumption the unit variable cost is unchanging once it has been determined.

7   HZ SELLING PRICE (SEPT 11)

(a)

The optimum selling price occurs where marginal cost = marginal revenue. Marginal cost is assumed to be the same as variable cost. From the data it can be seen that the costs of direct materials, direct labour and variable overhead total $18.75 per unit.

The price at which there is zero demand can be calculated to be $45 + ((130,000/10,000) × $1)) = $58. There is a change in demand of 10,000 units for every $1 change in selling price so the equation of the selling price is:

$58 − 0.0001x

And thus the equation for marginal revenue is **$58 − 0.0002x**

Equating marginal cost and marginal revenue gives:

18.75 = 58 − 0.0002x

39.25 = 0.0002x

39.25/0.0002 = x = **196,250**

If x = 196,250 then the optimum selling price is $58 − (0.0001 × 196,250) = $38.375

There is thus a contribution of $38.375 − $18.75 = $19.625 per unit.

Annual contribution = $19.625 × 196,250 units =	$3,851,406.25
Less annual fixed overhead costs	$360,000.00
Annual profit	$3,491,406.25

(b)

(i)   If the actual direct material cost per unit were lower than expected then the effect of this would be to reduce the variable cost and hence the marginal cost per unit. There would be no change to the price equation but this would impact on the solution of the optimal selling price and quantity, the result of which would be to lower the selling price and thus increase the quantity sold. The opposite would apply if the direct material cost per unit were to increase.

(ii)   Any change in the fixed overhead cost would have no effect on the optimal selling price and quantity sold.

8   HS (NOV 07)

Key answer tips

The high low method should be a well-practised technique for the prepared candidate. You will need to analyse the costs provided here using the high and low points method to separate them into their fixed and variable components.

(a) $p = a - bq$ where p is price and q is demand for product

When price = $1,350, demand = 8,000 units

When price = $1,400, demand = 7,000 units

So: (1) $1,350 = a - 8,000q$ and (2) $1,400 = a - 7,000q$

so subtracting equation (1) from equation (2)

$50 = 1,000b$

$b = 0.05$

and substituting in equation (2):

$1,400 = a - 0.05 \times 7,000$

$a = 1,750$

so Price = $1,750 - 0.05q$ and marginal revenue = $1,750 - 0.1q$

To find variable production cost per unit, we need to separate fixed and variable costs from the historic cost data. Using the high-low method, dividing the difference in cost for the highest and lowest activity levels by the change in activity:

Variable production cost per unit	= $(7,000 - 5,446) \times 1,000/(9,400 - 7,300)$
	= $1,554 \times 1,000/2,100 = $740
Direct material cost	= $270
Total variable cost	= $(270 + 740)$
	= $1,010

Price is maximised where marginal cost (= variable cost) = marginal revenue

$1,010 = 1,750 - 0.1q$

$q = 7,400$ units

and price = $1,750 - 0.05 \times 7,400 = $1,380

Optimum price is $1,380

(b)

Tutorial note

*Note that the question only asks for **two** reasons.*

There are a number of reasons why it may be inappropriate for HS to use this model in practice. The model depends on the market structure being one in which there is:

- Perfect competition (which is the closest situation to HS's market)

- Monopolistic competition

- Monopoly, or

- Oligopoly

Whilst the market is highly competitive, it is unlikely that there is perfect competition (in which the action of one company cannot affect the market price).

The model assumes that costs and demand follow a linear relationship and that there are no step changes in fixed costs. Again this may hold over a small range of volumes but is unlikely to be true for all possible volumes.

This model can only be used if the company has detailed knowledge of demand and cost curves. It is unlikely that in practice HS would be able to derive accurate cost and demand curves.

9 MULTI-PRODUCT BREAKEVEN ANALYSIS (SEPT 10)

(a) (i)

Tutorial note

The Examiner has communicated that 'most candidates do not fully understand a multi-product breakeven chart'. Such charts are usually constructed with the products with the C/S ratio first, or vice versa (as it is the case here).

The chart does not provide a useful summary of the data provided, because:

- It assumes that products are sold in the same order as the order of their C/S ratio. By convention, multi-product breakeven charts display and rank products by their C/S ratio (lowest first here); but, in reality, a mix of products will be sold each month.

- The different segments of line are not labelled with each product name.

- It simply shows cumulative profits and sales revenue of products in alphabetical order.

- It suggests that E should be deleted, but fails to highlight the linkage between Products A and E. Because A & E are linked, they should be combined as a single product. This would then mean that Product B had the highest contribution to sales ratio.

(ii)

Tutorial note

*X is not simply 'the breakeven point'. Because the chart is constructed starting with the product with the lowest C/S ratio first, X shows the **highest value of sales at which breakeven will occur**.*

X shows the highest value of sales at which breakeven will occur – the level of sales at which the company will make no profit or loss.

It looks like that breakeven point is achieved when all of E, all of D and some of Cs are sold.

It is not meaningful here, because:

- It shows an impossible sales combination whereby E is sold without A

- It is unlikely that in reality, all of D and Es products will be sold whilst none of As or Bs will.

(b)

Tutorial note

The only way to calculate a weighted average C/S ratio is shown below. Totalling all five ratios and dividing by five to obtain a weighted average C/S ratio is not correct and demonstrates poor maths skills.

In a multi-product context:

$$\text{Breakeven revenue} = \frac{\text{Fixed costs}}{\text{Weighted average contribution to sales ratio}}$$

$$\text{Breakeven revenue} = \frac{\$300,000}{24.16\% \text{ (W1)}}$$

Breakeven revenue = $1,241,935.

(W1) Weighted average contribution to sales ratio:

	A	B	C	D	E	Total
Sales ($000)	400	180	1400	900	200	3,080
CS ratio	45%	30%	25%	20%	–10%	
Contribution ($000)	180	54	350	180	–20	744
Average CS ratio						**24.16%**

10   Z MARKETING PACKAGE (MAY 13)

Tutorial note

Candidates needed to note that the figures provided were included to assist with answering the question. Additional calculations were not required. The requirement was quite specific and needed the four methods requested to be linked to "attitude to risk".

Z could use any of the following three approaches to dealing with uncertainty:

"**Maximin**": the decision maker will look at the options and choose the one that has the highest minimum return. This type of decision maker is a pessimist and will look at the worst outcome for each of the options and seeks to get the best of the worst.

"**Maximax**": the decision maker will look at the options and choose the one that has the highest return. This type of decision maker is an optimist.

"**Minimax regret**": the decision maker will analyse the options and choose the option so that if it is the wrong choice the regret will not be as big as if the others had been chosen and they were wrong. This type of decision maker seeks to minimise the post-event regret of having made a wrong decision.

If probabilities can be assigned to the outcomes then "uncertainty" will become "risk". It will then be possible to calculate "expected values". The decision maker will choose the outcome that has the highest expected value. This assumes that the decision maker is risk neutral.

The expected value of an option does not give any indication of the risk associated with the option. The risk, or spread, of the possible outcomes of each option can be measured by calculating the standard deviation. A risk minimiser would choose the option with the lowest standard deviation.

The trade off between risk and return can be evaluated by calculating the coefficient of variation (standard deviation divided by expected value).

COST PLANNING AND ANALYSIS FOR COMPETITIVE ADVANTAGE

11   JIT (NOV 12)

Tutorial note

Part (a) Carefully understand the details contained in the scenario and produce two plans which would identify which method of stock control/management would incur the lowest total cost.

A full costing approach could have been adopted, but the approach which made the most economical use of time was an incremental approach. Careful presentation of the figures was essential for this part of the question.

Part (b) asked candidates to explain two reasons why the decision reached in part (a) should not be based on this answer alone. (The marking schemes accommodated the answer given in part (a) in that reasons could be accepted for either eventuality).

(a)

Quarter	1	2	3	4
Production level using JIT (units)	19,000	34,000	37,000	50,000
Incremental production compared to constant level production	(16,000)	(1,000)	2,000	15,000
Standard unit variable production cost	$60	$60	$65	$70
Incremental production cost $ (excluding overtime)	(960,000)	(60,000)	130,000	1,050,000
Overtime production (units)			1,000	14,000
Overtime unit premium $			26.00	28.00
Overtime production cost $			26,000	392,000
Total incremental production cost	(960,000)	(60,000)	156,000	1,442,000

Net incremental production cost $578,000

Inventory costs saved by JIT system:

Units	1	2	3	4
Opening inventory	0	16,000	17,000	15,000
Production	35,000	35,000	35,000	35,000
Sales	19,000	34,000	37,000	50,000
Closing inventory	16,000	17,000	15,000	0
average inventory	8,000	16,500	16,000	7,500
Holding cost $	104,000	214,500	208,000	97,500

Total holding cost = $624,000

Therefore overall there is a saving of $46,000 by changing to a JIT system.

(b) On the basis of the above calculations CDE should change to a JIT production system but there are other factors that should be considered:

How long is the contract? What will the demand be for next year and subsequent years given the important features of the component? It would be foolish to make the decision based only on the first year's forecast if this is to be a long term contract. A full investment appraisal should be undertaken and the decision should be based on the net present value of the relevant cash flows.

Overtime will be needed in the final two quarters. Given the rising costs and the overtime premium, can alternative methods of production be found? What will be the impact of the overtime working on the workforce?

In a JIT production system there will be no inventory and consequently there is no margin for errors in production. Consequently CDE may need to invest in quality control systems in order to ensure that the units produced are of the appropriate quality.

Note: the question asked for two factors. Marks were awarded to other relevant comments.

12   JYT KAIZEN (MAY 11)

Tutorial note

Make sure you do not submit answers that are not disproportionate to the marks available: this is 'only' a 10-mark question.

Failing to plan your answer may result in duplication of several points. You could have approached this by explaining Target Costing, and how it operates; then explaining Kaizen Costing, and how it operates – then the differences between them.

Target costing is a system that is used when the company is unable to dictate the selling price of its products and (like JYT) is forced to accept the market price of the item it is planning to market. Once the specification of the product has been completed, then the company determines the price that the market is prepared to pay for its product. This may be discovered by market research or by considering the prices of similar items that are already available. The company then subtracts its profit target from this price to determine its cost target. If the expected product costs already meet the target cost over the lifecycle of the product, taking account of any cost reductions that may occur, for example due to the benefits of the learning and experience curves, then production commences. However, it is more likely that at this initial stage the expected product costs exceed the target costs and as a result major product/process changes are made in order to achieve the target cost. If it is not possible to achieve the target cost by making these changes then the product is abandoned.

Kaizen costing is a system that is used once production has commenced. Kaizen means improvement and it is applied by continually striving to improve. However, Kaizen does not look for large significant improvements; instead it is based around making small improvements continuously. It is a group effort in which everyone is involved. It should become part of every employee's daily routine to constantly look for ways to improve the workflow within the organisation. Kaizen is based around a continuous circle of Plan, Do,

Check, Act. Plan refers to the need to set a target for improvement as without a benchmark success cannot be measured. Do refers to the implementation of the plan. Check is the determination of whether the plan improved the process. Act means standardise the improved procedure so that it can be repeated.

One of differences is that Target Costing applies before production commences whereas Kaizen Costing applies once production has commenced. Another difference is that although both Target Costing and Kaizen Costing involve making changes to improve results, Target Costing looks at making significant changes in order to reduce the expected cost until it reaches the Target Cost necessary to achieve the Target Profit from the given selling price. Kaizen Costing deals with making a number of further small improvements as a result of involving everyone in the process.

> **Examiner's comments:** Many candidates were able to describe Target Costing, but were not able to correctly explain Kaizen Costing, and were not able to describe how either technique could improve the future performance of the company. The descriptions of Kaizen costing put forward by many candidates were simply detailed descriptions of JIT and TQM.

13 HT QUALITY (SEPT 10)

(a)

> *Tutorial note*
>
> *Keep an eye on the clock – only three marks are available. Also, note the verbs 'compare and contrast' and avoid writing at great length about the four types of quality costs. Markers will be looking for phrases such as 'as opposed to' or 'in contrast to' in your answer.*

Conformance and non-conformance costs make up the costs of quality; and there is an inverse relationship between conformance and non-conformance costs.

Conformance costs include prevention costs and appraisal costs. **Prevention costs** are the costs of trying to avoid having any errors/rejects, for example staff training costs. **Appraisal costs** represent the costs of checking that quality standards are being achieved, for example quality control staff. These conformance costs are both aimed at ensuring that zero defects are achieved in all aspects of a firm's operations. These costs are incurred before problems are found.

In contrast, **non-conformance** costs are incurred after the error has arisen. Again there are two elements here – **internal failure costs** arise when a faulty piece of work is detected before it is sold to the customer – e.g. reworking or scrap costs. **External failure costs** arise if a customer returns a faulty item that they have bought – the company must replace the item or possibly provide a refund.

As a company invests in preventing errors the conformance costs will increase, but, in contrast, this should cause the costs of non-conformance to fall as quality standards are improved and reject rates decline.

(b)

Tutorial note

Make sure you highlight HT's biggest challenge, which is to manage the trade-off between quality and price satisfactorily.

HT has developed a strong position in the market place – they have a 15% market share which is significantly greater than its closest rival. With such a large volume of sales, HT will be able to take advantage of economies of scale and learning curves effects that are not obtainable by competitors with much lower activity levels. The impact of this is to reduce the unit costs of production. By using a penetration pricing strategy, HT generates high volumes, which lowers unit costs and allows the company to generate a reasonable margin on its sales. So, it seems that the low price strategy is working for HT.

However, there are two main factors that consumers consider when buying the products; price is one, quality is the other. If quality is important for HT's customers then HT will need to invest heavily in conformance costs to achieve the high quality expected by their customers. If HT under-invests in conformance costs then customers will start to buy goods from one of HT's many rivals. If HT start to lose market share this will start to increase unit costs, profit margins will be eroded and the penetration pricing policy may quickly deliver losses for the firm.

In conclusion, for penetration pricing to deliver satisfactory profits, HT must deliver a quality product to its customers and to achieve this quality conformance is essential.

(c)   The Kaizen principle embraces the idea of continuous improvement throughout a product's life. It considers how processes, technology, quality and management culture can be gradually improved. Kaizen aims to make continuous small improvements all the time. It focuses on eliminating waste within a firm. The life cycle of many of HT's products is extremely short, partly because of the highly competitive environment in which HT operates with competitors continually launched new product lines. By adopting Kaizen principles HT will be continually questioning the product specification and looking for improvements. As the products and services evolve new customers will be attracted to the latest goods that HT is offering to the market. It should be possible to continually win new business, new customers – hence extending the product life cycle.

Likewise, Kaizen principles could be used to justify new versions and models of the same product – which would also extend the product life.

14   CONFORMANCE (NOV 12)

Tutorial note

*Part (a) required an explanation of each of the four quality cost classifications **using examples from the scenario.***

(a)   **Prevention costs** are costs that are incurred in order to prevent poor quality. Examples from the data provided are expenditure on staff training and preventative maintenance.

Appraisal costs are costs incurred to measure or appraise the quality of the items produced. An example from the data provided is finished goods inspection cost.

Internal failure costs are costs that are incurred in rejecting or correcting faulty goods where the quality failure is discovered before the item is despatched to the customer. An example from the data provided would be the costs related to the goods that are rejected before delivery.

External failure costs are costs that are incurred as a result of customers rejecting goods that have been delivered to them. In the data provided there are goods that have been rejected by customers. The costs associated with these rejects would include collection and re-delivery costs and the loss of customer goodwill.

Tutorial note

Part (b) required a discussion, using data from the scenario, to describe the relationship between conformance costs and non-conformance costs and its importance to this company.

(b)   Conformance costs are prevention and appraisal costs. Non-conformance costs are internal and external failure costs. The relationship is that higher conformance costs should in the long run lead to lower non-conformance costs.

In the data provided it can be seen that costs incurred on prevention and appraisal costs were a greater percentage of turnover in 2012 compared to 2011 and as a result the level of external failures reduced. This would improve the perception of the company in the market.

It can also be seen that the level of failures identified before despatch increased. This could be because of the greater expenditure on appraisal costs. However it would appear that there are far too many 'rejects' being manufactured and that the company needs to work towards improving the quality of its manufacturing processes rather than relying on quality inspections to identify sub-standard production. The company should work towards 'designing quality in' as opposed to 'inspecting poor quality out'.

15 KAIZEN AND STANDARD (SEPT 11)

Tutorial note

The verb in the question is to 'Discuss'. Listing the characteristics of Kaizen costing and standard costing will not be enough.

Kaizen costing is a system of costing that focuses on achieving small incremental improvements in the production process with the objective of reducing costs. Improvement is the aim and responsibility of every worker in every activity at all times in a Kaizen costing system. As a result of involving all workers significant overall cost reductions can be achieved over time.

Both standard costs and Kaizen costing may be used as part of a performance measurement process, however there are significant differences between their approach.

A standard cost is often set annually in advance of the budget year and is rarely updated during the year. Performance is measured against these standard costs and variances determined. If appropriate, planning and operational variance analysis is used to distinguish variances that are within the manager's control. It is quite common for only adverse variances to be further investigated since once the target has been achieved (or beaten with a favourable variance) no further action is required.

Kaizen costing is different in this respect because it exists in an environment of continual improvement. Therefore Kaizen cost goals are often updated monthly to reflect the improvement that has already been achieved and to challenge workers to improve still further.

Consequently rather than being a target to be achieved and then simply maintained, Kaizen costing provides a constantly moving target. If this technique were used to measure performance using traditional variance analysis it would be difficult to measure trends over time, however it would discourage workers from relaxing their efforts once a target has been achieved.

Examiner's comments: Some good, well constructed answers were submitted but far too many answers simply listed some of the characteristics of Kaizen costing and standard costing. No attempt was made to answer the question and discuss why Kaizen costing could be more useful for performance measurement than standard costing. Many candidates seemed to instead address the question 'discuss the characteristics of target costing'.

Candidates also failed to pick up and use key words in the scenario such as 'compete globally' and 'the modern environment'. These were vital clues and hints about how to structure the answer, but many candidates failed to recognise these points.

16   SW

REPORT

To: Managing Director

From: Management Accountant

Subject: JIT System

Introduction

Further to our brief meeting, I set out below the features of a JIT system and the effects of its introduction on our quality control procedures.

Findings

The present inventory control system is based upon the analysis of past inventory movement data to establish the likely pattern of usage in the future. The use of the three control levels for maximum, minimum and re-order levels, together with the economic order quantity model, ensures that there is a level of inventory of each chemical that is held as a minimum inventory. This provides SW with a safety inventory.

JIT is based on the principle that inventory is received just as it is required by production and therefore there is no safety inventory. It means that, as there is no inventory held, there is a significant reduction in costs in terms of storage space and other inventory-related costs such as insurance. However, to be able to achieve the goal of zero inventory levels, there must be knowledge of the chemical requirements and this must be communicated to the suppliers so that they may structure their production and deliveries accordingly.

Quality becomes a much more significant issue when a JIT system is being used. There are two areas to consider: the quality of the chemicals that are received, and the quality of the production facility in the use of those chemicals.

The chemicals that are received must be of acceptable quality when they are received, because if they are not, there is no safety inventory available. As a consequence, the cleaning material production facility will be stopped until replacement chemicals are received. This would incur large costs and would not be acceptable. There needs to be a quality control check on the incoming chemicals, but this may be considered to be too late if it is done when they arrive.

An alternative is to test their quality before the supplier despatches them, and this may have to be a condition of the supplier's contract. Ideally, both SW and its suppliers will build quality into their production systems rather than rely on inspecting poor quality out of the system at a post production stage.

A further issue concerns the usage of the chemicals. If there are faults within the conversion process that lead to the produced cleaning material being unsatisfactory, or if there is a spillage or other loss of the chemicals in processing, there is no safety inventory of chemicals that can be used. Thus, it is important to encourage an atmosphere of quality throughout the production process from handling of the chemicals, through their processing and eventual packaging for distribution to customers. There may need to be quality control checks at various stages of the production process too but, since a JIT system copes very badly with rectification of problems, the emphasis will be very much on minimising the need for such checks.

Conclusion

While there are potential cost savings through the use of a JIT system, there are many issues that need to be considered. I should be pleased to discuss this with you further if you wish.

Signed: *Management Accountant*

17 PT MANUFACTURING (MAY 11)

> **Examiner's comments:** It was surprising to note that many candidates were not fully conversant with the characteristics of a market skimming policy. Also, a significant number of candidates incorrectly believed that R&D, advertising, distribution and promotion costs were production costs. Some answers were extremely good with these answers relating closely to the scenario in the question.

(i)   **Growth stage**

Compared to the introduction stage the likely changes are as follows:

Unit selling prices

These are likely to be reducing for a number of reasons:

- The product will become less unique as competitors use reverse engineering to introduce their versions of the product

- PT may wish to discourage competitors from entering the market by lowering the price and thereby lowering the unit profitability

- The price needs to be lowered so that the product becomes attractive to customers in different market segments thus increasing demand to achieve growth in sales volume.

Unit production costs

These are likely to reduce for a number of reasons:

- Direct materials are being bought in larger quantities and therefore PT may be able to negotiate better prices from its suppliers thus causing unit material costs to reduce

- Direct labour costs may be reducing if the product is labour intensive due to the effects of the learning and experience curves

- Other variable overhead costs may be reducing as larger batch sizes reduce the cost of each unit

- Fixed production costs are being shared by a greater number of units.

(ii) **Maturity stage**

Compared to the growth stage the likely changes are as follows:

Unit selling prices

These are unlikely to be reducing any longer as the product has become established in the market place. This is a time for consolidation and while there may be occasional offers to tempt customers to buy the product the selling price is likely to be fairly constant during this period.

Unit production costs

Direct material costs are likely to be fairly constant in this stage. They may even increase as the quantities required diminish compared to those required in the growth stage, with the consequential loss of negotiating power.

Direct labour costs are unlikely to be reducing any longer as the effect of the learning and experience curves has ended. Indeed the workers may have started working on the next product so that their attention towards this product has diminished with the result that direct labour costs may increase.

Overhead costs are likely to be similar to those of the end of the growth stage as optimum batch sizes have been established and are more likely to be used in this maturity stage of the product life cycle where demand is more easily predicted.

18 PQ ELECTRONICS (MAY 10)

Key answer tips

Do not waste valuable time explaining the introductory phase of the product life cycle, or describing the market skimming approach to selling. These descriptions were not requested and earned no marks. Also, when asked to **explain** the changes, a fuller approach is required: an answer in the form of bullet points will reduce the number of marks that could be awarded.

Products and to some extent services have a recognisable life cycle. The life cycle will have considerable significance for the pricing decision (market skimming at introduction stage for PQ), because different pricing strategies will be appropriate for different stages in the cycle, depending on levels of demand and market structure. The life cycle has four stages:

In the growth phase:

(i) **Selling price**

This stage should offer the greatest potential for profit to PQ, whose aim should be to build market share, despite the fact that competitors will be prompted to enter the growing market. Price cuts should be put in place to remain competitive if competitors are starting to enter the market, and to appeal to new customers.

(ii) **Production costs**

Demand for the PQ product increases steadily and average unit variable costs fall with the economies of scale that accompany the greater production volume, and application of the learning curve.

(iii) **Selling and marketing costs**

Costs will still be high, because more promotion is needed to advertise the product more widely; distribution channels may be expanded to take up more market share.

In the maturity phase:

(i) **Selling price**

The price is certainly expected to fall in response to competition and in order to retain market share.

(ii) **Production costs**

Demand for the PQ product reaches a plateau and average unit variable costs fall further slightly, or stabilise with economies of scale being achieved.

(iii) **Selling and marketing costs**

Advertising costs should fall as product awareness is stronger, unless monies are spent reaching new customers or new markets or advertising upgrades or new versions of the PQ product.

In the decline phase:

(i) **Selling price**

PQ's product would have effectively reached the end of its life cycle. The fall in sales will accelerate when the market reaches saturation point. Although it is still possible to make profits for a short period during this stage with **reduced prices**, it is only matter of time before the rapidly dwindling sales volumes herald the onset of losses for PQ and all competitors who remain in the market.

(ii) **Production costs**

Economies of scale may begin to decline so the unit variable cost may actually rise again.

(iii) **Selling and marketing costs**

Advertising costs should fall as marketing support will gradually be withdrawn.

19   COST OF QUALITY REPORT (SEPT 12)

Tutorial note

*Knowledge is being tested here – there are four quality costs classifications that you **must** know. Reading carefully through (a) will enable you identify the category of quality cost each item belongs to. The format below is that of a traditional quality cost report and the safest presentation of quality costs.*

(a)

Statement of expected quality costs	$
Prevention costs	500,000
Appraisal costs	30,000
External failure costs (note 1)	286,880
Internal failure costs (note 2)	332,045
Total	1,148,925

Note 1

Customer demand = 24,000 units, however 13% of the units delivered are rejected by customers so 24,000 units = 87% of the units despatched to customers.

The number of units despatched to customers is therefore 24,000/0.87 = 27,586 units. This means that 3,586 units have to be replaced. The variable cost of producing these units is $75 per unit and there is a redelivery cost of $5 per unit so the total variable cost is 3,586 × $80 = $286,880.

Note 2

Since 10% of the items manufactured are discovered to be faulty before they are despatched then 27,586 units represents 90% of the items tested before despatch so the initial production = 27,586/0.9 = 30,651 units. Thus 3,065 units are produced and rejected. These have a variable production cost of $75 per unit = $229,875.

The cost of the components included in the units produced is 30,651 units × $30 = $919,530.

Since 10% of the components bought are damaged prior to their use then the cost of these damaged components = $919,530 × 10/90 = $102,170

Thus the total internal failure cost = $229,875 + $102,170 = $332,045.

(b)

Tutorial note

For a full answer and maximum marks, remember both perspectives – financial and non-financial.

On purely financial grounds the company should not accept the proposal because there is an increase of $163,040 in quality costs. However there may be other factors to consider as the company may enhance its reputation as a company that cares about quality products and this may increase the company's market share. On balance the company should accept the proposal to improve its long-term performance.

20   PRODUCT LIFECYCLE (SEPT 12)

Tutorial note

Carefully read the scenario and understand the pricing strategy chosen for this product. This company has elected to adopt a market skimming policy. This implies that the product is unique and will initially be made in small volumes.

Describe the likely effects on unit selling prices (gradual reductions) and why these would be expected.

The company has just launched an innovative new product using a market skimming pricing policy. This means that the selling price of the product is high and thus the product is only available to a small segment of the market that can afford to pay the high price for something that is unique and innovative.

There are four stages to the product life cycle: Introduction, Growth, Maturity and Decline.

In the Introduction stage the product is unique and hence the company can charge a high price. However the company's competitors will buy the product and carry out reverse engineering to see how it works and how they can develop their own similar, but different product. The competitors will be particularly attracted by the high unit selling price which should result in high unit profit. However, the company will seek to avoid this competition by lowering its selling price towards the end of the Introduction stage to deter competitors from entering the market and also to make its product more affordable to the wider market.

In the Growth stage the company will maintain its lower selling price to continue to attract new purchasers of the product. If competitors have entered the market there may need to be further reductions in selling price to maintain the growth unless the original product can be differentiated in other ways.

In the Maturity stage the selling price of the product is likely to be stable but may be reduced still further, possibly by short term one-off offers or discounts for multiple purchases so that the product continues to be financially viable for as long as possible.

In the Decline stage the product may continue to be sold provided its margin is positive. If it is not then the product may be bundled with other products or sold for less than its unit cost in order to clear the company's inventory of what has become an obsolete product.

21   CUSTOMER LIFECYCLE COSTING (SEPT 11)

Tutorial note

Be careful here – you are not asked to write all you know about product life cycle costing. Customer life cycle costing has a number of unique characteristics but the Examiner commented at the time that most candidates were obviously unaware of these and wrote, at length, about a completely different topic.

Life cycle costing collects the costs of the cost object (each client in DTG's case) over their lifetime, irrespective of accounting years. This allows the total profit of each client to be measured.

DTG would need to set up a system to record the time spent, its cost, the cost of disbursements and the fee income derived from its client so that these values could be accumulated over the client's lifetime.

This would start with the initial meeting with the potential client because although this cost could not be charged to the client it is still a cost that has been incurred. If they become a client then other costs will be incurred in setting them up on the system as a client. At this stage no fee income has been earned because no services have yet been provided so the client is loss making. DTG would hope to gradually recover these initial costs by providing services until the client becomes profitable to them.

For those clients where DTG is being engaged on a one-off basis for each assignment there will be non-chargeable set up costs before each assignment is agreed. These costs need to be reflected in the fees charged for the services that are to be provided. Where a continuous role is agreed then discounted fee rates may be applied to recognise the reduced amount of setup costs.

DTG will also need to record the cost of time spent on non-chargeable activities after the service has been provided such as chasing the client for payment. They will also need to record the value of referrals that the client has made to them. This is often difficult to measure but may perhaps be identified by the smaller amount of time required to convert a lead from an existing client into a new client compared with the time required to convert other prospects into clients.

DTG can then measure the profits of each of its clients since their initial appointment and consequently determine which of them are most and least profitable.

22 SF (NOV 11)

(a) Kaizen costing is a system of cost reduction based upon the concept of continuous review of systems and procedures to identify and implement small incremental cost savings. It is used in the production phase of a product and employees are both encouraged and empowered to recommend changes that they believe will reduce costs without affecting the quality of the products or otherwise adversely affecting the customer's perception of the products.

(b) Standard costing and variance analysis is used as a means of monitoring performance by comparing actual costs with the standard costs that have been set. SF currently sets its standards at the start of the financial year and then uses these standards as the basis of its comparisons. This implies that these standards are the targets to be achieved for the year.

This system does not allow for improvements during the year. Kaizen costing is based on continuous improvements being made throughout the year. Consequently the Kaizen cost is a moving target that changes each month.

This is in conflict with the concept of having a clear and fixed target against which performance is to be measured. If a changing standard were to be set based on the revised Kaizen cost and used as the basis of performance management this may confuse managers and would also affect the measurement of variance trends over time.

23 LEARNING CURVES AND LABOUR VARIANCES (MAY 10)

(a) Based on revised data:

Total time for 30 batches 30 × (Y_{30})	=	30 × (10 hours × $30^{-0.5146}$)	=	52.12 hrs
Add: Time for 30th batch × 20 batches	=	0.851 (W1) × 20	=	17.02 hrs

Total time for 50 batches (Actual production) = **69.14 hrs**

New product – revised out-turn performance report

	Flexed budget	Actual	Variance
Output (batches)	50	50	–
Direct labour hours	69.14	93.65	24.51 hours Adverse
Direct labour cost	$829.68	$1,146	$316.32 Adverse
Direct labour efficiency			$294.24 Adverse (W2)
Direct labour rate			$22.20 Adverse (W3)

Workings:

(W1) **Time for 30th batch**

Y_{30}	=	1.74	on average for 30 batches
		52.12	Total time for 30 batches
Y_{29}	=	1.77	on average for 29 batches
		51.27	Total time for 29 batches

Therefore time for 30th batch = 52.12 – 51.27 = 0.851 hours

(W2) **Direct labour efficiency variance**

24.51 hours adverse variance, @$12 per hour = $294.24 Adverse

(W3) **Direct labour rate variance**

93.65 hours should have cost 93.65 × $12	=	$1.123.80
93.65 hours did cost	=	$1.146.00
Rate variance	=	$22.20 Adverse

(b) Our report is more useful to the production manager because comparing the standard time and cost for the actual output is a fairer comparison then comparing performance for different levels of output.

Our report also highlights the operational effects of the labour hours variance. Original learning curve assumptions were inappropriate. By showing the true efficiency of the operations as opposed to an invalid application of the original target, our report shows that the revised learning period data has not ended as early as it was supposed to have based on revised standards.

These calculations show that the actual learning is worse and more costly than was expected whereas the original variance calculation showed that the time taken was more than it should have been.

Splitting the total labour cost variance into an efficiency and a rate variance enables the variances to be attributed to those managers responsible. For example, rather than congratulating the workforce of their efficiency, these revised figures should be shown to the appropriate manager and alternative strategies (or revised expectations) applied.

24 LEARNING CURVES, PLANNING AND OPERATIONAL VARIANCES (SEPT 10)

 Walk in the footsteps of a top tutor

(a)

Step 1

Calculate the revised standard hours for 6 batches.

Original standard hours for 6 batches		2,400
Revised standard hours for 6 batches (W 1)		1,827.8
Actual hours		1,950
Standard rate	$16,800/2,400	$7 per hour

(W1)

		y	=	$a.x^b$
where	time for first batch	a	=	2,400/6
			=	400 hours
		b	=	−0.1520
		x	=	6 batches
	average time per batch	y	=	$400 \times 6^{-0.1520}$
			=	304.6 hours per batch
	Total time for 6 batches		=	304.6 × 6
			=	1827.8 hours

Step 2

Calculate the planning variance caused by the learning effect.

Planning variance:

Efficiency:	(2,400 − 1,827.8) × $7	=	$4,005.40 Favourable

Step 3

Calculate the operational variance.

Operational variance:

Efficiency	(1,827.8 − 1,950) × $7	=	$855.40 Adverse
Rate			nil

(b)

Tutorial note

Keep an eye on the clock – with only 4 marks available, you are limited to what you can write in detail, and the answer below is sufficient. You could also have mentioned that target costing can apply to existing products as an ongoing cost reduction approach.

Differences between standard costing and target costing include:

Step 4

Explain target costing and contrast with standard costing.

Target costing focuses upon reducing costs for products over time, whereas standard costing is more concerned with cost control – simply achieving a standard cost that remains largely unchanged from one period to the next.

Standard costs tend to be set by senior staff and the accountants, whereas operational staff become much more involved in setting and agreeing their target staff. By being involved in the target setting process staff may be more accepting of the targets and strive to achieve them.

A standard cost is generally based upon a produce that has already been designed. The cost is based upon actual resources and costs that will be incurred as the item is manufactured. However, a target cost is generally derived from a target price. A desired profit margin is then deducted from this price to reveal the target cost. This target cost is originally calculated before the actual product has been designed in detail to a particular specification. The product is then designed in order to ensure that the target cost is achieved.

25   BATCHES, LEARNING CURVES AND VARIANCES (MAR 11)

Examiner's comments: The attempts for both parts were extremely poor. Part (a) tested the candidates' ability to use the learning curve formula and to use variances. Candidates had the option to use the traditional learning curve formula, or to use logs, to answer the question. Very few candidates attained the marks that were available, even allowing for the application of the 'own figure' rule.

(a)   The standard cost of the actual hours worked was $3,493 – $85 = $3,408. At $12 per hour the actual hours worked were $3,408/$12 = 284 hours.

So the average time per batch for the first 32 batches was 284/32 = 8.875 hours per batch.

32 batches represent 5 doublings of output.

The learning rate was therefore: $5\sqrt{8.875/20}$ = 0.85 = 85%

(b)

> **Examiner's comments:** Part (b) required candidates to use the output from part (a) (or their own, realistic figures) to calculate a total direct labour cost. A few candidates were able to submit meaningful answers. However, some candidates put forward figures that were simply not in context to the figures in the question. E.g. total labour cost equal to £690,000. Candidates need to check their answers for sense.
>
> The quality of most answers clearly indicates that prior knowledge had not been brought forward, especially relating to variances.

Actual labour rate paid = $3,493/284 = $12.30 per hour.

Learning index = log 0.85/log 2 = –0.2345

$Y = 20 \times 128^{-0.2345} = 6.41$ hours

Total cost of direct labour = 6.41 × 128 × $12.30 = $10,092

26 LEARNING CURVES AND VARIANCES (NOV 10)

> **Examiner's comments:** The attempts for both parts were generally poor. Part (a) tested the candidate's ability to use the learning curve formula and then link the answer to the calculation of variances. Very few candidates attained the marks that were available. One can only presume that the knowledge associated with variance analysis had not been brought forward from P1 (or its equivalent for those who gained exemptions from P1).

(a)   Average time per unit for the first 560 units: $Y = ax^b$

$Y = 8 \times 560^{-0.1520}$

$Y = 3.057$ hours

Total time for 560 units = 560 × 3.057 = 1,712 hours

Time allowed for actual production	1,712 hours
Actual hours	3,500 hours
Original standard hours	4,480 hours

Direct labour efficiency variances:
Planning variance:
(4,480 hours – 1,712 hours) × $15 $41,520 Favourable

Operating variance:
(3,500 hours – 1,712 hours) × $15 $26,820 Adverse

Direct labour rate variance:
(3,500 hours × $15) – $57,750 $ 5,250 Adverse

Tutorial note

Make sure you avoid the common pitfalls highlighted by the Examiner – not correctly labelling the variances, omitting the 'adverse' or 'favourable' signs, and putting forward figures that are not realistic.

(b)

> **Examiner's comments:** Part (b) asked candidates to explain the importance of the learning curve in the context of target costing. Most candidates were able to explain the term 'target costing' but few could form the link and explain how the reduction in the time to perform a task needed recognition when deciding whether to proceed with the production and selling of new products.

Target costing applies to organisations that are forced to accept the market price for a particular item. The organisation uses this market price together with a desired profit target to determine the cost at which the item must be produced. The organisation then sets out to achieve this cost as an average unit cost throughout the life of the product.

Learning curves may be an important part of target costing but it depends on the nature of the manufacturing process. In a machine intensive environment it may be that significant learning curves do not exist and therefore in these environments learning curves could be said to be irrelevant to target costing. However, in labour intensive environments the effect of learning may be extremely significant and important because target costs may only be achieved once a certain level of activity has been reached. It may only be during this post learning period that costs are lowered sufficiently to meet the desired target cost.

27 LEARNING CURVES AND SENSITIVITY (MAY 13)

Tutorial note

In part (i) candidates needed to calculate the maximum reduction in the labour rate that could take place to allow the company to generate a profit of $75,000. The change needed to be measured against the rate of $40 per labour hour.

(i) Cumulative average time for 64 units = 119.58 hours

Total time for 64 units = 119.58 * 64 = 7,653.12 hours

The target profit of $75,000 is 'earned' by 7,653.12 hours. This represents $9.80 per hour.

The hourly rate could rise by $9.80 before the profit is eroded.

The sensitivity is therefore 9.80/40.00 = 24.5%

Tutorial note

In part (ii) candidates needed to establish by how much the learning rate could fall, and still allow the company to generate a profit of $75,000. To fully answer the question the change (fall) in the learning rate needed to be measured against the original 90%.

(ii)   Total labour cost of 64 units = 7,653.12 * $40 = $306,124.8

The labour cost could rise to $306,124.8 + $75,000 = $381,124.8, before no profit is earned.

This equals $381,124.8/$40 = 9,528.12 hours

This is an average of 9,528.12/64 hours per unit = 148.88 hours per unit.

Cumulative average time for 64 units/average time for the first unit = 148.88/225 = 0.6617

An output of 64 units represents six 'doublings' and therefore the learning rate is the sixth root of 0.6617

$\sqrt[6]{0.6617}$ = 0.9335

Therefore the learning rate can fall to 93.35%.

The sensitivity is therefore 3.35/90 = 3.72%

28   LEARNING AND SENSITIVITY (SEPT 13)

Tutorial note

Candidates needed to carefully read the question to understand the data provided, and then answer the three parts of the question which dealt with the learning curve, the sensitivity of the budgeted profit related to a change in the price of materials, and a change in the learning rate.

(a)   Budgeted profit = $30 * 128 = $3,840

Material cost = $38,400

Material price can rise by 10%.

The sensitivity of the budgeted profit for the period to a change in the price per kg of materials is 10%.

(b)   Average time per unit after 128 units have been produced is 20 hours. Therefore:

20 = a * 0.97 (Alternatively: 20 = a * 128(−0.152))

20 = a * 0.4783

a = 41.81 hours

The time for the first unit is 41.81 hours

(c)   Labour cost can rise by $3,840. Therefore labour hours can increase by 384 hours.

Current labour hours = 20 * 128 = 2,560. Therefore labour hours can increase to 2,944 hours.

This would give an average time per unit for 128 units of 23 hours.

Calculation of learning rate that would give an average time of 23 hours for 128 units is:

$23 = 41.81 * r^7$

$0.5501 = r^7$

$r = 0.9182$

The budgeted learning rate was 90%. The rate can decrease to 91.82%.

Sensitivity to a change in the learning rate = 0.0182/0.9 = 2.02%

29   TOTAL COST PLUS PRICING AND TARGET COSTING (MAY 12)

(a)

Tutorial note

Read the question properly, and make sure you do not put forward more than two disadvantages, as it will not bring you extra marks.

Total cost plus pricing is a pricing technique based on determining the total cost of a product or service and adding a profit percentage to that total cost to determine the selling price.

In a competitive environment any cost inefficiencies or the use of too great a profit percentage will mean that the company is no longer able to compete and will start to lose its market share. As this happens and output volumes fall, then the total unit cost will rise due to the sharing of fixed costs among a smaller number of units. The total cost plus pricing formula will then result in increased selling prices thereby reducing still further the company's ability to compete.

Therefore one disadvantage of this approach to pricing is that it does not consider the nature of the market and as a result can lead to loss of sales and of course profits.

A second disadvantage is that the company is not motivated to save cost because if it does so this simply results in a lower selling price. Indeed if the market supports a total cost plus price then by increasing costs the size of the profit is increased!

(b)

Tutorial note

As always, make sure you relate the answers to the scenario in the question.

Target costing is useful in a competitive market such as this where a company is not dominant in the market and is forced to accept the market price for its products or services.

Thus target costing focuses on the achievement of a unit cost which will earn the company the financial return that it requires.

The starting point for the operation of Target costing is the unit selling price of the company's product or service. From this is deducted the required profit (to yield the company's required financial return) and the result is the target unit cost that is to be achieved. This target cost is then compared with the expected unit cost to see if the target cost is already being met or if the company needs to consider making changes which will result in a lowering of unit costs.

It may be that the effects of the learning and experience curves will reduce the present cost to the level of the target cost; or it may be that the company can achieve other cost savings provided they do not diminish the quality of the product or service as perceived by the customer.

If these cost savings cannot be made the company may have to lower its required return from the product or service or decide that it is not financially viable for it to sell this product or service in the market.

Thus target costing would benefit this company by forcing it to consider its internal processes and costs and to conduct these as efficiently as possible. If despite making these as efficient as possible the required return from the product cannot be achieved, then the company should cease to make a product that is not viable and therefore would be able to focus its resources on alternative sources of income.

30 LEARNING CURVES AND GAIN SHARING ARRANGEMENTS (NOV 08)

Key answer tips

In (i), a very easy calculation that should have been practised time and time again.

In (ii), more uncommon considerations for a small question carrying only two marks – do not waste any time here.

Requirement (b) had never examined before and only 5 marks anyway. To try and maximise marks, make sure the following is included in your answer:

(1)   A definition of gain-sharing arrangements

(2)   A definition of the learning curve.

With any time left over, three considerations on the possible link between the two can be added. We must insist on the importance of time-keeping here – it is easy to lose sight of the clock whilst trying to come up with suggestions.

(a)   (i)   From the formula sheet, the learning curve formula is given by Yx = aXb, where:

Y_x = the cumulative average time to produce X units

a = time required to produce the first unit of output.

X = the cumulative number of units and b = the index of learning

Here, $Y_x = 24 \: X^{-0.3219}$

Expected time for 8th unit is the difference between the total time to produce 8 units and the total time to produce 7 units.

Cumulative average time for 8 units:	Y_8	$= 24 \times 8^{-0.3219}$
		= 12.288 minutes on average
Total time for 8 units: 8 × 12.288		= 98.309 minutes in total
Cumulative average time for 7 units:	Y_7	$= 24 \times 7^{-0.3219}$
		= 12.828 minutes on average
Total time for 7 units: 7 × 12.828		= 89.799 minutes in total

Expected time to produce 8th unit = 98.309 minutes − 89.799 minutes = **8.5 minutes**.

(ii)   Time taken for the 1025th unit may be more than expected because:

- The steady state, at which the time taken per unit no longer declines, is reached before the 1025th unit is produced.

- The real learning curve is slower than the expected 80%.

(b)   In gain sharing agreements all costs savings, and costs overruns are shared between the customer and the contractor or supplier.

Very often, a target cost is negotiated and agreed. Any savings on this target cost are shared in agreed proportions.

However, any costs overruns based on target costs are also shared between the parties.

The learning curve effect states that the more times a task is performed, the less time will be required on each subsequent iteration, and therefore the costs per unit of output will decrease until a steady state is reached.

Considering the learning curve is important in gain sharing arrangements because:

(1)   It will allow an accurate calculation of financial benefits incurred by costs savings overtime −costs savings that can be shared between the parties.

(2)   A clear understanding by employees will be key to their motivation to achieve the forecast costs in order to reap the benefits of the gain sharing arrangements.

(3)   Gains will be achievable up until the steady state is reached − understanding the learning curve and forecasting costs accordingly will help to determine when the benefits linked to gain sharing arrangements will end.

31 LEARNING CURVES AND TARGETS (MAR 12)

(a)

	$
Direct material (6,400 units × $4)	25,600
Direct labour (see below)	8,503
Other variable costs (6,400 units × $2)	12,800
	46,903

Direct labour:

The time taken is expected to be:

$Y = ax^b = 25 \times 64^{-0.1520} = 13.286$ hours per batch, which is a total of 850.32 hours for 64 batches.

850.32 hours × $10 per hour = $8,503.20

(b) Assuming no other cost savings can be made the direct labour cost would have to reduce by $1,903 (i.e. the excess of cost above the target cost) to a total cost of $6,600 which is the equivalent of 660 hours at $10 per hour.

660 hours in total represents an average time of 10.3125 hours per batch (660/64 batches). Since the learning continued throughout the production of the 64 batches then this average can be used to determine the rate of learning required to achieve the target variable cost.

64 batches of production represent 6 doublings of cumulative output therefore:

10.3125/25 = 0.4125

$^6\sqrt{0.4125} = 0.8628$

The learning rate at which the target variable cost would be achieved is 86.3%

32 LIFETIME, LIFECYCLE (MAY 12)

(a) (i) Average cost for 4 batches: $y = ax^b$, with $y = \$40,000 \times 4^{-0.152} = \$32,400$

(ii) The total cost for the 4 batches = 4 × $32,400 = $129,600

Average cost for 3 batches: $y = ax^b$

$y = \$40,000 \times 3^{-0.152} = \$33,848$

The total cost for 3 batches = 3 × $33,848 = $101,544

(iii) Total labour cost over the product's life
= $129,600 + (4 × $28,056) = $241,824

Sales less non labour related cost over the product's life
= 8,000 × ($90 – $45) $360,000

CONTRIBUTION $118,176

Cost for 4th batch = $28,056

(b)　In order to achieve a contribution of $150,000 the total labour cost over the products lifetime would have to equal ($360,000 − $150,000) = $210,000.

This equals an average batch cost of $210,000/8 = $26,250.

This represents $26,250/$40,000 = 65.625% of the cost of the first batch.

8 batches represents 3 doublings of output

Therefore the rate of learning required = $3\sqrt{0.65625}$ = 86.9% = 87%

33　PR AND JIT (MAR 11)

(a)

> **Examiner's comments:** The answers put forward were generally good, but several problems were prominent in this question:
>
> 1　The major fault, and one that expended valuable time, is that many candidates wrote about JIT purchasing whereas the question related to JIT production.
>
> 2　Not including or mentioning that a JIT production system is based around the principle of zero inventories at all stages of production including finished goods. This is an important issue that specifically needed mentioning.

A JIT production system is based around the principle of zero inventory at all stages of the production cycle. This means that PR would:

- use a production control system so that there was no work in progress between the various stages of production; and

- not hold an inventory of finished goods because items would be completed just as the customer required them to be delivered.

(b)

> **Examiner's comments:** Failing to consider items that are costly and would have a negative impact on cash and profits including retraining, recruitment, possible redundancies, new machines, re-layout of the production area, idle time and overtime payments.

There are a number of reasons why the profitability of PR may not increase as a result of changing to a JIT production system. These include the following.

(i)　Rather than ordering materials in bulk to obtain lower supply prices, PR would place smaller, more frequent orders as items are required, thus eliminating inventory holdings. Charges made by suppliers for smaller more frequent deliveries may be greater than the cost saving from holding zero raw material inventory

(ii)　The need to use a production control system to match production and demand at all stages may necessitate overtime working. Overtime might be paid at premium labour rates, thus labour costs might be higher compared to those incurred when operating a constant flow production system.

34 OVERTIME WORKING (MAY 12)

(a)

Tutorial note

*It is a mistake to calculate the holding cost using the quarter-end inventory figures. The question specifically asked for the costs to be calculated based on **average** inventory levels.*

Annual demand = 540,000 units. (Quarterly capacity of 135,000 units × 4 quarters = 540,000 so no overtime is required.)

Current system – constant production

Quarter	1	2	3	4	Total
Opening inventory	0	35,000	60,000	5,000	
Production	135,000	135,000	135,000	135,000	
Sales	100,000	110,000	190,000	140,000	
Closing inventory	35,000	60,000	5,000	0	
Average inventory	17,500	47,500	32,500	2,500	
Inventory cost ($)	70,000	190,000	130,000	10,000	**400,000**

(b)

Tutorial note

Pay special attention to the layout of the answers and in particular attach an explanation to your figures.

JIT production system

Quarter	1	2	3	4	Total
Overtime production	0	0	54,000	5,000	
Lost sales			1,000		
Additional cost ($)*	0	0	1,107,000	102,500	
Lost contribution			15,000		
					1,224,500

The change in profit would be a reduction of $824,500

* Additional overtime cost per unit =

Direct labour $35 × 0.5 =	$17.50
Variable overhead $10 × 0.3 =	$ 3.00
	$20.50

35   LEARNING CURVES AND BREAKEVEN (SEPT 12)

(a)

> *Tutorial note*
>
> *Carefully read the data provided and recognise that the four figures required are simply a doubling of the time for the first batch. By use of the simpler doubling approach, or by use of the more complex learning curve formula, calculate the average time per batch for all 4 levels of production and multiply the resultant figures by the number of batches.*

No of units	No of batches	Average direct labour cost	Total direct labour cost	
100	1	$6,000	$6,000	
200	2	$4,800	$9,600	
400	4	$3,840	$15,360	
800	8	$3,072	$24,576	Ans (i)
1,600	16	$2,457.60	$39,321.60	Ans (ii)
3,200	32	$1,966.08	$62,914.56	Ans (iii)
6,400	64	$1,572.86	$100,663.30	Ans (iv)

(b)

> *Tutorial note*
>
> *Part (b) involved using the answer from part (a) to calculate the approximate break-even level of sales of the product. Only an approximate figure could be calculated as the direct labour cost per unit constantly reduces whilst a learning curve is in existence.*

No of units	3,200	6,400
	$	$
Sales	224,000	448,000
Direct material and other non-labour related costs	144,000	288,000
Direct labour cost	62,914.56	100,663.30
Fixed cost	60,000	60,000
Total costs	266,914.56	448,663.30
(Loss)	(42,914.56)	(663.30)

As can be seen from the table above the breakeven point seems to be slightly above 6,400 units.

(c)

Tutorial note

Part (c) required understanding of the workings of the learning curve in that labour cost per unit will increase (and the break-even point will also increase) if the rate of learning moves from 80% to 90%.

If the rate of learning were to be 90% instead of 80% this means that the labour time (and hence labour cost) per unit would reduce more slowly. Assuming that all other data remained unchanged then costs would be higher and hence the break-even level of sales would also be higher.

36   NEW PRODUCT (NOV 12)

Tutorial note

Carefully read and absorb the data provided, and by use of either the labour efficiency planning variance, or the labour efficiency operating variance, calculate the revised standard time to produce 32 units. The next step needed a calculation to arrive at the average time per unit, and express this as a percentage of the time for the first unit (25 hours). Then, by recognising that the number of 'doublings' is five, take the fifth root of the percentage earlier calculated to arrive at the expected learning rate.

Part (b) requested you to explain two reasons why it is important for production and control purposes to identify the learning curve, such as scheduling, control and resourcing.

(a)   The planning variance is $4,320. This represents 360 hours. Therefore the revised standard time to produce 32 units is (25 * 32) – 360 = 440 hours.

The cumulative average standard time per unit is 440/32 = 13.75 hours per unit

The time for the first unit was 25 hours.

The cumulative average time per unit for the first 32 units as a percentage of the time for the first unit is 55%.

32 units is 5 doublings of output (2, 4, 8, 16, 32) and therefore 55% is the fifth root of the learning rate

Therefore the expected learning rate was 88.7%

(b)   The identification of the learning curve is important because of its impact on the time taken to produce the output. This has implications in many areas of production planning and control:

Scheduling: it is important to know the expected time that the output will take so that realistic schedules can be produced. This is important for meeting deadlines and also for effective utilisation of resources (for example preventing under utilisation of capacity).

Resources: production planning is needed to ensure that sufficient resources are available (e.g. materials). If the workers can work faster because of the learning curve it is important that the resources they need are available.

Control: if the learning curve is not identified, the efficiency variance is of little use for control purposes. The impact of the learning curve will hide the true picture of the labour efficiency variance because the 'standard' will be unrealistic if it is based on the time taken for the first unit to be produced.

Note: the question asked for two reasons. Marks were awarded for reasons other than those shown above.

37   LEARNING CURVES AND BREAKEVEN (MAR 13)

Tutorial note

Candidates needed to carefully read and absorb the data provided and use the learning curve formula provided to establish the time taken to produce the 32nd batch.

Part (b) required candidates to use the data provided in the question, together with the output from part (a), to calculate the selling price of the final 500 units that would allow a certain level of profit to be earned.

(a)

	Output	
	31 batches	*32 batches*
Cumulative average time (y=ax–.152)	296.6764 hours	295.2482 hours
Total time (= c.a.t. * output)	9,196.9690 hours	9,447.9410 hours

Time for 32nd batch = 9,447.941 – 9,196.969 = 250.972 hours

(b)   Workings: labour cost of 40 batches

Labour hours for 32 batches	9,447.941
Labour hours 33 to 40 batches =250.9723 * 8	2,007.778
Total labour hours for 40 batches	11,455.719
Total labour cost = 11,455.719 * $24	$274,937

Total cost of 40 batches

	$
Labour	274,937
Other variable costs	240,000
Fixed costs	130,000
Total cost	644,937

Total revenue needed to earn target profit of $150,000 = $794,937

Revenue from 3,500 units = 3,500 * $215 = $752,500

Revenue needed from final 500 units = $42,437

Selling price per unit = $84.88

Examiner's note: Alternative ways of presenting the figures were/are acceptable.

38   XY COMPANY (MAY 10)

Key answer tips

The average inventory figure must be used in (a) to calculate the inventory cost, not the month end inventory levels.

(a)   (i)

	Month 1	Month 2	Month 3	Month 4	Month 5	Month 6	Total
Production (standard hours)	3,780	3,780	3,780	3,780	3,780	3,780	
Add: opening inventory	0	680	760	540	1,020	1,200	
Less: Sales/Demand	(3,100)	(3,700)	(4,000)	(3,300)	(3,600)	(4,980)	
= Closing inventory	680	760	540	1020	1,200	0	
Average Inventory for the month	340	720	650	780	1,110	600	
@ $6 per std hour	**$2,040**	**$4,320**	**$3,900**	**$4,680**	**$6,660**	**$3,600**	**$25,200**

(ii)

Month	Production Std hrs	Actual hours worked	OT hours	OT pay $15 ph
1	3,100	3,229.17 *	0	
2	3,700	3,854.17	0	
3	4,000	4,166.67	228.92	$3,433.8
4	3,300	3,437.5	0	
5	3,600	3,750	0	
6	4,980	5,187.5	1,249.75	$18,746.25
				22,180.05

Total saving $25,200 − $22,180.25 = $3,019.95

* 3,100/0.96 = 3,229.17

** any hours over 3,937.75 are OT hrs

(b)   Other factors to consider before moving to a JIT production system

1   Reliability of suppliers of direct material – would they be able to supply quality material on time and in full to ensure the JIT operations run smoothly with no production stoppages.

2   Labour efficiency ratio – were we in presence of a learning curve and have we reached the steady state yet.

3   As stock levels are lowered quality becomes essential, management should aim to improve quality at all levels:

- at source

- at design

- in process

- in people.

39   XY ACCOUNTANCY SERVICES (NOV 10)

> **Examiner's comments:** This question was generally well answered. Many candidates did not gain the marks available simply because they did not correctly answer the question. Candidates were asked to "prepare calculations to show the effect on fees", as a result of changing to an ABC system. Therefore a comparison was needed of the fees generated from both systems. A significant number of candidates simply produced a chart showing the costs using an ABC approach. The layout of the figures put forward by many candidates was extremely poor. A typical spreadsheet approach was required; simply three columns and a number of rows were required.

Cost driver rates:

Accounts preparation and advice	580,000/18,000 hours = $32.22 per hour
Requesting missing information	30,000/250 times = $120 per request
Issuing fee payment reminders	15,000/400 times = $37.50 per reminder
Holding client meetings	60,000/250 meetings = $240 per meeting
Travelling to clients	40,000/10,000 miles = $4 per mile

Client costs:

	Client A	B	C
	$	$	$
Accounts preparation and advice	32,222	8,055	10,955
Requesting missing information	480	1,200	720
Issuing fee payment reminders	75	300	375
Holding client meetings	960	240	480
Travelling to clients	600	2400	0
Total costs	34,337	12,195	12,530
Total costs on original basis*	40,280	10,070	13,695
Client fees – new basis	41,204	14,634	15,036
Client fees – original basis	48,336	12,084	16,434
Increase/(Decrease)	(7,132)	2,550	(1,398)

*$725,000/18,000 hours = $40.28 per hour

40   FACTORY ABC (SEPT 13)

Tutorial note

In part (a) two fixed overhead variances needed calculating and in part (b) two variances needed calculating that related to material handling costs.

(a)   (i)   Fixed production overhead expenditure variance = Actual – budget = $310,000 – $300,000 = $10,000 adverse.

     (ii)   Fixed production overhead volume variance = Budget – absorbed = $300,000 – (1,600 * $200) = $20,000 favourable.

(b)   The cost driver for the materials handling activity would be "material shipments". Analysis of the budgeted figures shows that the expected activity level is that one shipment should be 4 tonne and each shipment should cost $800.

     (i)   85 shipments should cost 85 * $800 = $68,000

          85 shipments did cost $69,000

          Therefore the materials handling shipment expenditure variance is $1,000 adverse

     (ii)   348 tonne of materials should have required 87 shipments but actually only needed 85 shipments. This is two shipments 'favourable'.

     The materials handling shipment efficiency variance is 2 * $800 = $1,600 favourable

41   HIERARCHY OF ACTIVITIES (SEPT 13)

Tutorial note

Candidates needed to carefully read the question to fully understand what was required. The requirement revolved around ABC but applied particularly to the context in which the question was set. A detailed discussion of the characteristics of ABC was not required.

Unit level activities

These would traditionally have been classified as variable costs and given the direct nature of these costs no improvements can be made to the linkage between cost control and responsibility accounting. Analysis through variances such as the materials usage variance and the materials price variance identify areas of responsibility.

Batch level activities

Some activities, for example machine set ups, consume resources in proportion to the number of batches produced rather than in proportion to the number of units produced. The cost driver for the set up activity is the request for the set up and not the number of units that are in the production run. Therefore a link can be established to the manager who has requested the set up and the appropriate charge made to the manager/product. Under a traditional system the charge would have been made based on, for example, the number of machine hours consumed by the production run and would have been considered as part of the general production overhead. It is in this area that ABC has the greatest impact: cost pools related to activities are identified and appropriate cost drivers are used to charge costs to the manager/product responsible for initiating the activity.

Product sustaining activities

These activities are performed to enable different products (or services) to be produced and sold (or performed). The resources consumed are independent of how many units or batches are produced although there may be some 'stepped costs' e.g. advertising. The costs can be identified directly with each product and the decision to incur them. The linkage to cost control and responsibility accounting should not be any different under ABC than traditional costing.

Facility sustaining activities

Even within an ABC system it is accepted that some costs simply relate to "being in business" and therefore cannot be directly linked with a specific product or service (examples include buildings maintenance and security). The linkage to cost control and responsibility accounting would not be any different under ABC than traditional costing.

42 DCPA (SEPT 10)

Key answer tips

Make sure you present a professional layout, and that your workings are clearly cross-referenced. In part (b), ensure you have actually answered the question and not just produced a brief description of DCPA; Another pitfall would be to discuss products, rather than customers.

(a) **Customer profitability analysis statement:**

	Customer B	Customer D
Factory Contribution	$75,000	$40,500
Less Cost of sales	$46,000	$12,500
Sales visit (24;12) (W1)	$6,000	$3,000
Processing orders (75;20) (W1)	$7,500	$2,000
Normal deliveries (45;15) (W1)	$22,500	$7,500
Urgent deliveries (5;0) (W1)	$10,000	$–
Net margin from customer	$29,000	$28,000

(W1) **Cost per driver**

Activity	Amount	Cost driver	Quantity	Cost per driver
Sales visits	$50,000	Sales visits to customers	200	$250
Processing orders	$70,000	Orders placed by customers	700	$100
Normal deliveries	$120,000	Normal deliveries	240	$500
Urgent deliveries	$60,000	Urgent deliveries	30	$2,000

(b) ST could use DCPA to build customer profitability profiles and charge customers according to the cost to serve them. In ST, an analysis of overheads per pack sold produces the following results:

	Customer B	Customer D
Total overheads/Cost of sales, as in (a)	$46,000	$12,500
Packs sold	50,000	27,000
Overhead per pack	**$0.920**	**$0.463**

Customers B and D do not cost the same to serve even if they require the same products. For example, Customer B may be more disruptive: it requires more urgent deliveries that could interrupt production scheduling and require immediate, special transport: it should therefore be charged more. Urgent deliveries cost 4 times as much as standard ones and this should be reflected in the 'cost to serve'.

Alternatively, profits could be increased by minimising or even eliminating these urgent deliveries and associated costs.

Likewise, the DCPA could be used to change customer behaviour and encourage customers to place larger orders and reduce processing costs and number of deliveries. A transparent DCPA system can therefore help operational cost reduction by listing customer-specific costs in a statement communicated to trading partners.

43 TREE FARM (MAY 13)

Tutorial note

Candidates need to carefully read the question and using the data provided, construct a customer profitability statement showing the profit for each customer. Candidates then need to perform a number of calculations to measure the performance of each customer, such as profit per order, profit per shrub. A brief discussion of the resulting figures is then required.

	B	C
	$	$
Gross revenue	57,600	39,000
Discounts allowed	8,640	7,800
Net revenue	48,960	31,200
Cost of shrubs	24,000	16,250
Delivery costs	4,000	0
Order processing	800	1,000
Net profit	20,160	13,950
No. of shrubs sold	960	650
Profit per shrub sold	$21	$21.46
Number of orders	8	10
Profit per order	$2,520	$1,395
Profit per $1 gross revenue	$0.35	$0.36

Comments:

There is very little difference between the profit per $ of gross revenue from customers B and C. Customer B earns the lower profit per shrub. This is despite the large discount given to C for using their own transport.

The discount offered to Customer C seems generous. The discount costs the farm $7,800 in lost revenue but only saves (based on the order frequency shown) $5,000 in delivery costs. Why has this discount been given? Is the transport being used to full capacity and it is not possible to make the sale unless the customer collects the shrubs themselves? Is C situated a large distance away from the farm?

The analysis shows that B earns the higher absolute profit for the farm because of the higher number of shrubs purchased. However C earns the highest profit per shrub.

The analysis could be used by the farm to assess the impact of the discounts it offers to the customers. For example, what would be the impact on delivery schedules and costs of reducing the discount offered on orders for more than 100 shrubs?

It would appear that the farm is happy to earn a profit margin of 35% and to offer incentives to achieve that margin.

44 SOFTWARE DEVELOPMENT (MAY 09)

Key answer tips

In part (a), do not produce only a general answer that could have applied to any company launching a new product.

In part (b) only showing the final profit position is not enough – you must show the impact of adopting the activity-based cost figures as a basis for setting selling prices. Presentation can make the difference between passing and not passing this question.

(a) VBG3 currently has a high market share because it appears to be under-priced: its selling price of $65.00 has not been calculated based on its 'truer' ABC cost of $75.00.

Indeed, VBG3 is loss making, at a rate of $10 per unit. In what appears to be price elastic conditions, VBG3's high market share, and appeal to customers, is therefore due to its low price.

This is particularly relevant in what we may assume is a highly competitive market, where competitors would have priced their output on a more accurate costing basis.

(b) **Using Activity Based Costing, current profitability:**

	AXPL1	FDR2	VBG3
ABC cost	$48	$42	$75
Current selling price	$50	$75	$65
Profit per unit	$2	$33	($10)
Market size in units	2,500	3,000	4,000
Market share in %	45%	15%	80%
Market share in units	1,125	450	3,200
Total profit per software product	$2,250	$14,850	($32,000)
Total profit		($14,900)	

Using Activity Based Costing, revised profitability:

	AXPL1	FDR2	VBG3
Revised selling price (W1)	$60	$52.50	$93.75
ABC cost as per question	$48	$42	$75
Revised profit per unit	$12	$10.50	$18.75
Revised number of units (working 2)	750	1,462.5	1,475
Revised total profit per software product	$9,000	$15,356	$27,656
Revised total profit		$52,013	
Current profitability	$2,250	$14,850	($32,000)
Revised profitability	$9,000	$15,356	$27,656
Difference – Increase in profitability	$6,750	$506	$59,656
Total increase in profitability		$66,913	

Workings:

(W1) **New selling price**

	AXPL1	FDR2	VBG3
ABC cost	$48	$42	$75
Mark-up 25%	$12	$11	$19
New selling price	$60	$52.50	$93.75

(W2) **Revised number of units**

	AXPL1	FDR2	VBG3
Revised number of units	AXPL1	FDR2	VBG3
Market size in units	2,500	3,000	4,000
Revised market share (W3)	30%	48.75%	36.875%
Number of units	750	1462.50	1475

(W3) **Revised market share**

	AXPL1	FDR2	VBG3
Increase/(Decrease) in selling price	$10	($22.50)	$ 28.75
$2 increase	5 times		14.375 times
$2 decrease		11.25 times	

Market share (reduction)/increase of:

	AXPL1	FDR2	VBG3
5 times × 3%	−15%		
11.25 times × 3%		33.75%	
14.375 times × 3%			−43.13%
Current market share – as per question	45%	15%	80%
New market share	30%	48.75%	36.875%

45   PQ BUILDING (MAR 13)

Tutorial note

In part (a) candidates simply needed to explain how absorption and allocation of costs differs in activity based costing compared to traditional absorption costing.

In part (b) candidates were required to explain how the introduction of ABC could help to increase the profits of the company. An understanding of ABC related to direct product profitability and customer profitability was required.

(a)   In traditional absorption costing costs are allocated to production and/or service departments and are then absorbed into products by the use of overhead absorption rates. The absorption rate base will be chosen to reflect the characteristics of the department in an attempt to establish causality and equity, and therefore labour hours or machine hours are typically used.

In activity based costing costs are allocated to cost pools. The costs allocated to a cost pool may be from different departments but the reason behind the grouping is that the costs will be caused by a particular type of activity i.e. a cost driver. The cost per driver can then be calculated and used to charge costs to products and/or service departments by looking at the number of times they give rise to the activity.

(b)   ABC can be used to identify the activities that are causing costs. The activities could be related to products and/or customers.

Direct product profitability necessitates that costs are attributed to the products that cause them. Activity based costing can help with this process by tracing costs through the identification of cost drivers which may be driven by specific products. Given this information PQ can investigate selling prices, inventory, display space, distribution costs and other factors that determine the profitability of each product or product group. For example the costs of Cutting Bay could be allocated to the products that are taken to the bay.

Customer profitability analysis is the "analysis of the revenue streams and service costs associated with specific customers or customer groups" (CIMA terminology). Activity based costing would enable PQ to do this. Activity based costing will lead to the identification of cost drivers and these could be traced to customers. For example, to identify which type of customers take advantage of the free delivery service.

When costs are traced to products/services/customers it will allow PQ to see the profits from each product and/or customer group and then make informed decisions about selling prices, products sold, inventory levels, etc.

46   QW (NOV 10)

(a)   QW is presently using a form of just-in-time (JIT) production system because each item that is produced is specific to the order placed by the customer. Consequently QW does not hold an inventory of finished items. QW does not use a JIT purchasing system because of the risk of being unable to fulfil customer orders due to lack of materials, however its raw material inventory levels are kept to a minimum which is in keeping with the JIT philosophy. This system encourages efficiency amongst the workforce because any delays may result in lost orders.

The proposed production system for the metal ornaments is a completely different system that is based on constant rates of production and fluctuating levels of finished goods inventory to smooth out the peaks and troughs of demand. This type of system would allow QW to predict the raw materials that it requires with greater certainty, but can lead to inefficient production and obsolete finished goods inventory. This is because managers often believe that it is good to produce as many of the item as possible without too much thought for the cost implications of holding high inventory holdings on cost. It is important that inventory levels are carefully monitored if losses due to obsolescence and damage are to be avoided.

(b)   A TQM system is essential if the production system is a JIT system because any failings cannot be remedied by supplying items from inventory. However the same is not true of a constant rate production system. In a constant rate production system, any failings can be hidden because items are sold from inventory. It is important therefore that such failings are reported via the performance reporting system.

As a consequence the focus on quality is less critical for a constant rate production system and as a result it is harder to convince employees of the need to be committed to such a philosophy.

47   VALUE AND FUNCTIONAL ANALYSIS (MAY 06)

Key answer tips

'Value Analysis' is totally different from 'Value Chain', so do not use Porter's model in your answer.

You must demonstrate that you understand the difference between Value Analysis, that relates to an **existing** product or service and functional analysis, more commonly applied to a product or service **before its production.**

(a)   Value analysis is an examination of the factors affecting the cost of a product or service with the objective of achieving the specified purpose most economically at the required level of quality and reliability.

Functional analysis is an analysis of the relationships between product functions, the cost of their provision and their perceived value to the customer. Functional analysis is applied to the design of new products and breaks the product down into functional parts. For example, a new washing machine may have the function to operate quietly. The value that the customer places on each component is considered and added to give a target cost.

Value analysis is thus a form of cost reduction which is based upon investigating the processes involved in providing a product or service whereas functional analysis focuses on the value to the customer of each function of the product or service and from this focuses resources on those functions that give the customer most value.

(b) There are a series of steps that the company of financial advisors needs to use to implement value analysis into the organisation:

(i) The company needs to identify the requirements of its clients so that it can ensure that the services it provides give value to its clients. It has been stated that many clients do not read the company's newsletters; clearly then the newsletters have no value to these clients in their present form. Perhaps the newsletters should be abandoned and their cost saved; or perhaps the newsletter could be changed to make it more valuable from a client perspective.

(ii) Once the company has identified the services that are valued by its clients it can then consider alternative ways of providing those services. Perhaps the newsletter could be emailed or could include competitions. The cost/benefit is then assessed.

(iii) The best option is chosen and implemented.

(iv) The change is then evaluated to determine whether the expected benefits have arisen.

> **Examiner's comments:** This question should have been quite straightforward, but far too many candidates wrote all they knew about JIT and TQM and did not address the question. Poor planning of the answer resulted in candidates repeating in part (b) details that appeared in part (a), and including details and explanations that did not relate to the question. Putting forward additional information did not attract marks and would have used up valuable time. Most candidates completely ignored the request to 'compare and contrast' the present and proposed systems. Words such as "in comparison to," or "whereas", needed to be used.

48 ZX AND TQM (MAR 11)

> **Examiner's comments:** This question should have presented candidates with very few problems as TQM is a major topic within the syllabus. Unfortunately a large number of the answers were simply a general essay on TQM, with no mention of or reference to the banking sector. When answering this question, candidates needed to explain clearly that TQM is a management philosophy, where quality is placed at the heart of the organisation's thinking and activities.
>
> The verb 'explain' was ignored by candidates and seemed to have been replaced with 'write all you know about'.

TQM is a management philosophy whereby quality is placed at the heart of the organisation's thinking and activities. The view is that the quality experience of the customer (whether internal or external) should be one of excellence. The organisation should strive for continuous improvement in the quality that it delivers with the ultimate aim of achieving zero defects in this quality.

It may be necessary to incur expenditure in order to improve quality. However, in TQM this expenditure is viewed as an investment that will yield future benefits, rather than as a cost that should be minimised.

By investing in TQM the ZX bank can improve its customers' experience in having their banking needs fulfilled. This should enable the bank to gain a competitive advantage.

There are many ways in which ZX can invest in TQM.

ZX could provide its employees with training in the technical aspects of banking practice as well as in customer care. Customers would therefore receive a better service not only technically but also from a customer care perspective. This should lead to fewer customer complaints and greater customer satisfaction. It could also encourage customers to recommend others to use this bank.

A TQM approach would require ZX to respond to its customers' comments, for example by providing more staff at busy times to reduce the lengths of queues. They could also open for longer hours to allow customers to complete their banking and have meetings with bank managers at a time that is more convenient for the customer. This should lead to more satisfied customers.

In the long run improved quality, despite incurring some additional expenditure, should enable ZX to gain competitive advantage and therefore generate higher profits for the bank.

49   TQM (MAY 09)

Key answer tips

The report presented here is longer than what is realistically feasible in 18 minutes. However, this remains an easy, straight off the textbook question where 10 marks were easily attainable.

REPORT

To: Managing Director   **From:** Assistant Management Accountant

Subject: Total Quality Management   **Date:** 20 May 2009

Introduction

Following our recent adoption of JIT principles, please find a report that briefly explains the Total Quality Management (TQM) principles and the four categories of quality costs. You will also find an explanation of the relationship between compliance and non-compliance costs in the context of TQM.

Total Quality Management

One of the main concepts behind TQM is that it is cheaper in the long run for a company to **'get it right first time'** and prevent quality problems, rather than allow the problems to continue and incur the cost of correcting these problems.

Continuous improvement is another key TQM principle: Managers may never be satisfied with the method used, because there always can be improvements. Certainly, the competition is improving, so it is very necessary to strive to keep ahead of the game. Working smarter, not harder, and taking into account every employee's suggestions on how to improve a process and eliminate waste is fundamental to the TQM philosophy.

Quality costs

Quality costs are divided into costs of control (or 'compliance costs') and costs of failure to control ('non-conformance costs').

Compliance costs are further divided into **prevention** costs and **appraisal** costs:

Prevention costs

These are costs incurred in preventing mistakes from happening. For example, the implementation of standards, staff training and the costs involved in setting up quality management programs are prevention costs.

Appraisal costs

These are the costs incurred in looking for mistakes before a product is manufactured. Appraisal costs include acceptance testing, the evaluation of purchased materials, checking of work by supervisors, vendor rating (the assessment of all suppliers of goods and services to determine their competence in meeting ours and our customers' needs).

Non-conformance costs are divided into 'internal failure' and 'external failure' costs:

Internal failure costs

These occur when the units produced fail to reach the set standard. They include:

- waste – the cost associated with unnecessary work as the result of errors, poor organisation or poor communication
- order re-entry
- unnecessary travel
- handling queries and complaints from the supplier.

External failure costs

These arise when the faulty product is not detected until after it reaches the customer. For example:

- the cost of handling, packing and returning faulty goods
- re-inspection of the product that has been replaced or rectified
- administration and other costs associated with non-compliance with the law.

Compliance and non-compliance costs

It is generally accepted that an increased investment in prevention and appraisal is likely to result in a significant reduction in failure costs. As a result of the trade-off, there may be an optimum operating level in which the combined costs are at a minimum. In short, an investment in "prevention" inevitably results in a saving on total quality costs.

One of our project managers should be responsible for determining the optimal amount to spend on conformance activities so that the overall cost of quality (conformance and non-conformance costs) is minimal. The optimal cost of quality is usually expressed as the cost per good unit of product produced or as a percentage of total development costs.

Conclusion

I hope that the above report clarifies the 'TQM' and 'Cost of Quality' concepts.

Signed: *Assistant Management Accountant*

50 CAL (NOV 10)

(a)

Quality conformance costs are costs that are deliberately incurred by an organisation in order to minimise quality failures. Quality non-conformance costs are costs that are incurred by an organisation as a consequence of quality failures that have occurred. There is a relationship between these categories of costs to the extent that the more that is spent on conformance costs the lower should be the level of quality failures and therefore the lower the non-conformance costs. Organisations must decide on their position in this quality/cost trade off. The scenario indicates that CAL has positioned itself in the middle of the range of possible positions because some of its competitors supply lower quality products whereas others supply higher quality products.

(b)

(i) Customer demand is 20,000 good items, but 2% of the items supplied are faulty therefore the total number of items to be supplied is:

20,000 × 100/98 = 20,408 so that 2% (i.e. 408) are returned for free replacement.

The cost of these 408 units that are replaced free of charge is $45 per unit = $18,360

However, there is a further cost of this failure because if it could be eliminated the market share would increase to 25%. This would result in an additional 5,000 units of sales which each earn a contribution of $15 = $75,000.

As a result the non-conformance cost of these faulty items is $93,360.

(ii) If these failures had been discovered before delivery some of these costs could have been avoided. Although the item might still have been faulty and needed replacement, the lost sales would be avoided as would the delivery cost of the faulty items. Thus the cost of this failure could potentially have been reduced to an internal failure cost of 408 units × $40 = $16,320 a saving of $77,040.

51   ZZ GROOMING (MAR 13)

(a)   Inbound logistics

Operations

Outbound logistics

Marketing and sales

Service

(b)   **Prevention** – operations: preventative maintenance and checking of the calibration of machinery. This would reduce the number of potentially faulty products being produced and therefore reduce guarantee claims.

Appraisal – inbound logistics: reduce costs of incoming inspections by building close links with suppliers and getting them to adopt TQM. If suppliers can guarantee their quality then inbound inspections could be eliminated.

Internal failure – operations: reduce costs of re-works by training employees on a continual basis e.g. quality circles. This would reduce failure costs and also improve quality.

External failure – service: design quality into the product to try to prevent guarantee claims and therefore the cost of servicing/repairing the product.

52   LCG (NOV 11)

Value analysis is a systematic interdisciplinary examination of the factors which affect the cost of a product in order to determine the means of achieving the specified purpose in the most economical manner while meeting the required level of quality and reliability.

Functional cost analysis is a method that can be applied to examine the component costs of a product or service in relation to the value as perceived by the customer. Functional cost analysis can be applied to new products and breaks the product down into its component parts. For example a garden table may have the function to fold completely flat and therefore require much less storage space. The outcome of the analysis is to improve the value of the product while maintaining costs and or reduce the costs of the product without reducing value.

Value analysis may therefore be viewed as a cost reduction and problem solving technique that analyses an existing product in order to identify and reduce or eliminate any costs which do not contribute to value or performance.

In contrast, functional cost analysis focuses on the value to the customer of each function of the product and consequently allocates resources to those functions from which the customer gains the most value.

It is clear from the scenario that LCG needs to be able to reduce its selling prices in order to compete in the market. This selling price reduction can only be sustained by a reduction in LCG's unit costs; however such a reduction must not be achieved by compromising on quality.

Both value analysis and functional cost analysis have potential to help LCG but value analysis is likely to be a more useful technique because garden tables and chairs are products that are sold more on the basis of their use value rather than their esteem value.

53 BUSINESS PROCESS RE-ENGINEERING (MAR 12)

Tutorial note

You must be able to describe how BPR examines business processes and makes substantial changes to the way in which an organisation operates.

Business process re-engineering involves examining business processes and making substantial changes to the way in which an organisation operates. It requires the redesign of how work is done through activities. A business process is a series of activities that are linked together in order to achieve the desired objective. For example material procurement might be viewed as a business process which could impact on the separate activities of production scheduling, storing materials, processing purchase orders, inspecting materials and paying suppliers.

The aim of business process re-engineering is to enhance organisational performance by achieving improvements in business processes by focusing on simplification, improved quality, enhanced customer satisfaction and cost reduction.

It may be that MLC needs to be able to reduce its selling prices in order to compete in the market. This selling price reduction can only be sustained by a reduction in MLC's unit costs, however such a reduction must not be achieved by compromising on quality.

Business Process re-engineering can be applied not only to manufacturing processes but also to an extensive range of administrative activities. In the case of material handling MLC might re-engineer the activity of processing purchase orders by collaboration with suppliers of timber and other components for their products by integration of their production planning system with that of their suppliers. This would enable purchase orders to be sent directly to their suppliers thereby obviating the need for any intermediate administrative activity.

Additionally scheduled orders might be agreed with suppliers which would reduce the need to hold inventories of timber and other components. In circumstances where suppliers are working in close collaboration with MLC, it may be possible to roll the quality back down the supply chain and agree quality control procedures with suppliers which would reduce the need to inspect incoming deliveries of timber and components. Thus savings in material handling costs could be achieved via reduced storage, processing and inspection costs. It must be recognised that such costs do not add value to the final product and thus are of no benefit to the customer.

In conclusion business process re-engineering may be useful to MLC because it may enable them to identify cost savings that do not directly affect their products and so would not have any effect on their customers' perception of the quality or value of the products.

54 INBOUND CALL CENTRES (SEPT 13)

Tutorial note

Candidates needed to carefully read the question and fully appreciate what was required in relation to the scenario described. An understanding of the modern business environment was required and the main principles associated with outsourcing customer liaison and support service operations.

A key feature of the modern business environment is that in order to compete organisations must recognise the need to achieve customer satisfaction. Organisations now operate in a global economy in which customers and competitors come from all over the world. Customers have far greater choice than ever before and are demanding ever improving levels of service in terms of cost, quality, reliability and delivery.

Advantages of outsourcing customer liaison and product support include:

*   Reduction in workload and non-core activities: this would allow the organisation to focus their time and resources on core activities and thereby increase the overall productivity.

*   24 × 7 support: most call centres offer a 'round the clock' service and therefore customers can obtain answers to enquiries outside of normal business hours.

*   Cost savings: training, development and technology investment costs will be the responsibility of the call centre. It is claimed that call centres can save organisations up to 70% of the overall cost of setting up, running and maintaining an in-house call answering centre.

*   Changing cost structure: what was previously viewed as a fixed cost is converted to variable cost and therefore impacts on operational costs and risks.

Disadvantages of outsourcing the service include:

*   The time and effort needed to ensure that the correct provider is chosen.

*   Resentment by customers: there is a chance that customers will view the use of a third party as a sign that the organisation does not view customer support as being important.

*   The possible loss of control over the quality of the service being received by callers. A close relationship should be built up with the call centre to ensure that all operatives have the detailed knowledge necessary to deal with callers.

BUDGETING AND MANAGEMENT CONTROL

55   ENGINEERING (NOV 12)

> **Tutorial note**
>
> *Carefully read and digest the relevant information and produce an amended statement that includes a flexed budget column. The variance column would now compare the flexed budget with the actual column.*
>
> *Part (b) asked for an explanation of a benefit and a limitation of the statement produced in part (a).*

(a)   **Performance report for the quarter ending October 2012**

	Budget	Flexed Budget	Actual	Variance	
Sales units	12,000	13,000	13,000		
Production units	14,000	13,500	13,500		
	$000	$000	$000	$000	
Sales	360	390	385	5	A
Direct materials	70	67.5	69	1.5	A
Direct labour	140	135	132	3	F
Variable overhead	42	40.5	43	2.5	A
Fixed overhead	84	84	85	1	A
Inventory adjustment	(48)	(12)	(12)	0	
Cost of sales	288	315	317	2	A
Gross profit	72	75	68	7	A

(b)   The original statement compared budgeted revenues and costs with actual revenues and costs. The resulting variances offer little insight into why the differences occurred. For effective performance review and control it is important the figures are compared on a 'like for like' basis: there is little point in comparing the actual costs of producing 13,500 units with the budgeted costs of producing 14,000 units. Therefore it is important that volume differences are taken out: this is the reason for flexing the budget.

The flexible budget does not offer enough detail for responsibility and control. The variances are 'total' variances and do not point to areas of individual responsibility. For example the total direct materials variance could be made up of a price variance and a usage variance. These variances will be the responsibility of different managers within the company.

56   DW TRANSPORT (NOV 10)

(a)

An annual budgeting system is a system of preparing a set of budgets for a 12 month period, usually coinciding with the financial year of the company.

A rolling budget system is a system of budgeting that is continuous. Once the budget has been prepared it is added to each month, or perhaps quarterly, thus ensuring that a budget always exists for the next 12 months and possibly for longer depending on the company's budgeting policy.

One of the key differences between these two systems is that, when a rolling budget system is being used, managers see budgeting as part of their ongoing planning and decision making processes, rather than as a separate exercise which is used to measure their performance.

In some organisations, where rolling budgets are used, the unexpired portion of the budget is also updated monthly or quarterly to reflect any changes in operational circumstances since the budget was originally prepared. There is much debate as to whether this amounts to changing the original budget or preparing a latest annual forecast.

(b)

The manager of the Southern depot has raised two specific issues with the current annual budgeting system.

One of these is his argument that the budgets become out of date due to changing operational circumstances. Whether or not rolling budgets provide a solution to this issue depends on the organisation's philosophy of the use of rolling budgets. If the view is that they should be used to plan for future budget years so as to ensure that managers can make better decisions for those years, but not change the current year's budget, then a rolling budget will not be the solution to this problem. However, the manager can now effect changes to future budget periods, as yet unapproved, in the light of those circumstances.

If the rolling budget system allows revision of the remaining part of the plan for the current budget year then their use will solve the argument that the original budget has become out of date.

It is important to consider the use of the budget. There are two main uses: operational control and strategic decision making. From an operational control perspective care must be taken to ensure that a rolling budget does not become a vehicle for eliminating variances caused by actual performance. Once a budget has been set and approved, then any unexpected changes to circumstances should be reported via the budgetary control system using variance analysis including planning variances as appropriate.

From a strategic decision making perspective, it is important to use the rolling budget process to determine whether strategies need to be revised in the light of the current operational circumstances.

The second of the manager's arguments relates to the lack of authority for actions in respect of future periods. The rolling budget method does have a role here because as it is continuously being updated then if each update is approved by the Board of Directors, managers will always have authority to carry out decisions in line with the approved budget for the next 12 months or more. This is a weakness of the annual budgeting system, especially towards the end of the current year when next year's budget is still to be approved. Managers can often find that they do not have authority for decisions which will impact on the early part of the next budget year until that year has almost started.

If DW were to introduce a system of rolling budgets then this would enable the depot manager to plan and improve their decisions, for example with regard to recruiting and training employees, and to evaluate alternative operating methods and possible capital investments based on the budgets that have been agreed for the next 12 months or more.

57 RESPONSIBILITY ACCOUNTING

(a) In responsibility accounting, a specific manager is given the responsibility for a particular aspect of the budget, and within the budgetary control system, he or she is often made accountable for actual performance. Managers are therefore made accountable for their area of responsibility.

The area of operations for which a manager is responsible might be called a responsibility centre. Within an organisation, there could be a hierarchy of responsibility centres:

- If a manager is responsible for a particular aspect of operating costs, the responsibility centre is a cost centre. A cost centre is defined as a production or service location, function, activity or item of equipment for which costs are accumulated. In Z, the Purchasing department (in charge of buying vinyl and metal) could be a cost centre.

- If a manager is responsible for revenues as well as costs, the responsibility centre is a profit centre, and the manager responsible is held accountable for the profitability of the operations in his charge. In Z, the Sales department could be a profit centre.

- If a manager is responsible for investment decisions as well as for revenues and costs, the responsibility centre is an investment centre. The manager is held accountable not only for profits, but also for the Return on Investment from the operations in his or her charge. There could be several profit centres within an investment centre.

Responsibility accounting is based on the application of the controllability principle: a manager should be made responsible and accountable only for the costs and revenues that he or she is in a position to control.

(b) The implications of the situation on Z limited could be that managers' targets, and their performance assessment, are partly based on uncontrollable elements. Uncontrollable factors linked to volatile demand or obsolete standards, for example, could mean that Z managers are judged unfairly and this may render Z's responsibility accounting system totally ineffective.

Z's purchasing manager may be able to influence the costs of purchasing raw material (vinyl, metal), however such costs are also dependent upon prevailing market conditions which are clearly beyond the manager's control. Likewise, Z's manufacturing manager may influence the quantities of metal and vinyl used, but quantities used may be influenced by the quality of raw materials purchased.

Furthermore, the majority of performance reports usually focus on a time period of one year or less, and this short term focus can mean that the current manager may have been experiencing problems and inefficiencies which were in fact a legacy from his predecessor. For example, Z's manufacturing manager may be constrained by a contract for the purchase of raw materials that was negotiated by his predecessor. This gives rise to the difficulty of separating what the incumbent actually controls from the outcomes of decisions made by others.

Changes that could be made to improve acceptance may include the following:

- Z's Management Accountant can attempt to eliminate the effects of uncontrollable items from the areas for which managers are held responsible. For example, a machine supervisor's performance report in the Production department might be confined to quantities (not costs) of vinyl and metal, direct labour, energy costs and related supplies.

- Reports can be prepared which clearly distinguish between controllable and uncontrollable items for any given area of responsibility. When assessing managers performance, reports could either show uncontrollable items in a separate section of a performance report, or exclude uncontrollable items from those reports altogether.

- Variance analysis could be used to analyse the factors that cause actual results to differ from pre-determined budgeted targets. The use of a planning and operational approach to variance analysis may distinguish between controllable and uncontrollable items. For example, any uncontrollable planning variances may be incorporated into future standards thereby improving business planning.

- Management may attempt to isolate the effects of uncontrollable factors by adopting the use of flexible performance standards in which targets are adjusted to reflect those uncontrollable factors arising from circumstances which were not recognised and allowed for at the time that the original targets were set. The use of flexible budgets is the most widely used flexible performance standard. Flexible budgeting aims to remove the uncontrollable effects of volume changes on cost behaviour from performance reports.

- Management may be able to use benchmarking to assess the performance of a responsibility centre. This method involves an evaluation of a responsibility centre relative to the performance of similar centres within Z, or with similar units outside the organisation. In order to prove a valid basis for comparison it is essential that the responsibility centres, which are the subject of comparison, perform similar tasks and are subject to similar environmental and business conditions.

58 CONTROLLABILITY (MAY 11)

(a)

> **Examiner's comments:** Very few candidates correctly interpreted what was required for part (a). Most candidates simply discussed issues such as customer satisfaction, whereas the main thrust related to the short-term nature of financial measures at the expense of long-term non-financial issues.

The modern service sector is extremely competitive and as a consequence if a business is to succeed it needs to ensure that it is both efficient and that is satisfies the needs of its guests. Financial performance is important but this is described as a "lagging measure" in that it reports on what has happened. Failing to meet targets can mean that profits are not achieved and that inadequate current returns are obtained. However, short term action to improve current financial performance might, in the long term, be at the expense of the company's interests. This is why modern thinking suggests that non-financial measures may be more appropriate in assessing performance. Non-financial "leading" measures indicate how well the company is doing things that can lead to future profits.

(b) One measure could consider customer satisfaction such as number of complaints and/or recommendations. In the short term saving money by cutting back on customer service might lead to long term loss of business due to a declining reputation.

Another measure might look at the number of new accommodation and events packages offered by the hotel. In the short term these would cost money to set up but in the long term they may lead to new business by achieving a competitive edge.

(c)

> **Examiner's comments:** Part (c) asked candidates to explain why, and how, non-controllable costs should be shown on profit reports. However, many candidates simply changed the emphasis and stated 'non-controllable cost should be shown on profit reports', and then went on to explain the reasons for this statement. This is a common fault and should be avoided i.e. changing the question.

Uncontrollable costs may be included in the performance report of a responsibility centre so that the report shows the final profit of that centre. This is sometimes done to make the manager aware of the other costs involved in running the business.

However, from a performance measurement perspective if it is the performance of the manager that is being measured then it is unfair to measure their performance on results that include items that are beyond their control. The solution to this is to include the non-controllable items in a separate section of the report and to measure the manager's performance based on only the controllable items.

59 SOLICITORS (MAY 10)

Tutorial note

In (a), note the verb 'Discuss' – it means there needs to be an argument. In other words, you need two or more differing (or opposing) viewpoints. Also, any discussion should, if possible, end in a conclusion. The first paragraph in our answer illustrates this approach.

(a) The present budgeting system includes elements of a participative (or bottom-up) system (whereby divisional partners are budget holders and are given the opportunity to participate in setting their own cost budgets). However, the senior partner's demand estimate for each division triggers the budgeting process and he again intervenes to approve cost budgets; his amendments are not open to negotiation. Therefore, we are in presence of an imposed budget, with pseudo involvement from the divisional partners.

Traditionally, imposed budgets have an adverse effect on morale. Divisional partners may feel like their opinion is not valuable. They will be less likely to accept the plans contained within the budget and strive to achieve the targets than if they had some say in setting the budget. Failure to achieve the target that they have been set would not be seen as a personal failure as much as it would if they felt they 'owned' the budget more.

Divisional partners also have a more detailed knowledge of their particular part of the business than senior managers, and thus would be able to produce more realistic budgets. An imposed budget could be seen as counterproductive is this situation. They may not feel motivated to prepare their own budgets in the future.

(b)

Tutorial note

Think about those typical 'Balanced Scorecard' indicators here, and note the verb 'Explain': If you're asked to explain something, write a sentence that makes your point, then write another to explain why the first sentence is so, or the consequences of the first sentence.

- **Staff turnover** could be used as a measure to indicate staff satisfaction in the different divisions. A high degree of staff retention will be a positive indicator for the firm, particularly if it is able to retain highly experienced lawyers. This would in turn influence financial indicators favourably.

- An indicator of **proportion of job offers accepted** will give a measure of the external reputation of the firm and that of its senior lawyers.

- **Number of press references** to the firm could also be treated as a key non-financial performance indicator as it would (hopefully favourably) affect the image of the firm.

60   SD KAIZEN (MAR 12)

(a)   Kaizen costing is a system of cost reduction based upon the concept of continuous review of systems and procedures to identify and implement small incremental cost savings. It is used in the production phase of a product and employees are both encouraged and empowered to recommend changes that they believe will reduce costs without affecting the quality of products or otherwise affect the customer's perception of products.

(b)   With regard to the use of standard costing and variance analysis, since Kaizen Costing is based on the concept of continuous small improvements to reduce costs then the original standard cost would no longer reflect the target that is achievable. Consequently the measurement of performance against this target would be of limited usefulness.

In order to prepare meaningful reports SD would need to determine the extent of the variances that have been caused by changes in the method of operations as a result of using Kaizen Costing. These variances would be reported as planning variances and the remaining cost differences would be reported as operational variances.

Although the managers of SD will have been involved in the Kaizen process it is important that the variances between the target that the managers believed would now be achievable and the actual results are reported separately. Then the managers can consider whether these variances have arisen due to operational factors or due to over ambitious revised targets. The variance between the original target and the new Kaizen target (the planning variance) measures the extent to which it is believed that Kaizen techniques have reduced SD's costs.

61   AIRLINE BSC (NOV 11)

(a)   The main principle of the balanced scorecard is that an organisation's performance should not be measured on the basis of its financial results alone. Other key performance indicators are relevant to an organisation's success.

The balanced scorecard typically identifies four groups (or perspectives) of performance indicator that would be suitable for most organisations, though each organisation is free to determine the performance indicators that are most relevant to its own needs. The typical perspectives are: customer perspective; internal business perspective; innovation and learning perspective; and financial perspective.

Many people believe that success in the non-financial performance measures will lead to success in the financial performance measures so that these other measures are leading measures whereas the financial measures are lagging measures.

The airline company could use the balanced scorecard to monitor its performance in other areas of its business. It is important for service businesses such as airlines to understand the needs of its customers and thus measures connected with the customer perspective are important. The airline may discover that particular destinations and flight times are demanded by their customers and this may lead the airline company to develop new routes which can be measured using the innovation and learning perspective.

The airline can also look at how it operates its processes both in relation to its staff and its customers. These could be used to improve the financial results because costs savings can be made.

(b) The airline could measure the number of new destinations that it has provided to its customers during the year. This measure relates to the innovation and learning perspective. The greater the number of destinations, the more choice it has provided to its customers and thus increased its potential customer base.

The airline company could measure the amount of time it takes for its staff to prepare the aircraft between flights, thus measuring the turnaround time. This is monitoring its internal business processes. The longer it takes to prepare the aircraft, the more expensive it is for the airline company because its asset is not earning revenue at that time.

62 COLLEGE (MAR 12)

(a) The main concepts of the Balanced Scorecard are that an organisation's performance should not be measured on the basis of its financial results alone. Other key performance indicators are relevant to an organisation's success.

The balanced scorecard typically identifies four groups (or quadrants) of performance indicator that would be suitable for most organisations, though each organisation is free to determine the performance indicators that are most relevant to its own needs. The typical quadrants are: customer perspective; internal business perspective; innovation and learning perspective; and financial perspective.

Many people believe that success in the non-financial performance measures will lead to success in the financial performance measures so that these other measures are leading measures whereas the financial measures are lagging measures.

The college could use the balanced scorecard to measure its success in other areas of its business. It is important for service businesses such as colleges to understand the wants of its customers and thus measures connected with the customer perspective are important. The college may discover that particular types of courses are demanded by their customers and this may lead the college to develop new courses which can be measured using the innovation and learning perspective.

The college can also look at how it operates its processes both in relation to its staff and its customers. Improvements in these processes could be used to improve the financial results, perhaps, because costs savings can be made.

(b) The college could measure the number of new courses that it has provided to its customers during the year. This measure relates to the innovation and learning perspective. The greater the number of courses, the more choice it has provided to its customers and thus increased its potential customer base.

The college could measure the time it takes for its staff to answer the telephone at the administration office. This is a measure of the effectiveness of its internal business processes. The longer it takes to answer the call the more likely is it that potential customers will be lost because they do not want to wait. If waiting time is significant, the customer may also deter others from making such calls thus losing the college even more business.

63 WX CONSULTANCY (NOV 11)

Feedforward control systems are the comparison of draft plans with the objectives of the company.

In the scenario provided the consultancy company has a number of objectives, two of which are related to their cash flow. The first of these is to reduce the overdraft to zero by 30 June 2012 and the second is to have a positive cash balance of $145,000 by 31 December 2012.

An initial draft of the cash budget will be produced based on the expected sales, costs, and other functional budgets of the company. It is usual for cash budgets to be prepared showing the cash inflows and outflows for each month so that the consultancy firm can identify its expected monthly cash balance. This can then be compared with the company's objectives to see if their cash balance objectives are being achieved. It is this comparison that is the process of feedforward control. It may be that if the objectives are not achieved by the first draft of the budget then the plans may need to be revised by delaying an investment or perhaps by changing the levels of receivables and payables.

Feedback control systems are the comparison of actual results against the budget that has been approved. Thus in the context of the consultancy firm a comparison of the actual monthly cash balance can be made against the budgeted cash balance for that month.

As with any budget and actual comparison there may be an adverse or favourable variance. If this is significant then further analysis may be required to determine its cause. It may be that an investment cost more than was expected, or receivables took less time to pay than expected, or payables were paid later than expected. This comparison process is feedback control.

Thus initially the difference between feedforward and feedback control systems is that feed-forward occurs in the budget setting stage whereas feedback control occurs during the year. This means that feedforward identifies potential problems before they occur (and may enable them to be prevented) whereas feedback identifies problems after they have happened.

64 FEEDBACK AND FEEDFORWARD (SEPT 13)

Tutorial note

Candidates needed to read the requirement carefully, paying particular attention to the verb used. As stated in the requirement, a budgeting system should have been used in explaining points.

Feedback control involves monitoring outputs achieved against desired (budgeted) outputs and taking whatever corrective actions are necessary if a deviation (i.e. a variance) exists. Feedback control establishes why there is a difference. If it is a negative situation steps must be taken to get operations back on track. If it is a positive position the reason must be understood so this favourable position can be maintained. Feedback is backward looking and is reactionary.

With feedforward control, instead of actual outputs being compared and controlled against desired outputs, predictions are made of what outputs are expected. If these predictions differ from the budgeted target, control action is taken immediately in order to minimise the differences. The objective is for control to be achieved before any deviations from the desired outputs actually occur.

With feedforward control likely steps are taken to prevent predicted variances, whereas with feedback actual errors are identified after the event and corrective action is taken to implement future actions to achieve the desired results, i.e. to get back on track. Feedforward is forward looking and is proactive.

A major limitation of feedback control is that errors are allowed to occur. This is not a significant problem (although it is obviously better if no errors occur) when there is a short term lag between the occurrence of an error and the identification and implementation of corrective action. Feedforward control is therefore preferable when a significant time lag occurs.

The budgetary planning process is a feedforward control system. To the extent that outcomes fall short of what is desired, alternatives are considered until a budget is produced that is expected to achieve what is desired. The comparison of actual results with budget, in identifying variances and taking remedial action to ensure that future outcomes will conform to budgeted outcomes is an illustration of a feedback control system. Thus accounting control systems consist of both feedback and feedforward controls.

65 TRANSPORT COMPANY (MAR 12)

Feedforward control systems are the comparison of draft plans with the objectives of the company.

In the scenario the company has to produce budgets showing acceptable cost targets in order to receive the first payment of its subsidy.

The first draft of the budget will need to be compared to the target costs that are acceptable to the government office to ensure that the company qualifies for the subsidy. This comparison process is the operation of a feedforward control system since the transport company will have this cost target as one of its objectives. It may be that the first draft of the budget does not achieve the required cost target. If this is the case then there will need to be revisions to the budget perhaps by changing the method of providing the transport service so that the cost target is achieved. Care must be taken however to ensure that the proposed budget changes do not cause the company to fail to meet its social objectives.

Feedback control systems are the comparison of actual results against the budget that has been approved. Thus in the context of the transport company a comparison of the actual monthly costs can be made against the budgeted costs for that month.

As with any budget and actual comparison there may be an adverse or favourable variance. If this is significant then further analysis may be required to determine its cause. This is particularly important in the context of the transport company because failure to achieve the cost target will result in not receiving the balance of the subsidy payment. If action is required to reverse an adverse variance this will need to be done as soon as possible before the size of the variance is too great to reverse before the end of the year. This comparison process is feedback control.

Thus the difference between feedforward and feedback control systems is that feedforward occurs in the budget setting stage whereas feedback control occurs during the year.

66 ZERO BASED BUDGETING (MAY 13)

Tutorial note

Candidates needed to carefully read the question and fully understand the scenario described. In particular, the question specifically requested candidates to discuss the disadvantages of implementing ZBB in a Research and Development setting. Both generic and specific disadvantages needed to be considered. A step-by-step description of the implementation of ZBB is not required, e.g. a description of a decision package.

Zero based budgeting (ZBB) can be an effective way of allocating resources and controlling discretionary costs. It is often thought that research and development is a discretionary cost. However the benefits of ZBB are often viewed from the company's perspective rather than that of the Director of a division or a budget holder.

Adopting ZBB could have major disadvantages for the Director. There are two immediate issues that the director needs to be aware of:

- it will involve a great deal of time.

- it requires management and accounting expertise. The Director may not have all of these skills.

There are four stages in the implementation of ZBB:

- Activities have to be specified and evaluated

- Decision packages have to be drawn up for each activity

- Each package has then to be evaluated and ranked

- Resources are then awarded to the preferred packages.

Possible disadvantages:

- The need to specify projects could stifle creativity. This could have a major impact on PP and consequently the Research and Development Division.

- The outcome of many projects could be difficult to forecast. Requesting funds for projects that do not have a clearly defined commercial outcome could be problematic given the use of decision packages within a zero based budgeting system.

- The Director would have to seek approval for funding for specified projects and would need to justify the request on a continuing basis. This loss of autonomy could be de-motivating and increase pressure to achieve results.

67   CW RETAIL (SEPT 10)

Key answer tips

Pay special attention to the verbs used in the requirements: **"explain"** for part (a) and **"discuss"** for part (b) can too often be incorrectly interpreted as "describe". Then, read the scenario carefully, or you may write at great length about motivation rather than a resource issue. Identify the type of business and its budgeting practice. Explain the problems of budgetary slack if it is allowed to be included in the final budgets and the problems of removing it from the budgets before they are finalised.

(a)   If the store managers overstate their budgets, essentially they are building a certain level of slack into the cost and revenue targets. These targets will not encourage the managers to operate their stores efficiently. For example:

- a major expense for a retailer would be the purchases of their ready made goods. An overstated purchases budget, which is easy to attain, would not encourage the store manager to search for good discounts with their suppliers; too many items could be bought in order to inflate inventory costs.

- Too many employees could be recruited in order to increase training costs.

- With access to debt finance, managers may borrow excessively to purchase unnecessary capital assets.

This lack of drive for cost efficiency will have a detrimental effect on the stores profits.

Additionally, easy to achieve revenue targets will not encourage the managers to push for higher sales and special promotions which may increase market share. Decisions made by the store managers will be sub-optimum, and whilst the stores may achieve a reasonable profit, they are unlikely to maximise their profits.

(b)   If the store managers participate in setting their own budgets, they are likely to overstate their costs in order to set a target that is easy to achieve without maximum effort and hard work. If the FD then removes or strips out these excess costs this is likely to have an adverse affect on the behaviour of the managers.

Store managers will feel that their budgets and indeed their work, is under close scrutiny from Head Office and senior managers. The staff in the stores may feel vulnerable and threatened by this scrutiny. Additionally, by stripping out budgetary slack, the store managers may feel that their budget preparation work is being undermined and questioned. They will not be happy to admit that their original budget was wrong. There may be a feeling of loss of power and they may end up disowning the budget.

The combined effect of all these factors is that staff may feel demotivated and as apathy and job dissatisfaction creeps in this will affect team spirit and the quality of customer service delivered. Additionally some staff may feel so dissatisfied that they may leave increasing staff turnover – an expense for CW and a loss of skills.

However, it should also be noted that some staff may feel motivated by a budget target that has to be strived for. By working hard staff achieve their goals and feel a great sense of fulfilment and achievement for a goal worth achieving.

68   BUDGETING IN COLLEGE (MAR 11)

> **Examiner's comments:** This question was extremely well answered with most candidates gaining the marks available.

There are potential advantages and disadvantages of the involvement of staff in the preparation of the budget.

Potential advantages include:

- Involvement would encourage senior staff to be motivated to achieve the target because they would take ownership of it as their budget.

- Senior staff may have a better knowledge of individual courses and how they may be delivered more efficiently and cost effectively. They would also have a better understanding of how to attract more students to the course thus increasing its profitability. This would improve the accuracy of the budget.

- Senior staff would feel that they are being respected for the value that their experience brings to the running of the college.

Potential disadvantages include:

- Senior staff may be excellent academically but could lack the knowledge and skills required to formulate their budget and to work together to form the budget for the college overall.

- Senior staff may spend a great deal of time arguing with each other (and with the college director) as to how to measure the benefits of a particular course and how the cost/benefit analysis of each course should be compared.

- Senior staff may agree among themselves to include unnecessary expenditure (budgetary slack) so that it is easier for them to achieve the cost targets they have set.

- Senior staff may underestimate the expected revenue in order to make their final target more achievable.

- The participative process can be very time consuming, thus delaying the availability of the budget for the forthcoming year.

69   KL RAIL TRANSPORT (NOV 12)

Tutorial note

Carefully read the scenario to identify the circumstances associated with the introduction of a participative budget. A report addressed to the new Director was required that needed to contain specific items such as potential benefits and disadvantages of involving new managers in this budget setting process. Finally the question asked for a recommendation to the new Director relating to the introduction of a participative budget.

REPORT

To: Managing Director

From: XX

Subject: Participative budgeting.

Date: November 2012

Introduction

The following report identifies two advantages and two disadvantages of involving managers in the setting of budgets.

Advantages

(1)   If managers are involved in setting budgets then the budgets may be more relevant to the business because the manager will have specialist knowledge of their area of the business and they can incorporate this into their budgets. As a result the budgets will provide a more realistic target and are a better indicator of likely results which can then be used in strategic planning and decision making with a view to meeting the terms of the contract.

(2)   If managers are involved in the budget setting process then they are likely to take ownership of the budget and feel that failing to achieve it is a personal failure. This means that managers will be motivated to achieve the targets they have set and agreed, and consequently the target is more likely to be achieved than one that is simply handed to them without their involvement.

(3)   The new managers may gain valuable knowledge of the business by working closely with the existing managers when preparing the budgets. The existing managers may have detailed knowledge of current operations and the availability of resources that are of benefit for the new contract.

Disadvantages

(1)   The managers may deliberately set themselves targets that are easier to achieve by the inclusion of budgetary slack. This may result in the company's performance being lower than it would have been had more difficult targets been imposed on the managers. However targets are set in the contract.

(2)   Some of the managers may have less experience than others in managing passenger transport operations. Consequently they may not understand the relationships that exist between different budgets and the impact that one has on the other and they may take decisions in their own area that are detrimental to another area of the business and to the company as a whole.

Recommendation

It is important that the managers work together as a team to prepare the company's budgets. In this way they can share their expertise and produce a set of budgets that are realistic and for the benefit of the company as a whole. In this way it is generally agreed that manager involvement in the budget setting process is likely to lead to better budgets and better performance.

70 SUMMARY STATEMENT (MAY 12)

(a)

	$000	$000
Sales (90,000 units)		
Production costs (100,000 units):		
Direct materials	400.00	
Direct labour	550.00	
Variable overhead	105.00	
Fixed overhead	230.00	
	1,285.00	
Inventory adjustment	128.50	
Cost of sales		1,156.50
Gross profit		(256.50)
Other overhead costs		200.00
Net loss		(456.50)

(b) If functional managers are involved in setting their own functional budget then this should have a positive motivational effect on their attempts to achieve it. These is because they will own the budget and accept it as being a fair target, seeing it as a personal failure if they do not achieve the target that they set (and therefore believed was achievable).

The difficulty with involving managers in the budget setting process is that if their performance is to be measured by comparing the actual results with the budget they have set then they may be tempted to set an easy budget by building in budget slack. This will prevent them from performing as well as they might do if a harder, but fair and achievable, budget had been set by someone else.

71 RECONCILING (MAR 13)

Tutorial note

Carefully read and understand the level of variance analysis required to reconcile the budgeted variable cost with the actual variable cost. A clearly labelled statement displaying the variances was required.

Reconciliation statement for February

	$ Fav	$ Adv	$
Budgeted variable production cost (1,100 units)			148,500
Planning variance (labour rate)			2,475 adv
Revised budgeted variable production cost			150,975
Materials price		11,540	
Materials usage	8,300		
Labour rate		2,065	
Labour idle time		4,347	
Labour efficiency	567		
Variable overhead expenditure		3,000	
Variable overhead efficiency	1,000		
Total variances	9,867	20,952	11,085 adv
Actual variable production cost			162,060

72 LINKS (SEPT 12)

Tutorial note

Reading carefully is important in part (a). You should take time to understand the question asked, confirm your knowledge of budgets, standard costs and flexible budgeting and explain the links between them.

For part (b) carefully read the question and then discuss the importance of your answer to (a), particularly how the use of planning and operational variances is important for management control.

(a) An original budget is determined by predicting the expected level of activity and using standard costs to determine the expected variable cost for that level of activity. To this would then be added the expected fixed cost. Standard costs are based on estimated resource requirements and the expected price of those resources for each unit. These values are then multiplied by the expected activity level to determine the expected variable cost of that level of activity.

Budgets are a statement of the total costs, revenues and resource requirements expected for the budgeted level of activity. It is this budget that is approved by the Board of Directors and used as the basis of comparison with actual results. However, it is most likely that the actual level of activity will differ from that budgeted. In such circumstances a simple comparison between the actual results and the original budget would be both meaningless and unfair because some of the costs and the revenues vary with the level of activity. In order to make a fair comparison flexible budgeting must be used.

Flexible budgeting recognises that, within the original budget, there are some costs and revenues that are affected by the level of activity (variable) and others that are not affected by activity levels (fixed). Using this analysis it is possible to produce a flexible budget showing the expected costs and revenues of the actual activity level. This can then be compared with the actual costs and the differences (variances) used as a measure of performance.

(b) In order to fairly measure performance actual activity must be compared with the original budget to understand why the actual activity level differed from those budgeted; and actual costs and revenues should be compared with the flexible budget to fairly measure the actual costs and revenues against those expected for the actual activity achieved. Thus it is important to understand the appropriate uses of each of the original and flexed budget and how standard costs are used to compile the original budget and assist in the preparation of the flexed budget for cost comparison purposes.

73 ZJET BALANCED SCORECARD (SEPT 11)

(a)

> **Examiner's comments:** This part of the question was poorly answered. Candidates were required to 'discuss'. Simply drawing up a table or describing each of the four perspectives did not meet the questions requirements. A small number of candidates believed that the measures included within the financial perspective were solely budgets, standard costing and variances.

A typical Balanced Scorecard measures the performance of an organisation from four perspectives: customer perspective; internal business perspective; innovation and learning perspective; and financial perspective.

The Balanced Scorecard demonstrates that the achievement of financial objectives is often the result of achieving other non-financial targets which lead to the financial targets being achieved. For example, if customers are happy with the products and services being provided then this will often result in increased sales which improve profits and therefore financial objectives are achieved.

Thus by measuring non-financial performance and taking action when targets are not achieved, the result will be improved financial performance. This is because the cause of the financial performance has been reviewed, whereas financial performance indicators alone do not identify the causes of performance, simply the effect of it.

(b) A number of non-financial indicators could be identified:

- The number of take-offs that are on time is a measure of the efficiency of the airline in preparing the aircraft for a flight. Aircraft do not earn revenue while they are standing on the tarmac. This is a measure of the efficiency of internal processes and is part of the internal business perspective.

- The number of new routes operated by the airline is a measure of the innovation of the airline to develop new services for its customers. The greater the number of routes the more customer choice, which also increases the number of customers that would consider ZJET for their flights. This measure is part of the innovation and learning perspective.

- Within the customer perspective, ZJET could use the number of missed calls due to all of the telephone operators being busy. Customers will expect a speedy answer when they telephone and undue delays may result in the customer ringing off before the call is answered. The negative impression gained by the customer may result in current and future business being lost.

74 PATHOLOGY LAB (MAR 13)

Tutorial note

Candidates needed to read the question carefully and understand the context in which this question is set.

An objective and suitable performance measure was required for each of the three non-financial perspectives.

Examiner's note: The following is an example of a scorecard. There are many that would be acceptable. The key element is that they must fit with the vision and strategy of the laboratory.

Four perspectives:

- Financial
- Internal processes
- Learning and growth
- Customer

Internal processes

Objective: to provide accurate results

Performance measure: percentage of spoiled tests. Reason: need to ensure accuracy and lack of contamination (and achieve external quality benchmark figures)

Learning and growth

Objective: to have highly qualified staff trained in the latest techniques

Performance measure: number of staff training days. Reason: provides a measure of continual professional development

Customer

Objective: to provide results that allow our customers to meet the stated minimum period for treatment

Performance measure: reporting time for each type of test. Reason: specific tests have specific treatment windows and therefore 'turn around' time is important for the doctors.

75   PLAYERS (MAY 11)

(a)

(i)

	Actual sales	Std Mix	Difference	Profit per unit	Variance
DVD	3,000	2,800	+200	$48.33 – $25	$4,667 A
Blu-ray	1,200	1,400	–200	$48.33 – $95	$9,334 A
	4,200	4,200			$14,000 A

The total sales mix profit margin variance is $14,000 A

Alternative method:

	Actual sales	Std Mix	Difference	Profit per unit	Variance
DVD	3,000	2,800	+200	$25	$5,000 F
Blu-ray	1,200	1,400	–200	$95	$19,000 A
	4,200	4,200			$14,000 A

(ii)   The sales volume profit variance relates only to Blu-ray players because the actual and revised budget volumes of DVD players are the same.

Therefore the variance is 300 players × $95 = $28,500 A

(b)

The market size is not within the control of the sales manager and therefore variances caused by changes in the market size would be regarded as planning variances. However, variances caused by changes in the selling prices and consequently the selling price variances and market shares would be within the control of the sales manager and treated as operating variances.

The market size variance compares the original and revised market sizes. This is unchanged for DVD players so the only variance that occurs relates to the Blu-ray players and is:

500 players × $95 = $47,500 F

It is important to make this distinction because as can be seen from the scenario the measurement of the manager's performance is distorted if the revised market size is ignored. The favourable volume variance of $19,000 referred to in the sales manager's e-mail is made up of two elements, one of which, the market size, is a planning variance which is outside their control. It is this that has caused the overall volume variance to be favourable, and thus the manager is not responsible for the overall favourable performance.

76 KHL RECONCILIATION (MAR 11)

> **Examiner's comments:** Many candidates failed to attempt this question and most of the answers submitted were extremely poor. Variance analysis is one of the main pillars upon which management accounting is built and questions relating to variances should require the application of basic knowledge from all management accounting candidates. The presentation of answers was extremely poor and figures were put forward without labels or titles. The result was that on many occasions the markers found it impossible to award marks.

Actual production during April 2011 was 6,000 units. There are two alternative proofs of this:

Fixed overhead absorbed = $60,000

Absorption rate = $10/unit

Therefore $60,000/$10 = 6,000 units

OR

Inventory has increased (production costs reduced to calculate cost of sales) by $15,000. In standard absorption costing inventory is valued at standard production cost ($12 + $20 + $8 +$10 = $50). $15,000/$50 = 300 units increase. Sales were 5,700 units therefore production = 6,000 units.

The production cost variances must therefore be calculated based on 6,000 units produced.

Reconciliation statement for April 2011

	$
Budgeted profit	84,000
Sales volume variance	4,200 (A)
Standard profit on actual sales	79,800
Selling price variance	34,200 (A)
	45,600

	Adverse	Favourable	
Direct material price		3,720	
Direct material usage	2,400		
Direct labour rate	13,800		
Direct labour efficiency		5,000	
Variable overhead expenditure	1,150		
Variable overhead efficiency		2,000	
Fixed overhead expenditure	7,000		
Fixed overhead volume		10,000	
Totals	24,350	20,720	3,630 (A)
Actual profit			41,970

Workings:

Direct material price = (18,600 × $4) – $70,680 = $3,720 favourable

Direct material usage = [(6,000 × 3) – 18,600] × $4 = $2,400 adverse

Direct labour rate = (11,500 × $10) – $128,800 = $13,800 adverse

Direct labour efficiency = [(6,000 × 2) – 11,500] × $10 = $5,000 favourable

Variable overhead expenditure = (11,500 × $4) – $47,150 = $1,150 adverse

Variable overhead efficiency = [(6,000 × 2) – 11,500] × $4 = $2,000 favourable

Fixed overhead expenditure = $50,000 – $57,000 = $7,000 adverse

Fixed overhead volume = (6,000 – 5,000) × $10 = $10,000 favourable

77 GRV MIX AND YIELD (SEPT 11)

Tutorial note

You will lose marks if you do not show a '$' sign before the variances you have calculated, or if you fail to adjust the price of chemical B before calculating the variances.

(a) **Mix variance**

	Standard mix	Actual	Difference	Price	Variance
A	450 litres	600 litres	+150 litres	($23.75 – $30)	$937.50 A
B	337.5 litres	250 litres	–87.5 litres	($23.75 – $30)	$546.875 F
C	562.5 litres	500 litres	–62.5 litres	($23.75 – $15)	$546.875 A
					$937.50 A

Mix variance – alternative calculation

	Standard mix	Actual	Difference	Price	Variance
A	450 litres	600 litres	+150 litres	$30	$4,500 A
B	337.5 litres	250 litres	–87.5 litres	$30	$2,625 F
C	562.5 litres	500 litres	–62.5 litres	$15	$937.50 F
					$937.50 A

Yield variance

1,350 litres of input should yield 1,125 litres of output, but output was only 1,000 litres so there is a shortfall of 125 litres.

125 litres of output at the revised standard direct material cost of $28.50 per litre of output = $3,562.50 Adverse.

(b)

Tutorial note

Your discussion must relate to the variances calculated in (a).

The Production Manager's decision to substitute some of chemical B with chemical A to avoid the increased cost caused by the worldwide price increase of chemical B has not been very successful as is shown by the adverse operational cost variances.

There was a significant increase in the total input volume needed to produce 1000 litres of output, possibly because the mix of chemicals being used was no longer optimum. This may have caused the adverse yield variance.

In addition, there was an adverse mix variance because a lower proportion of chemical C was used. It seems that the manager used chemical A instead of chemical B, but chemical A was originally the most expensive chemical and cost as much per litre as the revised price of chemical B that it replaced.

The Production Manager has taken action to reduce the effect of the worldwide price increase of chemical B, however, since the company has a separate purchasing department then it is they who are responsible for the purchasing function and therefore they should be responsible for the effect of price changes not the Production Manager.

Apart from the financial effects of the manager's decision there are a number of other issues to be considered. The manager may not have the authority to change the mix of the spray without consulting the company's chemical advisors. The alternative mix may not be as effective as a crop protector as the original mix and may even be harmful to the crops or to customers that consume them.

Examiner's comments: The answers to part (b) were poor and very few meaningful discussions were put forward. This demonstrated that mix and yield variances were not really understood.

78   BEYOND BUDGETING

The criticisms of traditional budgeting include the following:

- Budgets are a commitment which act as a constraint on doing anything different. In a rapidly changing business environment the budgets are usually based on out of date assumptions.

- Traditional budgets are seen as a mechanism for top-down control by senior management, but instead organisations should be empowering front-line managers.

- Traditional budgets restrict flexibility because individuals feel they are committed to achieving the budget targets. This is a deterrent to continual improvement and so is inconsistent with TQM.

- Budgeting reinforces the barriers between departments, instead of encouraging an organisation-wide sharing of knowledge.

- Budgets are internally focused, bureaucratic and time consuming to prepare.

The features of a more appropriate system of planning and control might be as follows:

- Managers should prepare rolling plans, usually on a quarterly basis. Forecasts would then be more up to date in a changing environment and they can be revised more frequently, without censure, if necessary. However the purpose of these plans is for cash forecasting, not for cost control.

- Instead of a comparison of actual with budget, performance measures should be based on:

  - achieving strategic milestones rather than detailed short-term targets

  - using relative measures of performance, for example by comparing actual results against a benchmark, in particular using external comparisons to avoid being too inward looking

  - an emphasis on maximising value, rather than on minimising costs.

79 CULTURAL FRAMEWORK (MAY 13)

Tutorial note

A careful read through the brief scenario was essential to understand the setting for this 'Beyond Budgeting' (BB) question. It was important that candidates did not simply write all they knew about BB, and fail to relate their answer to the scenario.

Beyond Budgeting (BB) is a responsibility culture in which managers are given goals that have been derived from benchmarks linked to competitors and world class performance. This culture requires an adaptive approach whereby authority is devolved to managers and the organisation's structure will be a 'network' rather than 'hierarchical'.

The principles of BB are:

- The organisation structure should have clear principles and boundaries. Everyone should have defined areas of responsibility.

- Managers should be given targets that are linked to the organisation's strategy. Such targets should be based on key performance indicators and should be part of a balanced scorecard.

- Managers should be given a high degree of freedom to make decisions. The organisation chart should be 'flat'.

- Responsibility for decisions that generate value should be placed with 'front line teams'. These teams should be made responsible for managing relationships with business partners (customers, suppliers, etc).

- Information support systems should be transparent. For example, an activity based accounting system would enable reports to be generated to show the costs/revenues for activities which are the specific responsibility of identified managers.

It can be argued that in the modern dynamic business environment it is vital that management can react to changes in the market and allocate resources accordingly. BB will allow this to happen. The benefits that should accrue from the adoption of the principles of BB are faster response times, better innovation, lower costs and improved customer and supplier loyalty. All of these are of great importance in the modern dynamic business environment.

CONTROL AND PERFORMANCE MEASUREMENT OF RESPONSIBILITY CENTRES

80 LMN (MAY 10)

(a) LMN should consider the following issues:

- Perceived fairness of the transfer pricing system

- Inclusion of controllable/non controllable costs from Head Office

- Perceived fairness of overhead apportionment

- Should only include the first $100,000 of investment, as this is all that they are able to control.

(b) An ABC system would have the following advantages:

(1) It would provide more accurate product line costings particularly if non volume related overheads are significant and a diverse product line is manufactured.

(2) It would provide a reliable indication of long-run variable product cost which is particularly relevant to managerial decision making at a strategic level, making the costs more controllable.

(3) It would provide meaningful financial (periodic cost driver rates) and nonfinancial (periodic cost driver volumes) measures which are relevant for cost management and performance assessment at an operational level.

(4) It would aids identification and understanding of cost behaviour and thus has the potential to improve cost estimation.

(5) It would provide a more logical, acceptable and comprehensible basis for costing work.

81 RETURN ON INVESTMENT

(i)

	20X3		20X2	
Division	RP	IP	RP	IP
	$000	$000	$000	$000
Cash flow	14,400	20,000	13,100	18,000
Depreciation (W1)	3,360	5,040	2,880	4,320
Profit	11,040	14,960	10,220	13,680
Average capital employed (40:60)	52,000	78,000	46,000	69,000
Return on investment (ROI) %	21.23	19.18	22.22	19.83

Workings:

(W1) **Depreciation**

Year	20X2	20X3
	$000	$000
NBV @ start of year	54,000	64,800
Add: Additions	18,000	19,200
Subtotal	72,000	84,000
Depreciation @ 10%	7,200	8,400
NBV @ end of year	64,800	75,600

Charged as follows:

	20X2	20X3
Division RP (40%)	2,880	3,360
Division IP (60%)	4,320	5,040

(ii) Response of divisional managers to results

Neither division has achieved the target rate of ROI of 22.5% per annum during either year. Hence managers would not have received a bonus payment.

Potential problem for Our Timbers

This might lead to dysfunctional behaviour by divisional managers who might be tempted to avoid investing capital in their respective divisions. This would reduce the average capital employed in order to achieve a level of ROI which will earn them a bonus payment. In circumstances where such disincentives to invest exist then it is probably going to be the case that the actions of divisional managers will not be in the best interests of the company as a whole.

Alternative measure

Residual income (RI) is an alternative measure of divisional performance. It encourages divisional managers to make new investments if they add to RI. A new investment might add to RI but reduce ROI. In such a situation, measuring the performance by RI would reduce the probability of dysfunctional behaviour.

82 DESIGNING BONUS SCHEMES (MAY 07)

A bonus scheme based on profit generated by each division must:

- be clearly understood by all personnel involved

- motivate the personnel. In order to be motivating a bonus scheme must be linked clearly to controllable costs and revenues

- not cause sub-optimal behaviour.

Ensuring goal congruence can be difficult when a transfer pricing system is in place.

If there is unlimited demand for the output of the two divisions in the market then the transfer price should equal the market price less any savings as a result of internal transfer. This then allows the divisions to report a profit on the transfers and will not cause any issue for the calculation of the bonus.

However, if there is a limit on the amount that can be sold on the external market and the supplying divisions have spare capacity then the transfer price should be based on marginal cost for the resulting decisions to be goal congruent. In this case they will have no contribution towards fixed costs or profit. This will mean that if the bonus is awarded on profit the divisional manager will not receive a bonus despite the fact that they have made internal supplies.

Therefore the company must ensure that in order for decisions to remain goal congruent the bonus scheme must allow for internal transfers that impact on the divisions' ability to earn bonuses.

Section 4

ANSWERS TO SECTION B-TYPE QUESTIONS

PRICING AND PRODUCT DECISIONS

83   ENGINEERING PROJECT (MAY 09) *Walk in the footsteps of a top tutor*

Key answer tips

This is a straightforward question that was a real gift from the Examiner. Remember the rule of thumb of relevant costs – to be relevant, a cost must be **future, cash** and **incremental**. You were asked to 'clearly explain', so merely stating in a working that a cost is 'sunk' or 'not relevant would not have got you full marks – you need to include a narrative and a nil value in the statement.

Step 1

Read the requirements, and split your time between (a) and (b) according to the mark allocation. Then, read the question.

Step 2

Try and layout your statement in (a) as neatly as possible. The highlighted *words are key phrases that markers are looking for.*

(a)

Item		Relevant cost
1	Specialised machine (W1)	$25,000
2	Machinery running cost $720 × 10 weeks	$7,200
3	Depreciation is not a relevant cash outflow	–
4	Skilled labour (W2)	$99,000
5	Unskilled labour 12,000 hours × $8	$96,000
6	Supervision (W3)	$500
7(a)	Material A	$15,000
7(b)	Material B (W4)	$35,000
8	Analysis of requirements is a sunk cost	–
9	Absorbed overheads (W5)	–
10	Profit is not a cost	–
	Total relevant costs	**$277,700**

Step 3

You must include an explanation in your statement for not including items 3, 8, 9 and 10. Credit will be given for a nil value as well as for its justification.

(b)   The financial profit reports at the end of the year would not show a profit of $125,000 because under absorption costing, the cost of the engineering project will be based on the cost of the resources used in completing the project. It will not be based on the relevant cost values.

In some cases these two values will be the same. For example the cost of the unskilled labour, will be $96,000 because this is an incremental cost to be incurred.

However, in other cases the financial accounting cost will differ. For example in the case of material B, the cost reported under absorption costing will be based on its historical inventory value, rather than its resale value.

In addition there will be some costs that are included under absorption costing which would not be included under relevant costing because they will be incurred regardless of the decision. Examples include a proportion of the supervision and overhead costs.

Step 4

Workings in an appendix would be a good idea here; note that they are cross-referenced in our statement.

Workings:

(W1) **Relevant cost of the specialised machine**

If we hire the machine for 10 weeks, the total hire cost would be $40,000.

If we purchase the machine:	Original cost	$250,000
	Less: Residual value	($150,000)
		$100,000
Less Rental income of $2,500 for 30 weeks		($75,000)
		$25,000

Tutorial note

Decision-making involves selecting the better of two alternatives. Here, the lowest cost option should be chosen by managers.

The relevant cost is the *lower* cost of $25,000. This is to buy the machine and rent it out when it is not being used.

(W2) **Relevant cost of skilled labour**

External project labour: 9,000 hours × $12   £108,000

External replacement labour   9,000 hours × $11 £99,000

The existing hourly rate is irrelevant, as the company would continue to pay its existing employees regardless of the decision. The relevant cost is the *lower* cost option: $99,000.

(W3) **Relevant cost of supervision**

'Existing salaries' is not an incremental cost, therefore irrelevant.

Overtime would not be paid in cash, therefore irrelevant.

Bonus of $500 is cash, incremental (only paid if the project goes ahead), and future, therefore a relevant cost of $500.

(W4)   **Relevant cost of Material B**

The historical cost of $100,000 is irrelevant (a sunk costs).

Remainder of material currently held in inventory: 5,000 metres. There is no other use for this material so the relevant cost is the foregone contribution this would otherwise bring, at $2/metre, ∴. $10,000

Add: 5,000 metres purchased on open market @ $5 a metre, $25,000

Total relevant cost of material B   **$35,000**

(W5)   **Absorbed overheads**

Absorbed overheads are not incremental, and are therefore not a relevant cost. They would be incurred regardless of the project going ahead, and are only a matter of company policy in the area of fixed costs allocation and apportionment.

The decision-making process should ignore overheads, unless overheads are specific to the project – which is not the case here.

84   THREE SEASONS HOTEL (MAY 11)

Key answer tips

This question illustrates the importance of proper, carefully thought-out planning and examines relevant costing in a new format.

A good idea would be to start by reading the 18-mark main requirement of the question. Then, you could adopt the following approach to part (a) of the question:

1   Carefully read the scenario to identify the relevant costs and their causes.

2   Prepare a statement that uses marginal costing principles (i.e., with prominent 'contribution' calculations) to show the relevant costs and revenues for each part of the hotel's operations for each season, as well as in total.

3   Identify the activities/seasons that have a negative contribution and recommend actions to the managers.

Examiner's comments: A relatively straightforward question which simply required a number of basic calculations, and arranging the figures in the most appropriate manner. Most candidates attained a high mark but easy marks were lost due to poor presentation of the figures.

(a)

Hotel closure

Workings Calculations ... **Gross Contributions**

Season	Days	Rooms	Occupants	Guests	Snacks	Restaurant
Peak	90	95	1.8	15,390	4,617	17,313.75
Mid	120	75	1.5	13,500	12,150	33,750
Low	150	50	1.2	9,000	8,100	47,250

	Peak	Mid	Low	Total
Room Revenue	855,000	720,000	412,500	1,987,500
Guest related costs	184,680	162,000	108,000	454,680
Room costs	68,400	81,000	82,500	231,900
Avoidable general costs	225,000	300,000	375,000	900,000
	478,080	543,000	565,500	1,586,580
Room/Guest contribution	376,920	177,000	−153,000	400,920

Snacks

	Peak		Mid		Low		Total	
Gross contribution	4,617		12,150		8,100		24,867	
Cook costs	5,000	−383	6,667	5,483	8,333	−233	20,000	4,867

Restaurant

	Peak		Mid		Low		Total	
Gross contribution	17,313.75		33,750		47,250		98,313.75	
Staff costs	13,500	3,813.75	18,000	15,750	22,500	24,750	54,000	44,313.75

	Peak	Mid	Low	Total
Total contribution	380,350.75	198,233	−128,483	450,100.75
Non avoidable general costs	75,000	100,000	125,000	300,000
Net contribution	305,350.75	98,233	−253,483	150,100.75
Hotel annual fixed costs				200,000
Hotel annual profit				−49,899.25

(b) Closure?   No   No   Yes

> **Examiner's comments:** The attempts for parts (b) (i) and (ii) were generally good but many candidates did not comment on the figures that they had produced in part (a) but instead gave generic answers that could have applied to many similar situations.

(i)   The statement shows that overall the hotel makes a loss. However further analysis shows that certain actions could make the hotel profitable.

The statement shows that the hotel makes a significant loss during the low season and therefore if it were to be closed for this part of the year the hotel would then be profitable.

Furthermore the snack service is only profitable during the mid season so if the service were to be closed during the other seasons of the year this would also add to the hotel's profitability.

(ii)   However, there are other factors to be considered before making the above short term changes. If the snack service were to be closed for parts of the year could it easily be re-opened just for the mid season or if it were to be closed entirely would this encourage more guests to use the hotel restaurant?

If the hotel were to be closed in the low season would the hotel retain its popularity during the other parts of the year or would its regular guests feel that the hotel was not customer focused and only interested in its own profits thus reducing the hotel's demand in other seasons?

85 CHOICE OF CONTRACTS

(a)

Note		North-East		South-Coast	
		£	£	£	£
Contract price			288,000		352,000
(1)	Material X: inventory	19,440			
(2)	Material X: firm orders	27,360			
(3)	Material X: not yet ordered	60,000			
(4)	Material Y			49,600	
(5)	Material Z			71,200	
(6)	Labour	86,000		110,000	
(8)	Staff accommodation and travel	6,800		5,600	
(9)	Penalty clause			28,000	
(10)	Loss of plant hire income			6,000	
			199,600		270,400
Profit			88,400		81,600

The company should undertake the North-East contract. It is better than the South-Coast contract by £6,800 (£88,400 – £81,600).

(b) **Notes:**

(1) Material X can be used in place of another material which the company uses. The value of material X for this purpose is 90% × £21,600 = £19,440. If the company undertakes the North-East contract it will not be able to obtain this saving. This is an opportunity cost.

(2) Although the material has not been received yet the company is committed to the purchase. Its treatment is the same therefore as if it was already in inventory. The value is 90% × £30,400 = £27,360.

(3) The future cost of material X not yet ordered is relevant.

(4) The original cost of material Y is a sunk cost and is therefore not relevant. If the material was to be sold now its value would be 24,800 × 2 × 85% = £42,160, i.e. twice the purchase price less 15%, however, if the material is kept it can be used on other contracts, thus saving the company from future purchases. The second option is the better. The relevant cost of material Y is 2 × 24,800 = £49,600. If the company uses material Y on the South-coast contract, it will eventually have to buy an extra £49,600 of Y for use on other contracts.

(5) The future cost of material Z is an incremental cost and is relevant.

(6) As the labour is to be sub-contracted it is a variable cost and is relevant.

(7) Site management is a fixed cost and will be incurred whichever contract is undertaken (and indeed if neither is undertaken), and is therefore not relevant.

(8) It is assumed that the staff accommodation and travel is specific to the contracts and will only be incurred if the contracts are undertaken.

(9) If the South-Coast contract is undertaken the company has to pay a £28,000 penalty for withdrawing from the North-East contract. This is a relevant cost with regard to the South-Coast contract.

(10) The depreciation on plant is not a cash flow. It is therefore not relevant. The opportunity cost of lost plant hire is relevant, however.

(11) It is assumed that the notional interest has no cash flow implications.

(12) It is assumed that the HQ costs are not specific to particular contracts.

86 JRL (MAR 12)

(a)

Tutorial note

You must practice constructing linear programming graphs. Most candidates are able to calculate the coordinates for the constraints, so make sure your graph is neat and accurate. When identifying the weekly production schedule that would maximise the profits, an arrow on the graph is not sufficient to gain the marks.

Workings for graph:

Iso contribution line: $41J + 47L = M$

Constraints:

Material A $\qquad$ $2J + 1L \leq 900$

Coordinates J = 0 and L = 900; J = 450 and L = 0 may be used.

Material B $\qquad$ $2J + 4L \leq 1,750$

Coordinates J = 25 and L = 425; J = 875 and L = 0 may be used.

Skilled labour $\qquad$ $2J + 1.5L \leq 1,250$

Coordinates J = 550 and L = 100; J = 475 and L = 200 may be used.

Machine hours $\qquad$ $3.5J + 4.5L \leq 2,400$

Coordinates J = 0 and L = 533.33; J = 25 and L = 513.88 may be used.

Demand $\qquad$ $0 \leq J \leq 400$

Demand $\qquad$ $0 \leq L \leq 450$

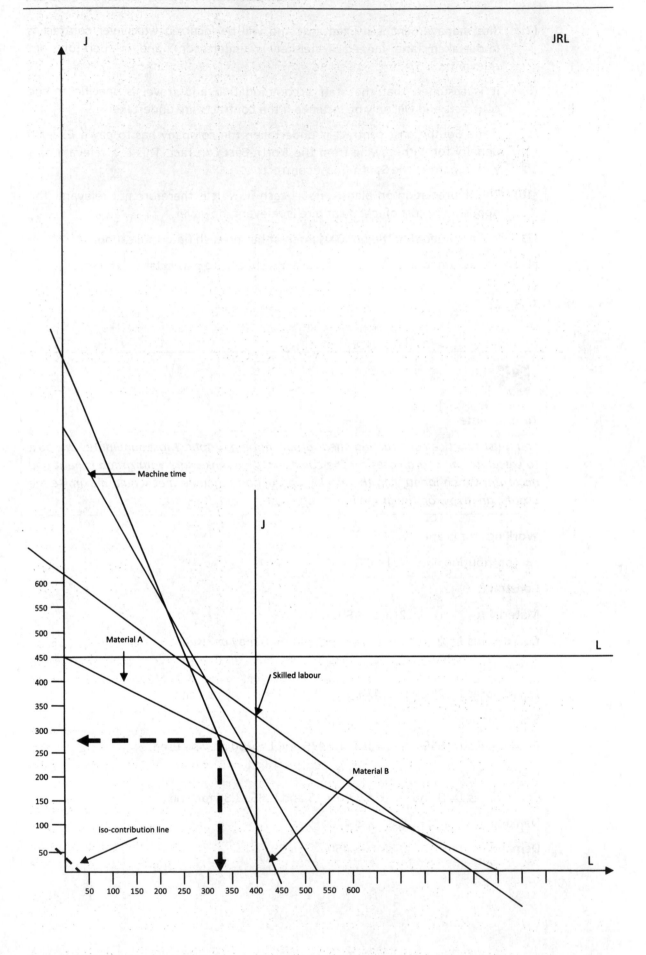

From the graph, it can be seen that the two binding constraints are those relating to Material A and Material B. The solution (from the graph) is to produce 310 units of J and 280 units of L. (A simplex solution shows the true optimum to be 308.333 units of J and 283.333 units of L).

(b)

Tutorial note

Being able to correctly describe a shadow price is a key skill in CIMA P2. A shadow price is the maximum premium that a company should pay for an additional unit of the scarce resource.

The shadow price equals the additional contribution that would be earned from one extra unit of a scarce resource. In a situation such as this, where a number of resources are scarce, the shadow price of any particular scarce resource will depend on whether or not the resource is binding.

The shadow price for skilled labour is NIL because although there is a shortage of skilled labour it does not have a constraining effect on output of JR as other resources are more scarce.

Since material A is one of the binding constraints, if the availability of material A could be increased by one unit, this would change the optimal plan. The increase in contribution as a result of this change is the value of the shadow price of material A. The shadow price thus represents the maximum premium that should be paid for an additional unit of material A.

(c)

Tutorial note

*Make sure you read and understand the requirement here. The question specifically asks you to **explain, using the graph**. You must therefore refer to the graph and to how the slope of the iso-contribution line would change if there was a change in the selling price of one of the products.*

If there was a change in the selling price of product J then assuming that there were no changes to the unit costs of either product or to the selling price of product L this would result in a change to their relative unit contributions. This would change the slope of the iso-contribution line, which may result in a different optimal solution.

In order to calculate by how much the selling price of product J would have to increase it would be necessary to identify each of the extreme points of the feasible region and then calculate the relative unit contributions of products J and L that would cause each of these extreme points to be chosen in preference to the existing optimal solution.

87 THS (MAR 13)

Tutorial note

Candidates needed to read the question carefully and gain a full understanding of the data presented and the specific requirements of each part of the question.

Part (a) required the construction of a graph to identify the optimal production plan, which would include the following actions.

- *Define the unknown*
- *Formulate the constraints*
- *Formulate the objective function*
- *Graph the constraints and objective function*
- *Manipulate the objective function to find the optimal feasible solution.*

(a) **Workings for graph**

Iso-contribution line: $35E + 66R$

Constraints:

Direct material A: $3E + 2R \leq 5,000$ ①

Direct material B: $4E + 3R \leq 5,400$ ②

Machine hours: $2E + 3R \leq 3,000$ ③

Skilled labour: $2E + 5R \leq 4,500$ ④

Demand: $0 \leq R \leq 1,500$ ⑤

From the graph, it can be seen that the two binding constraints are those relating to machine hours and skilled labour. The solution (from the graph) is to produce 375 units of E and 750 units of R.

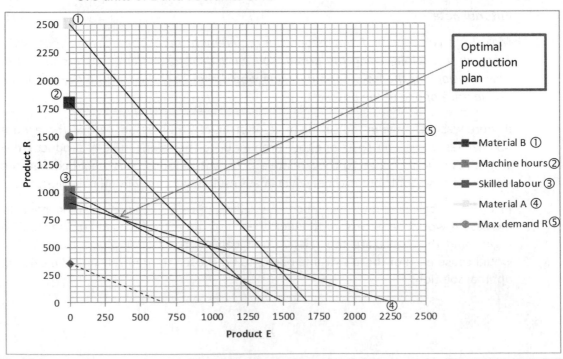

(b)   By inspecting the graph it can be seen that:

The extra labour would change the production plan to 0E and 1,000R

This would earn a contribution of $66,000 if the labour was paid $10 per hour but that rate only applies for 4,500 hours. The additional cost for the extra 500 hours will be $1,000 + (500 * $4) = $3,000. Therefore the contribution from 1000 R will be $63,000.

If the machine is hired the optimal production plan would be 225E and 1,500 R. At this level of output, 7,950 labour hours are needed.

If labour was paid $10 per hour the contribution would be $106,875

Extra labour cost = $1,000 + (3,450 * $4) = $14,800

Therefore contribution from 225E and 1,500R = $92,075

Maximum that should be paid next month to lease the machine is $29,075

(c)   Many factors would earn marks. Examples include:

Machine: the new machinery would increase the capacity to 5,000 machine hours. The production plan would require 4,950 hours and is therefore close to the capacity. If downtime was more than 50 hours the plan would not be achievable.

Labour: is it possible to supervise the additional labour given the current staff? The extra labour is an increase of 77% on current levels. Will there be any incremental overhead costs associated with the increased labour?

Labour: is it possible to recruit more labour without using the agency? Would the existing staff be prepared to work overtime? How will they feel about being paid $4 per hour less than the agency staff?

Management control: the revised plan requires a lot more resources. Can the existing staff control the extra resources?

Product E: if demand is unlimited at $99 per unit, could the selling price be increased?

88   CD COMPANY

(a)   (i)   First, identify whether the limiting factor is Department 1 hours; or Department 2 hours.

Dept 1 – maximum production:

Robroy   100,000 ÷ 5 = 20,000

Trigger   100,000 ÷ 7.5 = 13,333.

Dept 2 – maximum production:

Robroy   160,000 ÷ 7.5 = 21,333

Trigger   160,000 ÷ 10 = 16,000.

Therefore, without the use of sub-contractors Department 1 hours are the limiting factor.

Then, rank the contribution per dept 1 hour for each product:

	Robroy		Trigger	
	$	$	$	$
Selling price		300		430
Direct costs:				
Dept 1	85		135	
Dept 2	90		120	
Variable overhead:				
Dept 1	10		15	
Dept 2	18		24	
		(203)		(294)
Contribution/unit		**97**		**136**
Dept 1 hours/unit		5		7.5
Contribution/dept 1 hour		$19.40		$18.13
Ranking		1		2

Since Robroy has the highest contribution per Department 1 hour this product should be preferred.

Production is limited to 20,000 units which will yield profits of:

	$000
Contribution (20,000 × $97)	1,940
Fixed costs (800,000 + 400,000)	(1,200)
Profit	740

(ii) First, calculate the differences in cost between using the sub-contractors rather than manufacturing internally on a cost/unit basis.

	Robroy		Trigger	
	Internal	Sub-con	Internal	Sub-con
	$	$	$	$
Dept 1	95	110	150	170
Dept 2	108	120	144	154
Total	203	230	294	324

Because the internal cost is less than the buying price produce the maximum in-house and sub contract the remainder. The sub-contractors would be used as long as the contribution per unit is positive. The contribution earned if both sub-contractors were used would be:

		Robroy	Trigger
(W1)	Selling price	270	390
	Sub-contract price		
	Jason	(110)	(170)
	Nadira	(120)	(154)
	Contribution	40	66

As the contribution is positive use the sub-contractors to top up production to the maximum demand.

At the new level of sales, price would be reduced which would reduce contribution of in-house production to:

		Robroy	Trigger
(W2)	Selling price	270	390
	Direct costs	(203)	(294)
	Contribution	67	96

As there is spare capacity in department 2, at certain levels of production sub-contractors will be needed in department 1 but in-house production can be carried out in department 2. In this instance contribution will be:

		Robroy	Trigger
(W3)	Selling price	270	390
	Direct costs – dept 2	(108)	(144)
	Sub-contract costs	(110)	(170)
	Contribution	52	76

Revised profit

	Robroy $	Trigger $
Contribution from in-house production		
20,000 × $67 (W2)	1,340,000	
13,333 × $96 (W2)		1,280,000
Sub-contracting in dept 1 only		
1,333 × $52 (W3)	69,316	
2,667 × $76 (W3)		202,700
Sub-contracting in both departments		
667 × $40 (W1)	26,680	
2,000 × $66 (W1)		132,000
Total contribution	1,435,996	1,614,700

On the basis of the above Trigger should be the product sold, resulting in a profit of:

	$
Contribution	1,614,700
Less: Fixed costs	(1,200,000)
Profit	414,700

(b) (i) The conclusion is based on budgeted estimates of hours available. If these are found to be overstated (by as little as 6.25% in dept 2) then the production of 20,000 Robroy cannot be achieved.

(ii) Care must be taken to ensure that the quality of the work undertaken by the sub-contractors is acceptable.

(c) Marginal costing is a system of cost accounting which distinguishes between fixed and variable costs. In decision making relevant costs are those which are both future and differential. Such costs are most likely to be classified as variable costs because it is these costs which are related to the level of activity. Thus a system of marginal costing is likely to provide costs which are useful for decision-making purposes.

89   WTL DECISION (SEPT 11)

(a)

> **Examiner's comments:** In (a), many marks could not be awarded due to poorly presented statements. Such statements, which were to be used for decision making purposes, needed a 'gross' and net contribution' line, as well as final profit. For presentation and audit reasons, a 'total' column is always helpful. The overall layout and neatness of many of the statements was poor. Many rows were not labelled.

Product	W	X	Y	Z	Total
	$	$	$	$	$
Sales	1,300,000	2,260,000	2,120,000	1,600,000	7,280,000
Direct materials	300,000	910,000	940,000	500,000	2,650,000
Direct labour	400,000	1,040,000	640,000	600,000	2,680,000
Overhead:					
Machine related	80,000	78,000	32,000	120,000	310,000
Batch related	50,000	65,000	40,000	75,000	230,000
Gross contribution	470,000	167,000	468,000	305,000	1,410,000
Overhead:					
Product specific	500,000	50,000	100,000	50,000	700,000
Net contribution	(30,000)	117,000	368,000	255,000	710,000
General overhead					310,000
Profit				400,000	

(b)

> **Examiner's comments:** This requirement was generally well answered, although common errors included the lack of explanation about an ABC approach being adopted; some students also incorrectly stated that this was a relevant costing exercise.

(i)   The profit statement that is presented shows that two of WTL's products are profitable and the other two are loss making. However this statement is unsuitable for decision making. Although it shows the revenues and costs attributed to each product it makes arbitrary assumptions with regard to the company's overhead costs and uses these assumptions to attribute these overhead costs to each product.

The statement does not consider the causes of the overhead costs and the extent to which they are avoidable if the company were to decide on particular courses of action. For example, some of the overhead costs are product specific and would be avoided if the product were to be discontinued. This is not clear from the statement that has been presented.

(ii)   The profit statement shows that Product W has a negative net contribution and therefore from a financial perspective it should be discontinued as this would increase the company's profits by $30,000. This is in contrast to the original profit statement which showed that products W and Y were profitable and products X and Z were loss making. Products X, Y and Z should be continued because they all have a positive net contribution.

The discontinuance of product W will release resources that were previously used by that product. If there is sufficient demand for products X, Y, or Z then WTL may be able to increase its output of these other products and increase its profits by even more than $30,000.

(c)

The specific fixed cost of product W is $500,000.

The gross contribution to sales ratio of product W is $470,000/$1,300,000 = 0.36154

Therefore, the breakeven sales value is $500,000/0.36154 = $1,382,973; and the breakeven sales volume is $1,382,973/$13 = 106,383 units.

However, since production must be in batches of 100 units then to break even 1,064 batches would have to be produced and sold.

For every unit produced that was not sold there is a cost of $8.30, and the gross contribution from each unit sold is $4.70. Therefore the breakeven sales volume is:

106,383 + Z

Where $Z = 4.70x - 8.30 (17 - x) = 4.70x + 8.30x - 141.1 = 13x - 141.1$

$Z = 141.1/13 = 10.86$

Proof:

10.86 @ $4.7 = $51.04

17 − 10.86 @ 8.3 = $50.96

Therefore the breakeven sales volume is 106,383 + 11 = 106,394.

(d)

Value Analysis is a technique that improves the processes of production so as to achieve a reduction in cost without compromising the quality or usefulness of the product.

WTL would need to compare its products with those provided by its competitors to see if their products offer features that are not found in the products of their competitors. WTL it would then have to determine whether these features are important to their customers. If they are not important then these features could be removed without affecting the value of the product.

Alternatively, WTL should review the design of its products as it may be able to produce them using different, lower cost, materials without affecting the customer's perception of the product. This would enable WTL to reduce its costs and thereby increase its profit.

90 WZ MANUFACTURING (MAR 11)

(a)

Tutorial note

You must understand make or buy situations in the same context as limiting factors. Practice questions on the subject!

The internal manufacturing cost of the component is as follows:

	$/unit
Direct labour (1 hour @ $8/hour)	8.00
Direct material B (2 kgs @ $5/kg)	10.00
Variable overhead (working 1):	
Direct labour (1 hour @ $0.50/hour)	0.50
Machine hours (0.5 hours @ $0.25/hour)	0.125
	18.625

The buying price of the component is $35 per unit so if resources are readily available the company should manufacture the component. However, due to the scarcity of resources during the next 10 weeks the contribution earned from the component needs to be compared with the contribution that can be earned from the other products.

Tutorial note

You must make sure that your figures are supported by workings. 'Figures appearing with no explanation' is a common complaint amongst markers.

Workings:

Using product J (though any product could be used) the variable overhead rates per hour can be calculated:

Labour related variable overhead per unit = $1.25

Direct labour hours per unit = $20/$8 = 2.5 hours

Labour related variable overhead per hour = $1.25/2.5 hours = $0.50 per hour

Machine related variable overhead per unit = $1.25

Machine related variable overhead per hour = $1.25/5 hours = $0.25 per hour

Both material A and material B are limited in supply during the next 10 weeks, but calculations are required to determine whether this scarcity affects the production plans of WZ. The resources required for the maximum demand must be compared with the resources available to determine whether either of the materials is a binding constraint.

All figures in kg:

Resource	Available	Total	J	K	L	M	P
Direct material A	21,000	20,150	2,200	3,700	0	14,250	0
Direct material B	24,000	31,050	2,200	0	8,850	19,000	1,000

It can be seen from the above that the scarcity of material B is a binding constraint and therefore the contributions of each product and the component per kg of material B must be compared. At this point product K can be ignored because it does not use material B.

	J	L	M	P
	$	$	$	$
Selling price/buying cost	56	78	96	35
Direct labour	20	24	20	8
Material A	6	0	9	0
Material B	10	15	20	10
Overhead:				
Labour	1.25	1.50	1.25	0.50
Machinery	1.25	0.75	1	0.125
	——	——	——	——
Contribution	17.50	36.75	44.75	16.375
Contribution/kg of material B	8.75	12.25	11.19	8.19
Rank	3	1	2	4

Since the component is the lowest ranked usage of material B then WZ should continue to purchase the component so that the available resources can be used to manufacture products L, M and J.

(b)

Tutorial note

This was not asking you to repeat points 2-5 from part (a). Also, you must calculate what the new contract requires before allocating the remaining quantity of material B.

The optimum usage of material B is based on the ranking shown above:

	J	L	M	P	Total
Minimum (units)	100	150	250		
Uses (kg)	200	450	1,000		1,650
Balance (units)		2,800	3,487.5		
Uses		8,400	13,950		22,350
					24,000
Production (units)	100	2,950	3,737.5	0	

(c) (i) The decision concerning the purchase of the component would change if the contribution from its manufacture were equal to the least best contribution from the products using material B. Apart from the minimum demand constraint the least best usage is derived from product M which has a contribution per kg of $11.19 which is $3 per kg higher than that from component P. Since each unit of P requires 2 kgs of B then the buying price would have to be 2 × $3 = $6 per component higher than at present before it would have the same rank as product M. Thus the buying price at which the decision would change = $35 + $6 = $41.

(ii) A number of factors could be explained:

- The control of the production if it were to be manufactured internally

- The quality of the component produced

- The skill set of the employees

- The exposure of WZ to pressure from the external supplier to withhold supplies/assist a competitor

(d)

Examiner's comments: A common error here was to use total quantities in the equations, rather than the individual quantities for each product.

Objective function:	Maximise 17.5J + 36.75L + 44.75M = C
Material A:	2J + 1K + 0L + 3M <21,000
Material B:	2J + 0K + 3L + 4M <24,000

91   EXE

(a)

	Note	$
Direct materials:		
Steel	(1)	55.00
Brass	(1)	20.00
Direct labour:		
Skilled	(2)	300.00
Semi-skilled	(3)	–
Overhead	(4)	7.50
Estimating time	(5)	–
		382.50
Administration	(6)	–
Profit	(7)	–
Lowest cost estimate		382.50

Notes (that is, brief reasons for using each of the values above):

(1)   The steel will eventually be replaced at a cost of $5.50 per square metre: the brass is included at its future purchase cost.

(2)   Cost of working overtime = 25 × $8.00 × 1.5 = $300.00

Cost of substituting this order is that cash inflow of 25 × ($8.00 + $13.00) = $525.00 is lost. It is more economic to work overtime.

(3)   No incremental cost since there is paid idle time.

(4)   The power cost is based on the expected usage of power by the machine.

(5)   Estimating time-related costs have already been incurred; they are sunk costs.

(6)   Administration costs are not incremental cash flows.

(7)   The profit mark-up is not a future cash flow.

(b)   The two way data table shows the effect of alternative combinations of three values of each of two input variables on the final outcome solution.

In this question the two variables are the skilled labour rate per hour and hourly power costs and, where the values of these items are as set out in part (a) of the question, there is no effect on the solution that has already been found. However, alternative combinations of the values of these input variables will cause the output value (the minimum cost price) to either increase or decrease.

The table can thus be used to illustrate the range of values that may arise given the uncertainty of the values of these input variables. In this question the minimum cost price may be as low as $344.50 ($382.50 – $38.50) or as high as $459.00 ($382.50 + $76.50).

By introducing the probability estimates as well, the likelihood of the minimum cost price being more or less than the value in the original calculation can also be determined. The combined probabilities of each combination are as follows:

Skilled labour rate $	Hourly power cost $	Probability	
10	0.90	0.3 × 0.25 = 0.075	
10	0.75	0.3 × 0.55 = 0.165	
10	0.65	0.3 × 0.20 = 0.060	
8	0.90	0.6 × 0.25 = 0.150	0.45 chance that costs will be higher than those determined in part (a)
8	0.75	0.6 × 0.55 = 0.330	0.33 chance that the costs are as determined in part (a)
8	0.65	0.6 × 0.20 = 0.120	
7	0.90	0.1 × 0.25 = 0.025	
7	0.75	0.1 × 0.55 = 0.055	
7	0.65	0.1 × 0.20 = 0.020	0.22 chance that costs will be lower than those determined in part (a)

By also introducing the effective results of these combinations on the minimum cost price an expected value can be determined:

Skilled labour rate $ per hour	Hourly power cost $	Probability	Effect $	Expected value $
10	0.90	0.3 × 0.25 = 0.075	+76.50	+5.7375
10	0.75	0.3 × 0.55 = 0.165	+75.00	+12.3750
10	0.65	0.3 × 0.20 = 0.060	+74.00	+4.4400
8	0.90	0.6 × 0.25 = 0.150	+1.50	+0.2250
8	0.75	0.6 × 0.55 = 0.330	0	0.000
8	0.65	0.6 × 0.20 = 0.120	−1.00	−0.1200
7	0.90	0.1 × 0.25 = 0.025	−36.00	−0.9000
7	0.75	0.1 × 0.55 = 0.055	−37.50	−2.0625
7	0.65	0.1 × 0.20 = 0.020	−38.50	−0.7700
Sum of expected values				+18.925

(That is expected increase/decrease in cost compared to part (a) of the solution.)

This means that the expected value of the minimum cost price is $401.43. This table can thus be used to provide the following information to the manager:

If the most likely combination of skilled labour rates and hourly power costs occurs, the minimum cost price is $382.50. However, given the alternative values of these input resources, the cost could be as low as $344.00 or as high as $459.00. The likelihood of the cost being more than $382.50 is 45%, whereas there is only a 22% chance of it being less than $382.50. Using an expected value approach the expected minimum cost price is $401.43. The manager may then make a decision depending upon his or her attitude to risk.

92   ELECTRICAL APPLIANCES (SEPT 10)

(a)   (i)   The selling price that should be charged is the one that maximises total contribution, i.e. a price of $75 for a demand of 1,400 units:

Selling price per unit	$100	$85	$80	$75
Variable cost	$38	$38	$38	$38
Unit contribution	$62	$47	$42	$37
Demand units	600 units	800 units	1200 units	1400 units
Total weekly contribution	**$ 37,200**	**$ 37,600**	**$ 50,400**	**$ 51,800**

(ii)   1,400 units will use up 1,400 standard hours; in order to utilise all of the spare capacity, we now need to use 600 hours for Product L, for the first 10 weeks.

$$\frac{600 \text{ hours}}{1.25 \text{hours}} = 480 \text{ units will use all the spare capacity.}$$

To maximise profits, the optimum price P will be expressed as P = a – bQ.

Here, a = $100 + ($\frac{1,000}{200}$ × $10)

So a = $150 and b = $\frac{\$10}{200}$ = –0.05

P = $150 – 0.05Q

P = $150 – 0.05 × 480 units

P = $126 for the first 10 weeks.

For the following 10 weeks when the extra capacity becomes available, the optimum price P will be expressed as P = a – bQ and we need to equate MC = MR to maximise profits, with MR = a – 2bQ.

Profit maximised when	MC = MR
When	$45 = a – 2bQ
When	$45 = $150 – 0.10Q
When	Q = 1,050 units
And	P = $150 – 0.05 × 1,050
	P = $97.50

(b)   **Skimming**

- Given that the product is innovative and unlike any current products on the market, then a skimming strategy would seem a very good fit.

- As the product in new and exciting, charging a high early price would help target the early adopters in the introduction stage.

- This would also have the advantage of allowing product M to be produced in relatively low volumes, whilst still generating good cashflows to recoup the substantial R&D and launch costs traditionally linked to this kind of products.

- Finally, as the market is untested for the product, it allows the firm to start with a high intro price and adjust downwards accordingly.

Penetration pricing

- Represents the alternative approach when launching a new product; it involves charging an initial low price to quickly gain market share.

- It offers the advantage of scaring off potential entrants to the market and may allow the firm to exploit economies of scale.

- However, given that the product is differentiated and there will be little, if any, immediate competition, we think the company is right to adopt a skimming strategy for its pricing.

(c)

Tutorial note

Don't forget to relate your answer to the scenario in the question. Mentioning the learning/experience curve effect will also get you marks.

The remaining stages of M's product life cycle are:

Growth

(i) Assuming M successfully negotiates the perils of the introduction stage it will enter the growth phase, where demand for M will increases steadily and average costs fall with the economies of scale that accompany the greater production volume. Learning and experience curves also impact favourably on production costs.

(ii) This stage should offer the greatest potential for profit to the producer, despite the fact that competitors will be prompted to enter the growing market. The unit selling price should be maintained or slightly eroded to remain competitive.

Maturity

(i) By this stage, M will reach the mass market, and the increase in demand will begin to slow down. The sales curve will flatten out, and eventually start to decline. Profitability will generally be at a lower level than in the growth phase, because production costs will remain constant, as the learning curve will have ended by then.

(ii) M's selling price may need to be cut down to remain competitive. M may be modified or improved, as a means of sustaining its demand.

Decline

(i) The fall in sales accelerates when the market reaches saturation point, but production costs may increase due to lower volumes.

(ii) Although it is still possible to make profits for a short period during this stage, it is only matter of time before the rapidly dwindling sales volumes herald the onset of losses for all producers who remain in the market. The product has effectively reached the end of its life cycle, and selling prices are usually slashed to exploit the last remnants of the market.

93   PRICING STRATEGIES (NOV 08)

(a)   (i)   Using a tabular approach:

- Total revenue at different levels of price and demand:

Selling price per unit	Annual demand (units)	Total sales revenue
$100	50,000	$5,000,000
$120	45,000	$5,400,000
$130	40,000	$5,200,000
$150	25,000	$3,750,000
$160	10,000	$1,600,000
$170	5,000	$850,000

- Using the formula whereby $Z = 70x + 80y + \$240,000$, total cost may be calculated as follows:

Annual demand (units) x	Annual demand (batches) y	Total cost Z
50,000	500	$3,780,000
45,000	450	$3,426,000
40,000	400	$3,072,000
25,000	250	$2,010,000
10,000	100	$948,000
5,000	50	$594,000

- Total profit can be calculated as follows:

Annual demand (units)	Total sales revenue	Total cost Z	Profit
50,000	$5,000,000	$3,780,000	$1,220,000
45,000	$5,400,000	$3,426,000	$1,974,000
40,000	$5,200,000	$3,072,000	**$2,128,000**
25,000	$3,750,000	$2,010,000	$1,740,000
10,000	$1,600,000	$948,000	$652,000
5,000	$850,000	$594,000	$256,000

Profit is maximised when annual demand reaches 40,000 units, i.e. when the selling price is $130.

(ii)   Our chosen selling price of $130 may not result in the highest possible profit from this product if:

- The initial data provided by market research proves inaccurate or fails to incorporate the consequences of competitors' actions on our level of demand

- The estimate of fixed costs of $240,000 is inaccurate at a level of demand of $40,000

- Total costs are not only correlated with the level of activity but with other factors such as inflation, number of machine breakdowns, change in VAT rates, etc.

(b) (i) Alternative pricing strategies that may be adopted when launching a new product are:

- *Price skimming*

  Initially, it may be possible to charge a very high price if the product is new, innovative and different. This is the case for our new product. Furthermore, as we expect demand to be inelastic, price skimming is particularly appropriate so that we can exploit those sections of the market which are insensitive to price

- *Penetration pricing*

  Initially, we may want to sell at a very low price to discourage competition from entering the market. This would also encourage high volumes, and we may benefit from economies of scale. Low prices would help to gain rapid acceptance of the product, and, therefore, a significant market share.

- *Demand based pricing*

  With this method, our company could utilise some market research information to determine the selling price and level of demand to maximise company's profits. This relies heavily on the quality of market information and the estimate of the demand curve. Also, this method assumes that price is the only factor that influences the quantity demanded and ignores other factors such as quality, packaging, advertising and promotion.

- *Cost based pricing*

  Cost based pricing is the simplest pricing method. We would calculate the cost of producing the product and add on a percentage (profit) to give the selling price. This method although simple has two flaws; it takes no account of demand and there is no way of determining if potential customers will purchase the product at the calculated price.

(ii) I recommend that we adopt a price skimming strategy to benefit from the lack of competition in the first six months. In such a competitive market, it is unlikely that competitors would be deterred from entry by low prices, so a penetration strategy seems unsuitable.

Introduction stage

As our product is the first of its type, and incorporates the latest technology, we could initially set very high prices to take advantage of its novelty appeal during the introduction stage, as demand would be inelastic.

This method would help to recover the significant level of development costs quickly, and is recommended when the product life is short and competition is intense, as high initial returns and maximum profits can be gained before competitors enter the market.

Growth stage

During this stage of the product's lifecycle, the sales of our product in garages would be expected to grow rapidly. As the product starts to become accepted and established by the mass market, competition usually increases significantly. In order to maintain market share and dominance, we may find it necessary to lower the initial market skimming launch price, thereby reducing our profits margins.

Maturity stage

As product sales growth begins to slow down and level off, an established market price for our product will become apparent. An average price may be charged. The price will often reach its lowest point during this stage. However, if our company has a good reputation and is respected worldwide, we may be able to charge a premium price based on its reputation and a certain level of brand loyalty.

We may want to extend the maturity phase by launching upgrades, or by trying to sell in new markets. The product must achieve its lowest unit cost during this stage. Profits are likely to be highest in the maturity stage.

Decline

The decline stage is the final stage of the product's lifecycle. The initial new innovative technology would have, by now, been superseded by superior products. Our own product may hold on to a small niche market, and the group of loyal garages still purchasing our product may be willing to pay a price that will ensure continued profitability.

94 WRX (MAY 12)

(a)

Product	W	R	X
	$/unit	$/unit	$/unit
Selling price	90	126	150
Variable costs	61	92	106
Contribution	29	34	44
Kgs of material B	4	6	5
Contribution/kg of B	$7.35	$5.67	$8.80
Ranking	2nd	3rd	1st

The major customer order is for 400 units of each of W, R and X and therefore uses 6,000 kgs of material B (400 × (4 + 6 + 5)). This leaves 11,500 kgs of material B to be used for other sales.

Production plan:

Make (units)	500	250	1,600
Uses (kg of B)	2,000	1,500	8,000

Optimum plan (including major customer order) is therefore:

W   900 units

R   650 units

X   2,000 units

(b)   By completing the order for the major customer WRX is giving up sales of 550 units of R (800 − 250) to the full price market. These units would yield of a contribution of $34 each = $18,700

In order to produce these units and thus not fulfil the major customer order in full WRX would need to release 3,300 kg of material B from the major customer order (550 units × 6 kgs per unit). This material would be released as follows:

Major customer sales:

Product	W $/unit	R $/unit	X $/unit
Selling price	80	116	140
Variable costs	61	92	106
Contribution	19	24	34
Kgs of material B	4	6	5
Contribution/kg of B	$4.75	$4.00	$6.80
Ranking	2nd	3rd	1st

Thus the additional contribution that can be earned and therefore the penalty value at which WRX would decide not to supply the major customer order in full is $4,825 ($18,700 − $13,875).

(c)   (i)   The objective function (P) is to maximise $29w + 34r + 44x$ where

w = number of units of W

r = number of units of R

x = number of units of X

And the constraints are:

Material B: $4w + 6r + 5x <= 11,500$

Direct labour: $2w + 4r + 5x <= 5,400$

Demand W: $0 <= w <= 500$

Demand R: $0 <= r <= 800$

Demand x: $0 <= x <= 1600$

(ii)   Two constraints are binding:

Demand W − because the optimal solution is to produce 500 units of W

Direct labour hours − because the optimal solution uses 5,400 direct labour hours (500w uses 1,000 hours and 880 x uses 4,400 hours; total 5,400 hours)

95   RAB CONSULTING

(a)   (i)

	Type A	Type B
	$	$
Revenue per project	1,700	1,500
Direct expenses	(408)	(310)
Qualified researchers	(600)	(360)
(20, 12 hours @ $30/hr)		
Junior researchers	(112)	(210)
(8, 15 hours @ $14/hr)		
Contribution per project	580	620

Administration costs are not a direct cost, so are excluded.

(ii)   Let A = number of Type A projects undertaken in the period

Let B = number of Type B projects undertaken in the period

Maximise contribution: 580A + 620B

Subject to constraints:

20A	+	12B	≤ 1,344	(qualified researchers' hours)
8A	+	15B	≤ 1,120	(junior researchers' hours)
A			≥ 20	(agreement)
B			≤ 60	(maximum)
A, B			≥ 0	(non-negativity)

(iii)   **Projects undertaken by RAB Consulting, four weeks ending 30 June 20X0**

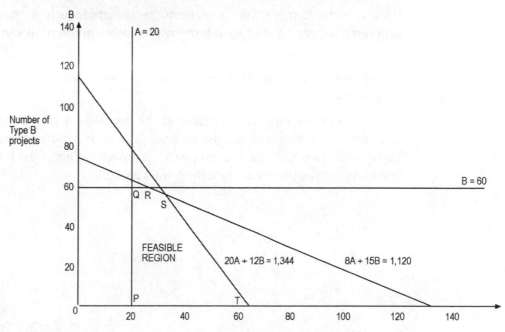

The vertices of the feasible region are:

	Co-ordinates	Contribution = 580A + 620B
		$
P	(20, 0)	11,600
Q	(20, 60)	48,800
R	(27.5, 60)	53,150
S	(33, 57)	54,480 ← maximum
T	(67.2, 0)	38,976

Therefore the mix of projects that will maximise profit for RAB Consulting Ltd for the four-week period ending 30 June 2000 is to undertake 33 Type A projects and 57 Type B projects.

(b) Optimal profit is given by:

	$
Contribution (as above)	54,480
Less: Administration costs	(28,000)
Profit for the period	26,480

(c) In practice, the available quantities of some resources will be limited in the short run. When budgets are produced if this is not taken into consideration the budget may be impossible and therefore not relevant. Each resource to be used in the forthcoming budget period must be investigated, and scarce resources identified.

If there is only one scarce resource, contribution can be maximised by ranking the products according to the contribution earned per unit of the scarce resource consumed. Those products with the highest contribution per unit should be produced first.

Where there is more than one resource simultaneously in scarce supply, linear programming can be used to determine the optimum use of resources.

Linear programming considers the set of all feasible production plans, then identifies where, within this set, an objective function (such as the contribution earned) is maximised.

Where there are only two variables in the problem, a graph can be drawn of the problem which clearly shows the situation in a clear pictorial form. Where there are more than two variables, a graphical approach is not possible, and alternative methods such as the Simplex method must be used.

96   RT LINEAR (MAY 10)

(a)   First, we will need to check if any of our resources are a limiting factor:

Resource	Amount needed for order	Amount needed for normal production	Total amount needed	Amount available	Limiting Factor?
Labour hours	(250 R × 3 hrs) + (350 T × 5 hrs) = 2,500 hours	(500 R × 3 hrs) + (800 T × 5 hrs) = 5,500 hours	8,000 hours	7,500 hours	Yes
Material A	(250 R × 5 kgs)+ (350 T × 4 kgs) = 2,650 kgs	(500 R × 5 kgs) + (800 T × 4 kgs) = 5,700 kgs	8,350 kgs	8,500 hours	No
Material B	(250 R × 2 ltrs)+(350 T × 1 ltr) = 850 litres	(500 R × 2 ltrs) +(800 T × 1 ltr)= 1,800 litres	2,650 litres	3,000 litres	No
Machine hours	250 R × 3 hours + 350 T × 4 hours = 2,150 hours	(500 R × 3 hrs) +(800 T × 4 hrs) = 4,700 hours	6,850 hours	7,500 hours	No

Therefore 'Direct Labour Hours' represent a limiting factor. Contribution per unit of the limiting factor are calculated as follows:

	R	T
Unit selling price	$130	$160
Direct labour	$(24)	$(40)
Material A	$(15)	$(12)
Material B	$(14)	$(7)
Machine hours	$(30)	$(40)
Contribution on normal units	**$47**	**$61**
Direct labour hours	3 hours	5 hours
Contribution per direct labour hour	**$15.67**	**$12.20**
Rank	**1st**	**2nd**

We have 7,500 hours available. Completing the order for the commercial customer will use:

R : 250 × 3 hours		750 hours
T : 350 × 5 hours	=	1,750 hours
Total	=	**2,500 hours**

This leaves 5,000 hours in which to complete 'normal' production, starting with priority product R:

R : 500 units × 3 hours	=	1,500 hours
T : $\dfrac{3,500 \text{ hours}}{5 \text{ hours per unit}}$ = 700 units	=	3,500 hours β

Summary:

Units	Units	Unit contribution	Total Contribution
Commercial order	R : 250 units	$17 (W1)	$4,250
Commercial order	T : 350 units	$36 (W1)	$12,600
Normal	R : 500 units	$47	$23,500
Normal	T : 700 units	$61	$42,700
Total contribution			**$83,050**

(W1) **Contribution per unit on commercial customer order**

	R	T
Unit selling price	$100	$135
Direct labour	($24)	($40)
Material A	($15)	($12)
Material B	($14)	($7)
Machine hours	($30)	($40)
Contribution per unit	**$17**	**$36**

Tutorial note

A crucial point on exam technique here: long calculations will get you to the right answer but, for only three marks, it is likely that 'shortcuts' will be available.

(b)

	'Normal' production		Commercial Customer order	
	R	T	R	T
Contribution per unit	$47	$61	$17	$36
Direct Labour	3 hours	5 hours	3 hours	5 hours
Contribution per DL hour	$15.67	$12.20	$5.67	$7.20
Rank	1st	2nd	4th	3rd

We have 7,500 hours available. Production based on the above rankings will use:

R for 'normal' production	: 500 × 3 hours	=	1,500 hours
T for 'normal' production	: 800 × 5 hours	=	4,000 hours
T for commercial customer order	: 350 × 5 hours	=	1,750 hours
Total		**=**	**7,250 hours**

This leaves 250 hours in which to complete product R for the commercial customer:

$$R : \frac{250 \text{ hours}}{3 \text{ hours per unit}} = 83 \text{ units (we 'lose' 167 units by doing so)} = 250 \text{ hours } \beta \text{ (*)}$$

Tutorial note

You could have stopped here and noticed that the only benefit of following the above production plan is to supply an extra 100 T's for 'normal' production, compared to what you have worked out in (a). This would only bring in 100 × $61 = $6,100 extra contribution; not enough to justify the $10,000 financial penalty (particularly since 100 T's for the commercial order would also be lost). Therefore, the order should be fulfilled. Another, equally valid view would be to calculate the lost contribution attached to the 167 lost R's and add this to the $10,000 financial penalty – still far too much to offset the $6,1000 benefit of an extra 100 T's.

We need to calculate what the contribution would be if we did not fulfil the customer order fully and incur the financial penalty. We could then compare this with the contribution calculated in (a).

Units	Units	Unit contribution	Total Contribution
Normal	R : 500 units	$47	$23,500
Normal	T : 800 units	$61	$48,800
Order	T : 350 units	$36	$12,600
Order	R : 83 units	$17	$1,411
Total contribution			**$86,311**
Financial penalty			**$(10,000)**
Net benefit			**$76,311**

Conclusion: We should complete the order for the commercial customer as doing so incurs a net benefit ($76,311) that is higher that the option of not doing so ($83,050) by $6,739.

(c)   If resources are 10 % lower than originally predicted:

Direct Labour hours:	7,500 hours × (1–10%)	=	6,750 hours
Material A:	8,500 kgs × (1–10%)	=	7,650 kgs
Material B:	3,000 litres × (1–10%)	=	2,700 litres
Machine hours:	7,500 hours × (1–10%)	=	6,750 hours

Step 1: define the variables

Let 'R' be the number of R units to produce on top of the 250 units required for the order

Let 'T' be the number of T units to produce on top of the 350 units required for the order

Step 2: state the objective function

We want to maximise contribution. Each R generates a contribution of $47 and each T generates a contribution of $61, so we want to maximise **C = $47R + $61T**

Step 3: Define constraints

R, T ≥ 0; R ≤ 500 and T ≤ 800

Direct labour hours

Direct labour hours used by order = (250 Rs × 3 hours) + (350 Ts × 5 hours)

Direct labour hours used by order = 2,500 hours

Therefore, 6,750 hours − 2,500 hours = 4,250 hours are available for June

3R + 5T ≤ 4,250

Material A

Material A used by order = (250 Rs × 5 kgs) + (350 Ts × 4 kgs)

Material A used by order = 2,650 hours

Therefore, 7,650 kgs − 2,650 kgs = 5,000 kgs are available for June

5R +4T ≤ 5,000

Material B

Material B used by order = (250 Rs × 2 litres) + (350 Ts × 1 litre)

Material B used by order = 850 litres

Therefore, 2,700 litres − 850 litres = 1,850 litres are available for June

2R +T ≤ 1,850 litres

Machine hours

Machine hours used by order = (250 Rs × 3 hours) + (350 Ts × 4 hours)

Machine hours used by order = 2,150 hours

Therefore, 6,750 hours − 2,150 hours = 4,600 kgs are available for June

3R +4T ≤ 4,600

Step 4: Draw the graph (see next page)

Step 5: Finding the optimum solution

Graphically, the iso-contribution line can be pushed up until it reaches Vertex B at the intersection of Direct Labour hours and R = 500. This represents an optimum solution of 500Rs and 550 Ts.

Solving simultaneous equations, coordinates for B are to be found at the intersection of the DL and R= 500 when **3R + 5T ≤ 4,250**

i.e. when (3 × 500) + 5T = 4,250

i.e. when 5T = 2,750, i.e. T = 550 units.

(d)   The graph can be used to show the upper and lower boundaries of the optimum production plan.

R will stay at 500 units so the feasible region will not expand right off the R = 500 line; but we may be able to increase our number of T units: the DL and Material constraints would slide upwards, the optimum corner would be affected and the feasible region would expand up to the managers' most optimistic prediction.

Many lines could be moved and inputting the constraints in a computer package would enable the graph to be reproduced and simulations (or 'what-if' analysis) to be performed.

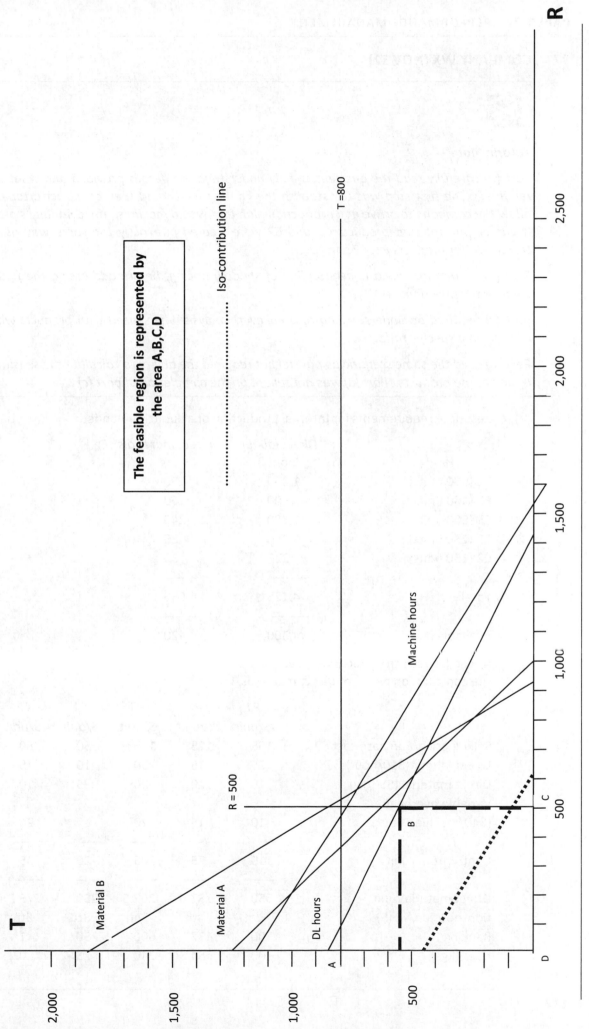

The feasible region is represented by the area A,B,C,D

········· Iso-contribution line

97 COMPANY WX (NOV 12)

Tutorial note

Part (a) carefully read the question to fully understand the details provided and what was required. The first step was to establish the limiting factor and then construct a table to allow the company to arrive at a production plan that would maximise the company's profit. It was important that products C1 and C2 were treated in exactly the same way as the treatment for products P1, P2 and P3.

Part (b) required a sound understanding of shadow pricing, before addressing the figures given in the question.

Part (c) required an understanding of breakeven analysis when faced with products which are sold in a specific ratio.

Part (d) used the same scenario as part (c) but required the ability to calculate the sensitivity of one of the products. Part (d) was not reliant on the completion of part (c).

(a) Resource requirements for internal production of all units demanded:

	Direct labour (hours)	*Direct materials* (kg)
P1 (500 units)	1,250	100
P2 (400 units)	600	160
P3 (600 units)	1,800	240
C1 (250 units)	250	25
C2 (150 units)	225	30
Total	4,125	555
Available	4,300	420

As can be seen the direct materials are the scarce resource so the ranking is based on the contribution per kg of direct materials.

	P1 $/unit	*P2* $/unit	*P3* $/unit	*C1* $/unit	*C2* $/unit
Selling price/Purchase cost	155	125	175	50	80
Direct labour ($10/hour)	25	15	30	10	15
Direct material ($50/kg)	10	20	20	5	10
Variable overhead ($40/machine hour)	10	15	20	10	20
Contribution/unit	110	75	105	25	35
Direct material/unit	550	187.5	262.5	250	175
Contribution/kg ($)	1st	4th	2nd	3rd	5th
Ranking	500	137	600	250	1
Uses (kgs)	100	54.8	240	25	0.2

(b)   If there was an extra 0.2 kgs of direct material then the production of P2 would increase by 1 unit and the production of C2 would reduce by 1 unit with a resulting increase in contribution of $40, thus the shadow price of the next 0.2 kgs of direct material is $200 per kg.

Then, until the demand for P2 is fully satisfied the shadow price would be $187.5 per kg provided it could be purchased in multiples of 0.4 kgs. The demand for P2 would be fully satisfied once a further 105.2 kgs had been obtained ((400 units – 137 units) × 0.4 kg).

Thereafter any further materials would be used to produce C2 so the shadow price would reduce to $175 per kg.

(c)   Consider a 'bundle' of products in the mix 9L:6M:5N

	L	M	N	Total
Sales mix	9	6	5	1 bundle
	$	$	$	
Selling price per unit	300	600	230	
Variable cost per unit	100	300	50	
Contribution per unit	200	300	180	
Total contribution	1,800	1,800	900	4,500

Number of bundles needed to break even = 2,700,000/4,500 = 600

Therefore the sales plan to break even is 5,400L, 3,600M and 3,000N

(d)

	L	M	N	Total
Sales budget (units)	6,300	4,200	3,500	
	$	$	$	
Contribution per unit	200	300	180	
Total contribution	1,260,000	1,260,000	630,000	3,150,000
Fixed costs				2,700,000
Profit				450,000

Contribution from L can drop by $450,000.

The contribution per unit, and therefore selling price per unit, can fall by $450,000/6,300 = $71.43 per unit.

The current selling price per unit is $300.

Therefore the sensitivity is $71.43/$300 = 23.8%

98   DFG (NOV 07)

Key answer tips

The question does not specify whether the resource limits given are for the weekly availability or for the total for the four week period. The answer below assumes the former. A quick check of the requirements for material A at the maximum demand gives a figure of 2,500 kg and a comparison with the resource limit of 1,800 kg suggests that this is likely to be the correct assumption. If you have similar problem in the exam, make an assumption, state that assumption clearly and stick to it throughout all your calculations.

(a)   The following answer is based on the assumption that the resource limits given are the weekly availability of each resource. Profit will be maximised by maximising contribution.

Fixed costs do not vary with quantity produced and are therefore not relevant to the decision.

Let: d = quantity of product D produced and g = quantity of product G produced

Contribution per unit of product D	= selling price – variable cost
	= $115 – $(20 + 12 + 28 + 14)
	= $41
Contribution per unit of product G	= selling price – variable cost
	= $120 – $(10 + 24 + 21 + 18)
	= $47

	Product D	Product G
Contribution/unit ($)	41	47
Usage of material A/unit (kg)	20/5 = 4	10/5 = 2
Usage of material B/unit (kg)	12/3 = 4	24/3 = 8
Usage of skilled labour/unit (hours)	28/7 = 4	21/7 = 3
Usage of machine/unit (hours)	14/2 = 7	18/2 = 9
Maximum weekly demand (units)	400	450

Objective function: Contribution C = 41d + 47g

Constraints:

Material A	$4d + 2g \leq 1,800$	Material B	$4d + 8g \leq 3,500$
Skilled labour	$4d + 3g \leq 2,500$	Machine hours	$7d + 9g \leq 6,500$
$d \leq 400$	$g \leq 450$		
$d \geq 0$	$g \geq 0$		

Plotting these lines on the graph:

Material A:

d = 0, g = 900	d = 450, g = 0

Material B:

d = 0, g = 437.5	d = 75, g = 400	d = 875, g = 0

Skilled labour:

d = 250, g = 500	d = 400, g = 300	d = 0, g = 833.33
d = 625, g = 0		

Machine hours:

	d = 0, g = 722.22	d = 928.57, g = 0

To plot iso-contribution line, say C = 19270 = 41d + 47g, then:

d = 0, g = 410 or d = 470, g = 0

From the graph, contribution will be maximised on the iso-contribution line furthest from the origin which touches the edge of the feasible region and is furthest from the origin. This point, point P, is at the intersection of the constraint lines for material A and material B.

This point is the solution of the simultaneous equations:

(1)   4d + 2g = 1,800 and (2) 4d + 8g = 3,500

Subtracting equation (1) from equation (2)

6g	= 1,700	
g	= 283 units	

and substituting this in (1)

4d + 2 × 283	= 1,800
4d	= 1,234
D	= 308 units

Weekly production schedule to maximise contribution = 308 units of D and 283 units of G.

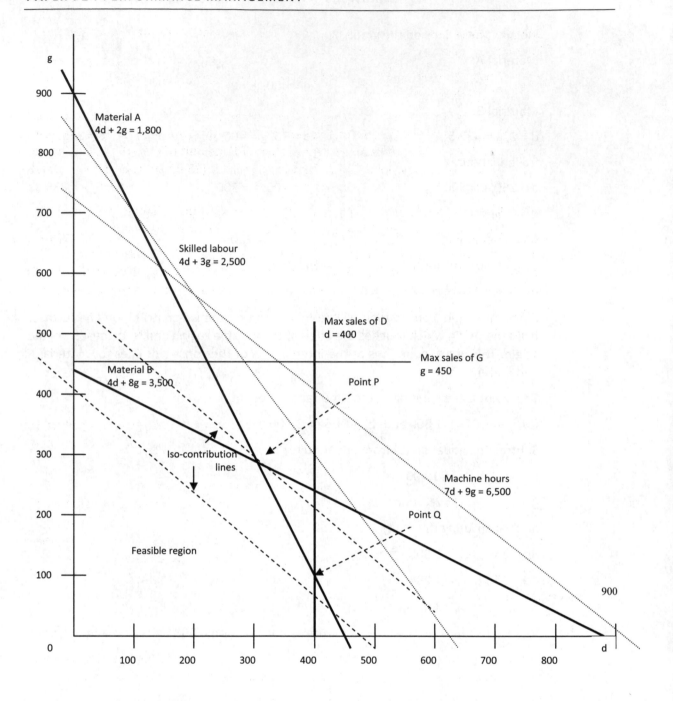

(b)   The shadow price of a resource is an increase in value which would be created by having available one additional unit of a limiting resource at its original cost. (CIMA, Official Terminology, 2000).

This means that there would be an increase in value of $5.82 for every unit of material A which is available. However there will be no increase in value of additional skilled labour, as it has a shadow price of $Nil and availability of skilled labour is not a binding constraint at the optimum solution. It can be seen from the graph that this is indeed the case as the constraint line for the skilled labour lies outside the feasible region.

Shadow prices (also known as opportunity costs or dual prices are one of the most important aspects of linear programming.

- The shadow price is the extra profit that may be earned by relaxing each of the constraints by one unit.

- It therefore represents the maximum premium that the firm should be willing to pay for one extra unit of each constraint. In the case of material A the firm should be willing to pay $5.82 for each additional unit of material A, i.e. should be willing to pay anything up to $10.82 per kg ($5.82 on top of the normal price of $5).

- Since shadow prices indicate the effect of a one unit change in each of the constraints, they provide a measure of the sensitivity of the result.

(c) Changes in the price of product D will change the slope of the contribution line. As the contribution line is moved further from the origin, the same point as calculated previously will still be the last point of the feasible region that it touches, unless the slope of the contribution line alters considerably.

In general, the contribution can be expressed as C = 47g + xd where x is the contribution from product D. Rearranging this:

47g = C – xd

g = C/47 – (x/47)d

This graph has a negative gradient, which means that as the price of product D increases, the contribution from D (= x) will increase and the slope of the contribution line will steepen.

Point P will continue to be the optimum solution until the contribution line steepens to the point where point Q becomes the last point of the feasible region that it touches. This will happen when the gradient of the contribution line equals the gradient of the line representing the constraint on material A. From this, the revised contribution and a revised selling price for product D can be calculated.

99 LM (NOV 10)

(a)

> **Examiner's comments:** Most candidates scored well with this question and gained most of the marks that were on offer, but common faults in part (a) included:
>
> 1 Ranking the products on profit or contribution as opposed to contribution per unit of limiting factor.
>
> 2 Failing to calculate the contribution from the optimal mix.
>
> 3 Poor presentation of answers.

Resources required to meet demand:

	L	M	Total
Maximum demand (units)	400	700	
Direct labour (hours)	1,600	1,400	3,000
Direct material (kg)	800	6,300	7,100
Machine hours	400	1,400	1,800

Direct material is the limiting factor.

Product	L	M
	$	$
Unit selling price	70	90
Variable costs per unit:		
Direct labour ($7 per hour)	28	14
Direct material ($5 per kg)	10	45
Machine hours ($10 per hour)	10	20
Contribution per unit	22	11
Contribution per kg	11	1.22
Ranking	1	2
Make (units)	400	577
Uses(kg of material)	800	5,193
Contribution	$8,800	$6,3477

Total contribution $15,147

(b)

> **Examiner's comments:** Common faults in part (b) included:
>
> 1   Presenting a graph. This was not requested.
>
> 2   Failing to subtract the resources needed for the special order before presenting the revised resource constraints.

Direct labour	4L + 2M < 2,300
Direct material	2L + 9M < 2,550
Machine hours	1L + 2M < 1,100

Z = 22L + 11M

Product L   400   Other value **0**

The value of 400 represents the optimum production of product L in units, the other value is the unsatisfied demand which can be seen to be zero because the output from the plan is 400 units which is the same as the maximum demand for the product.

Product M   194   Other value 506

The value of 194 represents the optimum production of product M in units, the other value is the unsatisfied demand which can be seen to be 506 because the output from the plan is 194 units and the maximum demand for the product was 700 units, hence the unsatisfied demand is 700 – 194 = 506 units.

Machine hours   312

The value of 312 is the number of unused machine hours. This can be proven by comparing the outputs to the machine hours available:

400 units of L use 1 hour each =	400 hours
194 units of M use 2 hours each =	388 hours
Total hours used	788 hours
Hours available	1,100 hours
Hours unused	312 hours

Direct material $ 1.22

The value of $1.22 is the shadow price of the direct materials. This is the maximum additional price that should be paid for an extra kg of direct material above the resource's base cost of $5 per kg. The fact that there is a shadow price for this resource confirms that it is a binding constraint.

This shadow price can be proven because 1 extra kg of direct material would be used to increase the output of product M. Each unit of M requires 9 kg so 0.11 additional units of M could be produced from 1 extra kg of material. Each unit of M yields a contribution of $11 so 0.11 units yields $1.22 contribution.

Labour hours 312

The value of 312 is the number of unused direct labour hours.

Contribution $**10,934**

The value of $10,934 is the contribution earned from the optimum production plan. It can be proved by:

400 units of L earn $22 each =	$8,800
194 units of M earn $11 each =	$2,134
	$10,934

100   D, E AND F (MAY 13)

Tutorial note

Part (a): Carefully read the question to understand clearly what is required and complete two limiting factor calculations to identify the financial impact of making component F internally as opposed to buying it.

Part (b) Understand the changes to the figures in part (a) and apply linear programming skills to construct the objective function and the constraints to be used in a linear programming model and address the issue described in part b(ii).

(a) **Buying in the component**

	D	E	F	Total
Contribution per unit	54	72	35	
Skilled labour hours per unit	1	1.5	0.5	
Contribution per skilled labour hour	54	48	70	
Rank	2nd	3rd	1st	
Output (units)	2,400	1,000	3,000	
Contribution $	129,600	72,000	105,000	306,600

Making the component

	D	E	F	Total
Contribution per unit	54	72	78	
Skilled labour hours per unit	1	1.5	1.5	
Contribution per skilled labour hour	54	48	52	
Rank	1st	3rd	2nd	
Output (units)	2,400	0	2,000	
Contribution $	129,600	0	156,000	285,600

In Month 1 the optimum production plan is to buy in the component and make 2,400, 1,000 and 3,000 units of D, E and F respectively. This will earn a profit of $156,600

(b) (i) Objective function: Maximise 54D + 72E, where D and E are the number of units of those products to be produced.

Subject to:

Direct materials	$3D+4E \leq 16,000$
Skilled labour	$1D+1.5E \leq 5,400$
Unskilled labour	$1.5D+1E \leq 5,000$
Machine hours	$4D+4E \leq 19,600$
Demand for D	$D \leq 3,000$
Demand for E	$E \leq 3,000$

(ii) The optimum will be at the point where the binding constraints intersect. The binding constraints are:

$1D + 1.5E = 5,400$ (Equation 1)

$1.5D + 1E = 5,000$ (Equation 2)

Multiply equation 1 by 1.5 gives:

$1.5D + 2.25E = 8,100$ (Equation 3)

Equation 3 – Equation 2 gives: $1.25E = 3,100$ and therefore E = 2,480

Therefore by substitution into any of the equations gives D = 1,680

The resulting profit is (1,680 * $54) + (2,480 * $72) – $150,000 = $119,280.

(c)   The stages in a value analysis exercise are:

- Determine the function of the product and of each part/component in the product. The main issue is to identify the function of each component.

- Determine the costs of each part/component that makes up the function.

- Develop alternative ways of performing the function of each part.

- Evaluate the alternatives.

- Recommend/implement the results.

101   X, Y AND Z PRODUCTION PLANNING (SEPT 13)

Tutorial note

Part (a)

Candidates needed to carefully read the question to gain a full understanding of what was required. Firstly, there was a need to identify the limiting factor, and then maximise the profit by making best use of the limiting factor.

Part (b)

This part required candidates to calculate the shadow prices for labour hours using the outcome of part (a).

Part (c)

Required candidates to understand the data provided and to use it to show a revised optimum production position by use of a marginal contribution approach.

(a)

	X	Y	Z	Total	Available
Labour hours per unit	0.5	1.5	1.5		
Machine hours per unit	1	2	0.75		
Production and sales (units)	10,000	6,000	10,000		
Labour hours needed for budget	5,000	9,000	15,000	29,000	12,500
Machine hours needed for budget	10,000	12,000	7,500	29,500	30,000

From the above table it can be seen that labour hours are the limiting factor.

	X	Y	Z
Selling price ($ per unit)	24	41	42
Variable cost ($ per unit)	8	8	14
Contribution per unit ($)	16	33	28
Labour hours per unit	0.5	1.5	1.5
Contribution per labour hour ($)	32.00	22.00	18.67
Rank	1st	2nd	3rd

	X	Y	Total
Output (units)	10,000	5,000	
	$	$	$
Revenue	240,000	205,000	445,000
Variable costs	80,000	40,000	120,000
Contribution	160,000	165,000	325,000
Fixed costs			402,000
Loss			(77,000)

(b) The shadow price of labour is $22 per hour for the next 1,500 hours (up to a total 14,000 hours) and then $18.67 per hour for the subsequent 15,000 hours (up to a total of 29,000 hours). After that the shadow price will be zero because of the lack of demand.

(c) (i) It is necessary to compare the marginal contribution earned from each batch and recognise the labour hours used.

Product X

Sales	Price	Cont per unit	Total cont	Marginal contribution	Marginal cont/lhr	Hours used	Rank	Cumulative hours
	($)	($)	($)	($)	($)			
2,000	28	20	40,000	40,000	40	1,000	1	1,000
4,000	27	19	76,000	36,000	36	1,000	2	2,000
6,000	26	18	108,000	32,000	32	1,000	4	6,000
8,000	25	17	136,000	28,000	28	1,000	5	7,000
10,000	24	16	160,000	24,000	24	1,000	7	11,000
12,000	23	15	180,000	20,000	20	1,000	8	12,000
13,000	22	14	182,000	2,000	4	500	9	12,500

Product Z

Sales	Price	Cont per unit	Total cont	Marginal contribution	Marginal cont/lhr	Hours used	Rank	Cumulative hours
	($)	($)	($)	($)	($)			
2,000	66	52	104,000	104,000	34.67	3,000	3	5,000
4,000	60	46	184,000	80,000	26.67	3,000	6	10,000
6,000	54	40	240,000	56,000	18.67			
8,000	48	34	272,000	32,000	10.67			
10,000	42	28	280,000	8,000	2.67			
12,000	36	22	264,000	−16,000	−5.33			

The revised optimum production plan is 13,000 X and 4,000 Z

(ii) The total contribution from the revised plan is (13,000 * $14) + (4,000 * $46) = $366,000.

102   CDF (SEPT 12)

(a)

	Note	$
Material D	1	1,520
Components	2	49,920
Direct labour	3	11,050
Specialist machine	4	10,000
Machine operating costs	5	12,000
Supervision	6	500
Development time	7	NIL
General fixed overhead	8	NIL
Total relevant cost		84,990

Notes:

1   Material D is in regular use by CDF and must be replaced. Consequently its relevant value is its replacement cost. The historical cost is not relevant because it is a past cost and the resale value is not relevant because CDF is not going to sell it because the material is in regular use.

2   CDF could obtain the components externally at a cost of $15 each which totals $60,000 or they could be obtained from RDF. The transfer price from RDF is ($8 + 30%) + 20% = $12.48 per component. Thus the internal cost to CDF is $12.48 × 4,000 = $49,920. The opportunity cost to RDF is not relevant to CDF because from CDF's viewpoint the relevant cost is the price they have to pay to their supplier. Since this is lower than the external buying price the relevant cost for the contract is $49,920.

3   The employees in department W will continue to paid for their full hours regardless of how the work is completed because they are working at 100% capacity. Therefore their cost is irrelevant. The choice is between using employees from department Z at a cost of $15 per hour (total $12,750) or engaging sub-contract workers at a cost of $13 per hour (total $11,050). Since the use of sub-contract employees is the cheaper option this is the relevant cost.

4   CDF has a number of options: (a)If the machine were to be hired it would have a cost of $15,000; (b) if the machine were bought and then sold at the end of the work it would have a net cost of $20,000; or (c) if the machine were bought and then modified to avoid the need to buy the other machine it would have a net cost of $10,000 ($50,000 plus $5,000 modifications less $45,000 cost of another machine). Thus the most economic approach is buy the machine and then modify it so the relevant cost is $10,000.

5   The machine operating costs are future costs of doing the work and therefore are relevant.

6   The supervisor's salary is irrelevant, but the bonus needs to be included because it is dependent on this work and therefore is relevant.

7   The development time has already been incurred. Therefore it is a past cost and not relevant.

8   General fixed overhead costs and their absorption are not relevant because they will be incurred whether the work goes ahead or not. Depreciation is also not relevant because it is an accounting entry based on the historical purchase of assets. It is not affected by the work being considered.

(b)   Two main issues arise when pricing work based on relevant costs:

- Profit reporting; and

- Pricing of future work.

With regard to profit reporting, the decision as to whether to proceed with the work will have been based on the use of relevant costs, but the routine reporting of the profit from the work will be based on the company's normal accounting system. Since this system will be based on total cost, it is probable that the costs of the work reported will be greater than its relevant cost. Consequently the amount of profit reported to have been made on this order will be lower than expected and may even be a loss. This may cause difficulties for the manager who accepted the work as an explanation will be required of the reasons why there is such a difference in profit.

With regard to the pricing of future work the difficulty lies in increasing the price for similar items for the same customer in future. Once a price is set, customers tend to expect that any future items will be priced similarly. However, where a special price has been offered based on relevant cost because of the existence of spare capacity the supplier would not be able to continue to price on that basis as it does not recover its long term total costs. There may also be difficulties created by this method of pricing as other customers are being charged on a full cost basis and if they were to discover that a lower price was offered to a new customer they would feel that their loyalty was being penalised.

COST PLANNING AND ANALYSIS FOR COMPETITIVE ADVANTAGE

103 VWXYZ COMPANY

(a)   (i)   Pareto analysis of sales revenue (see diagram on next page)

Product	Sales revenue	Cumulative sales revenue	%
	$000	$000	
Tables and chairs	340	340	35
Sheds	200	540	56
Barbecue equipment	140	680	70
Garden seats	120	800	82
Pavilions	70	870	90
Gates	50	920	95
Lawnmowers	30	950	98
Tools, toys etc	15	965	99
Café	5	970	100
	———		
	970		
	———		

80% of 970 = 776. This is within the first four product groups.

(ii)   Pareto analysis of contribution

Product	Contribution	Cumulative contribution	%
	$000	$000	
Sheds	46	46	31
Pavilions	29	75	50
Barbecue equipment	20	95	64
Garden seats	17	112	75
Gates	13	125	84
Tables & chairs	12	137	92
Lawnmowers	8	145	97
Café	3	148	99
Tools, toys, etc	1	149	100
	149		

80% of 149 = 119. This is within the first five product groups.

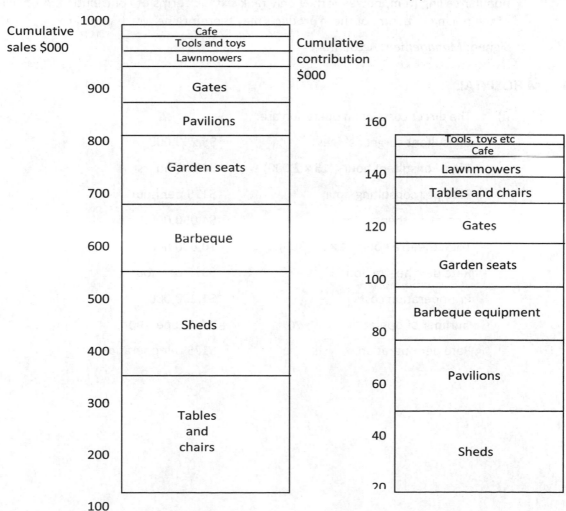

(i)   **Sales**   (ii)   **Contribution**

(b) **Report on the Pareto analysis of sales revenue and contribution**

To: All Managers

From: Management Accountant

Date: 29/4/X4

Terms of reference: A report was requested by the sales and marketing director reviewing the company's product groups in terms of sales revenue and contribution.

Procedure: A Pareto analysis (80/20 rule) was carried out.

Findings: The analysis revealed that 80% of the company's sales derive from four of the product groups: tables and chairs, sheds, barbecue equipment and garden seats. 80% of the company's contribution is generated by only five of the nine product groups, three of which overlap with the 'sales' generating group-namely sheds, barbecue equipment, garden seats, the other two being pavilions and gates. The three products common to both groups obviously represent our key products. However, pavilions, which rank only fifth in terms of sales revenue, represent our second most important product in terms of contribution.

Recommendations: It would seem appropriate to concentrate our promotional activities on pavilions i.e. the highest margin product. Tables and chairs are our most popular selling item, however they only rank sixth in terms of contribution. A review of the pricing structure of these products may therefore be worth pursuing.

Signed: *Management Accountant*

104 LM HOSPITAL

(a) (i) The direct costs of an operation are:

Consultant surgeons' fees	$5,250,000
Total consultant hours (15 × 2,000)	30,000 hours
Rate per consulting hour	$175 per hour
Operating theatre costs	$4,050,000
Total theatre hours (4 × 9 × 300)	10,800 hours
Rate per theatre hour	$375 per hour
Pre-operation costs	$1,260,000
Number of operations	7,200 operations
Rate per operation	$175 per operation

Indirect costs under the three categories are as follows:

	Caring for patients $000	Admissions and record keeping $000	Facility sustaining costs $000
Nursing services and admin	9,936		
Linen and laundry	920		
Kitchen and food	2,256		
Insurance of buildings			60
Depreciation of building and general equipment			520
Medical supplies	1,100		
Pathology laboratory	920		
Updating patient records		590	
Patient and bed scheduling		100	
Invoicing and collections		160	
Housekeeping activities			760
Total indirect costs	15,132	850	1,340
Cost driver:			
Caring for patients – Patient days	44,000 days		
Admissions and records – No. of patients		9,600 patients	–
Cost per cost driver	$343.91/day	$88.54/patient	

As the 15% mark-up covers facility sustaining costs a cost driver was not identified for this. As cost of caring for patients is heavily dependent on the length of stay, no of patient days was selected as the appropriate cost driver for this. The number of patients drives the admissions and record keeping costs.

Price charged under existing method:

	ENT operation $	Cataract operation $
Direct costs:		
Consultant's fee @ $175 per hour	525.00	148.75
Operating theatre costs @ $375 per hour	750.00	187.50
Pre-operation costs @$175 per operation	175.00	175.00
Total direct costs	1,450.00	511.25
Mark-up @ 135%	1,957.50	690.19
Price	3,407.50	1,201.44

Price charged using ABC:

	ENT operation $	Cataract operation $
Total direct costs (as above)	1,450.00	511.25
Indirect costs:		
Patient care costs @ $343.91 per day	1,375.64	343.91
Admissions and records		
@ $88.54 per patient	88.54	88.54
Total cost	2,914.18	943.70
Mark-up @ 15%	437.13	141.56
Price	3,351.31	1,085.26

(ii) Prices under the ABC method are lower for both types of operations. The 15% mark-up should be questioned – is it sufficient to cover both the facility sustaining costs and the current level of profit?

The cataract operation, which does not require an overnight stay, is charged a patient care cost at the same rate per day as an ENT operation. This may require further refinement to obtain realist costs of both operations.

On the other hand the hospital may be over pricing its operations under the existing method and perhaps losing customers. LM Hospital should compare its prices with other private hospitals providing a similar service.

(b) LM Hospital groups all its costs under three activities and uses two cost drivers. For a more accurate costing it needs to analyse its costs under several categories and select an appropriate cost driver for each.

As the number of pathology tests is available, pathology costs can be charged at a rate per test rather than per patient day. The tests required will depend on the requirements of each patient rather than the length of stay in hospital.

Under the proposed ABC system nursing services are also charged at a rate per patient day. The type of nursing care required can vary from operation to operation. This can be further analysed into intensive care, day care etc. and charged accordingly.

(c) The concept of throughput accounting is based on the management of bottlenecks. A hospital could have several bottlenecks – operating theatre facilities, surgeons' time, intensive care beds etc. Throughput accounting would enable a hospital to identify its bottlenecks and ensure optimal use is made of these resources.

Throughput accounting is used in a manufacturing environment to improve the flow through its process. It is questionable if a hospital should advocate such a policy – hurrying patients through its surgical and aftercare processes!

105 S & P PRODUCTS COMPANY

Key answer tips

There is a lot of material in the question; it is a good idea to highlight information in the question as you slot it into your answers. If, when you reach the end, you find that there is a piece of information given to you by the examiner that you have not taken account of, you will have a chance to correct your answer.

(a) (i)

		Department store		S & P shops	Post	Phone	Internet	Total
		$		$	$	$	$	$
Sales revenue	1.3x	50,000	1.4x	1,000,000	150.00	300.00	100.00	
Less: purchase cost (W1)	x	38,462	x	714,286	107.14	214.29	71.43	
Gross margin per type of sale	0.3x	11,538	0.4x	285,714	42.86	85.71	28.57	
Overheads				300,000				
Telephone queries @ $15.00		600		5,250				
Sales visits @ $250		500		1,000				
Shop orders @ $20		500		3,000				
Packaging @ $100		2,800		15,000				
Delivery to shops @ $150		4,200		22,500				
Processing mail orders					5.00	6.00	3.00	
Dealing with queries					4.00	4.00	1.00	
Packaging & delivery @ $10.00 per package					20.00	20.00	10.00	
Internet cost $80,000/(80,000 × 10%)							10.00	
Total costs		8,600		346,750	29.00	30.00	24.00	
Net margin		2,938		(61,036)	13.86	55.71	4.57	
% Net margin to sales		5.9%			9.2%	18.6%	4.6%	
Ranking		3		5	2	1	4	
Number of outlets/orders (30/60/10)		50		10	24,000	48,000	8,000	
		$		$	$	$	$	$
Total revenue		2,500,000		10,000,000	3,600,000	14,400,000	800,000	31,300,000
Total net margin/loss		146,900		(610,360)	332,640	2,674,080	36,560	2,579,820
% Net margin to sales								8.2%

Workings:

(W1) 1.3x = 50,000 ∴ x = 38,462

(ii) The figures show that the different parts of the business generate very different amounts of profit. S & P's own shops make a substantial loss which effectively more than wipes out the profits of the department stores, postal orders and internet orders together. The telephone orders are both the biggest revenue generators (46%) and the most profitable source of business. The department stores, while profitable, are not as profitable as the traditional mail order side of the business. The internet sales are profitable but are both small in number and on a low net margin because of the internet costs. Increased sales here will improve the overall profitability of each sale, as the high fixed cost is spread over more sales.

(b)   (i)   The information prepared shows that, while there is a fairly respectable net margin of 8.2%, the business overall will make a loss because of the high Head Office and Warehousing costs – particularly Warehousing.

As the information prepared is based on the short term – one year ahead only – it is most useful as a means of drawing attention to areas of immediate cost or revenue concern, rather than as a basis for making strategic decisions. For instance, the knee-jerk' reaction would be to discontinue S & P's own shops as they generate a loss, and perhaps transfer the business to the department stores and the mail order side. This could be a disaster for the following reasons:

(1)   The information that we have used is based on an absorption system (ABC) which necessarily makes generalisations. It could be that only one or two of the shops are actually causing problems, and that their removal from the portfolio would go a lot of the way to solving the overall problem of poor profitability.

(2)   It could be that the presence of the shops in the marketplace has a substantial 'PR' effect and that the company's complete withdrawal from this method of distribution would remove the opportunity that shoppers take to browse among the goods, even if they later take advantage of the opportunity to actually shop by mail order. This may be compensated for by the department stores, but the matter needs careful investigation.

Another possible conclusion would be to expand the telephone mail order side. Again, more investigation is needed on this – in particular, will telephone sales gradually decline in the light of increased internet sales? If this is a possibility then the company does not want to take on high fixed and semi-fixed costs to expand this mature business.

For both these possible strategic moves the company must not only look at costs and revenues but at the overall consumer market and at the activities of competitors.

However, the analysis is useful when it comes to looking at the level of costs in particular operations. For instance, the warehousing costs and the establishment costs of the shops are very high and cost reduction might be a possibility here.

Finally, it may be possible to apportion the head office and warehousing costs to the business units. This would help when it came to any decisions about discontinuing any operations. If some methods make more use of the personnel of warehousing functions, for example, then removal of those operations would mean that these high costs would have to be spread out.

(ii) Information on the following matters would aid more informed judgement and more strategic decision-making:

- the overall economic climate and the state of the consumer market in particular

- the activities of direct competitors and the possibility of new entrants into the market

- fashion and consumer tastes

- exchange rates as some goods are imported, and the possibilities of price rises if some of the source markets are experiencing economic problems such as inflation

- the perception of the brand in consumer eyes, and in particular whether S & P's own shops help to promote that brand

- the future prospects for internet selling.

Some of this information may be available from an analysis of past data already held by the company.

In addition, a more detailed analysis of each shop's performance would have to be undertaken to ascertain whether some are actually performing quite well but are affected by the poor performance of the others.

106 RS COMPANY

(a)

	Baked beans	Ice cream	White wine
	$	$	$
Selling price per item	0.32	1.60	3.45
Bought-in price	(0.24)	(0.95)	(2.85)
Gross margin	0.08	0.65	0.60
Warehouse costs:			
Labour and other costs (W1)	(0.013)	(0.130)	(0.222)
Refrigeration costs (W2)	–	(0.148)	–
Supermarket costs:			
Labour and other costs (W3)	(0.015)	(0.153)	(0.131)
Refrigeration costs (W4)	–	(0.333)	–
Transport costs:			
Standard vehicles (W5)	(0.019)	–	(0.083)
Refrigerated vehicles (W6)	–	(0.127)	–
Direct product profit per item	0.033	(0.241)	0.164

Workings:

(W1) Total labour and other costs = 220 + 340 = $560,000

Volume of goods sold per week = 20,000m^3

$\therefore$ Cost = $560,000 ÷20,000 = $28 per m^{3}per week

Baked beans: $28 ÷ 28 ÷ 80 = $0.013 per unit

Ice cream: $28 ÷ 24 ÷ 18 × 2 weeks = $0.130 per unit

White wine: $28 ÷ 42 ÷ 12 × 4 weeks = $0.222 per unit

(W2) Total warehouse refrigeration cost = $160,000

Volume of refrigerated goods sold per week = 5,000m3

$\therefore$ Cost = $160,000 ÷ 5,000 = $32 per m^3 per week

Ice cream: $32 ÷ 24 ÷ 18 × 2 weeks = $0.148 per unit

(W3) Total labour and other costs = 16 + 28 = $44,000

Volume of goods sold per supermarket per week = 20,000 ÷ 15 = 1,333 m^3

$\therefore$ Cost = $44,000 ÷ 1,333 = $33 per m^3 per week

Baked beans: $33 ÷ 28 ÷ 80 = $0.015 per unit

Ice cream: $33 ÷ 24 ÷ 18 × 2 weeks = $0.153 per unit

White wine: $33 ÷ 42 ÷ 12 × 2 weeks = $0.131 per unit

(W4) Total supermarket refrigeration cost = $24,000

Volume of refrigerated goods sold per supermarket per week
= 5,000 ÷ 15 = 333 m^3

$\therefore$ Cost = $24,000 ÷ 333 = $72 per m^3 per week

Ice cream: $72 ÷ 24 ÷ 18 × 2 weeks = $0.333 per unit

(W5) Standard vehicle cost per m^3 = $3,750 ÷90 = $41.67 per week

Baked beans: $41.67 ÷ 28 ÷ 80 = $0.019 per unit

White wine: $41.67 ÷ 42 ÷ 12 = $0.083 per unit

(W6) Refrigerated vehicle cost per m^3 = $4,950 ÷90 = $55 per week

Ice cream: $55 ÷ 42 ÷ 18 = $0.127 per unit

(b)   The company's current method would report the profitability of the three items as follows:

	Baked beans	Ice cream	White wine
Selling price per item	$0.32	$1.60	$3.45
Bought-in price	$0.24	$0.95	$2.85
Gross margin	$0.08	$0.65	$0.60
Gross margin %	25%	40.63%	17.39%
Ranking	2	1	3

Ice cream appears to be the most profitable product, followed by baked beans and then white wine.

A direct product profitability method as in part (a) would report results as follows:

	Baked beans	Ice cream	White wine
Selling price per item	$0.32	$1.60	$3.45
Direct profit per item	$0.033	($0.241)	$0.164
Direct profit %	10.31%	(15.06%)	4.75%
Ranking	1	3	2

Baked beans are now reported as being the most profitable product, followed by white wine, with ice cream making a loss.

The direct product profitability (DPP) method aims to report a more accurate profitability since all direct costs are charged to the product ranges on as fair a basis as possible.

In the given situation, the differences in the methods have arisen due to:

(i) the refrigeration costs being charged to the ice cream items in the DPP method, while they are treated as a fixed cost in the current method and not charged against any product items

(ii) the periods of time that items are held in inventory in both the warehouses and the supermarkets.

Profitability could be improved by reducing the inventory holding periods. For example, if inventory of ice cream could be held on average for just one week at both warehouse and supermarket, then refrigeration costs would be halved to save $\frac{0.148+0.333}{2}$ = $0.24 per item, and the loss per item of ice cream would be eliminated.

Profitability could also be improved by obvious methods such as increasing the selling price and reducing the bought-in cost paid.

(c) Traditional overhead absorption totals up all overheads (including head office costs and administration) and then seeks to absorb these into the product cost on the basis of an overhead absorption rate. This rate will use a basis of absorption such as direct labour hours worked which results in an arbitrary absorption of head office costs, etc, since these are not incurred on the basis of hours worked.

The direct product profit method only considers the costs (both fixed and variable) that are directly attributed to the products, so avoids the arbitrary apportionment of the traditional method.

In the traditional method, costs are allocated to cost centres (typically the departments of the business) for which absorption rates are devised. The DPP method gathers costs into pools classified by activities, in a similar way to activity-based costing (ABC). Cost control is therefore the responsibility of departmental managers in the traditional method, while DPP takes the better approach of controlling costs by examining the activities that give rise to costs.

107 X COMPANY

(a)

	Original budget			JIT
	$000	$000		$000
Set ups	42,660			
$13,000 × 3,500	45,500	88,160	−30%	61,712
Materials handling	52,890			
$4,000 × 14,600	58,400	111,290	−30%	77,903
Inspection	59,880			
$18,000 × 3,500	63,000	122,880	−30%	86,016
Machining	144,540			
$40 × 4,560,000	182,400	326,940	−15%	277,899
Distribution and warehousing	42,900			
$3,000 × 14,600	43,800	86,700		–
		735,970		503,530
Direct material				
($2,520 × 75,000) + ($2,924 × 75,000) + ($3,960 × 75,000)				
[189,000 + 219,300 + 297,000]	705,300			705,300
Direct labour				
($1,120 × 75,000) + ($1,292 × 75,000) + ($1,980 × 75,000)				
[84,000 + 96,900 + 148,500]	329,400	1,034,700		395,280
Total costs		1,770,670		1,604,110
Total saving ($000)			$166,560	

(b)   **Variable cost per car**

Car		C1		C2		C3
		$		$		$
Set up						
$13,000 \times 0.7 = \$9,100$		121		121	$\times \dfrac{1,500}{75,000}$	182
Materials handling						
$4,000 \times 0.7 = \$2,800$	$\times \dfrac{4}{75}$	149	$\times \dfrac{5}{75}$	187	$\times \dfrac{5.6}{75}$	209
Inspection						
$18,000 \times 0.7 = \$12,600$	$\times \dfrac{1}{75}$	168	$\times \dfrac{1}{75}$	168	$\times \dfrac{1.5}{75}$	252
Machining						
$40 \times 0.85 = \$34$	$\times \dfrac{1,080}{75}$	490		816	$\times \dfrac{1,680}{75}$	762
Variable OH		928		1,292		1,405
Material		2,520		2,924		3,960
Labour		1,344		1,550		2,376
Variable cost per car		4,792		5,766		7,741

It is now possible to determine the optimum demand level:

Car: C1

Price	Demand 000s	Variable Cost	Contribution per car	Total contribution $000
$5,000	75	$4,792	$208	15,600
$5,750	65	$4,792	$958	62,270
$6,000	50	$4,792	$1,208	60,400
$6,500	35	$4,792	$1,708	59,780

∴ To maximise contribution from C1 sell 65,000 cars at $5,750.

Car: C2

Price	Demand 000s	Variable Cost	Contribution per car	Total contribution $000
$5,750	75	$5,766	(16)	(1,200)
$6,250	60	$5,766	484	29,040
$6,500	45	$5,766	734	33,030
$7,500	35	$5,766	1,734	60,690

∴ Sell 35,000 C2 cars at $7,500

Car: C3

Price	Demand 000s	Variable Cost	Contribution per car	Total contribution $000
$6,500	75	$7,741	(1,241)	(93,075)
$6,750	60	$7,741	(991)	(59,460)
$7,750	45	$7,741	9	405
$8,000	30	$7,741	259	7,770

∴ To maximise contribution sell 30,000 C3 cars at $8,000.

(c) **Optimum production plan**

	C1 $000	C2 $000	C3 $000
Contribution	62,270	60,690	7,770
Attributable fixed costs			
4% of 231,660 (W1)	9,266		
5% of 231,660		11,583	
8% of 231,660			18,533
Decision	Continue	Continue	Do not continue

(W1) **Total fixed costs with JIT**

		$000
42,660	× 0.70	29,862
52,890	× 0.70	37,023
59,880	× 0.70	41,916
144,540	× 0.85	122,859
		231,660

(d) **To:**　　Management of X Company

From:　Management Accountant

Date:　21 November 2002

Subject:　Successful implementation of JIT

In order for any company to be able to successfully implement a Just-In-Time system several conditions must be met.

Supplier relationships

JIT systems require a huge reduction in inventory levels. In order to facilitate this, inventory order sizes must be small. Hence suppliers must be capable of AND willing to deliver small quantities on a regular basis. X Company will need to have a good relationship with its accredited suppliers.

JIT systems aim to eliminate raw material inventory. In order to do this suppliers must be capable of achieving all aspects of quality – delivering the correct quantity to the correct location at the correct time. Ideally suppliers should also deliver defect-free items.

Quality issues

For JIT to be effective achieving the highest possible levels of quality is essential. Production scheduling becomes demand based and in order to meet customers' requirements quality problems need to be eliminated. It is often necessary to implement a quality programme such as Total Quality Management. The aim is to prevent the problems in the first place.

Quality should be considered from several angles:

- from suppliers – as mentioned above

- in machinery – equipment should be well maintained to avoid breakdown and the manufacture of sub-standard output

- in staff – all staff should be appropriately trained and skilled to carry out the task required of them.

Education and training

JIT will only be successful if our employees are willing to make it so. All levels of staff throughout the organisation should be appropriately trained and educated as to the objectives of the new system and the benefits that it will bring to X Company.

Work scheduling

Cellular manufacturing or group technology brings great benefits for JIT companies. This is where whole products are made within each manufacturing cell. X Company appears to have this system already as each car has its own production line.

Information systems

The new management systems that will be put in place will require new information systems. There will be major changes in the communication line with suppliers and the work scheduling system may need redeveloping in order to cope with the new pull-system.

Financing

Appropriate funds must be available to finance the development and implementation of JIT. Without sufficient funding JIT will fail.

Should you require any further advice, then please do not hesitate to contact me.

Signed: *Management Accountant*

108 GAIN SHARING (MAY 07)

Key answer tips

In questions such as this one it is important to take care and go through the calculations systematically to ensure that you make all necessary changes to convert the figures to actual cash flows – it is easy to miss one.

(a) Depreciation must be deducted from production costs since it is not a cash flow. Annual depreciation on $150,000 (initial investment less residual value) over 3 years is $50,000. This depreciation charge also needs to be added to the profit figure before calculating the tax due.

The analysis also needs to reflect the cash flows due to changes in receivables and payables and the timing of taxation payments.

Year	0	1	2	3	4
	$	$	$	$	$
Investment	(200,000)			50,000	
Sales		230,000	350,000	270,000	
Less closing receivables		(20,000)	(30,000)	(25,000)	
Add opening receivables		0	20,000	30,000	25,000
		210,000	340,000	275,000	25,000
Production costs:					
Materials		(54,000)	(102,000)	(66,000)	
Labour		(60,000)	(80,000)	(70,000)	
Other		(30,000)	(40,000)	(30,000)	
Less closing payables		6,000	9,000	8,000	
Add opening payables		0	(6,000)	(9,000)	(8,000)
		(138,000)	(219,000)	(167,000)	(8,000)
Pre-tax net cash flow	(200,000)	72,000	121,000	108,000	17,000
Taxation at 30%		(25,800)	(38,400)	(31,200)	
Less tax payable following year		12,900	19,200	15,600	
Add tax b/f		0	12,900	19,200	15,600
		(12,900)	(32,100)	(34,800)	(15,600)
Post-tax net cash flow	(200,000)	59,100	88,900	123,200	1,400
Discount factor	1.000	0.943	0.890	0.840	0.792
PV	(200,000)	55,731	79,121	103,488	1,109

NPV = $39,449

(b) If inflation became more significant it would be necessary to include all the cash flows in real money terms, with each item inflated by an inflation rate reflecting the inflation expected for that particular cost or revenue. It is unlikely that all elements will be subject to the same level of inflation.

Where cash flows relate to costs or sales from previous years it is important to ensure that they are inflated by the rate relating to the year in which the costs or sales arose.

The discount rate used needs to be a money rate which takes account of the effect of inflation. The relationship between the real rate (excluding the effect of inflation) and the money rate is given by:

$$(1 + r) = \frac{(1 + m)}{(1 + i)}$$

where r, m and i are the real, money and inflation rates, respectively.

(c)   If the resources are limited and only $400,000 is available for investment, the mix of projects chosen should be that which maximises the NPV.

As all projects are non-divisible there are insufficient funds to carry out the investment in the new product in combination with project W. Possible combinations are:

	Total initial investment	Total NPV
W & Y	$400,000	$102,000
New product and Y	$300,000	$66,449

Investments W & Y should be undertaken as this maximises NPV.

(d)   (i)   A gain-sharing arrangement is a form of contract in which the two parties share the risks and returns of a project. For example, vendors may guarantee customers will achieve a certain amount of cost savings or top-line improvement. If targets are not met, the vendor commits to making up the difference in cash. If targets are exceeded, the vendor may also receive a pre-specified percentage of the gains.

These agreements are attractive to vendors because they can provide insulation from the cut-throat price competition that characterises today's technology marketplace. Vendors that guarantee cost savings and top-line improvement can command a price premium in the marketplace. Such risk-sharing agreements are attractive to customers because they reduce the business risk and cost associated with implementing new technologies, systems, and services.

In a case such as this example where X has insufficient funds, the company could join with another company in a gain-sharing arrangement where the second company provides investment capital in return for a share in the profits arising.

(ii)   There are a number of possible reasons why X might not want to enter into such an arrangement:

- Such agreements can be difficult to put into practice and require management expertise which X may not have.

- Mutual trust and co-operation is essential between the two parties – this may be difficult if the two companies are competitors.

- Sharing of information is also required – again X may be unwilling to do this if the second company is a competitor.

- Such an arrangement involves sharing the management of the project as well as the risk and profit and X may not want to relinquish total control.

109 AVX (MAY 06)

Key answer tips

The learning curve model states that, as the number of units made doubles, the cumulative average time per unit falls by a constant percentage. The first task is therefore to find the actual cumulative average time per batch. As output doubles on a monthly basis, the learning rate can be found by calculating the percentage reduction in time for each month.

(a) (i)

Month	Batches		Standard hours		Actual hours	
	This month	To date	This month	Variance in hours	This month	To date
Nov	1	1	50	0	50	50
Dec	1	2	50	17	33	83
Jan	2	4	100	45.22	54.78	137.78
Feb	4	8	200	108.93	91.07	228.85
Mar	8	16	400	171.15	228.85	457.70
Apr	16	32	800	342.3	457.70	915.40

Month	Average actual hours per batch (year to date)	Comment
Nov	50	
Dec	41.5	83% of November average
Jan	34.445	83% of December average
Feb	28.61	83% of January average
Mar	28.61	100% of February average
Apr	28.61	100% of March average

(ii) The learning period ends at the end of February; the rate of learning is 83%. This means that from March onwards the time taken per batch is constant or steady state and therefore decisions involving costs such as resource allocation and pricing should be based on this constant labour time per batch.

(b)

Tutorial note

The profit-maximising price and quantity could be calculated using a tabular approach but it is much quicker to equate MC and MR and solve the equation for quantity. The profit-maximising quantity can then be input into the original demand equation to find the profit selling price.

The marginal cost and selling price per batch are as follows:

Marginal cost = $672.72

Demand at price of $1,200 = 16 batches and demand increases by 1 unit for every $20 reduction in selling price

Therefore, Price = $1,520 – 20q

Marginal revenue = $1,520 – 40q

Equating marginal cost and marginal revenue:

672.72 = 1,520 – 40q

40q = 847.28

q = 21.182

Price = $1,520 – (20 × 21.182) = $1,096.36

(c)　(i)　A standard cost is a predetermined unit cost of a product and is used for planning and control. It usually represents attainable costs based on known production methods and prices.

A target cost is a planned cost which is determined by identifying a market price then deducting a target profit. Target costing is a strategic tool which focuses on cost reduction prior to production of a product by identifying and attempting to eliminate a cost gap.

The main differences are that standard costing is used for short-term control and does not emphasise continual improvement whereas target costing is driven by external market price and may not be attainable in the short term.

(ii)　Now that the product has been in the market place for six months it is no longer unique. AVX plc is facing increasing competition, hence its difficulty in selling the circuit boards for $1,200 per batch. AVX plc may wish to adjust prices to reach sectors of the market which have previously been unwilling to pay the high price. It will also have to reduce the price to the market price to remain competitive.

110　RETAIL OUTLET (NOV 07)

(a)　Assuming that overheads will be incurred throughout the redecoration even if floor space is not used, the overhead cost will not be relevant to the decision.

The two options will be assessed by considering the lost contribution from closure of retail space.

Option 1

No sales for first 4 week period　　Weeks 5 – 8: 30% of sales lost

Weeks 9 – 12: 20% of sales lost　　Weeks 13 – 16: 10% of sales lost

10% reduction in price of basic and canned foods for 12 weeks. Assuming that all four freezers are kept running and stocked throughout the period:

Change in contribution per week due to lower sales ($)	Weeks 1 – 4 100% of budgeted contribution	Weeks 5 – 8 30% of budgeted contribution	Weeks 9 – 12 20% of budgeted contribution	Weeks 13 – 16 10% of budgeted contribution
Basic foods	(200)	(60)	(40)	(20)
Newspapers	(300)	(90)	(60)	(30)
Frozen foods	(950)	(285)	(190)	(95)
Canned foods	(1,200)	(360)	(240)	(120)
Further change in contribution due to price reduction ($)	10% of sales price on actual sales			
Basic foods		(56)	(64)	(72)
Canned foods		(168)	(192)	(216)
Power costs not incurred ($)	100			
Loss per week ($)	(2,550)	(1,019)	(786)	(553)

Total loss over 16 week period = 4 × 2,550 + 4 × 1,019 + 4 × 786 + 4 × 553

= $19,632

Cost of redecoration = $2,500

Total cost = $22,132

Option 2

Total floor area = 400 m^2

Option 2 used 40% of floor area = 160 m^2

Basic foods and newspapers and magazines use 100 m^2. Remaining 60 m^2 to be split between frozen and canned foods based on profitability per unit of area.

Comparing contribution per m^2 of normal space:

Frozen foods: contribution per m^2 = 950/100 = $9.5 per m^2

Canned foods: contribution per m^2 = 1,200/200 = $6.0 per m^2

As frozen food space must be allocated in complete freezer units of 25 m^2, contribution will be maximised by allocating as much space as possible to frozen foods, i.e. 50 m^2 frozen foods, 10 m^2 canned foods.

40% floor space for first 3 week period. No change in sales of basic foods and newspapers.

0.5 week closure

40% floor space for next 3 week period. No change in sales of basic foods and newspapers.

Assuming no changes to prices in this period:

	6 weeks at 40%	Closure period (0.5 weeks)
Change in contribution per week due to lower sales ($)		
Basic foods	0	(200)
Newspapers	0	(300)
Frozen foods (50% of budget)	(475)	(950)
Canned foods (95% of budget)	(1,140)	(1,200)
Power costs not incurred ($)	(50)	(100)
Loss per week ($)	(1,565)	(2,550)

Total loss over period = $(6 × 1,565 + 0.5 × 2,550) = $10,665

Cost of redecoration and moving products = $(3,500 + 1,000) = $4,500

Total cost of option 2 = $15,165

Losses will be minimised by option 2 with two freezer units running.

(b) Activity-based costing (ABC) has its origins in the 1950s, when some US manufacturing firms made efforts to allocate their selling and distribution overheads between products in a more 'accurate' and meaningful way. Over time, as manufacturing methods changed, growing attention was given to overhead costs, and the problem of how overhead costs should be allocated between products or services, in order to obtain a more reliable assessment of the profitability of different products or services. It was recognised that traditional absorption costing did not necessarily provide a reliable analysis of product costs and profitability. ABC was later adopted by a range of non-manufacturing organisations including retail businesses.

ABC attempts to charge overhead costs more accurately to the products or services that, directly or indirectly, consume resources and give rise to the expenditures. It does this by charging overhead costs in a way that reflects the activities that influence those costs:

The collection of overhead costs is done in the same way as with traditional overhead costing.

The next step is to allocate overhead costs to cost pools or activity pools. There is a cost pool for each activity that consumes significant amounts of resources. Costs in each cost pool might arise in a number of different departments. (Costs are not allocated or apportioned to production and service departments, so in this respect ABC differs significantly from traditional absorption costing.)

Examples of resource-consuming activities might be deliveries of goods from warehouses to stores and checking purchases through tills, or for an internet-based retailer, processing customer orders. The selection of cost pools will vary according to the exact nature of the retailer's operations and management's judgement.

For each activity pool, there should be a cost driver. A cost driver is an item or an activity that results in the consumption of resources, and so results in costs being incurred. For the costs in the cost pool, overheads are then allocated to product costs on the basis of a recovery rate per unit of cost driver.

Examples of activity pools and cost drivers in the retail industry could be:

Activity pool	Cost driver
Checkouts	Number of customers
Deliveries to stores	Number of deliveries
Order processing (for mail order)	Number of orders

There is no rule governing the identification of cost pools and drivers – this will depend on the nature of the business. For example, in the case of checkout costs, a store may have separate checkouts for baskets and trolleys.

The time taken to check out a basket may be much shorter than the time taken for a trolley, and therefore the cost per customer will also be less. The company may decide to separate the costs of the two different types of till into to cost pools, with the respective numbers of customers passing through checkouts as the cost driver.

Having established the total costs for an activity pool, and having chosen the cost driver for that pool, a cost per unit of cost driver is then calculated. This is an overhead recovery rate that will be used to allocate overhead costs to products or services, calculated as:

$$\frac{\text{Budgeted costs for the cost pool}}{\text{Budgeted activity level (units of cost driver)}}$$

For each activity pool, costs are allocated to products and services, on the basis of:

Units of cost driver used up × Cost per unit of cost driver.

ABC is a form of absorption costing, and so has similarities with traditional absorption costing. However, the cost driver represents the factor that has the greatest influence on the behaviour of costs in the activity pool, and the consumption of resources. For example, if 50% of orders received and processed are for one particular product and there is a cost pool for order handling costs, the product should attract 50% of the total costs of order handling.

ABC can be used to identify activities and costs that are not contributing to the value of the products an organisation makes or the services it provides. The following questions can be asked:

• What is the purpose of this activity?

• Who benefits from the activity, and how?

• Why are so many people needed?

• What might reduce the number of staff needed?

• Why is overtime needed?

ABC can also be used as the basis for one-off exercises to identify activities that do not add value to products or services, or to identify ways in which activities might be re-organised. One-off investigations using ABC analysis are referred to as 'activity-based management'.

There are a number of disadvantages to ABC:

Setting up and operating an ABC system is costly, as the activities in each cost pool have to be monitored and measured. The system should also be reviewed periodically, to check that the selection of activity pools and cost drivers is still appropriate.

There can be a danger of taking the analysis of activities and cost pools to excessive detail. This would add to the complexity of the system, and the cost of operating it. To prevent an ABC system from becoming too complex and expensive, the number of cost pools and cost drivers should be kept to a small and manageable number.

There is a risk that ABC costs will be seen as 100% accurate economic costs of activities. This is not the case. ABC is a form of absorption costing, and although it attempts to trace overhead costs to products and services more accurately, there will inevitably be some element of shared cost apportionment. It is impossible to trace all costs objectively to specific products or services.

Activity based costing can be used as a basis for other areas of financial management: Activity based management is a 'system of management which uses activity based cost information for a variety of purposes including cost reduction, cost modelling and customer profitability analysis'. (CIMA Official Terminology, 2000) The activity-based approach brings costs out into the open and helps management see what they get for the commitment of resources.

Activity-based budgeting is a method of budgeting based on an activity framework and utilising cost-driven data in the budget setting and variance feedback process.

BUDGETING AND MANAGEMENT CONTROL

111 AHW

Key answer tips

Part (a) involves a lot of number crunching, and a clear layout should help you here in saving time and avoiding silly mistakes. Parts (b) to (d) are fairly straightforward knowledge-type questions, though you should try to apply your knowledge to AHW to gain extra marks.

(a)   First we need to calculate the budgeted cost driver rates:

Budgeted total activities

Activity	Budgeted cost $	Product A	Product B	Product C	Product D	Product E	Total	Rate $
W	160,000	80	150	30	120	25	405	395
X	130,000	60	60	75	40	100	335	388
Y	80,000	60	90	30	160	50	390	205
Z	200,000	80	180	120	80	75	535	374

Now we calculate the actual number activities and the flexible budget figures:

Actual total activities

Activity	Product A	Product B	Product C	Product D	Product E	Total	Flexible budget (rate × actual activities) $000
W	72	165	32	105	28	402	159
X	54	66	80	35	112	347	135
Y	54	99	32	140	56	381	78
Z	72	198	128	70	84	552	206

Budgetary control statement for October 20X2

Activity	Original budget	Flexible budget	Actual	Variance (actual from flexible)
	$000	$000	$000	$000
W	160	159	158	1 F
X	130	135	139	4 A
Y	80	78	73	5 F
Z	200	206	206	0
Total	570	578	576	2 F

(b) The main reasons why it may be preferable for managers NOT to be involved in the setting of budgets are as follows:

- Budget setting is often a very time-consuming task and it may be that operational managers do not have the time available to make a significant contribution to the budget-setting process.

- Budget setting in complex environments such as that of AHW is a skilled task and it may be that operational managers do not have the necessary skills to take part, and that time is not available to provide them with those skills.

- Budget setting is often a very political process with operational managers trying to lay off responsibility for 'difficult' areas onto their colleagues or superiors. Centralised budgeting prevents this, and the resultant bad feeling, from happening.

- There is always a very strong temptation for operational managers to set as 'soft' a budget as possible, so they cannot fail to meet it and so will be assessed positively by senior managers. Soft budgets means that there is a degree of slack in there, so managers are not motivated to achieve their best possible performance, but rather one that is simply adequate.

(c) (i) A fixed budget is one that is typically set at the beginning of the budget period, based on a particular level of activity. A flexible budget, on the other hand, takes account of the fact that the actual level of activity achieved affects the level of costs, and adjusts the fixed budget costs accordingly. Thus the rates and efficiency targets may be maintained, but the total figures are adjusted for the actual level of activity achieved.

Flexible budgets are particularly useful for monitoring the costs which are directly affected by changes in activity levels. Fixed budgets, however, are better placed to help monitor costs which are unaffected by the level of activity, i.e. non-production costs. Hence in AHW plc, a flexible budget is useful for activities W to Z, while a fixed budget will help to control discretionary non-production costs such as marketing costs.

(ii) As AHW is a manufacturer serving the retail trade, it will probably be able at the beginning of a period to set a fixed amount of money to be spent on advertising. Even if actual activity levels fluctuate over the period, this fixed budget should represent the maximum expected expenditure. In some organisations it would be possible to talk about 'having funds left in the budget' to allocate to a particular campaign. Once these funds are spent, there will be no more available.

Another example of a cost that falls into this category is training. Usually the training budget is set at the beginning of the period and it is then up to the training managers to allocate the funds as they see fit.

112 PRODUCTS R, S AND T

(a) A cost driver is any factor that causes a change in the cost of an activity, so the most important factor when selecting a cost driver is to identify a causal relationship between the cost driver and the costs. Such a relationship may arise because of some physical relationship or because of the logic of the situation.

For example, quality inspection costs are caused by the action of carrying out an inspection to ensure quality standards are being achieved, so the appropriate cost driver would be the number of inspections carried out. Some activities may have multiple cost drivers associated with them; in such a situation it is best if the costs can be analysed into separate cost pools for each of which a single driver can be identified.

(b) (i) The budgeted costs are:

Activity	Total	Appropriate cost driver
	$000	
Power	1,250	Power (kj) per batch
Stores	1,850	Purchase orders per batch
Maintenance	2,100	Machine hours per batch
Machinery cleaning	800	Machine set-ups per batch
Indirect labour	1,460	Standard labour hours per batch

For each activity we must calculate a cost driver rate.

Power

Total budgeted power $= (1.4 \times 36) + (1.7 \times 10) + (0.8 \times 40)$

$= 99.4$ kj

$\therefore$ Cost driver rate $= \dfrac{\$1.25m}{99.4}$ $= \$12,575$ per kj

Stores

Total budgeted purchase orders = $(5 \times 36) + (3 \times 10) + (7 \times 40)$

= 490 orders

$\therefore$ Cost driver rate = $\dfrac{\$1.85m}{490}$ = $3,776 per order

Maintenance

Total budgeted machine hours = $(10 \times 36) + (7.5 \times 10) + (12.5 \times 40)$

= 935 hours

$\therefore$ Cost driver rate = $\dfrac{\$2.1m}{935}$ = $2,246 per machine hour

Machinery cleaning

Total budgeted machine set-ups = $(3 \times 36) + (2 \times 10) + (5 \times 40)$

= 328 set-ups

$\therefore$ Cost driver rate = $\dfrac{\$0.8m}{328}$ = $2,439 per set-up

(ii)   The actual output is 30 batches of R, 12 batches of S and 40 batches of T.

$\therefore$ Actual output uses $(1.4 \times 30) + (1.7 \times 12) + (0.8 \times 40)$

= 94.4 kj of power

and $(5 \times 30) + (3 \times 12) + (7 \times 40)$

= 466 purchase orders

and $(10 \times 30) + (7.5 \times 12) + (12.5 \times 40)$

= 890 machine hours

and $(3 \times 30) + (2 \times 12) + (5 \times 40)$

= 314 machine set-ups

The production overhead budgetary control report can therefore be redrafted using an activity based approach as follows:

Production overhead budgetary control report – April

	Original budget $000		Flexed budget $000	Actual $000	Variances $000
Power	1,250	($12,575 × 94.4)	1,187	1,295	108 (A)
Stores	1,850	($3,776 × 466)	1,760	1,915	155 (A)
Maintenance	2,100	($2,246 × 890)	1,999	2,100	101 (A)
Machinery cleaning	800	($2,439 × 314)	766	870	104 (A)
Indirect labour	1,460	($1,460 × $\dfrac{1,710}{1,800}$)	1,387	1,510	123 (A)
	7,460		7,099	7,690	591 (A)

(c) An organisation such as X plc should benefit from an activity based approach to budgetary control since it offers a conceptually valid method of flexing a budget. The method recognises that different costs have different causes, rather than assuming that all costs can be absorbed on the basis of labour hours (the more traditional approach). The ABB approach should therefore produce more accurate budgeted figures against which actual costs can be compared, to yield meaningful variances.

Looking at the figures above, we can see that the ABB variances for power, stores and maintenance are significantly different to what was reported originally, although all the reported variances remain adverse. These more accurate ABB variances should enable management to concentrate their attention on the areas of the business where costs should be reduced – a message that might be lost using the less accurate variances produced using the traditional approach.

113 KEY METRICS

Key answer tips

There are sometimes different opinions as to how some of these metrics are calculated. The safest thing would be to show your formulae as well as clear workings, so that the marker can see how you have derived your results.

(a) (i) Return on capital employed $= \dfrac{\text{Profit}}{\text{Net assets}} \times 100\%$

$$= \dfrac{295}{(1{,}280 + 800 - 280 - 50)} \times 100\%$$

$$= 16.9\%$$

This is lower than the target and would not be acceptable.

(ii) Profit/sales ratio $= \dfrac{\text{Profit}}{\text{Revenue}} \times 100\%$

$$= \dfrac{295}{4{,}885} \times 100\%$$

$$= 6.0\%$$

This is exactly as required, therefore the profitability of sales is acceptable.

(iii) Net asset turnover $= \dfrac{\text{Revenue}}{\text{Net assets}}$

$$= \dfrac{4{,}885}{(1{,}280 + 800 - 280 - 50)}$$

$$= 2.8 \text{ times}$$

This is lower than the target and would not be acceptable.

(iv)   Non-current asset turnover $\quad = \dfrac{\text{Revenue}}{\text{Non-current assets}}$

$$= \dfrac{4,885}{1,280}$$

$$= 3.8 \text{ times}$$

This is lower than the target and would not be acceptable.

(v)   Current ratio $\qquad\qquad = \dfrac{\text{Current assets}}{\text{Current liabilities}}$

$$= \dfrac{800}{(280+50)}$$

$$= 2.4 \text{ times}$$

This is higher than the target. Although this is acceptable from a point of view of liquidity, it may indicate a wasteful level of current assets which requires further investigation.

(vi)   Quick ratio $\qquad\qquad = \dfrac{\text{Current assets excluding inventory}}{\text{Current liabilities}}$

$$= \dfrac{465}{330}$$

$$= 1.4 \text{ times}$$

This is exactly equal to the target and so would be acceptable.

(b)   The key metrics which are not acceptable can be summarised as follows.

Key metric	Target	Master budget result
Return on capital employed	19.0%	16.9%
Net asset turnover	3.2 times	2.8 times
Non-current asset turnover	4.5 times	3.8 times
Current ratio	2.1 times	2.4 times

The return on capital employed should be higher. The profitability of sales is acceptable therefore an improvement is needed in the net asset turnover, as indicated above. These two ratios could both be increased by generating higher sales for a given level of net assets, or by reducing the level of net assets without affecting sales.

Opportunities for increasing sales without the need for further investment in net assets should be investigated.

The non-current asset turnover ratio indicates again that insufficient sales are being generated compared to the investment in the assets. An increase in sales would help again here and in addition the utilisation of every group of non-current assets should be investigated to see whether the non-current asset base can be reduced or alternatively used more effectively.

Although the current ratio is higher than target it may indicate a wasteful level of investment in current assets compared with the commitment to current liabilities. When the inventory is removed from the calculation the quick ratio reveals an acceptable level of current assets relative to current liabilities. This suggests that inventory levels are unnecessarily high.

If inventory levels can be reduced this would also lead to an improvement in the net asset turnover and the return on capital employed.

(c) Critical success factors are those areas of a business and its environment which are critical to the achievement of its goals and objectives. A company may, for example, express its main goal as being a world-class business in its chosen areas of operation. Management should identify critical success factors since failure in any one such factor may prevent or inhibit the advancement of the company and the achievement of its goals.

The balanced scorecard is one approach where managers identify critical success factors in four different aspects of performance – customer perspective, internal business perspective, innovation and learning perspective and the financial perspective.

The key metrics calculated in (a) are examples of financial measures. Critical success factors can be identified in the other areas and performance measures developed to monitor their progress.

114 M PLC (MAY 06) Walk in the footsteps of a top tutor

Key answer tips

A major theme throughout the scenario is that the Manager of the Assembly Department is new to the job but he does have many years' experience as a supervisor and will therefore have considerable knowledge about assembling furniture.

Step 1

The starting point for this answer is to think "What is wrong with the current control statement?"

The major problems are that it does not compare like with like (the budget is based on 6,400 hours but the actual results are for 7,140 hours), and that fixed and variable costs are not shown separately.

Step 2

It is therefore necessary to identify and separate the fixed and variable costs and then prepare a flexed budget (in a working).

Step 3

Variances should then be based on the flexed statement.

(a)   The current statement is against an original fixed budget which needs to be flexed to reflect the increased assembly hours.

	Original budget	Flexed budget	Actual	Variance	
Assembly labour hours	6,400	7,140	7,140		
Variable costs	$	$	$	$	
Assembly labour	49,920	55,692	56,177	485	Adv
Furniture packs	224,000	249,900	205,000	44,900	Fav
Other materials	23,040	25,704	24,100	1,604	Fav
Variable overheads (W1)	34,560	38,556	76,340(W2)	37,784	Adv
Total variable costs	331,520	369,852	361,617	8,235	Fav
Departmental fixed costs					
Manager	2,050	2,050	2,050	–	
Overheads (W1)	18,500	27,000	27,000	–	
Total departmental fixed costs	20,550	29,050	29,050	–	
Central costs	9,000	9,000	9,000	–	
	361,070	407,902	399,667	8,235	Fav

Note: The variable costs have been flexed in relation to the number of assembly hours worked.

Workings:

(W1) **Step 2:** Using the high low method at 10,000 and 7,500 units so that the impact of the stepped fixed cost does not distort the analysis.

	Units	$
	10,000	90,000
	7,500	76,500
Difference	2,500	13,500

Variable cost = $13,500/2,500 = $5.40 per unit

Fixed cost = 90,000 – (10,000 × 5.40) = 36,000. This is made up of a fixed cost of $9,000 for services from head office which are uncontrollable and should therefore be shown separately in the statement.

Overhead at 5,000 units = 5,000 × $5.40 + Fixed cost = $54,500

Fixed cost = $27,500 – $9,000 = $18,500

(W2) Actual overhead cost $112,340

Less fixed cost   36,000 ($27,000 controllable cost + $9,000 HQ cost)/76,340

(b)

Step 4

Ensure you provide evidence from the scenario to support your answer.

(i)   The revised format of the statement is more helpful to the management and managers of M plc for performance measurement because:

- it is flexed to the actual level of activity and therefore actual costs are measured against expected costs for the level of output achieved

- it separates controllable and uncontrollable items to facilitate responsibility accounting

- it separates variable and fixed costs so that managers are more aware of how a change in activity levels will impact on profit.

(ii)

Step 5

Think, "will costs vary with labour hours?" Is there any indication in the scenario that labour hours might not be the most appropriate base to use for flexing the budget?

The company has used labour hours to flex all variable costs but it is possible that furniture packs do not vary directly with labour hours as the furniture made varies considerably in size and complexity. There is a significant favourable variance for furniture packs and this may reflect more labour-intensive work (hence more labour hours) in producing more complex but less furniture. The company may consider identifying the activities that drive costs to allow for flexing to be more accurate.

(c)

Step 6

Avoid giving descriptive answers rather than discussing the pros and cons of a change and making a recommendation.

Benefits of participative budgeting for M plc potentially include:

- improved communication of aims and objectives which can lead to improved goal congruence

- managers can widen their experience and develop the skills necessary for more senior posts

- improved accuracy as managers will have better knowledge of operations

- improved motivation if targets are discussed and agreed.

The main disadvantages of a participative approach are:

- budgetary slack. Managers may include allowances for unforeseen events to make achievement of the budget easier

- managers may not be sufficiently skilled to participate in the budgetary process.

CONTROL AND PERFORMANCE MEASUREMENT OF RESPONSIBILITY CENTRES

115 SPORTS EQUIPMENT (MAY 09)

Key answer tips

Part (a) of this question should be straightforward and merely tests your understanding of the scenario and of how transfer pricing works. The crux of the question comes in part (b). It relies on an understanding that the TP for the receiving division and also the relationship between contribution and profit. You then have to find the transfer price that gives the result required in the requirement. Part (c) is much more straightforward and the key to success will be to relate the answer to the results found in part (b).

(a) Without the transfer the Wheels Division would make a profit of:

$($950-$650) \times 30{,}000 - $8m = $1m$

With the transfer the profit would increase to:

$$300 \times 35{,}000 - $9m = $1.5m$

The internal transfer would lead to an increase in cost for the Frames Division of:

$15{,}000 \times ($900 - $870) = $0.45m$

The net impact on profit for the group would be:

Wheels Division	Frames Division	Group
Increase of $0.5m	Reduction of $0.45m	Increase of $50,000

(b) (i) Let TP = transfer price required

Maximum capacity is 35,000 units so to supply the Frames Division with 15,000 units only 20,000 units can be sold externally. Fixed costs would rise to $9m. In order to maintain the current profit level of $1m and to cover the fixed costs of $9m, the total contribution would have to be $10m after the introduction of the new transfer price.

Contribution per unit on external sales = $950 - $650 = $300

If contribution remains the same when the transfer price is $900 then the variable cost per unit relating to internal transfers must be $900 - $300 = $600.

The new total contribution would be a combination of the contribution from new sales and the contribution from external sales:

Contribution from internal sales + contribution from external sales = $10m

$15{,}000 \times (TP - 600) + 20{,}000 \times 300	=	$10m
$15{,}000 \times (TP - 600)$	=	$4m
$TP - 600$	=	$4m/15,000
TP	=	266.67 + 600

So TP = $866.67

(ii) Return on assets consumed is calculated as profit divided by fixed costs. The revenue/transfer price (TP) from internal transfers is unknown, but the return must come out at 35%. Therefore the missing TP is calculated as follows:

$$\frac{15{,}000 \times (TP - 600) + 20{,}000 \times $300 - $9m}{$9m} \times 100 = 12.5\%$$

$15{,}000 \times (TP - 600) = (12.5\% \times $9m) - (20{,}000 \times $300) + $9m$	
$15{,}000 \times (TP - 600)$	= $4,125,000
$TP - 600$	= $4,125,000m/15,000
$TP - 600$	= $275

So **TP = $875**

(c)

REPORT

To: Managing Director   **From:**   Management Accountant

Date: 20 May 2010   **Subject:**   Transfer pricing

This report discusses issues raised by the directive and the introduction of performance measures.

(i)   **Existing problems**

Spare capacity

The Wheels Division has 5,000 units of spare capacity and should, in principle, be prepared to supply these at any price which exceeds incremental costs. For 5,000 units this would be $600 + $1m/5,000 = $800 per units. (Note that the variable cost of internal transfers is lower than that of external sales – see part (b).

This would give the Frames Division a profit of $70 per set, and the overall company profit would rise by $350,000 ($70 × 5,000 units).

The Frames Division would be prepared to accept any price under $870, the price at which the chips can be purchased from a local supplier. For the first 5,000 units there is a range of possible transfer prices which would be acceptable to both divisions of $800 to $870. This would result in sharing the $350,000 extra company profit between the divisions.

However, care should also be given to the performance measure that is chosen. Part b) shows that if a profit measure is used then the Wheels Division will want at least $866.67 per set. But if the return on assets measure is used the minimum acceptable price for the Wheels Division will be $875 – a figure that is above the highest acceptable price for the Frames Division. It would be impossible to set a transfer price that would be acceptable to both divisions. So, if this measure is used the divisions will either not transact or end up de-motivated.

The proposed transfer price by the Wheels Division is $900. This is outside the range and will incur a loss for the Frames Division of $450,000. Overall company profit will rise by only $50,000 – and only if the policy of buying wheels from the Wheels Division is imposed on the Frames Division.

Existing sales

The Frames Division requires 15,000 units however and the additional 10,000 units could only be supplied by reducing the supply to external customers. The minimum transfer price acceptable to the Wheels Division would be $900 as this would earn the same contribution per chip as external sales. At this price the Frames Division would be paying $30 per chip more than from the external market and so would not be motivated to buy internally.

It is good for the company overall for each market to deal externally rather than internally. Although the Frames Division is paying $70 more externally than the price at which the Wheels division can produce the sets, this would allow the Wheels Division to continue to make its own external sales which generate a contribution of $300 per set.

The calculations show that the Wheels Division would be happy with a lower transfer price, but only if this transfer price was applied to all units transferred (both those that had previously been sold externally and the spare capacity).

Other issues with the performance measures

It should also be noted that noted that the performance measures that have been proposed have other problems outside of the goal congruence reported above. For example, they focus solely on profit. This could lead to short-termism (such as from reductions in R&D), and it ignores the range of a managers responsibilities (as production companies the divisions are likely to have responsibility for assets as well as profits). The measures are also very inward looking so that there is no consideration of non-financial factors such as customer satisfaction and market share, for example.

Conclusion

The proposed transfer price of $900 per set is inappropriate and will not maximise company profits. An alternative transfer price should be introduced which encourages divisional managers to maximise the profits for the company overall. The performance measures should also be reconsidered in order to ensure goal-congruence, long-term thinking and better responsibility accounting.

(ii) **Potential solutions**

The problems could be resolved by allowing the Wheels Division to set the transfer price at full external selling price for the first 30,000 units. As the division faces excess demand, any price below market price would be unacceptable for the first 30,000 units.

The remaining 5,000 units could be transferred at a price at incremental cost of $000. This spare capacity has no opportunity cost – if the Frames Division does not use the capacity it will not be used at all.

This will mean that the profits of the Wheels Division are left unaffected, but for the 5,000 units spare capacity that the Wheels division has, the Frames Division can buy this at a cost of $800 rather than the external cost of $870. So the Frames Division should experience an increase in profit of ($870 – $800) $70/unit for these 5,000 units, meaning an overall increase in group profits of $350,000.

In terms of the performance measures it may simply be a case of extending them beyond financial measures – perhaps by using a balance scorecard approach.

116 KDS

(a) **Divisional administrator's proposal**

Effect on 20X5 ROCE

It will have been assumed in arriving at the 31/12/X5 net assets that the debt will have been paid. Reversing this assumption has the effect of increasing liabilities and has no effect on assets, as cash is excluded. Thus net assets will be reduced by $90,000 (to $4,310,000).

Whether the $2,000 late payment penalty is accounted for in 20X5 or 20X6 will depend to some extent on the company's accounting policy. The accruals concept would, however, lean towards it being accounted for in 20X5. Thus operating profits would be reduced by $2,000 (to $647,000).

The new ROCE would thus be $\dfrac{\$647,000}{\$4,310,000} \times 100 = 15.01\%$

Thus the target will have been achieved and bonuses paid. This is, of course, no indication of improved performance, but simply an arithmetical anomaly arising as a result of one side of the transaction being ignored in the calculation. In fact, the finance cost of the late payment is extremely high.

Longer term effects

There would be no quantifiable long-term effects, although relationships with the supplier may be adversely affected by the late payment.

The works manager's proposal

Effect on 20X5 ROCE

Assuming no depreciation charge in 20X5, net assets would be increased by the cost of the new assets, $320,000 (to $4,720,000), and operating profits would be unaffected.

The new ROCE would thus be $\dfrac{\$649,000}{\$4,720,000} \times 100 = 13.75\%$

This represents a reduction of ROCE in the short term.

Longer term effects

In 20X6 and beyond, the full impact of the cost savings and depreciation charge would be felt – operating profits would be increased by a net $(76,000 - 40,000) = $36,000. Net assets value will be increased, but the increase will be smaller each year as the asset is depreciated.

In 20X6, the equipment's own ROCE would be $\dfrac{\$36,000}{\$(320,000 - 40,000)} \times 100 = 12.86\%$

This will still not help the division to achieve its target of 15%, although it does exceed the company's cost of capital and thus may be desirable overall.

However, by the end of 20X7, the equipment WDV will be $(320,000 - 80,000) = $240,000, giving a ROCE of 15%, exactly on target. As it increases above this level it will help the division to achieve its overall target.

This illustrates one of the major problems with using book values for assets in performance measures – as the assets get older, they appear to give better performance. This can have the effect of deterring managers from replacing assets even though this may be of benefit in the long term through cost savings (as above), increased productivity etc.

(b)   Residual income (RI) is an absolute measure of performance, and is arrived at by deducting a notional interest charge at the company's cost of capital on the net assets. Appraising the two divisions' performance forecasts under this method would have the following results:

	20X5 operating profit	Interest charge (12% net assets)	Residual income
	$	$	$
Division K	649,000	528,000	121,000
Division D	120,000	57,600	62,400

The performance rankings of the two divisions are now apparently reversed. However, the RIs of the two divisions are not directly comparable – whilst Division K has produced nearly twice the level of RI than that of Division D, the net asset base required to do this is over nine times as large. RI cannot be meaningfully used to compare investments of differing sizes, as ROCE can.

One could also question the use of the company's average cost of money in computing the notional interest charge. The two divisions have been set a target well above this – this may be because they are considered riskier than average. If 15% had been used in the computation, Division K would have negative RI, whilst Division D has positive RI – reflecting the same information as the ROCE, that K is not achieving its target return.

The RI uses the same principles for establishing profit and asset values as the ROCE, and thus shares the same problems. As assets get older and their WDV falls, the imputed interest falls and RI rises.

However, RI can be of greater benefit than ROCE in management decision making. Management may only feel inclined to undertake new investment if doing so improves their performance measure. For example, Division D currently enjoys a ROCE of 25% and its manager may only consider new projects that give a return at least as good as this (although this may depend upon the particular structure of the bonus scheme – a fixed bonus provided the target of 15% is reached may not provoke such an attitude).

However, the RI measure will improve with new investment, i.e. increase, provided the investment's returns are at least covering the rate used in computing the notional interest (12% or 15%). This will ensure that projects that are worthwhile from the company's point of view will also be seen as such by the divisional manager (goal congruence).

In summary, RI has advantages and disadvantages over ROCE as a performance measure, and both suffer from common valuation problems. One of these can be used as part of a package of performance indicators – market share, productivity, employee satisfaction, technological advancement, etc – but neither is perfect in isolation.

(c)   Financial measures taken in isolation are unlikely to tell the whole story of a division's or company's performance. They must be put into context, taking account of the circumstances in which they were achieved – new products being introduced, market changes, technological changes, competitors' moves, availability of resources, etc.

For example, one might question why the two divisions in KDS are apparently performing at such different levels. Whilst quality of management may well be a contributory factor, it is unlikely to explain a difference of over 10 percentage points in ROCE.

The age profile of assets used should be considered, as discussed above. Division K may have recently invested in new machinery, possibly in response to technological advances. Not to do so would put them at a disadvantage over their competitors, and thus is for long-term benefit. The industry of the much smaller Division D may be more static, requiring less asset changes.

Performance relative to the market and competitors should be considered (market share, product leadership, etc) and the degree of innovation achieved. Level of complaints received may also be monitored.

Finally, employee measures are relevant when assessing the effectiveness of a manager – labour turnover, staff morale, managers' relationships with both subordinates and superiors. The level of job satisfaction felt by employees at all levels is an important consideration in the plan for achievement of company objectives.

117   CNJ (MAR 13)

Tutorial note

Candidates needed to carefully read the question to gain a full understanding of what was required.

Part (a) required candidates to compare the performance of two divisions for two accounting periods, and comment on the performances by use of appropriate measures e.g. ROCE

Part (b)(i) required candidates to calculate the net present value of the investment described in the scenario.

Part (b)(ii) required a comparison of the ROCE of one of the divisions before and after the investment, and a discussion of the results.

(a)

	2012		2011	
	Eastern	Western	Eastern	Western
ROCE %	38.0	41.7	29.3	26.7
Staff costs/revenue %	63.9	57.7	62.1	58.2
Other operating costs/revenue %	25.6	27.2	26.3	27.6
Asset turnover	3.6	2.8	2.5	1.9
Operating profit/revenue %	10.6	15.1	11.6	14.2
Depreciation $000	250.0	300.0	250.0	300.0
Op costs-depreciation $000	210.0	375.0	250.0	320.0
Op costs-depreciation/revenue %	11.7	15.1	13.2	14.2
Revenue per member $	265	267	266	267
Staff costs per member $	169	154	165	156

In 2011 the Eastern Division generated the higher ROCE and the Managing Director of that division would have received the bonus. The revenue for the Eastern division was lower than that of the Western Division but so was its capital employed. This is because it had a lower investment in non-current assets and its assets are older (assuming that all assets in each particular division were acquired at the same date).

Revenue at the Eastern division has fallen by 5.3% between 2011 and 2012. As revenue per member of $266 has been maintained at broadly the same level during the period it can be concluded that the decline in revenue is due to the fall in number of members. The opposite is true for the Western division, as revenue has increased by 10.2% over the period. Revenues per member are in line with the Eastern division at $267 and have been maintained over the period.

The operating profit has fallen over the period at the Eastern division due to a fall in revenue and also less effective cost management with operating profit margins decreasing from 11.6% to 10.6%. Conversely, in the Western division, the operating profit margin has increased from 14.2% to 15.1%. However further information can be obtained from a deeper analysis of the figures:

- Staff expenses as a percentage of revenue have increased for the Eastern Division but decreased for the Western Division. Given that revenue is almost directly linked to the number of members it could be argued that this is to be expected given that it is highly likely that many of the staff costs are fixed.

- Operating costs as a percentage of revenue have fallen for both divisions but if depreciation is excluded it can be seen that they have increased for the Western Division.

The Managing Director of the Western Division would earn the bonus in 2012.

(b)　(i)

	Year	$000	Disc factor	PV $000
Investment	0	−800	1.000	−800
Cash inflow	1–5	234	3.352	784
Sales of assets	5	350	0.497	174
NPV				158

Note: 234 = 144 + (450/5)

The NPV of the project is $158,000.

(ii)　The NPV of the investment is positive and therefore this investment should have been made. However the Managing Director of the Western Division will want to earn a bonus and knows that this is determined by the ROCE of the division. Without the investment the ROCE for the Western Division would rise to 41.7% from 26.7% the previous year.

With the investment the operating profit for the Western Division would rise to $519,000 and the capital employed to $1,610,000. This would give a ROCE of 32.2% ($519,000/$1,610,000). Although this is above the 2011 figure it is significantly below what it would be if the investment was not made. Consequently the Managing Director of the Western Division would make a decision that is not in the best interests of the group and would reject an investment that should be undertaken as it has a positive NPV.

ROCE is not an appropriate measure for several reasons: it is based on profit and will increase without any effort being made due to the effects of depreciation on the capital base, and can be distorted by accounting policies. As can be seen it also focuses on the short term: the Divisional Manager focussed on the immediate impact. Another major criticism of ROCE is that it ignores the time value of money.

118　DIVISION A

(a)　(i)　Profit required by division A to meet RI target:

	$
Cost of capital $3.2m @ 12%	384,000
Target RI	180,000
Target profit	564,000
Add fixed costs	1,080,000
Target contribution	1,644,000
Contribution earned from external sales 90,000 @ ($35–$22)	1,170,000
Contribution required from internal sales	474,000
Contribution per bit on internal sales ($474,000/60,000)	$7.90
Transfer price to division C $22.00 + $7.90	$29.90

(ii)　The two transfer prices based on opportunity costs:

40,000 units (150,000 − 110,000) at the marginal cost of $22.00

20,000 units (110,000 − 90,000) at the external selling price of $35.00

(b)   Where divisional managers are given total autonomy to purchase units at the cheapest price and where divisional performance is assessed on a measure based on profit, sub-optimal behaviour could occur i.e. divisional managers could make decisions that may not be in the overall interests of the group.

Impact of group's current transfer pricing policy

Division C's objective is to maximise its RI in order to achieve its target RI. It will therefore endeavour to find the cheapest source of supply for Bits.

As C requires 60,000 Bits and X is willing to supply them at $28 each, C would prefer to buy them from X rather than division A. However this will not benefit the group, as division A will be unable to utilise its spare capacity of 40,000 Bits.

The effect on the group's profit will be as follows:

	$
Additional payment by division C 60,000 Bits@ ($28 – $22)	(360,000)
Gain in contribution by Division A 20,000 Bits @ $13	260,000
Net loss to group	(100,000)

Impact of group's proposed transfer pricing policy

If division A was to set transfer prices based on opportunity costs the effect on its divisional profit would be as follows:

	$
Reduction in profit 40,000 Bits @ ($29.90 – $22.00)	(316,000)
Increase in profit 20,000 Bits @ ($35 – $29.90)	102,000
Net loss to division	(214,000)

Division C has the following two purchase options:

	$
Purchase from division A 40,000 Bits @ $22	880,000
Purchase from Z 20,000 Bits @ $33	660,000
Total cost of Bits	1,540,000
Or Purchase 60,000 from X 60,000 Bits @ $28	1,680,000

As division C will opt to source the Bits from the cheapest supplier/s it will choose to purchase 40,000 Bits from division A at $22 per Bit and the remaining 20,000 Bits from Z at $33 per Bit.

This also benefits the group, as there is no opportunity cost to division A on the 40,000 units transferred to division C.

When marginal cost is used as the transfer price division C will make the correct decision and the group will maximise profits.

However division A would suffer. This can be overcome by changing the way it measures the performance of its divisions – rather than using a single profit based measure it needs to introduce a variety of quantitative and qualitative measures.

(c) **Purchase of 60,000 Bits from division A**

	Contribution $	Taxation $	Net effect $
A – external sales 90,000 Bits @ ($35 – $22)	1,170,000		
– internal sales 60,000 Bits @ ($30 – $22)	480,000		
Total contribution from A	1,650,000		
Taxation @ 55%		(907,500)	
C – purchases 60,000 Bits @ $30	(1,800,000)		
Taxation @ 25%		450,000	
Net effect	(150,000)	(457,500)	(607,500)

Purchase of 60,000 Bits from X

	Contribution $	Taxation $	Net effect $
A – external sales 110,000 Bits @ ($35 – $22)	1,430,000		
Taxation @ 55%		(786,500)	
C – purchases 60,000 Bits @ $28	(1,680,000)		
Taxation @ 25%		420,000	
Net effect	(250,000)	(366,500)	(616,500)

The group will maximise its profits if division C purchased the Bits from division A.

119 DE TRANSFER (MAY 11)

> **Examiner's comments:** Overall the attempts were poor, especially for parts (c) (i) and (c) (ii). Part (a) was generally well answered but the answers to the discursive parts (b) and (d) were weak. Questions relating to transfer pricing have appeared quite regularly at recent sittings and each time the marks have been disappointing. It leads one to suppose that many candidates do not understand this area of the syllabus and ignore it in their revision programme.

(a) The internal sales volume is 70,000 components. Division E could have sold a further 42,000 components to the external market if it had extra capacity or were to reduce its internal sales. Therefore this volume of components was sold to Division D at market price and the balance was sold at variable cost.

An analysis of the sales is therefore as follows:

	Internal @ cost	Internal @ MV	External	Total
Number of components	28,000	42,000	70,000	140,000
0000	$000	$000	$000	$000
Variable cost	28,000	42,000	70,000	140,000
Sales value	28,000	65,100	108,500	201,600

(b)   Division E has sold components to Division D without deriving any financial benefit. If Division D had bought them at market value the cost to Division D would have been $43.4m which is $15.4m greater than the current transfer price.

While it may not be appropriate for Division D to pay the full market price (since Division E could not sell these components externally) it does seem unfair that all of the profit from the use of these components accrues to Division D and therefore a transfer price that accrues some reward to Division E for the supply of the components would be fairer to both divisions. Any transfer price above variable cost would reduce the profits of Division D and increase those of Division E by the same amount. For example if the difference between variable cost and market price were shared equally then the change in profit of each division would be $7.7m.

If the external demand for the components were to decrease, then more of the components supplied to Division D would be transferred at variable cost thus lowering the profits of Division E, but increasing the profits of Division D. If the external demand were to increase then the opposite effect would occur until all of the internal transfers were being made at the external selling price.

(c)   The investment has two effects: the increase in E's capacity by 10% and the 20% reduction in its variable cost. From Division E's perspective the benefit of these effects is diluted due to the internal sales and the transfer pricing policy.

If the capacity of Division E is increased by 10% then it will increase its external sales, but in doing so will reduce the volume of external sales foregone by selling the components to Division D. Therefore the effect of the additional capacity would be to transfer an additional 10% by volume at cost. Thus there is no financial benefit to Division E.

E sells 50% of its present capacity internally, and 28/70 of this is transferred to Division D at variable cost therefore any cost savings arising in respect of this proportion will be passed on to Division D due to the transfer pricing policy.

The cost saving that will accrue to Division E will therefore be limited to items sold at market value. This amounts to:

Variable cost of items sold at market value = 80% × $140m = $112m per annum

20% cost saving thereon = $22.4m per annum

Using the 8% annuity factor for 5 years this saving has a present value of:

$22.4m × 3.993 = $89.4432m

Since the capital cost of the equipment is $120m with no residual value the investment is not financially viable from Division E's perspective.

However, if the investment were to be evaluated from the position of the whole organisation then consideration would be given to the benefits that accrue to Division D as a consequence of the transfer pricing policy. These benefits can be identified as the difference between the original and revised values of internal sales. The original value was $93.1m ($28m + $65.1m – see above). The revised transfer value will be:

42,000 components @ revised cost of $42m less 20%	$33.6m
28,000 components @ market value of $1,550	$43.4m
	$77.0m

A saving to Division D of $16.1m per annum.

If this were added to the Division E saving of $22.4m the total saving is $38.5m per annum which would have a present value of $153.73m which clearly makes the investment of $120m worthwhile.

Note: Alternative methods of deriving the same solution are also acceptable.

(d) A number of factors should be considered when designing divisional performance measures. These include:

Each measure should be simple to calculate and to understand so that managers can see the effect of the decisions that they make on the measurement of their division's performance.

Each measure should be fair to the manager of the division and only include items that are within their control.

120 SWZ (NOV 10)

> **Examiner's comments:** This was a poorly answered question, especially parts (b) and (c). It was patently obvious that many candidates did not understand this area of the syllabus or had not included it in their revision programme. The question clearly stated that ROI was the main measure of each division's performance, but many candidates described other measures such as return on deliveries. The presentation of figures for parts (b) and (c) was particularly poor with markers not being able to award marks on many occasions due to figures being set down at random, and figures appearing with no explanation and no workings to support them.

(a) The ROI for each of the last three years was:

> **Examiner's comments:** Common Errors in part (a) included:
>
> 1   Failing to appreciate that the method of depreciation was a key factor.
>
> 2   Failing to realise that the operating costs, excluding depreciation, increased each year.
>
> 3   Commenting on other, non relevant, performance measures.
>
> 4   Failing to note from the question that there had been no additions or disposals of fixed assets during the period under review.

2008   40/400 = 10.00%

2009   56/320 = 17.50%

2010   62/256 = 24.22%

There has been a gradual improvement in ROI throughout the three year period. However, this summary ratio hides the detailed performance of S division.

(1) It is stated that the values have been adjusted to remove the effects of inflation. It can thus be seen that sales and cost of sales are constant throughout the period and therefore there has been no significant change in the volumes of activity during the period:

(2) The gross profit margin has been constant at approximately 67% mark-up throughout the three year period

(3) Other operating costs have increased throughout the three year period. These costs are inclusive of depreciation which is being calculated using 20% reducing balance and in fact if depreciation is excluded the underlying operating costs have increased by $4,000 in 2009 and more significantly in 2010.

In conclusion the improvement in ROI during the three year period is a function of the depreciation policy rather than of the performance of the division.

(b)

> **Examiner's comments:** Common errors in part (b) included:
>
> 1 Simply comparing the figures for 2011 with the new investment, against the figures for 2010 as given in the question.
>
> 2 Failing to show two sets of figures for 2011. One being if the investment did not go ahead, the other being figures assuming the investment did go ahead.
>
> 3 Numerous errors in the calculation of the profit and capital invested under each method.
>
> 4 No explanation for figures shown within the answer.
>
> 5 No reference to workings.
>
> 6 Poorly presented answers.

The investment has a positive net present value of $24,536 and therefore from a company perspective it should go ahead.

However, the investment needs to be looked at from the divisional manager's point of view. Assuming that the results of 2011 are the same as those of 2010 (other than the specific changes as a result of the investment and ignoring inflation), we can put forward the following calculations:

If the investment **does not go ahead** then the results in 2011 will be:

	$000	
Sales	400	
Cost of sales	240	
Gross profit	160	
Other operating costs	85.2	($98 – $64 + $51.2)
Pre-tax operating profit	74.8	
Capital invested	204.8	($256 – $51.2)

ROI $74.8/$204.8 = 36.5%

But if the investment **does go ahead**, the results will be:

	$000	
Sales	400	
Cost of sales	216	($240,000 × 0.9)
Gross profit	184	
Other operating costs*	97.2	
Pre-tax operating profit	86.8	
Capital invested**	252.8	

The ROI in 2011 if the investment in the new machine goes ahead would be $86,800/ $252,800 = 34.3%

This is lower than the ROI that would be achieved in 2011 by continuing with the existing equipment and therefore the manager is unlikely to go ahead with the investment.

* In 2010 the other operating costs value of $98,000 includes $64,000 depreciation of equipment and $34,000 of other costs. The new depreciation charge for 2011 will be $63,200 so assuming the other costs remain unchanged the total other operating costs for 2011 will be $97,200.

		$000
** Original NBV	256	
Less NBV of replaced machine	40	
		216
Cost of new machine	100	
		316
Depreciation at 20%	63.2	
NBV at the end of 2011	252.8	

(c)

<table>
<tr><td colspan="2">Examiner's comments: Common errors in part (c) included:</td></tr>
<tr><td>1</td><td>Not appreciating that a Residual Income is an absolute figure and not a percentage.</td></tr>
<tr><td>2</td><td>Not calculating the RI using figures from (b).</td></tr>
<tr><td>3</td><td>Not appreciating that a comparison was called for, rather than simply a decision based on a positive RI from one set of figures.</td></tr>
<tr><td>4</td><td>5 and 6 as for part (b). 2. Failing to subtract the resources needed for the special order before presenting the revised resource</td></tr>
</table>

Using the figures from part (b) above:

Without investment:

	$
Pre-tax operating profits	74,800
Notional capital charge ($204,800 × 8%)	16,384
Residual Income	58,416

With investment:

	$
Pre-tax operating profits	86,800
Notional capital charge ($252,800 × 8%)	20,224
Residual Income	66,570
Increase in Residual Income	8,160

This is consistent with the company's NPV based decision above.

Alternative calculation based on incremental values:

	$
Increase in capital $48,000 × 8% ($60,000 – $12,000 depreciation)	(3,840)
Savings in direct costs	24,000
Increase in depreciation ($60,000 × 20%)	(12,000)
Increase in Residual Income	8,160

121   H PERFUMES (MAY 10)

Tutorial note

A debit entry on the T account indicates that a process is making a profit of $18,800. The other entry would be a credit in the income statement, therefore a profit.

(a)   (i)

$$\text{ROI (Annualised)} = \frac{\text{Earnings before interest and tax}}{\text{Capital Employed}} \times 100\%$$

In this context, $\text{ROI} = \dfrac{\text{Profit or loss from T account}}{\text{NBV of capital equipment at the start of the year}}$ × 12 months

Process B

The NBV of capital equipment at the start of the year = original cost $800,000 × $(1-20\%)^{5 \text{ years}}$ = $262,144

Therefore $\text{ROI}_B = \dfrac{\$18,800}{\$262,144}$ × 12 months

∴ ROI_B = 7.17% × 12 months

ROI_B = 86.04%

Process C

A credit entry on the T account indicates that Process C is making a loss of $15,550.

NBV of capital equipment at the start of the year = original cost $500,000 x $(1-20\%)2^{\text{years}}$ = $320,000

Therefore $\quad ROI_c = \dfrac{\$(15,550)}{\$320,000} \times 12 \text{ months}$

$\therefore \quad$ **ROI $_c$ = −4.48% × 12 months**

$\therefore \quad$ **ROI $_c$ = −58.08%**

Process D

A credit entry on the T account indicates that Process D is making a loss of $5,000. The NBV of capital equipment at the start of the year = original cost $300,000 \times (1-20\%)^{10 \text{ years}}$ = $32,212

Therefore $\quad ROI_D = \dfrac{\$(5,000)}{\$32,212} \times 12 \text{ months}$

$\therefore \quad$ ROI $_D$= −15.52% × 12 months

$\therefore \quad$ **ROI $_D$= −186.24%**

(ii) As a relative measure, ROI enables comparisons to be made up with divisions of different sizes (i.e. with asset bases of different values). For Division B, it is unfair to use ROI as a performance measure, because the Division cannot influence its sales revenue. Production is processed internally and external sales of its by-product sales are less than 3% of the divisional total revenue. Furthermore, divisional profits or losses are dependent on a somewhat arbitrary or debatable transfer pricing policy.

The division cannot influence the value of assets either, as it must follow H's group policy on depreciation and does not seem to be able to make its own investment decisions (we are not told it is a investment centre like C and D).

Processes C and D are investment centres so managers are able to influence parameters such as investment decisions and selling prices – ROI seems more appropriate. However, when NBVs are used, ROI increases artificially with the age of the assets. This could lead to dysfunctional behaviour and prevent further investments from managers with an ROI that is already negative. Managers are operating with assets bought at different times; therefore, the value of their assets is inconsistent when Head Office has to make cross-divisional comparisons.

Last, overhead costs include a share of Head Office costs which are taken into account when calculating divisional ROIs, but outside the control of the divisions. All three divisional managers could argue that a performance appraisal based on such an indicator is unfair.

(b) (i) We will calculate 2011's ROI assuming that the investment does NOT go ahead; then we will recalculate it, assuming it does.

With **no investment**, and assuming that all other things remain equal, a lower depreciation will be charged monthly in 2011, and the $15,550 loss slightly reduced.

$$ROI_c = \frac{\$(15,550) + [\text{Monthly Depreciation charge for 2010} - \text{Monthly depreciation charge for 2011}]}{\$NBV \text{ of capital equipment at 1st January 2011}} \times 12$$

$$ROI_c = \frac{\$(15,550) + \$5,333\,(W1) - \$4,267\,(W2)}{\$320,000 \times (1-20\%)} \times 12 \text{ months}$$

$$ROI_c = \frac{\$14,484}{\$256,000} \times 12 \text{ months}$$

$$ROI_c = -67.89\%$$

Compared to 2010, this represents a worsening of ROI for Division C.

If the **investment goes ahead**, revenue in 2011 will be increased as follows:

'Abnormal loss' units revenue: 1,500 litres × $20	$30,000
Less loss of abnormal loss scrap revenue	$(750)
Net monthly increase in revenue in 2011	**$29,250**
2010 Profit, as per question	$(15,550)
2011 Profit per month before depreciation	**$13,700**
Less: increase in monthly depreciation charge (W1)	($11,334)
2011 Profit per month, after depreciation	**$2,366**
This represents a yearly profit of $2,366 × 12 months	$28,392

$$\text{Therefore } ROI_{C\text{-}2011} = \frac{\$28,392}{\$1,000,000}$$

Therefore ROI $_{C\text{-}2011}$ =2.84%

Conclusion: The effect of the investment on Division C's ROI is 67.89% + 2.84% = 70.73% increase. Therefore, the investment should go ahead.

Workings:

(W1) **Increase in monthly depreciation charge:**

2010 depreciation charge =	$\dfrac{\$64,000}{12 \text{ months}} =$	$5,333
2011 depreciation charge =	$\dfrac{\$1,000,000 \times 20\%}{12 \text{ months}} =$	$16,667
Net increase in monthly depreciation charges		**$11,334**

(W2) **Monthly depreciation charge in Division C if no investment**

$$2011 \text{ depreciation charge} = \frac{\$320,000 \times (1-20\%) \times 20\%}{12 \text{ months}} = \$4,267$$

(ii) The ROI indicates that Division C should go ahead with the investment in new processing equipment. This, however, is still quite a low return. It could be contradicted by the use of the NPV investment appraisal method if the sum of discounted cash flows is negative. The NPV investment appraisal method states that an investment is accepted if it yields a positive NPV.

(c)   Currently, Division B will be satisfied with the Transfer Pricing Policy being applied as it enables the division to make a profit. Division B can recover all variable and fixed costs, as the Transfer Prices are calculated based on the total budgeted costs of process, to which a mark-up of 15% is added.

Because a **budgeted** cost base is used, Division B's manager will be rewarded for any efficiencies that are achieved and the managers of Processes C and D are protected against inefficiencies of process B.

The Manager of Division D will be unhappy with the Transfer Pricing policy as the Division is loss making and its ROI negative. The choice of an appropriate Transfer Pricing policy is particularly important for an investment centre such as Division D and it is likely that its manager will view H's current practice as a concern.

Division D is currently forced to pay more than external prices when purchasing internally from Division B; However, it could save $9.20 − $7.50 = $1.70 per litre if it were allowed to make its own purchasing decision. Division D is foregoing total possible savings of $1.70 × 10,000 litres = $17,000 by sourcing its litres from Division B.

Two alternatives are possible for the Manager of Division D:

(1)   D could chose, if H allows, to purchase externally – and Process Division B would still have to produce for Process Division C. This could work at a group level, assuming that all of B's production can be absorbed by C.

(2)   A system a dual prices, whereby the selling price recorded by Division B would not be the same as the buying price recorded by Division D, could be suggested. Typically, Division D would include the company's variable costs as its costs and be charged a competitive price of $7.50; Division B would include a value closer to market value as its sales and still charge at $9.20.

122   ALPHA GROUP (SEPT 10)

(a)

Key answer tips

A diagram may help to clarify the relationship between the three divisions, and has attracted marks in the past. Also note the requirement verb 'Discuss'. It is a Level 4 verb:' *Examine in detail by argument'*.

Technically, remembering that ROCE = Operating profits × Asset turnover (the 'triangular relationship') will serve you well. Remember that the asset turnover ratio is expressed in 'times', not percentages.

	X Consultancy	X Production	Y
Operating profit	$210,000	$140,000	$370,000
Capital employed	$800,000	$2,000,000	$4,000,000
ROCE	**26.25%**	**7%**	**9.25%**
Sales	$710,000	$1,260,000	$750,000
Operating profit margin	**29.57%**	**11.11%**	**49.33%**
Asset turnover	**0.88 times**	**0.63 times**	**0.1875 times**

(i) **ROCE**

- To be able to discuss the performance of these three divisions, we would need to know the target ROCE set by Alpha in order to assess whether this is achieved. A comparison of these three divisions may also seem unfair as the nature of their business is very different: consultancy (services), component manufacturing and machinery assembly.

- For a fairer assessment, we would need to know what proportion of Admin costs are controllable by each division and what proportion is a result of an allocation from Alpha's Head Office; we would also need to know if the same accounting policies are applied consistently throughout the 3 divisions (for example, on depreciation.)

- **X Consultancy** is the most profitable division from a ROCE point of view; its returns are higher than Y. This is not a surprise: healthy margins can be expected from a consultancy business. We will need to determine whether X Consultancy's performance is due to a higher profit margin, a better use of assets, or both.

- **X Production** returns the lowest ROCE of all 3 divisions, which seems to be due to a low operating profit margin.

(ii) **Operating profit margin**

- **X Production** is the division performing the least well. This could be due to high prices charged by Y as well as to the nature of its activities.

- **Y** is doing better than both of X's divisions. This may be due to a healthy price being maintained for its units (almost half of which are sold to X Production) as well as a good control of costs. A very healthy margin explains the division's ROCE but the high price charged to another of the Group division is likely to prove controversial.

- Also, as Y uses imported components, exchange rates may have played in the division's favour and reduced Y's equivalent costs in $.

(iii) **Asset turnover**

- **Y** has the largest asset base but shows a particularly low return on every $ of assets used in its business. This could be due to recent purchases of fixed assets.

- Management should concentrate on a better use of assets in Y.

- **X Consultancy** has the highest A/T indicator, which confirms a high ROCE. There seems no use in using asset turnover in a non-manufacturing division where there is no use of Fixed Assets; however, a higher A/T here may suggest a better use of non-fixed assets, i.e. a better working capital management process.

(b) (i)
- The current transfer pricing policy, whereby the transfer price is the market price for both internal and external sales, is affecting the group performance in what seems like a price sensitive market (X's competitor won the order with a price that was less than 10% lower than X's).

- In other words, the current TP policy is making X uncompetitive and damages Alpha's profits. It is therefore not a goal-congruent policy, even if Y Division maximises its profits.

- The manager of Division X may feel demotivated because of the high prices he has to pay Y, and the loss of orders that explain his/her comparatively low performance.

- From Y's perspective, selling to X means the sacrifice of further external sales so opportunity costs justify a market price to internal sales; however, Y sells its components globally so an adjustment for sales to X, situated in the same country, should have been implemented.

- Alpha needs to determine what would be the most goal-congruent price, and whether or not to encourage Y to expand its external sales.

(ii) In a context where there are production constraints, Y should charge a transfer price equal to its marginal cost + the shadow price of its unit. By supplying X, Y Ltd satisfies only 80% of its external markets; External Sales currently amount to \$400,000 so potentially, could rise as much as $\dfrac{\$400,000}{0.8}$ = \$500,000. In other words, supplying X means that Y has to forego \$100,000 of sales.

Tutorial note

The key point here is that unsatisfied external demand needs different treatment from the remainder of sales to X Ltd.

There should be two separate prices:

– Y should charge X \$100,000 for some of its units, less all the adjustments due to distribution costs savings linked to internal transfers. This would ensure that Y doesn't 'lose out' by selling internally.

- For the other units, i.e. the remainder \$250,000 of internal sales, the minimum cost would be Y's marginal cost.

- Currently, marginal costs in Y = 60% × \$250,000 = \$150,000.

- We therefore have Marginal costs of \$150,000 for sales of \$750,000: a ratio of 1 to 5, or 20%.

- Therefore, for the remainder of the sales of \$250,000, Y should charge a fifth as a transfer price, i.e. \$50,000.

- Total Internal receipts = **\$100,000 + \$50,000 – savings linked to internal transfers.**

- Problems with this TP will remain: using the MC as the TP will demotivate Y's manager, who will not get at a reward.

- Alpha needs to implement a compromise TP system that will still bring about competitive prices from for X Production, but will give some return to the seller, Y.

Possible solutions include:

- A system whereby a market price less any internal cost savings is charged to X by Y. This in itself may help to make X more competitive.

- A dual transfer pricing system whereby Y charges a price and Division X pays another. The difference would be charged to a central reconciliation account in Alpha. This would make the Manager of Division Y happy, Division X would be able to set a profit-maximising price and win more profitable orders.

- A two-part tariff system whereby X would pay the marginal costs for its transfers ($50,000) but also a contribution towards Y's fixed costs once a year for example.

- The Alpha profit – maximising price that should be set so that MC = MR for Y's external and internal sales. From a Performance Evaluation point of view, Alpha should ensure that divisions are not penalised by a change in calculations.

(c)   The potential tax consequences of the internal TP policy if Y Ltd were to relocate would be as follows:

1   Alpha's tax liability overall would be reduced, as the highest earning division would be taxed at a lower rate.

2   This would increase Y's and Alpha's total profits after tax, and therefore make business sense

3   Governments might get suspicious and force the transfer price charged by Y to be at arms' length – although this is currently satisfied as TP = market price.

123   PZ GROUP (MAR 11)

(a)

Examiner's comments: In part (a), common errors included:
1   Not knowing that pre-tax profit % and the asset turnover are secondary ratios to the ROCE.
2   Using incorrect profit figures in the calculations.
3   Incorrectly showing asset turnover as a percentage (as opposed to "times").
4   Putting forward unrealistic answers e.g. asset turnover = 699%.

Company	P Limited	Z Limited
ROCE	10/459.6 = 2.2%	30/453.216 = 6.6%
Pre-tax profit %	10/200 = 5.0%	30/220 = 13.6%
Asset turnover	200/459.6 = 0.435	220/453.216 = 0.485

(b)

> **Examiner's comments:** In part (b) (ii), common errors included:
>
> 1   Failing to recalculate the figures that appeared in part (a), i.e. eliminate the effect of the internal transactions. Virtually every candidate failed to complete this task.
>
> 2   Failing to mention the gearing (loan) for P Limited, and then to calculate relevant, supporting figures.
>
> 3   Failing to fully explain the original cost and the written down value of non-current assets, and then to explain how this affected the ROCE.
>
> 4   Putting forward general (and weak) comments relating to revenue and cost of sales.
>
> 5   Including motivational issues that did not relate to the question.

The value of the group transaction can be identified by comparing the group results with the sum of the two individual company results: the sales value was $20,000 and the cost of sale value was $10,000 thus Z Limited made a profit of $10,000 on this transaction which is equal to a gross margin of 50%.

The gross margin on the external sales was $50,000 / $200,000 = 25%. Thus there is a significant difference in the margins being achieved. If this transaction had not occurred and assuming that P Limited had sold these items using its normal mark-up then the ratios would have been:

Company	P Limited	Z Limited
ROCE	6.47/459.6 = 1.4%	20/453.216 = 4.4%
Pre-tax profit %	6.47/176.47 = 3.7%	20/200 = 10%
Asset turnover	176.47/459.6 = 0.384	200/453.216 = 0.441

These calculations show that the relative performance of the two companies is significantly different.

> ***Tutorial note***
>
> *The sales and profit figures used in the ratios above may need a bit more explanation: P would want the profit excluding anything to do with the transfer. We can work out that the transfer price must have been $20,000, as the total revenue is $400,000, which is $20,000 less than the divisions combined.*
>
> *This $20,000 will be in P's cost of sales figure, so it needs stripping out ($170,000 − $20,000 = $150,000).*

> *P, of course, will have also sold these in the year so some of their revenue will be related to this. This also needs stripping out. Without any other information, we would have to assume that they made a similar profit on the goods as they would any other. So, looking at their sales of $200,000 compared to their cost of sales of $170,000, the average margin achieved is 15%. Therefore, on goods costing $20,000, a sale revenue of $23,529 would have been obtained.*
>
> *In summary, the adjusted sales should be $200,000 − $23,529 = $176,471. The adjusted Cost of Sales should be $170,000-$20,000 = $150,000. Take away admin and interest costs, and profit amounts to $6,471.*

Further analysis identifies two key reasons for this:

Gearing

P Limited is financed partly by borrowing and partly by equity and the interest charge made by the lenders amounts to a 6.7% return (10/150). This is a significant cost to P Limited and amounts to a higher return than is being achieved before interest is paid which is 4.4% (20/459.6).

Non-current asset values

Although there are differences in the original cost of the non-current asset values (P Limited is two thirds of Z Limited) which reflects the relative sizes of the companies there is also a difference in the age of the assets which can be identified by the proportion of the non-current asset that has depreciated. Both companies use the same depreciation policy of 20% per annum on a reducing balance basis yet the non-current asset value of P Limited has been depreciated by 59.0% of its original cost whereas the non-current asset value of Z Limited has been depreciated by 73.8% of its original cost. Thus the non-current assets of P Limited are newer and because they have a higher net book value, this reduces the apparent ROCE.

(c)

> **Examiner's comments:** In part (c), common errors included incorrectly describing the various methods of transfer pricing, such as dual pricing.

Three factors that should be considered when setting the transfer pricing policy are:

- The policy should lead to transfer prices that are fair to both the internal supplier and the internal customer and should provide them both with an incentive to carry out the internal transaction where it is worthwhile from the Group's viewpoint to do so.

- The policy should reflect the capacity constraints and market demand for the item being transferred. Therefore the transfer price should take account of the supplier's opportunity cost.

- The policy should provide autonomy to both the internal supplier and the internal customer to make their own decisions concerning internal transactions.

124   TY NPV (SEPT 11)

(a)

Tutorial note

Ensure you do not make the mistake of including only the sales figures; contribution must also be shown.

	Internal	External	Total
Number of components	50,000	150,000	200,000
	$000	$000	$000
Sales value	768,000	3,072,000	3,840,000
Variable cost	384,000	1,152,000	1,536,000
Contribution	384,000	1,920,000	2,304,000

(b)

(i)   Currently Division Y is operating at 80% capacity and producing 200,000 components each year. Division Y therefore has existing capacity for up to a further 50,000 components. The increase in division T's capacity by 25% equals 12,500 units which will be sold at a unit selling price of $60,000.

Division Y has sufficient capacity to supply the additional components to division T.

Tutorial note

You must adopt an incremental approach here and show contribution figures (a common error was to show sales figures instead of contribution).

Assuming that the current transfer pricing policy continues and that there are no other cost changes the variable cost per unit of these sales will be $28,800 thus yielding a unit contribution of $31,200.

This has a present value of	$969,930,000
$31,200 × 12,500 units × 2.487	
The residual value of the equipment has a present value of 400m × 0.751	$300,400,000
	$1,270,330,000
But the capital investment cost is	$1,350,000,000
Resulting in an NPV of	($79,670,000)

The manager of Division T will not want to go ahead with the investment.

(ii)

Tutorial note

Your written statement must be supported by figures.

From an overall perspective TY will also consider the effect of the investment on Division Y. It has already been stated above that Division Y has sufficient capacity to produce the additional 12,500 components.

It has also been determined above that the transfer price represents a 100% mark up on their variable cost so Division Y's contribution would increase by:

12,500 components × $7,680 = $96,000,000 per annum.

This has a present value of $96,000,000 × 2.487 = $238,752,000.

Therefore the investment is worthwhile overall because it has an NPV of $159,082,000. Consequently the decision would be different if it were being made from the perspective of TY.

(c)

Examiner's comments: The answers were generally poor and in most cases did not relate to the scenario in the question. The figures contained in part (a) allowed candidates to easily calculate the transfer price, the external market price and the variable cost of production for Division Y. Most of the answers were general in nature and only gained a few marks.

Many candidates interpreted the question as 'suggest alternative transfer pricing techniques' and then carefully described 'dual pricing'.

The variable cost per component incurred by Division Y is $1,536,000,000/200,000 = $7,680. If this were used as the transfer price then the internal sales value would be $3,840,000,000 so it seems that the transfer price is based on variable cost plus a 100% mark up.

At the current level of operations (80% of capacity), the fixed cost is equal to $9,750 per unit, so the total unit cost is $17,430.

As a result it can be seen that Division Y has sold components to Division T which yield a positive contribution but which are being sold at below total cost and at a discount to the market price of $20,480.

The manager of Division T would argue that since Division Y has spare capacity then it does not have any unsatisfied external demand. Therefore the transfer price should reflect the opportunity cost to Division Y of those sales. This is their variable cost, since the fixed cost would be incurred whether the internal sales took place or not. The manager of Division T will therefore feel that they are being overcharged and the transfer price should be $7,680 per component.

The manager of Division Y would argue that the internal sales are making a loss. The full cost is $17,430 per unit and they would not be able to manufacture the components without incurring the fixed costs. The manager of Division Y would also be keen to point out that the internal price is significantly lower than the market price that Division Y is charging on its external sales.

For the company as a whole the transfer price that is used has no effect unless it changes the decisions being made by the divisional managers so that they are sub-optimal for the company. As shown in part (b) above the transfer price does change the decision made by the manager of Division T so that it is a sub-optimal decision. Consequently the transfer price is not appropriate if sub-optimal decision making is to be avoided.

125   RFT (NOV 11)

(a)

	Note	$
Production director – meeting	1	NIL
Material A	2	1,375
Material B	3	360
Components	4	3,000
Direct labour	5	2,100
Machine hours	6	175
Fixed overhead	7	NIL
Total relevant cost		7,010

Notes:

1   The production director has already had this meeting with the potential client, therefore the relevant cost is NIL firstly because it is a past cost, and secondly because even if it were future the director is paid an annual salary and therefore there is no incremental cost to RFT.

2   Material A is in regular use by RFT and consequently its relevant value is its replacement cost. The historical cost is not relevant because it is a past cost and the resale value is not relevant since RFT is not going to sell it since the material is in regular use and therefore must be replaced.

3   Material B is to be purchased for the contract therefore its purchase cost is relevant. Although only 30 litres are required for the work the minimum order quantity is 40 litres and as RFT has no other use for this material and there is no indication that the unused 10 litres can be sold, the full cost of purchasing the 40 litres is the relevant cost.

4   The components are to be purchased from HY at a cost of $50 each. This is a relevant cost because it is future expenditure that will be incurred as a result of the work being undertaken.

5   Since 75 hours of spare capacity are available which have a zero relevant cost, the relevant cost relates only to the other 160 hours. RFT has two choices: either use its existing employees and pay them overtime at $14 per hour which is a total cost of $2,240; or engage the temporary staff which incurs their cost of $1,920 plus a supervision cost of $180 which equals $2,100. The relevant cost is the cheaper of these alternatives which is to use the temporary employees.

6   The machine is currently being leased and it has spare capacity so it will either stand idle or be used on this work. The lease cost will be incurred regardless so the only relevant cost is the incremental running cost of $7 per hour.

7   Fixed overhead costs are incurred whether the work goes ahead or not so it is not a relevant cost.

(b)   The factors that would be considered by HY to determine the opportunity cost of the component are its available capacity and the extent to which it has unsatisfied demand for its products.

If HY has spare capacity then if the components can be produced for RFT using the capacity that is available there is no opportunity cost so the relevant cost to the group would be the same as the relevant cost to HY, i.e. the variable cost.

If HY does not have sufficient spare capacity to produce all of the components demanded by RFT then to the extent that the internal sales are utilising capacity that would have been used to produce more units for external customers there is an opportunity cost to the group equal to the contribution forgone by not making those external sales.

Once there is no further unsatisfied external demand then the opportunity cost reverts to NIL because there is no loss of contribution.

(c)   (i)   When a cost based transfer pricing policy is used it is usual for it to be on a cost plus basis so that the "plus" provides an incentive to the supplier to make the internal sale. If it is on a cost only basis then there is no profit to the supplier, nor is there any incentive for them to be efficient because the cost (and therefore the inefficiency) is simply passed on to the buyer. When a cost plus transfer price is used then the efficiency issue is made even worse as illustrated by the following example:

Assume that the transfer price is actual cost + 30%. If the cost to the supplier is $10 then the transfer price would be $13 ($10 + 30%) and thus the supplier would record a profit of $3 from the internal sale.

However, if the supplier were to become inefficient so that the cost of the item increased to $12, then the new transfer price would be $15.60 ($12 + 30%) with the result that the new supplier profit would be $3.60.

This means that the supplier profit increases as a result of the supplier's inefficiency, and therefore the transfer pricing policy encourages such inefficiency to occur.

(ii) If standard costs are used instead of actual costs then the problem is solved provided the standard that is used is fair to both the supplier and the buyer.

Firstly it is important that both the supplier and buyer agree the standard cost for the item as being a fair standard. This may be difficult to achieve without the intervention of head office as it may be affected by the negotiating skills of the managers of the respective responsibility centres.

Secondly, there is the need to review the standard in the light of changing conditions that are beyond the control of the supplier. It would not be fair for the transfer price to be based on an out of date standard if the reason it has become out of date is outside the control of the supplier. This would require a renegotiation of the standard.

Using the above example and assuming that the standard cost of the item is $10. This would mean that initially the supplier was achieving the standard cost and there would be no change to the transfer price. However if the supplier was to become inefficient the transfer price would remain at $13 and so the supplier's profit reduces to $1. Conversely, if the supplier were to become more efficient and produce the item for $9 then their profit would increase to $4.

This would seem to solve the problem identified in (i) above as it encourages the supplier to be efficient.

126 THE OB GROUP (NOV 12)

Tutorial note

Part (a)(i) Carefully digest the details in the question and calculate the revenue generated by the complete cameras when viewed by the Optics divisional manager.

The main aim was to calculate the selling price the Optics division would transfer the optical device to the Body division.

Part (a)(ii) a required similar calculations but the transfer price needed to generate the maximum profit for the OB group.

Part (b) considered the transfer of items between two divisions of the same company and required calculations to address the two situations described in the questions.

Part (c) required a discussion relating to the use of opportunity costs as a basis for transfer pricing.

All parts of this question required answers to relate to the scenarios in the question.

(a)   (i)   **Optics division** Price equation is $P = 6,000 - 0.5x$

Profit maximised when MC = MR

$1,200 = 6,000 - x$

$x = 4,800$

Therefore $P = 6,000 - 2,400 = \$3,600$

Body Division Price equation is $P = 8,000 - (1/3)x$

Profit maximised when MC = MR

The marginal cost for the complete camera will be $1,750 + 3,600 = 5,350$

$5,350 = 8,000 - (2/3)x$

$(2/3)x = 2,650$

$x = 3,975$

$P = 8,000 - (1/3)3,975$

$P = \$6,675$

Revenue generated by the complete cameras = $3,975 * \$6,675 = \$26,533,125$

   (ii)   If the transfer price was set to maximise the profits of the group it would be $1,200 and the marginal cost of a complete camera would be $2,950

MC = MR

$2,950 = 8,000 - (2/3)x$

$(2/3)x = 5,050$

$x = 7,575$

$P = 8,000 - (1/3)7,575$

$P = \$5,475$

Revenue generated by the complete cameras = $7,575 * \$5,475 = \$41,473,125$

(b)   (i)   Return required by PD = $\$2.4m * 12\% = \$288,000$

Therefore total contribution needed = $\$2,688,000$

Total contribution = $(x - 1.40) * 4,480,000$

$2,688,000 = (x - 1.40) * 4,480,000$

$x - 1.40 = 2,688,000/4,480,000 = 0.60$

Therefore the minimum selling price per box that PD would be willing to charge is $2.00.

   (ii)   Return required by SD = $\$6m * 12\% = 720,000$

Total contribution needed = $\$6,720,000$

$6,720,000 = 13,500,000 - (x * 500,000)$

$x*500,000 = 6,780,000$

$x = 13.56$

The maximum variable cost that would allow SD to earn a return of 12% is $13.56. The variable costs from within SD are $12.00 and therefore the maximum that it would be willing to pay for a box is $1.56

(c) The possible extreme transfer prices are:

Marginal cost: no 'reward' is given to the supplying division. This method could be acceptable to the supplying division if there was spare capacity but there would be a reluctance to trade at this price because of the lack of a reward. Under this system PD would supply the boxes to SD at $1.40 each. However PD is operating very close to capacity and if demand from external customers increased the opportunity cost would be the external sales that would be forgone.

Market price: this should be used if there is a perfectly competitive market. The selling division will, if operating efficiently, be expected to earn a profit and the buying division should be happy to buy at this price as the only alternative is the open market. The price should be reduced for any 'internal' savings. This is what PD wants to do (charge SD the external selling price).

Using opportunity cost as the transfer price would enable the above extremes to be recognised. Therefore the view of the Manager of SD is worthy of support. If PD can sell all of its output externally then the opportunity cost would be the selling price. Consequently PD should not be penalised by having to accept a lower price from SD. If there is spare capacity then SD should be allowed to benefit and could then be charged just the marginal cost.

However the performance appraisal will have an impact on the behaviours of the managers and their willingness to 'trade' must be considered. One solution to this could be to use a 'dual pricing' system.

127 SHG (NOV 11)

(a) (i)

Year	2011		2010	
Division	Northern	Southern	Northern	Southern
	$m	$m	$m	$m
Cash flow	42.000	60.000	37.000	55.000
Depreciation (W1)	8.750	16.250	8.050	14.950
Profit	33.250	43.750	28.950	40.050
Average capital employed	122.500	227.500	115.500	214.500
Return on capital employed (ROCE) %	27.14	19.23	25.06	18.67

Workings:

(W1) **Depreciation**

Year	2011		2010	
Division	Northern	Southern	Northern	Southern
	$m	$m	$m	$m
NBV @ start of year	72.45	134.55	70.00	130.00
Add: Additions	15.05	27.95	10.50	19.50
Subtotal	87.50	162.50	80.50	149.50
Depreciation @ 10%	8.75	16.25	8.05	14.95
NBV @ end of year	78.75	146.25	72.45	134.55

(ii)

Year	2011		2010	
Division	Northern	Southern	Northern	Southern
	$m	$m	$m	$m
Turnover	168.00	240.00	148.00	220.00
Capital employed	122.50	227.50	115.50	214.50
Profit	33.25	43.75	28.95	40.05
Asset turnover	1.37	1.05	1.28	1.03
Profit/Sales %	19.79	18.23	19.56	18.20

(iii)   The Southern division has not been able to achieve a ROCE of 20% in either year and therefore their manager would not receive a bonus payment in respect of either 2010 or 2011, whereas the Northern division has achieved this target return in both years.

The manager of the Southern division might well argue that the division's non-current asset values are higher since the assets were more recently acquired than those of the Northern division. Hence the capital employed of the Southern division is much higher than that of the Northern division and consequently the ROCE of the Southern division might inevitably be lower and therefore having the same percentage target as the Northern division is unfair.

However, while this may be true, it is not the only factor that may have caused the difference between the divisions' performances. It can be seen from the secondary ratio calculations that both divisions have improved their asset turnover and profit to sales % between 2010 and 2011, even though there were net increases in the values of capital employed. This suggests that newer equipment may produce better yields in terms of sales than old equipment so that the argument of the Southern division manager may be only partly valid.

In both divisions for both years the operating cash flow is 25% of the turnover. This suggests that both divisions have the same gross profit percentages and the same operating costs to sales revenue percentages (or that their differences compensate for each other) if depreciation is ignored. Thus the differences between the divisions' profit to sales percentages between each other and between years is a function of the depreciation policy rather than of the actions of the divisional management.

(b) **Cost of quality report for the year ending 31 May 2011**

	Quantity	Rate	Total costs
Prevention costs:		$	$000
Design engineering	66,000	75	4,950
Training			150
Total prevention costs			5,100
Appraisal costs:			
Inspection (manufacturing)	216,000	40	8,640
Product testing			49
Total appraisal costs			8,689
Internal failure costs:			
Rework (manufacturing)	1,500	3,000	4,500
Total internal failure costs			4,500
External failure costs:			
Customer support (marketing)	1,800	200	360
Transportation costs (distribution)	1,800	240	432
Warranty repair	1,800	3,200	5,760
Total external failure costs			6,552
Total costs (P, A, IF and EF)			24,841
Opportunity costs	1,400	6,000	8,400
Total quality costs			33,241

128 HTL (MAR 12)

(a)

Hotel	Northern	Southern	Eastern
Return on net assets	20%	15%	13%
Residual income ($000)	412	360	136

All three hotels are making profits, though analysis shows that the Southern hotel is making a loss on its restaurant operation which is having a negative effect on its overall performance.

If the Southern hotel restaurant costs were to be similar to those of the Northern hotel restaurant (i.e. 60% of its revenue) then the profits of the Southern hotel would increase by almost $480,000 which would increase its return on assets to 21% (1,580/7,400) and its residual income would increase to $840,000.

The Southern hotel restaurant is of concern because it is loss making, this may be caused by its poor utilisation even though its selling prices ($44 per meal) are similar to those of the Northern hotel restaurant ($40 per meal) and the Eastern hotel restaurant ($45 per meal).

An analysis of the bed and breakfast room rates and room related costs is as follows:

Hotel	Northern	Southern	Eastern
Room rates per night	$95	$124	$80
Room and breakfast costs per night	$81	$106	$70

The differing prices being charged by the Northern and Southern hotels may be the effects of the market in each of those areas as the price difference does not seem to have significantly affected the market share achieved by each of the hotels (15% and 16% respectively). This further suggests that the poor utilisation of the restaurant in the Southern hotel is not caused by its prices. The Eastern hotel has a low market share and this might indicate that its room rate is too high although its restaurant prices are similar to those of the Northern hotel restaurant and it achieves the same 60% utilisation percentage so perhaps the lack of market share is caused by other establishments that offer cheaper accommodation, perhaps as loss leaders.

The hotels are not of the same size as measured by their number of bedrooms, so it is not fair to compare them on the basis of their residual income values.

Overall the Northern hotel has the highest return on assets, and the Eastern hotel has the lowest. The latter is caused by its poor occupancy rates which are related to its poor market share. The performance of the Southern hotel would be much improved if it could take actions to make its restaurant operation profitable.

(b) The investment has a positive net present value and therefore will increase the value of the Northern hotel and of HTL. It is therefore appropriate that the investment goes ahead. However, since the bonus of the manager of the Northern hotel is determined by the hotel's Return on Assets, this must be considered to determine the likely action of the manager.

The net assets values of the new investment at the end of each of the next 5 years together with the investment profits and the corresponding Return on Investment will be as follows:

	Incremental net assets $000	Incremental profit $000	RONA %
2012	750	110	14.7
2013	700	120	17.1
2014	650	155	23.8
2015	600	145	24.2
2016	550	130	23.6

The above calculations show that the investment yields a return in excess of the cost of capital of 10% in all years. However, it is not until 2014 that it yields a return greater than the current Return on Net Assets of 20%. This would mean that, in the first two years, the investment would cause the hotel's Return on Net Assets to be lower than its present level. As a consequence the manager is unlikely to want to proceed with the investment because it will adversely affect the bonus receivable in the immediate future.

Indicative workings:

Number of room nights:

Northern Hotel: 120 × 80% × 365 days = 35,040

Number of restaurant meals:

Northern Hotel: 100 × 60% × 365 days = 21,900

Room rates per night:

Northern Hotel: $3,328,000/35,040 = $95

Room and breakfast costs per night:

Northern hotel: $2,847,000/35,040 = $81

Restaurant selling price per meal:

Northern hotel: $876,000/21,900 = $40

129 GHYD (MAY 12)

(a) (i) Currently the selling price is $375 and this gives demand of 2,000 units. For every $25 increase in selling price demand reduces by 500 units so if the price was increased by (4 × $25) to $475 then demand would be zero.

Hence, the price equation P = $475 – 0.05x; And therefore Marginal Revenue = $475 – 0.1x

Marginal cost = Variable cost = $310

So, equating marginal revenue and marginal cost gives: 475 – 0.1x = 310

0.1x = 165

X = 1,650

And thus selling price = $475 – (0.05 × 1,650) = $392.50

(ii)

Tutorial note

In order to maximise your marks here, take extra care about the layout of your answers, and make sure you include explanations and workings.

This would yield a monthly contribution for YD as follows:

	$/unit	$
Selling price	392.50	
Variable cost	310.00	
Contribution	82.50	
Total monthly contribution: 1,650 units × $82.50		**136,125**

GH would now sell fewer components to YD. The new level of internal sales is 1,650 x2 = 3,300. As a result GH monthly contribution from these components would be $181,500 (3,300 × $55) so that the revised contribution of the company from these sales would be $317,625 ($181,500 + $136,125).

(b)   (i)   From a company perspective optimal decision making will occur if the transfer price is at company variable cost + any opportunity cost due to lost external sales.

It is stated that there is sufficient capacity within the company so no opportunity cost arises.

If the transfer price were to be at the variable cost of $70 per component this would change YD's perspective of its own variable costs (which would now be $200 per unit) and lead it to a different external price for its own product:

The price equation is unchanged P = $475 – 0.05x

And therefore marginal revenue = $475 – 0.1x

Marginal cost = Variable cost = $200

So, equating marginal revenue and marginal cost gives:

475 – 0.1x = 200

0.1x = 275

x = 2,750

And thus selling price = $475 – (0.05 × 2750) = $337.50 per unit

(ii)   This would yield a monthly contribution for YD as follows:

	$/unit	$
Selling price	337.50	
Component cost	140	
Other Variable cost	60	
Contribution	137.50	
		378,125

However, GH is no longer making any contribution on its internal sales

The monthly contribution of the GHYD company is now
($Nil + $378,125)   **378,125**

(c)

Tutorial note

The pitfall to avoid here is a general discussion of the principles of transfer pricing: you must make sure you relate your discussion to the question. You should also avoid expanding valuable time describing alternative transfer pricing methods such as dual pricing or two-part tariff – this was not requested.

The original company contribution from the sale of CX was $350,000. ($220,000 + $130,000).When the optimum price for the component was determined in part (a) above the total company contribution decreased to $317,625 but as shown in part (b) above with an internal transfer price based on company variable cost the total company contribution increased to $378,125.

Clearly therefore the effect of the transfer price is to distort the decision making processes in such a way as to not be beneficial to the company as a whole.

The use of a company variable cost as the transfer price yields a better result for the company as a whole and also for YD. However the manager of GH will not be happy with this transfer price because all of the additional contribution has accrued to YD and it is GH that has forgone contribution on its internal sales. Thus while the transfer price should be set at variable cost to enable the optimum decision to be made from a company perspective there needs to be a separate transfer price paid by YD to GH (as a fixed cost element) to compensate them for their lost contribution.

If the transfer price were to be the external price, but the decision in (ii) above were made on a company optimisation basis then the company contribution from product CX would still be $378,125 but it would be shared YD $75,625 and GH $302,500. This means that the increased activity for YD reduces its contribution but increases that of GH. YD will not be happy with this because their efforts result in a reduction of their divisional contribution. They will therefore expect a transfer price that is lower than the external price because GH is not giving up any external sales to meet the internal demand and consequently can only sell extra units to YD.

Clearly it can be seen that different transfer prices have an effect on both the company contribution and on the contributions of each division.

130 HPS TRANSFER PRICING (SEPT 13)

Tutorial note

A careful read through the scenario was essential to understand what was required. In part (a) a clear statement was required to show the profit for each division using the present pricing policy. In part (b) a statement was required using an opportunity cost approach to transfer pricing.

(a) (i)

	Division P $	Division R $	Working
Internal transfer	4,812,500		1
External sales	4,125,000	10,000,000	2
Total sales	8,937,500	10,000,000	
Internal transfers		4,812,500	
Variable costs	7,000,000	1,250,000	3
Fixed costs	1,500,000	1,000,000	
Profit before tax	437,500	2,937,500	
Tax	196,875	734,375	
Profit after tax	240,625	2,203,125	

Workings

(W1) 625T * $7,000 * 1.1

(W2) P: 375T * $11,000   R: 500T * $20,000

(W3) P: 1,000T * $7,000.   R: 625T * $2,000

(ii) The inter-company transfer price for processed coffee beans is equivalent to $7,700 per tonne. This is significantly below the market price for processed coffee beans of $11,000 per tonne and the difference of $3,300 per tonne equates to $2,062,500 on the 625 tonnes transferred to Division R. Setting the transfer price at $7,700 compared to $11,000 has the effect of reducing profit before tax at Division P by $2,062,500 and increasing profit before tax at Division R by the same amount.

This will be of particular interest to tax authorities as HPR are moving $2,062,500 of taxable profit from country Y (where a tax rate of 45% is operation) to country Z (where a lower tax rate of 25% is in operation) by the use of their chosen transfer price for processed coffee beans. Country Y's tax authorities would argue the transfer price of $7,700 does not represent an arm's length transaction as it is below $11,000 per tonne, the market price for processed coffee beans. The tax authorities in Country Y may require that an arm's length transfer price be introduced to ensure tax is not avoided in that country.

(b)

	Division P	Division R	Working
	$	$	
Internal transfer	6,075,000		1
External sales	4,125,000	10,000,000	2
Total sales	10,200,000	10,000,000	
Internal transfers		6,075,000	
Variable costs	7,000,000	1,250,000	3
Contribution	3,200,000	2,675,000	

Workings

(W1) (200T * $7,000) + (425T * $11,000)

(W2) P: 375T * $11,000   R: 500T * $20,000

(W3) P: 1,000T * $7,000.   R: 625T * $2,000

(c) Two issues that could arise by the imposition of a transfer pricing policy on divisional managers are:

One of the purposes of decentralisation is to allow managers to exercise greater autonomy. There is little point in granting autonomy and then imposing transfer prices. Such imposition may make the managers feel that they are deemed to be incompetent and consequently undermine their confidence.

If the performance measure for the divisional managers is based on the profits of their respective divisions it is essential that the transfer pricing policy allows an equitable portrayal of the performance of each division to be presented. Managers should be held responsible for what they can control; they should not be held responsible for profits or losses generated by an imposed transfer price. One way to overcome this problem is to use "dual prices".

131 S AND R DIVISIONS (MAY 13)

Tutorial note

For part (a), carefully read and understand the data provided and assemble the figures to show the profitability of two divisions, at three different levels of output with one division supplying to a second division. Part (b) requests candidates to consider the impact of the receiving division deciding to purchase components externally as opposed to purchasing from the other division. Part (c) requires an explanation of "arm's length" pricing and the methods that can be used to determine an "arm's length" price.

(a) **S Division**

External demand for components	15,000	19,000	35,000
	$000	$000	$000
Loss before internal sales	−2,050	−2,050	−2,050
Internal sales	2,100	2,480	4,000
Profit	50	430	1,950

R Division

External demand for components	15,000	19,000	35,000
	$000	$000	$000
Profit before cost of components	4,600	4,600	4,600
Cost of components	2,100	2,480	4,000
Profit	2,500	2,120	600

Workings

Given the demand figures for the finished product and the components it can be seen that both divisions will be working at full capacity. The only changes to the profits of both divisions will be caused by the transfer prices used for the components.

S Division

		$000
External sales	15,000 @ $200	3,000
Variable costs	35,000 @ $105	3,675
Fixed costs		1,375
Loss before internal sales		−2,050

R Division

		$000
Revenue	10,000 @ $800	8,000
Own variable costs	10,000 @ $250	2,500
Fixed costs		900
Profit before cost of components		4,600

The transfer prices used will generate revenues for S Division and costs for R Division. The prices used will be based on opportunity cost and these will be determined by reference to the demand made by external customers for the components and S Division's capacity. For example if external demand is for 19,000 components, S will only be able to supply 15,000 and therefore there is an opportunity cost of 4,000 components at $200 each because of the fixed capacity of 35,000 components.

External demand for components	15,000	19,000	35,000
Components transferred at $200	0	4,000	20,000
Components transferred at $105	20,000	16,000	0
Internal revenues and costs $000	2,100	2,480	4,000

(b)

External demand for components	15,000	19,000	35,000
	$000	$000	$000
Extra cost of external purchases 20,000*(170–105)	1,300	1,300	1,300
Extra contribution by S external	0	380	1,900
Total impact	–1,300	–920	600

(c) The OECD guidelines are based on the "arm's length" price principle, that is a price that would have been arrived at by two unrelated companies acting independently. There are three methods that the tax authorities can use:

(1) The comparable uncontrolled price method (which uses externally verified prices of similar transactions involving unrelated companies)

(2) The resale price method (which deducts a percentage from the selling price from the final product to allow for profit) can be used when goods are 'sold on' with little further processing

(3) The cost-plus method: an arm's length gross margin is established and is applied to the seller's manufacturing cost.

The OECD guidelines state that whenever possible the comparable uncontrolled price method should be used and if there is no market price, preference should be given to cost-plus.

132 HJ AND KL (SEPT 12)

(a)

Tutorial note

Make sure you identify the age of the non-current assets – they are four years old. There is no need to recalculate the three original KL ratios, which was a common mistake in this Exam.

An analysis of KL's non-current assets shows that they are four years old:

	$000
Cost	1,800
Depreciation @ 25% in year 1	450
	1,350
Depreciation @ 25% in year 2	337
	1,013
Depreciation @ 25% in year 3	253
	760
Depreciation @ 25% in year 4	190
	570

570   as shown in the question

If the non-current assets of HJ are depreciated at the rate of 25% on a reducing balance basis (i.e. the same method as is used by KL) and its assets aged forward to year 4 then its depreciation charge for the year will be $211,000 (see below) thus increasing its profits to $469,000; and its non-current asset value will reduce by $967,000 so that its capital employed is $833,000.

As a result of these changes to HJ's results its revised ratios (and the original ratios of KL for ease of comparison) would be:

Tutorial note

The same profit figure must be used to calculate those ratios that included profit figures. Likewise, the same Capital Employed figure must be used for those ratios that need it. This is the basis of 'triangulation'.

		HJ
ROCE	469/833	56.30%
Operating Profit margin	469/1,600	29.31%
Asset Turnover	1,600/833	1.92

HJ depreciation	$000
Original cost	2,000
Depreciation @ 25% in year 1	500
	1,500
Depreciation @ 25% in year 2	375
	1,125
Depreciation @ 25% in year 3	281
	844
Depreciation @ 25% in year 4	211
	633

(b)   KL's contribution to sales ratio is $590,000/$990,000 = 59.6%. KL's fixed costs (excluding depreciation) are $280,000 ($200,000 + $80,000).

If KL continues to use the same method of depreciation in 2012 and 2013 then its depreciation charge in 2012 will be 25% of $570,000 = $142,500; and in 2013 it will be 25% of $427,500 ($570,000 – $142,500) = $106,875.

Tutorial note

Make sure you are comfortable with the following revised fixed cost figure. Very few candidates managed it in the exam.

Thus for 2013 KL's fixed costs including depreciation are $386,875 ($280,000 + $106,875).The break-even sales value is therefore: $386,875/0.596 = $649,119.

Tutorial note

One last check – ensure your breakeven point or revenue is realistic.

(c)   (i)   The effect of the investment in the new equipment is to change the cost structure. Fixed costs (excluding depreciation) are to increase by 30% this equals ($390,000 – $190,000) × 30% = $60,000.

Variable costs are to decrease by 20%; this equals $400,000 × 20% = $80,000.

Thus there is a net cash inflow from cost savings of $20,000 per annum; The present value of these future cost savings when discounted at 10% per annum for 5 years is $20,000 × 3.791 = $75,820.

Tutorial note

Do not ignore the trade-in value of the old machine.

The residual value of the equipment in five year's time is $285,000, this has a present value of $285,000 × 0.621 = $176,985.

Since the capital cost is $1.2m less the trade in of $427,500 there is a negative NPV of $519,695.

As a result KL would not wish to replace its equipment.

(ii)

Tutorial note

You must try, as much as possible, to support your answers with figures.

If KL replaces its non-current assets with new equipment that has a cost of $1.2m then this will also cause a significant increase in the depreciation charge for the year. The depreciation charge for 2013 would be $300,000 whereas the depreciation on the existing equipment would only be $106,875. This is an increase of $193,125. In addition the other fixed costs are expected to increase by $60,000 (see(c) (i)).

The fixed costs for 2013 will now be $200,000 + 80,000 + 60,000 + 300,000 = $640,000.

Variable production costs are expected to reduce by 20% (see (b) above) which will improve the contribution to sales ratio from 59.6% (590/990) to 67.7% (670/990).

If the investment goes ahead the breakeven sales value for 2013 will be $640,000/.677 = $945,668.

Without the investment the breakeven sales value is $649,119 (see (b) above).

This means that KL would need to increase its sales by 45.7% in order to break-even.

Section 5

SPECIMEN EXAM PAPER QUESTIONS

1 DT GROUP

You are engaged as a consultant to the DT group. At present the group source their raw materials locally, manufacture their products in a single factory, and distribute them worldwide via an international distribution company. However, their manufacturing facilities are restricting them from expanding so they are considering outsourcing some of their manufacturing operations to developing economies.

Required:

(a) **Discuss the concept of the value chain and how the changes being considered by the DT group may impact on the management of contribution/profit generated throughout the chain.** **(6 marks)**

(b) **Discuss how gain sharing arrangements might be used by the DT group in the context of the changes being considered. Suggest one non-financial target that may be used as part of these gain sharing arrangements.** **(4 marks)**

(Total: 10 marks)

2 S COMPANY

S uses a standard absorption costing system to control its production costs and monitors its performance using monthly variance reports.

S has recently launched a new product which is being manufactured in batches of 100 units. An extract from the standard cost details per unit for this new product is as follows:

5.3 hours of direct labour @ $10 per hour $53.00

It is now realised that the standard cost details were based on an average learning period target of 5.3 hours per unit, and that a batch related period of learning was expected. The time expected for the initial batch was 1,000 hours and 90% learning rate was anticipated.

During August production commenced on the product, and 400 units were produced in four batches of 100 units using 2500 hours of direct labour at a cost of $26,000. The direct labour variances that were reported in respect of this product were:

Direct labour rate variance $1,000 Adverse

Direct labour efficiency variance $3,800 Adverse

Required:

(a) Calculate the expected length of the learning period in batches (to the nearest whole batch). **(4 marks)**

(b) Calculate planning and operating variances for August. **(4 marks)**

(c) Explain why the variances you have calculated in (b) above provide more meaningful information to the managers of S. **(2 marks)**

(Total: 10 marks)

3 BUDGET PLANNING AND COST CONTROL

A firm of solicitors is preparing its budgets for 2010. The structure of the firm is that it has a managing partner who is responsible for client and staff management, the firm's accounts and compliance matters and three other partners who each take responsibility for case matters depending on the branch of law that is involved in each case.

For a number of years the managing partner has prepared the budgets for the firm. These include budgets for fee income and costs analysed by each partner, and a cash budget for the firm as a whole. The firm has overdraft facilities which are renewable in June each year and sets cash balance targets for each month that reflect the seasonality of some of its work. At the end of each month there is a partners' meeting at which the managing partner presents a statement that compares the actual results of the month and the year to date with the corresponding budget. At this meeting all partners are asked to explain the reasons for the variances that have arisen.

The managing partner recently attended a course on "Budget Planning and Cost Control" at which the presenter argued that each of the partners in the firm should be involved in the budget setting process. However, the managing partner is not convinced by this argument as she believes that this could lead to budget manipulation.

Required:

(a) Explain feedback and feed-forward control systems and give an example of each in the context of the firm of solicitors. **(5 marks)**

(b) Discuss ONE potentially beneficial consequence and ONE potentially adverse consequence of involving the firm's other partners in the budget setting process of the firm. **(5 marks)**

(Total: 10 marks)

4 W AND XYZ

W is a manufacturing company that produces three products: X, Y and Z. Each uses the same resources, but in different quantities as shown in the table of budgeted data for 2010

Product	X	Y	Z
Budgeted production	1,500	2,500	4,000
Direct labour hours per unit	2	4	3
Machine hours per unit	3	2	3
Batch size	50	100	500
Machine setups per batch	2	3	1
Purchase orders per batch	4	4	6
Material movements per batch	10	5	4

W's budgeted production overhead costs for 2010 are $400,000 and current practice is to absorb these costs into product costs using an absorption rate based on direct labour hours. As a result the production overhead cost attributed to each product unit is:

Product X $32   Product Y $64   Product Z $48

The management of S are considering changing to an activity based method of attributing overhead costs to products and as a result have identified the following cost drivers and related cost pools:

Cost pool	$	Cost driver
Machine maintenance	100,000	machine hours
Machine setups	70,000	machine setups
Purchasing	90,000	purchase orders
Material handling	60,000	material movements

The remaining $80,000 of overhead costs are caused by a number of different factors and activities that are mainly labour related and are to be attributed to products on the basis of labour hours.

Required:

(a)   **Calculate the production overhead cost attributed to each product unit using an activity based approach.** **(7 marks)**

(b)   **Explain how W has applied Pareto Analysis when determining its cost drivers and how it may continue to use Pareto Analysis to control its production costs.**

(3 marks)

(Total: 10 marks)

5   HJ PRINTING

HJ is a printing company that specialises in producing high quality cards and calendars for sale as promotional gifts. Much of the work produced by HJ uses similar techniques and for a number of years HJ has successfully used a standard costing system to control its costs.

HJ is now planning to diversify into other promotional gifts such as plastic moulded items including key fobs, card holders and similar items. There is already a well established market place for these items but HJ is confident that with its existing business contacts it can be successful if it controls its costs. Initially HJ will need to invest in machinery to mould the plastic, and it is likely that this machinery will have a life of five years. An initial appraisal of the proposed diversification based on low initial sales volumes and marginal cost based product pricing for year 1, followed by increases in both volumes and selling prices in subsequent years, shows that the investment has a payback period of four years.

Required:

(a)   **Explain the relationship between target costs and standard costs and how HJ can derive target costs from target prices** **(5 marks)**

(b)   **Discuss the conflict that will be faced by HJ when making pricing decisions based on marginal cost in the short term and the need for full recovery of all costs in the long term.** **(5 marks)**

(Total: 10 marks)

6   M GROUP

M is the holding company of a number of companies within the engineering sector. One of these subsidiaries is PQR which specialises in building machines for manufacturing companies. PQR uses absorption costing as the basis of its routine accounting system for profit reporting.

PQR is currently operating at 90% of its available capacity, and has been invited by an external manufacturing company, to tender for the manufacture of a bespoke machine. If PQR's tender is accepted by the manufacturing company then it is likely that another company within the M group will be able to obtain work in the future servicing the machine. As a result, the Board of Directors of M are keen to win the tender for the machine and are prepared to accept a price from the manufacturing company that is based on the relevant costs of building the machine.

An engineer from PQR has already met with the manufacturing company to determine the specification of the machine and he has worked with a non-qualified accountant from PQR to determine the following cost estimate for the machine.

	Note	$
Engineering specification	1	1,500
Direct material A	2	61,000
Direct Material B	3	2,500
Components	4	6,000
Direct Labour	5	12,500
Supervision	6	350
Machine hire	7	2,500
Overhead costs	8	5,500
Total		91,850

Notes:

1   The engineer that would be in charge of the project to build the machine has already met with the manufacturing company, and subsequently prepared the specification for the machine. This has taken three days of his time and his salary and related costs are $500 per day. The meeting with the manufacturing company only took place because of this potential work; no other matters were discussed at the meeting.

2   The machine would require 10,000 square metres of Material A. This material is regularly used by PQR. There is currently 15,000 square metres in inventory, 10,000 square metres were bought for $6 per square metre and the remainder were bought for $6.30 per square metre. PQR uses the weighted average basis to value its inventory. The current market price of Material A is $7 per square metre, and the inventory could be sold for $6.50 per square metre. TURN OVER

3   The machine would also require 250 metre lengths of Material B. This is not a material that is regularly used by PQR and it would have to be purchased specifically for this work. The current market price is $10 per metre length, but the sole supplier of this material has a minimum order size of 300 metre lengths. PQR does not foresee any future use of any unused lengths of Material B, and expects that the net revenue from its sale would be negligible.

4   The machine would require 500 components. The components could be produced by HK, another company within the M group. The direct costs to HK of producing each component is $8, and normal transfer pricing policy within the M group is to add a 50% mark up to the direct cost to determine the transfer price. HK has unused capacity which would allow them to produce 350 components, but thereafter any more components could only be produced by reducing the volume of other components that are currently sold to the external market. These other components, although different, require the same machine time per unit as those required by PQR, have a direct cost of $6 per component and currently are sold for $9 each. Alternatively PQR can buy the components from the external market for $14 each.

5   The machine will require 1000 hours of skilled labour. The current market rate for engineers with the appropriate skills is $15 per hour. PQR currently employs engineers that have the necessary skills at a cost of $12.50 per hour, but they do not have any spare capacity. They could be transferred from their existing duties if temporary replacements were to be engaged at a cost of $14 per hour.

6   The project would be supervised by a senior engineer who currently works 150 hours per month and is paid an annual salary of $42,000. The project is expected to take a total of one month to complete, and if it goes ahead is likely to take up 10% of the supervisor's time during that month. If necessary the supervisor will work overtime which is unpaid.

7   It will be necessary to hire specialist machine for part of the project. In total the project will require the machine for 5 days but it is difficult to predict exactly which five days the machine will be required within the overall project time of one month. One option is to hire the machine for the entire month at a cost of $5,000 and then sub-hire the machine for $150 per day when it is not required by PQR. PQR expects that it would be able to sub-hire the machine for 20 days. Alternatively PQR could hire the machine on the days it requires and its availability would be guaranteed at a cost of $500 per day.

8   PQR's fixed production overhead cost budget for the year totals $200,000 and is absorbed into its project costs using a skilled direct labour hour absorption rate, based on normal operating capacity of 80%. PQR's capacity budget for the year is a total of 50,000 skilled direct labour hours. PQR's latest annual forecast is for overhead costs to total $220,000, and for capacity to be as originally budgeted.

Required:

(a)   **You are employed as assistant Management Accountant of the M group. For each of the resource items identified you are to:**

(i)   **discuss the basis of the valuation provided for each item**

(ii)   **discuss whether or not you agree with the valuation provided in the context of the proposed tender**

(iii) **prepare a revised schedule of relevant costs for the tender document on behalf of the M group.**   **(15 marks)**

(b) Assume that PQR successfully wins the bid to build the machine for a selling price of $100,000 and that the costs incurred are as expected. Discuss the conflict that will arise between the profit expected from the project by the Board of M on a relevant cost basis and the project profit that will be reported to them by PQR using its routine accounting practices. Use at least two specific examples from the bid to explain the conflict that you discuss. **(5 marks)**

(c) Discuss two non-financial matters that you consider relevant to this decision. **(5 marks)**

(Total: 25 marks)

7   DEF

DEF is a trading company that is divided into three divisions: D, E and F. Each division maintains its own accounting records and prepares an annual summary of its results. These performance summaries are shown below for the year ended 30 September 2009.

Division	D	E	F
	$000	$000	$000
Sales (net of returns)	150	200	400
Variable production costs	50	70	230
Fixed production costs	60	50	80
Administration costs	30	25	40
Profit	10	55	50
Capital Employed	400	550	415

The following additional information is available:

1   Divisions are free to trade with each other without any interference from Head Office. The managers of the respective divisions negotiate transfer prices between themselves. During the year and included in the above costs and revenues are the following transactions:

- Division D sold goods for $20,000 to Division E. The price negotiated was agreed on a unit basis between the managers of the two divisions. The variable production cost of these items in Division D was $18,000. Division D was operating under capacity and agreed to a transfer price that was little more than its own variable cost.

- Division F sold goods for $15,000 to Division E. The price negotiated was agreed on a unit basis between the managers of the two divisions. The variable production cost of these items in Division F was $9,000. Division F was operating under capacity and negotiated a transfer price based on its total production cost.

2   Included in the Administration costs for each division are the following management charges from Head Office:

D: $10,000   E: $8,000   F: $15,000

3   At the start of each year Head Office sets each division a target Return on Capital Employed. The target depends on their nature of the work and their industry sector. For the year ended 30 September 2009 these targets were:

D: 6%   E: 3%   F: 15%

Required:

(a) Discuss the shortcomings of the above performance summaries when measuring the performance of each division. (5 marks)

(b) Discuss the potential problems of negotiated transfer pricing, and how these have impacted on the performance of each of Divisions D, E, and F for the year ended 30 September 2009. (6 marks)

(c) Prepare an alternative statement that is more useful for measuring and reporting the performance of Divisions D, E, and F. (8 marks)

(d) Discuss how the use of "Dual" transfer prices could affect the measurement of divisional performance within DEF. Illustrate your answer with suggested dual prices. (6 marks)

(Total: 25 marks)

Section 6

ANSWERS TO SPECIMEN EXAM PAPER QUESTIONS

1 DT GROUP

(a) The Value Chain is the concept that there is a sequence of business factors by which value is added to an organisation's products and services. Modern businesses cannot survive merely by having efficient production facilities, they must also have a thorough understanding of the importance of the relationship between all of the elements in the value chain. These include: research & development, design, manufacturing, marketing, distribution and customer service.

The DT group currently has an internal manufacturing facility, this makes communications between different parts of that manufacturing process relatively straight-forward, however, if part of this process is to be outsourced this will place as added burden on the production management to ensure that all parts of the production process operate smoothly. Aside from communication difficulties, there may be different work ethics to contend with, and delays in receiving items and quality issues may disrupt the flow of goods to customers. This will lead to difficulties in identifying where profits/contributions are being earned (and lost) within the value chain.

(b) Gain sharing arrangements are based on the concept of sharing profits, however, if they are to be successful both parties must be willing to share the information necessary to determine the extent of any gain (or loss) that has arisen.

The DT group may seek to enter a gain sharing arrangement with the suppliers of the components that they have outsourced. This would require both organisations to establish some clear targets which could include quality specifications and delivery schedules. The gain from lower levels of rejects and earlier delivery of components can then be determined and shared between DT and the external supplier.

2 S COMPANY

(a)

Number of batches completed	Average time per batch
1	1,000 hours
2	900 hours
4	810 hours
8	729 hours
16	656 hours
32	590 hours
64	531 hours

It seems that the average time equals 5.3 hours per unit (i.e. 530 hours per batch after 64 batches had been completed.

(b) 4 batches were produced so the average time per batch should have been 810 hours (as shown in the answer to (a) above.

Therefore the total time should have been 4 × 810 hours =	3,240 hours
Actual hours taken were	2,500 hours
Operating efficiency difference	740 hours Favourable

By comparing the standard with the revised target time, the planning variance can be identified:

Original standard (5.3 hours × 400 units)	2,120 hours
Time allowed per learning curve	3,240 hours
Planning efficiency difference	1,120 hours Adverse

Each of these differences in hours is valued using the standard hourly rate of $10 per hour, so the revised efficiency variances are:

Planning variance	$11,200 Adverse
Operating variance	$7,400 Favourable

The rate variance remains unchanged at$ 1,000 Adverse

(c) The analysis of the efficiency variance into planning and operational effects provides more meaningful information because it shows the true efficiency of the operations as opposed to an invalid application of the original target. As production has only reached four batches by the end of August and the learning period seems to continue to around 64 batches it is clear that the learning has not yet been completed and therefore it is unfair to measure performance against the post learning standard. These revised calculations show that the actual learning is better than was expected whereas the original variance calculation showed that the time taken was more than it should have been. Rather than accusing the workforce of being inefficient they should be congratulated on their efficiency.

3   BUDGET PLANNING AND COST CONTROL

(a) Feedback control is the comparison of actual performance with an agreed target such as the budget set by the Managing partner. An example would be a comparison of the fees earned by each partner compared to those budgeted to be earned.

Feed-forward control is the comparison of a draft version of a target with a rule or objective. An example would be the comparison of the draft cash budget with the target cash balances and the overdraft facility. As a result of this comparison it may be necessary to defer some expenditure until a later period or reduce it so as to stay within the firm's existing cash balances/overdraft facility. This will lead to a second draft of the cash budget being prepared.

(b) One beneficial consequence of involving the other partners in the preparation of the firm's budgets is that they will accept ownership of their budget and accept responsibility for achieving their target. However, one adverse consequence is that since they will effectively be setting their own targets they may be tempted to set a target that is more easily achieved than that which would have been set by the Managing partner. This is known as the inclusion of budgetary slack.

4 **W AND XYZ**

(a) Calculation of cost driver rates:

Machine maintenance

$100,000/((1,500 × 3) + (2,500 × 2) + (4,000 × 3)) = $4.65 per machine hour

Machine setups

$70,000/[{(1,500/50) × 2} + {(2,500/100) × 3} + {(4,000/500) × 1}] = $489.51 per setup

Purchasing

$90,000/[{(1,500/50) × 4} + {(2,500/100) × 4} + {(4,000/500) × 6}] = $335.82 per order

Material handling

$60,000/[{(1,500/50) × 10} + {(2,500/100) × 5} + {(4,000/500) × 4}] = $131.29 per movement

Other costs

$80,000/((1,500 × 2) + (2,500 × 4) + (4,000 × 3)) = $3.20 per labour hour

Product	X	Y	Z
Batch costs:			
Machine setup	979	1,468.5	489.5
Purchasing	1,343	1,343	2,015
Material handling	1,313	656.5	525
	3,635	3,468	3,029.5
Batch size	50	100	500
Unitised batch costs	72.70	34.68	6.06
Machine maintenance	13.95	9.30	6.06
Other costs			
Product overhead costs	93.05	56.78	29.61

(b) Pareto Analysis is also known as the 80:20 rule. In this context it means that 80% of the production overhead costs are caused by 20% of the total number of causes. W has identified the causes of 80% of its overhead costs (i.e. $320,000 out of the total of $400,000) and linked these with just four cost drivers. The remaining $80,000 is said to be caused by a number of factors.

By focusing attention on controlling these four cost causes in the future, and minimising the costs of cost control, W will be controlling 80% of its production overhead costs.

4 **W AND XYZ**

5 HJ PRINTING

(a) Standard costs are the estimated costs of providing one unit of goods or service. They are determined by identifying the resources expected to be required for the completion of the unit and the price expected to be paid for each unit of those resources.

Target costs are determined by taking the market price of a product or service and deducting the required profit margin to determine the cost at which the product or service must be provided in order to meet the required profit margin.

HJ is diversifying into a well established market place where it is likely to be a price taker rather than a price maker. HJ will therefore be able to determine the selling price of its range of plastic moulded items. HJ must then determine the profit that it wishes to achieve to make a reasonable return on its investment in the new machinery. By deducting the profit required from the selling price HJ will determine the target cost for its plastic moulded products. HJ will then have to consider its production methods and the impact of any learning and experience efficiencies that may arise to determine whether it is capable of producing the items for their target cost.

(b) Short-term marginal cost based pricing is often necessary to enter into a new market that is already well established and mature. However, this form of pricing is unlikely to be financially viable in the longer term because of the need to recover the fixed costs of the business and deliver a suitable return for the business owners.

The difficulty lies in making the switch from one pricing model to the other without losing the customer base that has been built up using the marginal cost based prices. It will therefore be necessary for HJ to develop new items which have the perception of adding value to the original product range so that they can be sufficiently differentiated to allow the new prices to be introduced.

6 M GROUP

(a) 1 The cost of the engineering specification is based on the time spent (i.e. 3 days) multiplied by the salary and related employment costs of $500 per day. However, this is not a relevant value because the time has already been spent and is therefore a sunk cost. The relevant value is $NIL.

2 The cost of Direct Material A is based on 10,000 square metres valued using the weighted average basis. This can be shown to be calculated by:

10,000 square metres × $6 = $60,000

5,000 square metres × $630 = $31,500

15,000 square metres total = $91,500 = an average of $6.10 per square metre

This is not the correct valuation because the material is in regular use by PQR. Consequently its relevant cost is its cost of replacement which is $7 per square metre which is therefore $70,000 in total.

3 The cost of Direct Material B is based on 250 metre lengths being bought at a price of $10 per metre length. This is not the correct valuation because the sole supplier has a minimum order size of 300 metre lengths and the remainder has no foreseeable use or net sales revenue. Therefore the relevant cost is the cost of the minimum order of 300 lengths, i.e. 300 × $10 = $3,000

4   The cost of the components is based on the normal transfer pricing policy of $8 plus a 50% mark-up = $12 per component. 500 components × $12 = $6,000. However, this is not the relevant cost to the M group. The relevant cost to the M group is the variable cost of manufacturing the components plus any lost contribution from the reduction in external sales by HK. Thus: 350 components × variable cost only = 350 × $8 = $2,800 150 components × variable cost + lost contribution = 150 × ($8 + $3) = $1,650 Total relevant cost of the components = $2,800 + $1,650 = $4,450 The external market price of $14 is not relevant because it is cheaper to manufacture them internally, even if there is lost contribution caused by reduced external sales.

5   The cost of direct labour is the cost of the existing employees; 1000 hours × $12.50 per hour. This is not the relevant cost. The relevant cost is the lower of:

(a)   Recruiting engineers to do the work at $15 per hour; and

(b)   Transferring the existing employees and recruiting replacements to do their work at $14 per hour.

The second of these is the lower cost option so the relevant cost is 1000 hours × $14 per hour = $14,000.

6   The cost of the supervisor is based on a monthly salary of $3,500 (annual salary of $42,000/12 months) multiplied by 10% as the project time estimate = $350. This is not the relevant cost. The supervisor is already employed and will continue to be employed whether the project goes ahead or not. If the supervisor cannot complete this work within his normal hours he will work overtime but he is not paid for this so there is no incremental cash flow. The relevant cost is $NIL.

7   The machine hire cost is based on 5 days multiplied by a hire charge of $500 per day. However, this is not the relevant cost because there is a lower cost option available. If the machine is hired for an entire month at a cost of $5,000 and then sub hired for $150 per day for 20 days (total $3,000) the net cost of this option is $2,000. Therefore the relevant cost is $2,000.

8   The overhead cost value is based on the latest annual forecast of overhead costs and capacity levels as follows:

$220,000/80% of 50,000 hours = $5.50 per hour

1,000 hours of skilled labour × $5.50 per hour = $5,500.

However, this is not a relevant cost. There is no indication that these overhead costs are incurred as a result of undertaking the project, indeed being based on an absorption rate implies that they are not project specific and will be incurred whether the project goes ahead or not. The relevant cost is therefore $NIL.

	Note	$
Engineering specification	1	NIL
Direct material a	2	70,000
Direct material B	3	3,000
Components	4	4,450
Direct Labour	5	14,000
Supervision	6	NIL
Machine hire	7	2,000
Overhead costs	8	NIL
Total		93,450

(b)   The difference between the reported profit and that which would be expected based on the relevant cost schedule is caused by the differing nature of the accounting techniques used for decision making compared to those used for profit reporting and inventory valuation. For example:

(i)   The usage of material A on the project will be valued using its average cost of $6.10 per square metre rather than the replacement cost of $7 per square metre.

(ii)   The accounting system will attribute overhead costs to the project using an absorption rate that would normally be based on the budgeted costs and activity levels. This is relevant for profit reporting and is required by external reporting rules, but is not appropriate for short term decision making as these costs are not affected by the decision.

(c)   There are a number of non-financial factors that need to be considered, these include:

(i)   Will there be any long term impact on the external market of HK as a result of them choosing to make an internal supply in preference to their external customers. Does this mean that their external customers will find a permanent alternative supplier?

(ii)   Will there be any conflicts between the temporary replacement workers being paid $14 per hour to do the work of employees who are currently being paid $12.50 per hour?

7   DEF

(a)   The performance statement does not show the actual return on capital employed achieved by each division which is:

D: 2.5%   E: 10%   F: 12%

It can thus be seen that only Division E achieved the target that had been set for it by Head Office. However, there are a number of other factors that need to be considered in relation to the performance report.

1   The management charges from Head Office are presumed to be non-controllable at divisional level, it is therefore inappropriate to include them in any measure of divisional performance.

2   The basis of valuing the Capital Employed by each division is not stated. It is assumed to be based on the original cost of the assets less accumulated depreciation. As a consequence older assets will have lower original costs (due to price inflation) and lower book values (due to more years depreciation charges). As a result comparisons between divisions may not be a fair comparison. This may also explain the different cost structure that seems to exist in Division F where fixed production costs are approximately 25% of total production costs whereas in divisions D and E the fixed production costs are around 50% of total production costs. This may imply that the equipment used in Divisions D and E is newer and more automated.

(b)   The problem with negotiated transfer prices is that the results of the negotiations is as much affected by the personalities of the managers of each division as it is by the circumstances surrounding the transaction. If one manager has a stronger personality than another, or is a better negotiator then this will act to the detriment of the weaker division and may not be in the best interests of the company as a whole.

The inter-divisional trading affects the performance of all of the divisions. Assuming that the goods sold between the divisions were similar to those that the supplying division sold into the external market, then the following analysis can be made.

1   *Goods sold by Division D*

The external sales of Division D were $130,000 during the year for which the variable cost was $32,000, a mark-up of just over 300%. If the same mark – up were applied to the internal sale then Division D's profits would have increased by $52,000 to $62,000 and the profits of Division E would reduce by $52,000.

2   *Goods sold by Division F*

The external sales of Division F were $385,000 during the year for which the variable cost was $221,000, a mark-up of 75%. The mark-up added to the internal sale was 67% so there is not a significant impact on the profit reported by the divisions as a result of these internal transactions.

(c)

	D	F	F
	$000	$000	$000
Net sales – External	130	200	385
Sales – Internal	72	0	15
Total sales	202	200	400
Variable production costs			
– External	50	35	230
– Internal **		27	
– Internal mark-up**		60	
Fixed production costs	60	50	80
Divisional administration costs	20	17	25
Divisional profit	72	11	65
Non-controllable Head Office management charge	10	8	15
Profit	62	3	50
Capital employed	400	550	415
Return on Capital Employed (based on profit)	15.5%	0.5%	12.0%
Return on Capital Employed (based on divisional profit)	18%	2%	15.7%

* Internal sales have been valued at their equivalent external prices by applying the mark-up calculated earlier.

** These values show the variable cost to the company of these internal transactions and the mark-up that would normally apply to these transactions.

(d) A system of dual prices would mean that the selling price recorded by the selling division would not be the same as the buying price recorded by the buying division. Typically, the buyer would include the company variable cost as their cost and the seller would include a value closer to market value as their sales.

If this were done here, then the "Internal mark-up shown under Variable Production cost" would not appear and as a result the divisional profit of division E would have increased by $60,000 to $71,000 which would give the division a Return on Capital.

Performance Pillar

P2 – Performance Management

20 November 2013 – Wednesday Afternoon Session

Instructions to candidates

You are allowed three hours to answer this question paper.
You are allowed 20 minutes reading time **before the examination begins** during which you should read the question paper and, if you wish, make annotations on the question paper. However, you will **not** be allowed, **under any circumstances**, to open the answer book and start writing or use your calculator during this reading time.
You are strongly advised to carefully read ALL the question requirements before attempting the question concerned (that is all parts and/or sub-questions).
ALL answers must be written in the answer book. Answers written on the question paper will **not** be submitted for marking.
You should show all workings as marks are available for the method you use.
ALL QUESTIONS ARE COMPULSORY.
Section A comprises 5 questions and is on pages 2 to 6.
Section B comprises 2 questions and is on pages 8 to 11.
Maths tables and formulae are provided on pages 13 to 16.
The list of verbs as published in the syllabus is given for reference on page 19.
Write your candidate number, the paper number and examination subject title in the spaces provided on the front of the answer book. Also write your contact ID and name in the space provided in the right hand margin and seal to close.
Tick the appropriate boxes on the front of the answer book to indicate which questions you have answered.

P2 – Performance Management

TURN OVER

© The Chartered Institute of Management Accountants 2013

[You are advised to spend no longer than 18 minutes on each question in this section.]

ANSWER *ALL* FIVE QUESTIONS IN THIS SECTION. EACH QUESTION IS WORTH 10 MARKS. YOU SHOULD SHOW YOUR WORKINGS AS MARKS ARE AVAILABLE FOR THE METHOD YOU USE.

Question One

PWR is a manufacturing company that is about to launch a new product: Product Z. Details of the variable costs incurred in producing one unit of Product Z are as follows:

Labour $25 per hour

Materials $52 per unit

Variable overheads $5 per labour hour

Learning curve

Product Z is produced in batches of 10 units. The first batch of 10 units is expected to take 15 labour hours. There will be 95% learning curve that will continue until 64 batches have been produced.

Note: The learning index for a 95% learning curve = -0.074

Required:

(a)

(i)   **Calculate** the time required to produce the 64th batch of Product Z.

(3 marks)

(ii)   **Calculate** the total variable cost of the 64th batch of Product Z.

(2 marks)

(b)   **Explain** THREE conditions that must exist in the production process of Product Z for the learning curve effect to be realised.

(5 marks)

(Total for Question One = 10 marks)

Question Two

SXL is a specialist car manufacturer that produces various models of car. The organisation is due to celebrate its 100th anniversary next year. To mark the occasion, SXL intends to produce a sports car; the Model S. As this will be a special edition, production will be limited to 1,000 Model S cars.

SXL is considering using a target costing approach and has conducted market research to determine the features that consumers require in a sports car. Based on this market research and knowledge of competitors' products, SXL has decided to price the Model S at $19,950. SXL requires an operating profit margin of 25% of the selling price of the car. Details for the forthcoming year are as follows:

Forecast direct costs for a Model S car

Labour $5,000
Material $9,500

Forecast annual overhead costs

	$	Cost driver
Production line cost	4,630,000	See note 1
Transportation costs	1,800,000	See note 2

Note 1
The production line that would be used for Model S has a capacity of 60,000 machine hours per year. The production line time required for Model S is 6 machine hours per car. This production line will also be used to make other cars and will be working at full capacity.

Note 2
Some models of cars are delivered to showrooms using car transporters. 60% of the transportation costs are related to the number of deliveries made. 40% of the transportation costs are related to the distance travelled.

The car transporters are forecast to make a total of 640 deliveries in the year and carry 10 cars each time. The car transporter will always carry its maximum capacity of 10 cars.

The total annual distance travelled by car transporters is expected to be 225,000km. 50,000km of this is for the delivery of Model S cars only. All 1,000 Model S cars that will be produced will be delivered in the year using the car transporters.

Required:

(a)

(i) **Calculate** the forecast total cost of producing and delivering a Model S car using activity based costing principles to assign the overhead costs.

(4 marks)

(ii) **Calculate** the value of any cost gap that currently exists between the forecast total cost and the target total cost of a Model S car.

(2 marks)

(b) **Explain** TWO potential advantages to SXL of using target costing for the Model S car.

(4 marks)
(Total for Question Two = 10 marks)

Question Three

HRS is a food producer that makes low cost processed food that it sells to supermarkets. HRS produces only one type of processed food product and production techniques have remained largely unchanged for a number of years.

Over recent months, sales have been falling steadily. Consumer tastes are changing to favour natural ingredients and supermarkets have reflected this in the products that they offer for sale.

HRS is keen to address the decline in sales and recently held a meeting to discuss the performance of the organisation. The Management Accountant suggested to the Managing Director that the performance of HRS could be improved by implementing Total Quality Management (TQM) principles and adopting Kaizen costing concepts. Currently the control systems of HRS focus on material price and usage.

The Managing Director is sceptical of the Management Accountant's suggestions and is unclear as to whether they are suitable for the company.

Required:

(a)   **Explain** TWO concepts of Kaizen costing.

(4 marks)

(b)   **Explain** THREE conditions that must exist for TQM to be successfully implemented at HRS.

(6 marks)

(Total for Question Three = 10 marks)

Section A continues on the opposite page

Question Four

CHX is a retail bank. The lending division within CHX sells a loan product, Product L.

CHX is part owned by the Government and is required by the Government to produce 'Low' and 'High' gross profit forecast scenarios each year for comparison against actual performance.

Gross profit is calculated as:

Total lending income less **total funding cost**

Total lending income = total average balance multiplied by customer lending rate

Total funding cost = total average balance multiplied by funding rate

In order to calculate the total average balance for the 'Low' and 'High' forecast scenarios, CHX uses its actual total average balance from the previous year as a starting point.

	Product L
Previous year actual total average balance	$1,650m
'High' scenario assumptions	
Total average balance (movement on previous year's actual)	+2%
Customer lending rate	8.8%
Funding rate	4.15%
'Low' scenario assumptions	
Total average balance (movement on previous year's actual)	-25%
Customer lending rate	**See note**
Funding rate	4.55%

Note: It is expected that during the year it will be necessary to lower the customer lending rate in order to compete with other banks. Therefore it is expected, that under the 'Low' scenario, that the customer lending rate will be 7.90% on 40% of the total average balance and 5.90% on the remainder of the total average balance.

Required:

(a) **Produce** calculations to determine the forecast gross profit for Product L, under both the 'Low' forecast scenario and the 'High' forecast scenario.

(6 marks)

(b) **Explain** the potential advantages and disadvantages of the use of spreadsheets by CHX in developing forecast scenarios.

(4 marks)

(Total for Question Four = 10 marks)

Section A continues on the next page

Question Five

HIJ is a cosmetics company that produces perfume. The perfume market is very competitive and subject to frequent changes.

The finance team at HIJ prepare monthly rolling budgets as part of their planning and management control process.

The data for the forthcoming new budget period are as follows:

The variable cost of producing a bottle of perfume is $21.

The planned selling price of a bottle of perfume is $45 and at this selling price the demand for perfume is expected to be 125,000 bottles. Information from the marketing division at HIJ suggests that for every $3 increase in the selling price the customer demand would reduce by 10,000 bottles, and that for every $3 decrease in the selling price the customer demand would increase by 10,000 bottles.

Note: If $P = a - bx$ then $MR = a - 2bx$

Required:

   (a)   **Calculate** the revenue that HIJ would earn if the selling price of a bottle of perfume was set so that profits would be maximised for the forthcoming budget period.

                                                 (6 marks)

   (b)   **Discuss** the use of rolling budgets in the planning and management control process at HIJ.

                                                 (4 marks)

                    (Total for Question Five = 10 marks)

                    (Total for Section A = 50 marks)

End of Section A
Section B starts on page 8

This page is blank

[You are advised to spend no longer than 45 minutes on each question in this section.]

ANSWER *BOTH* QUESTIONS IN THIS SECTION. EACH QUESTION IS WORTH 25 MARKS.   YOU SHOULD SHOW YOUR WORKINGS AS MARKS ARE AVAILABLE FOR THE METHOD YOU USE.

Question Six

DLW is a company that builds innovative, environmentally friendly housing. DLW's houses use high quality materials and the unique patented energy saving technology used in the houses has been the result of the company's own extensive research in the area.

DLW is planning to expand into another country and has been asked by a prominent person in that country for a price quotation to build them a house. The Board of Directors believes that securing the contract will help to launch their houses in the country and have agreed to quote a price for the house that will exactly cover its relevant cost.

The following information has been obtained in relation to the contract:

1. The Chief Executive and Marketing Director recently met with the potential client to discuss the house. The meeting was held at a restaurant and DLW provided food and drinks at a cost of $375.
2. 1,200 kg of Material Z will be required for the house. DLW currently has 550 kg of Material Z in its inventory purchased at a price of $58 per kg. Material Z is regularly used by DLW in its houses and has a current replacement cost of $65 per kg. The resale value of the Material Z in inventory is $35 per kg.
3. 400 hours of construction worker time are required to build the house. DLW's construction workers are paid an hourly rate of $22 under a guaranteed wage agreement and currently have spare capacity to build the house.
4. The house will require 90 hours of engineer time. DLW engineers are paid a monthly salary of $4,750 each and do not have any spare capacity. In order to meet the engineering requirement for the house, DLW can choose one of two options:

   (i)   Pay the engineers an overtime rate of $52 per hour to perform the additional work.

   (ii) Reduce the number of engineers' hours available for their existing job, the building of Product Y. This would result in lost sales of Product Y.

   Summary details of the existing job the engineers are working on:

   Information for one unit of Product Y
Sales revenue	$4,860
Variable costs	$3,365
Engineers' time required per unit	30 hours

5. A specialist machine would be required for 7 weeks for the house build. DLW have 4 weeks remaining on the 15 week specialist machine rental contract that cost $15,000. The machine is currently not in use. The machine can be rented for an additional 15 weeks at a cost of $15,250. The specialist machine can only be rented in blocks of 15 weeks.

   Alternatively, a machine can be purchased for $160,000 and sold after the work on the house has been completed for $140,000.

6.	The windows required for the house have recently been developed by DLW and use the latest environmentally friendly insulating material. DLW produced the windows at a cost of $34,950 and they are currently the only ones of their type. DLW were planning to exhibit the windows at a house building conference. The windows would only be used for display purposes at the conference and would not be for sale to prospective clients.

	DLW has had assurances from three separate clients that they would place an order for 25 windows each if they saw the technology demonstrated at the conference. The contribution from each window is $10,450. If the windows are used for the contract, DLW would not be able to attend the conference. The conference organisers will charge a penalty fee of $1,500 for non-attendance by DLW. The Chief Executive of DLW can meet the clients directly and still secure the orders for the windows. The meetings would require two days of the Chief Executive's time. The Chief Executive is paid an annual salary of $414,000 and contracted to work 260 days per year.

7.	The house build requires 400kg of other materials. DLW currently has none of these materials in its inventory. The total current purchase price for these other materials is $6,000.

8.	DLW's fixed overhead absorption rate is $37 per construction worker hour.

9.	DLW's normal policy is to add a 12% mark-up to the cost of each house.

Required:

(a)	**Produce** a schedule that shows the minimum price that could be quoted for the contract to build the house.

	Your schedule should show the relevant cost of each of the nine items identified above. You should also explain each relevant cost value you have included in your schedule and why any values you have excluded are not relevant.

	(17 marks)

(b)	**Explain** TWO reasons why relevant costing may not be a suitable approach to pricing houses in the longer term for DLW.

	(4 marks)

(c)	**Recommend**, with justifications, a pricing strategy for DLW to use to price the innovative, environmentally friendly houses when they are launched in the new country.

	(4 marks)

	(Total for Question Six = 25 marks)

Section B continues on the next page

Question Seven

CD is a producer of soft drinks. The company has two divisions: Division C and Division D.

Division C manufactures metal cans that are sold to Division D and also to external customers. Division D produces soft drinks and sells them to external customers in the cans that it obtains from Division C.

CD is a relatively new company. Its objective is to grow internationally and challenge the existing global soft drinks producers. CD aims to build its brand based on the distinct taste of its soft drinks.

Division C annual budget information	$
Market selling price per 1,000 cans	130
Variable costs per can	0.04
Fixed costs	2,400,000
Net assets	4,000,000

Production capacity	40,000,000 cans
External demand for cans	38,000,000 cans
Demand from Division D	20,000,000 cans

Division D annual budget information	$
Selling price per canned soft drink	0.50
Variable costs per canned soft drink (excluding the can)	0.15
Cost of a can (from Division C)	At transfer price
Fixed costs	1,750,000
Net assets	12,650,000

Sales volume	20,000,000 canned soft drinks

Transfer Pricing Policy
Division C is required to satisfy the demand of Division D before selling cans externally.
The transfer price for a can is full cost plus 20%.

Performance Management Targets
Divisional performance is assessed on Return on Investment (ROI) and Residual Income (RI).
Divisional managers are awarded a bonus if they achieve the annual ROI target of 25%.
CD has a cost of capital of 7%.

Required:

(a) **Produce** a profit statement for each division detailing sales and costs, showing external sales and inter-divisional transfers separately where appropriate.

(6 marks)

(b) **Calculate** both the ROI and the RI for Division C and Division D.

(4 marks)

The directors of CD are concerned about the future performance of the company and, together with the divisional managers, have now agreed the following:

- A machine that would increase annual production capacity to 50,000,000 cans at Division C will be purchased. The purchase of this machine will increase the net assets of Division C by $500,000. Assume that there is no impact on unit variable costs or fixed costs resulting from this purchase.

- Inter-divisional transfers will be priced at opportunity cost.

Required:

(c) **Produce** a revised profit statement for each division detailing sales and costs, showing external sales and inter-divisional transfers separately where appropriate.

(6 marks)

It has now been decided that inter-divisional transfers are not required to be priced at opportunity cost.

(d) **Calculate** the minimum transfer price per can that Division C could charge for the 20 million cans required by Division D in order for Division C to achieve the target ROI.

(5 marks)

(e) **Explain** TWO non-financial measures that could also be used to monitor the performance of the manager of Division D against the objectives of CD company.

(4 marks)

(Total for Question Seven = 25 marks)

(Total for Section B = 50 marks)

End of question paper

Maths tables and formulae are on pages 13 to 16

This page is blank

PRESENT VALUE TABLE

Present value of 1 unit of currency, that is $(1+r)^{-n}$ where r = interest rate; n = number of periods until payment or receipt.

Periods	Interest rates (r)									
(n)	1%	2%	3%	4%	5%	6%	7%	8%	9%	10%
1	0.990	0.980	0.971	0.962	0.952	0.943	0.935	0.926	0.917	0.909
2	0.980	0.961	0.943	0.925	0.907	0.890	0.873	0.857	0.842	0.826
3	0.971	0.942	0.915	0.889	0.864	0.840	0.816	0.794	0.772	0.751
4	0.961	0.924	0.888	0.855	0.823	0.792	0.763	0.735	0.708	0.683
5	0.951	0.906	0.863	0.822	0.784	0.747	0.713	0.681	0.650	0.621
6	0.942	0.888	0.837	0.790	0.746	0705	0.666	0.630	0.596	0.564
7	0.933	0.871	0.813	0.760	0.711	0.665	0.623	0.583	0.547	0.513
8	0.923	0.853	0.789	0.731	0.677	0.627	0.582	0.540	0.502	0.467
9	0.914	0.837	0.766	0.703	0.645	0.592	0.544	0.500	0.460	0.424
10	0.905	0.820	0.744	0.676	0.614	0.558	0.508	0.463	0.422	0.386
11	0.896	0.804	0.722	0.650	0.585	0.527	0.475	0.429	0.388	0.350
12	0.887	0.788	0.701	0.625	0.557	0.497	0.444	0.397	0.356	0.319
13	0.879	0.773	0.681	0.601	0.530	0.469	0.415	0.368	0.326	0.290
14	0.870	0.758	0.661	0.577	0.505	0.442	0.388	0.340	0.299	0.263
15	0.861	0.743	0.642	0.555	0.481	0.417	0.362	0.315	0.275	0.239
16	0.853	0.728	0.623	0.534	0.458	0.394	0.339	0.292	0.252	0.218
17	0.844	0.714	0.605	0.513	0.436	0.371	0.317	0.270	0.231	0.198
18	0.836	0.700	0.587	0.494	0.416	0.350	0.296	0.250	0.212	0.180
19	0.828	0.686	0.570	0.475	0.396	0.331	0.277	0.232	0.194	0.164
20	0.820	0.673	0.554	0.456	0.377	0.312	0.258	0.215	0.178	0.149

Periods	Interest rates (r)									
(n)	11%	12%	13%	14%	15%	16%	17%	18%	19%	20%
1	0.901	0.893	0.885	0.877	0.870	0.862	0.855	0.847	0.840	0.833
2	0.812	0.797	0.783	0.769	0.756	0.743	0.731	0.718	0.706	0.694
3	0.731	0.712	0.693	0.675	0.658	0.641	0.624	0.609	0.593	0.579
4	0.659	0.636	0.613	0.592	0.572	0.552	0.534	0.516	0.499	0.482
5	0.593	0.567	0.543	0.519	0.497	0.476	0.456	0.437	0.419	0.402
6	0.535	0.507	0.480	0.456	0.432	0.410	0.390	0.370	0.352	0.335
7	0.482	0.452	0.425	0.400	0.376	0.354	0.333	0.314	0.296	0.279
8	0.434	0.404	0.376	0.351	0.327	0.305	0.285	0.266	0.249	0.233
9	0.391	0.361	0.333	0.308	0.284	0.263	0.243	0.225	0.209	0.194
10	0.352	0.322	0.295	0.270	0.247	0.227	0.208	0.191	0.176	0.162
11	0.317	0.287	0.261	0.237	0.215	0.195	0.178	0.162	0.148	0.135
12	0.286	0.257	0.231	0.208	0.187	0.168	0.152	0.137	0.124	0.112
13	0.258	0.229	0.204	0.182	0.163	0.145	0.130	0.116	0.104	0.093
14	0.232	0.205	0.181	0.160	0.141	0.125	0.111	0.099	0.088	0.078
15	0.209	0.183	0.160	0.140	0.123	0.108	0.095	0.084	0.079	0.065
16	0.188	0.163	0.141	0.123	0.107	0.093	0.081	0.071	0.062	0.054
17	0.170	0.146	0.125	0.108	0.093	0.080	0.069	0.060	0.052	0.045
18	0.153	0.130	0.111	0.095	0.081	0.069	0.059	0.051	0.044	0.038
19	0.138	0.116	0.098	0.083	0.070	0.060	0.051	0.043	0.037	0.031
20	0.124	0.104	0.087	0.073	0.061	0.051	0.043	0.037	0.031	0.026

CUMULATIVE PRESENT VALUE TABLE

Cumulative present value of 1 unit of currency per annum, Receivable or Payable at the end of each year for n years $\frac{1-(1+r)^{-n}}{r}$

Periods (n)	Interest rates (r)									
	1%	2%	3%	4%	5%	6%	7%	8%	9%	10%
1	0.990	0.980	0.971	0.962	0.952	0.943	0.935	0.926	0.917	0.909
2	1.970	1.942	1.913	1.886	1.859	1.833	1.808	1.783	1.759	1.736
3	2.941	2.884	2.829	2.775	2.723	2.673	2.624	2.577	2.531	2.487
4	3.902	3.808	3.717	3.630	3.546	3.465	3.387	3.312	3.240	3.170
5	4.853	4.713	4.580	4.452	4.329	4.212	4.100	3.993	3.890	3.791
6	5.795	5.601	5.417	5.242	5.076	4.917	4.767	4.623	4.486	4.355
7	6.728	6.472	6.230	6.002	5.786	5.582	5.389	5.206	5.033	4.868
8	7.652	7.325	7.020	6.733	6.463	6.210	5.971	5.747	5.535	5.335
9	8.566	8.162	7.786	7.435	7.108	6.802	6.515	6.247	5.995	5.759
10	9.471	8.983	8.530	8.111	7.722	7.360	7.024	6.710	6.418	6.145
11	10.368	9.787	9.253	8.760	8.306	7.887	7.499	7.139	6.805	6.495
12	11.255	10.575	9.954	9.385	8.863	8.384	7.943	7.536	7.161	6.814
13	12.134	11.348	10.635	9.986	9.394	8.853	8.358	7.904	7.487	7.103
14	13.004	12.106	11.296	10.563	9.899	9.295	8.745	8.244	7.786	7.367
15	13.865	12.849	11.938	11.118	10.380	9.712	9.108	8.559	8.061	7.606
16	14.718	13.578	12.561	11.652	10.838	10.106	9.447	8.851	8.313	7.824
17	15.562	14.292	13.166	12.166	11.274	10.477	9.763	9.122	8.544	8.022
18	16.398	14.992	13.754	12.659	11.690	10.828	10.059	9.372	8.756	8.201
19	17.226	15.679	14.324	13.134	12.085	11.158	10.336	9.604	8.950	8.365
20	18.046	16.351	14.878	13.590	12.462	11.470	10.594	9.818	9.129	8.514

Periods (n)	Interest rates (r)									
	11%	12%	13%	14%	15%	16%	17%	18%	19%	20%
1	0.901	0.893	0.885	0.877	0.870	0.862	0.855	0.847	0.840	0.833
2	1.713	1.690	1.668	1.647	1.626	1.605	1.585	1.566	1.547	1.528
3	2.444	2.402	2.361	2.322	2.283	2.246	2.210	2.174	2.140	2.106
4	3.102	3.037	2.974	2.914	2.855	2.798	2.743	2.690	2.639	2.589
5	3.696	3.605	3.517	3.433	3.352	3.274	3.199	3.127	3.058	2.991
6	4.231	4.111	3.998	3.889	3.784	3.685	3.589	3.498	3.410	3.326
7	4.712	4.564	4.423	4.288	4.160	4.039	3.922	3.812	3.706	3.605
8	5.146	4.968	4.799	4.639	4.487	4.344	4.207	4.078	3.954	3.837
9	5.537	5.328	5.132	4.946	4.772	4.607	4.451	4.303	4.163	4.031
10	5.889	5.650	5.426	5.216	5.019	4.833	4.659	4.494	4.339	4.192
11	6.207	5.938	5.687	5.453	5.234	5.029	4.836	4.656	4.486	4.327
12	6.492	6.194	5.918	5.660	5.421	5.197	4.988	4.793	4.611	4.439
13	6.750	6.424	6.122	5.842	5.583	5.342	5.118	4.910	4.715	4.533
14	6.982	6.628	6.302	6.002	5.724	5.468	5.229	5.008	4.802	4.611
15	7.191	6.811	6.462	6.142	5.847	5.575	5.324	5.092	4.876	4.675
16	7.379	6.974	6.604	6.265	5.954	5.668	5.405	5.162	4.938	4.730
17	7.549	7.120	6.729	6.373	6.047	5.749	5.475	5.222	4.990	4.775
18	7.702	7.250	6.840	6.467	6.128	5.818	5.534	5.273	5.033	4.812
19	7.839	7.366	6.938	6.550	6.198	5.877	5.584	5.316	5.070	4.843
20	7.963	7.469	7.025	6.623	6.259	5.929	5.628	5.353	5.101	4.870

FORMULAE

PROBABILITY

$A \cup B$ = **A or B**. $A \cap B$ = **A and B** (overlap).
$P(B \mid A)$ = probability of B, **given** A.

Rules of Addition
If A and B are mutually exclusive: $P(A \cup B) = P(A) + P(B)$
If A and B are not mutually exclusive: $P(A \cup B) = P(A) + P(B) - P(A \cap B)$

Rules of Multiplication
If A and B are *independent*: $P(A \cap B) = P(A) * P(B)$
If A and B are **not** *independent*: $P(A \cap B) = P(A) * P(B \mid A)$

$E(X) = \sum$ (probability * payoff)

DESCRIPTIVE STATISTICS

Arithmetic Mean

$$\bar{x} = \frac{\sum x}{n} \qquad \bar{x} = \frac{\sum fx}{\sum f} \quad \text{(frequency distribution)}$$

Standard Deviation

$$SD = \sqrt{\frac{\sum(x - \bar{x})^2}{n}} \qquad SD = \sqrt{\frac{\sum fx^2}{\sum f} - \bar{x}^2} \quad \text{(frequency distribution)}$$

INDEX NUMBERS

Price relative = $100 * P_1/P_0$ Quantity relative = $100 * Q_1/Q_0$

Price:

$$\frac{\sum w * \left(\frac{P_1}{P_o}\right)}{\sum w} \times 100$$

Quantity:

$$\frac{\sum w * \left(\frac{Q_1}{Q_o}\right)}{\sum w} \times 100$$

TIME SERIES

Additive Model

Series = Trend + Seasonal + Random

Multiplicative Model

Series = Trend * Seasonal * Random

FINANCIAL MATHEMATICS

Compound Interest (Values and Sums)
Future Value S, of a sum of X, invested for n periods, compounded at $r\%$ interest
$$S = X[1 + r]^n$$

Annuity
Present value of an annuity of £1 per annum receivable or payable for n years, commencing in one year, discounted at $r\%$ per annum:

$$PV = \frac{1}{r}\left[1 - \frac{1}{[1+r]^n}\right]$$

Perpetuity
Present value of £1 per annum, payable or receivable in perpetuity, commencing in one year, discounted at $r\%$ per annum:

$$PV = \frac{1}{r}$$

LEARNING CURVE

$$Y_x = aX^b$$

where:
Y_x = the cumulative average time per unit to produce X units;
a = the time required to produce the first unit of output;
X = the cumulative number of units;
b = the index of learning.

The exponent b is defined as the log of the learning curve improvement rate divided by log 2.

INVENTORY MANAGEMENT

Economic Order Quantity

$$EOQ = \sqrt{\frac{2C_oD}{C_h}}$$

where: C_o = cost of placing an order
$\quad\quad\quad C_h$ = cost of holding one unit in inventory for one year
$\quad\quad\quad D$ = annual demand

This page is blank

This page is blank

LIST OF VERBS USED IN THE QUESTION REQUIREMENTS

A list of the learning objectives and verbs that appear in the syllabus and in the question requirements for

each question in this paper.

It is important that you answer the question according to the definition of the verb.

LEARNING OBJECTIVE	VERBS USED	DEFINITION
Level 1 - KNOWLEDGE What you are expected to know.	List State Define	Make a list of Express, fully or clearly, the details/facts of Give the exact meaning of
Level 2 - COMPREHENSION What you are expected to understand.	Describe Distinguish Explain Identify Illustrate	Communicate the key features Highlight the differences between Make clear or intelligible/State the meaning or purpose of Recognise, establish or select after consideration Use an example to describe or explain something
Level 3 - APPLICATION How you are expected to apply your knowledge.	Apply Calculate Demonstrate Prepare Reconcile Solve Tabulate	Put to practical use Ascertain or reckon mathematically Prove with certainty or to exhibit by practical means Make or get ready for use Make or prove consistent/compatible Find an answer to Arrange in a table
Level 4 - ANALYSIS How are you expected to analyse the detail of what you have learned.	Analyse Categorise Compare and contrast Construct Discuss Interpret Prioritise Produce	Examine in detail the structure of Place into a defined class or division Show the similarities and/or differences between Build up or compile Examine in detail by argument Translate into intelligible or familiar terms Place in order of priority or sequence for action Create or bring into existence
Level 5 - EVALUATION How are you expected to use your learning to evaluate, make decisions or recommendations.	Advise Evaluate Recommend	Counsel, inform or notify Appraise or assess the value of Advise on a course of action

Performance Pillar

Management Level Paper

P2 – Performance Management

November 2013

Wednesday Afternoon Session

Management Level Paper

P2 – Performance Management
November 2013 examination

Examiner's Answers

SECTION A

Answer to Question One

Rationale

The question examines candidates' knowledge and understanding of the learning curve. The learning outcome tested is B1(e), *apply learning curves to estimate time and cost for new products and services.*

Suggested Approach

Candidates needed to carefully read the question and use the information to relate their answers to the scenario. In part (a) candidates needed to calculate the time required to produce the 64th batch and the variable cost. The time for batch number 64 was required; candidates then needed to apply the variable costs to calculate the cost of the batch rather than the cost of a unit.

In part (b) candidates were required to give three conditions that must exist in the production process of Product Z for the learning curve effect to be realised. Full explanations, relating the conditions to Product Z production, were needed to score the highest marks.

(a) (i)

Cumulative average time for first 64 batches

$y = ax^b$	x = 64	y = 11.03 hours
a = 15 hours	b = -0.074	

Total time for first 64 batches

11.03 hours * 64 = 705.92 hours

Cumulative average time for first 63 batches

$y = ax^b$	x = 63	y = 11.04 hours
a = 15 hours	b = -0.074	

Total time for first 63 batches

11.04 hours * 63 = 695.52 hours

Time for batch 64 = 705.92 - 695.52 = 10.40 hours

(ii)

	$	Working
Labour	260	1
Material	520	2
Variable overhead	52	3
Total variable cost	832	

Workings

1   10.40 hours x $25 per hour

2   $52 * 10 units per batch

3   10.40 hours x $5 per hour

(b)

In order for the learning curve effect to be realised at PWR a number of conditions must be satisfied.

The production process must be labour intensive. The Product Z production process should have direct involvement from the company's labour force rather than being largely automated. The process must be labour intensive in order for the learning curve effect to apply.

The production process should be complex in its composition. Complicated production processes will allow scope for learning. This seems to be the case for Product Z with the first batch expected to take 15 hours.

The production process should be continuous without extended stoppage periods. The reduction in production time stated by the learning curve effect can only be achieved if production occurs without significant breaks. A prolonged stoppage in production risks the learning from previous units being lost and production time increasing back towards the time for the first unit.

There should be a low turnover of production labour. A high number of production staff leaving the organisation will mean that new staff need to be employed. These new staff members will have no experience of the production at PWR and consequently take a longer time to produce units than more experienced PWR employees. The steady state production time per unit of Product Z will be achieved once all production staff have sufficient experience to realise the learning effect.

Answer to Question Two

Rationale

The question examines candidates' knowledge and understanding of target costing.
The learning outcome tested is B1(h), *explain how target costs can be derived from target prices and the relationship between target costs and standard costs.*

Suggested Approach

It was important for candidates to carefully read the question in order to calculate the cost of producing and delivering a Model S car. Part (a) required candidates to use the cost driver information in the notes to calculate both the production line and delivery cost for a Model S car.
In part (b) candidates should use the information in the question, for example highlighting the limited production numbers of Model S and the importance of using target costing to achieve the required profit figures.

(a) (i)

Forecast cost	$
Labour	5,000
Material	9,500
Overhead	791.75
Total cost	15,291.75

Workings

$4,630,000 / 60,000 annual production line machine hours = $77.17 per machine hour

$77.17 x 6 machine hours for a Model S = $463

Transportation cost
60% delivery related = $1,080,000
40% distance travelled related = $720,000

$1,080,000 / 640 deliveries = $1,687.50 per delivery
$1,687.5 / 10 cars = $ 168.75 per car

$720,000 / 225,000km = $3.20 per km travelled
$3.20 x 50,000km = $160,000
$160,000 / 1,000 Model S cars = $160 per car

(ii)

	$
Target selling price	19,950
Profit margin	25%
Target cost	14,962.50
Forecast cost	15,291.75
Cost gap	**329.25**

(b)

A target costing approach for the Model S car has significant potential advantages for planning and control at SXL. Model S is a special edition and production numbers will be limited. As such, it is important that revenues and costs are carefully planned to ensure Model S generates the required profit over its short production life.

Target costing is a market focussed approach that bases the target price on customer requirements to achieve a specified level of demand. This market led and price driven approach offers a greater degree of accuracy in profit planning.

The majority of manufacturing cost for model S will be committed at the design stage. Adopting target costing enables cost reductions to be planned before costs are committed whilst ensuring the product still fits the requirements of the customer.

The team based approach to target costing requires staff from all departments at SXL involved in the Model S project to input into the process to close the cost gap. Cost savings are sought in the production of Model S together with transportation efficiency savings in the achievement of the target cost.

Examiner's Note: candidates were required to explain only two advantages.

Answer to Question Three

Rationale

The question examines candidates' knowledge and understanding of Kaizen costing and Total Quality Management principles when set in a food production environment.
The learning outcome tested is B1(c) *explain the concepts of continuous improvement and Kaizen costing that are central to total quality management.*

Suggested Approach

Part (a) required the explanation of two concepts of Kaizen costing and did not require candidates to relate their answers to the scenario in the question.

Part (b) needed candidates to carefully read through the scenario in order to identify the conditions that must exist for TQM to be successfully implemented at HRS. Citing generic conditions without relevance to the situation described at HRS would earn only limited marks.

(a)

Kaizen costing is a system of cost reduction based upon attaining incremental cost reductions by making small changes in the product or the method of operations.

Kaizen costing is a system of cost reduction rather than cost control. Kaizen goals are often updated monthly and targets set based on achievement of a cost reduction.

Kaizen costing is based on the assumption that the manufacturing process is always able to improve. Perfection is never achieved and the organisation should continually seek to improve its processes and production conditions.

Examiner's Note: only two concepts are required by the question.

(b)

In order for Total Quality Management to be successfully implemented at HRS, the whole organisation must adopt a quality culture. This includes the managing director of HRS. It is imperative that the managing director adopts and espouses the principles of Total Quality Management as the company's ethos will dictate to what extent the philosophy is committed to by the employees of HRS.

HRS must get much closer to its customers. HRS's supermarket customers have reduced their purchases as consumer tastes have changed. HRS must foster and deepen its relationship with supermarkets to understand the customer requirements.

HRS should seek continuous improvement in its production, processes and employees. Production techniques have remained largely unchanged at HRS and production is limited to one type of product. HRS must aim to meet the quality requirements of its customers and not be satisfied with current production techniques.

Answer to Question Four

Rationale

The question examines candidates' knowledge and understanding of "what if" scenarios and the use of spreadsheets in facilitating these analyses.

The learning outcome tested is C2(b) *evaluate the consequences of "what if" scenarios and their impact on the master budget.*

Suggested Approach

Part (a) required candidates to read the question carefully to understand the method to calculate gross profit. A clear layout and methodical approach to calculations were required to ensure all information in the scenario was incorporated.

Part (b) required an explanation of potential advantages and disadvantages of the use of spreadsheets in developing forecast scenarios. The wording of the requirement should be noted as it was the advantages and disadvantages of the use of spreadsheets that was required and not answers focussing on advantages and disadvantages of developing the scenarios.

(a)

High scenario	Product L
Total average balance	$1,683m
Customer lending rate	8.80%
Lending income	$148.104m
Funding rate	4.15%
Funding cost	$69.845m
Gross profit	$78.260m

Low scenario	Product L
Total average balance	$1,237.6m
Customer lending rate (7.9%*0.4+5.9%*0.6)	6.70%
Lending income	$82.913m
Funding rate	4.55%
Funding cost	$56.306m
Gross profit	$26.607m

(b)

Scenario analysis using spreadsheets offers users a high degree of flexibility. By splitting the spreadsheet into input, processing and output areas, assumptions can be managed and held separately. This functionality is useful in CHX as a number of key assumptions in the high and low scenarios differ from those in the base case, and the spreadsheet allows their effect to be measured easily.

The flexible nature of the spreadsheet also allows different scenarios to be readily developed. The spreadsheet used for the base scenario can be used to develop high and low scenarios as the processing and output areas and the lending income and cost calculations for CHX, will stay the same and only assumptions in the input area will change.

However, inaccuracies are potentially difficult to detect in spreadsheets. A developer entering complex formulae into the spreadsheet could make a mistake. As the error in the formula is held in the processing area of the spreadsheet it may not be detected by other users and go unnoticed. The implications of inaccuracies in forecast scenarios are obviously significant for THX, a bank that is part owned by the government.

Answer to Question Five

Rationale
The question examines candidates' knowledge and understanding of pricing based on profit maximisation in imperfect markets and the use of rolling budgets.

The learning outcomes tested are:
Part (a) A3(a) *apply an approach to pricing based on profit maximisation in imperfect markets.*

Part (b) C3(d) *discuss the criticisms of budgeting, particularly from the advocates of 'beyond budgeting' techniques.*

Suggested Approach
Part (a) required candidates to use the relevant formulae to calculate the price at which profit would be maximised. Candidates should note the requirement to 'calculate the revenue' and use the profit maximising price and associated demand to calculate the total revenue.

Part (b) required a discussion of the use of rolling budgets in the planning and management control process at HIJ. This required candidates to discuss advantages and disadvantages of the budgeting approach at HIJ. The frequent changes in the perfume market should have been noted and linked to the advantage of rolling budgets in these specific circumstances.

(a)

To calculate the marginal revenue function the demand function must first be established.

$P = a - bx$

$b = 3 / 10,000 = 0.0003$

$45 = a - 0.0003*125,000$. Therefore, $a = 82.50$

$P = 82.50 - 0.0003x$

$MR = a - 2bx$, $MR = 82.50 - 2*0.0003x$

Profit is maximised when $MR = MC$

$MC = \$21$

$21 = 82.50 - 2*0.0003x$. Therefore $x = 102,500$

Substitute the value of x into the demand function to get price

$82.50 - 0.0003*102,500 = \$51.75$

Revenue $= \$51.75 * 102,500 = \$5,304,375$

(b)

Rolling budgets are updated each period, usually a month, adding a further month on to the end of the forecast period, usually one year, when the current month has expired. Rolling budgets in HIJ will mean that the frequent changes in the perfume market can be reflected in the company's financial plans. This results in performance management against more meaningful budgets and management able to take better-informed decisions.

However, rolling budgets are time-consuming to prepare. Rather than preparing a fixed budget once for use throughout the following year, a rolling budget is revised each month with an additional month added to the forecast period once the current one has elapsed. The budget process will require a significant amount of administration and input from finance and other department staff.

SECTION B

Answer to Question Six

Rationale

The question examines candidates' knowledge and understanding of pricing strategies and of relevant costing in the production of a minimum price quotation.

The learning outcomes tested are:

Part (a) A1(a), *discuss the principles of decision-making including the identification of relevant cash flows and their use alongside non-quantifiable factors in making rounded judgements.*

Part (b) A1(c), *discuss the particular issues that arise in pricing decisions and the conflict between 'marginal cost' principles and the need for full recovery of all costs incurred.*

Part (c) A3(b), *discuss the financial consequences of alternative pricing strategies.*

Suggested Approach

Part (a)

Carefully read the question to understand the relevant cost impact of each item of information. For each item, 1 to 9, candidates were required to show the relevant cost along with an explanation of their treatment of the costs. A clear layout and full explanation of cost treatment were required.

Part (b)

Candidates needed to explain two reasons why relevant costing may not be a suitable approach to pricing houses in the longer term and relate their explanation to the scenario.

Part (c)

Justified recommendations were required. The recommendation must be specific and relevance to the innovative environmentally friendly houses produced by DLW explained. Explanations of unrelated pricing strategies would not earn marks.

(a)

	$	Note
Food and drink at meeting	-	1
Material Z	78,000	2
Construction workers	-	3
Engineers	4,485	4
Specialist machine	15,250	5
Windows	1,500	6
Other materials	6,000	7
Fixed overhead	-	8
Profit margin	-	9
Total relevant cost	105,235	

Notes

1) The food and drink costs are sunk. The meeting with the client has already occurred and therefore the costs not relevant.

2) Material Z is regularly used by DLW. The 550kg currently in inventory will need to be replaced and therefore should be valued at replacement cost. $65 x 550kg = $35,750 The remaining 650kg required for the contract is not owned by DLW and therefore will need to be purchased at the replacement cost. $65 x 650 = $42,250.

Total relevant cost $78,000

3) The construction workers have spare capacity to complete the work and are employed under a guaranteed wage agreement. Construction workers will be paid whether or not they work on the contract; therefore the cost is not relevant.

4) Engineers are salaried and this is not an incremental cost. However, they are currently at full capacity and do not have time within their normal hours to complete the 90 of hours work required. The engineers' additional time should be valued at opportunity cost.
If overtime is paid, the cost would be 90 hours x $52 = $4,680

Alternatively, switching engineers from their existing job:

90 hours / 30 hours to produce a unit = 3 units valued at contribution per unit $1,495 = $4,485.

The lower cost of the two options is $4,485 and this is the relevant cost.

5) The first rental period is part way through and the payment of $15,000 has already been made. Therefore, this is a sunk cost and not relevant. In order to obtain the machine for the required seven week period another 15 week standard rental agreement would have to be entered into, therefore the relevant cost is $15,250.

If the machine was to be purchased, the relevant cost would be $20,000 (sales price less resale value). The lower relevant cost of the two options is to rent the machine for another rental period, $15,250.

6) The cost to produce the windows has already been incurred and is therefore sunk and not relevant.

If DLW use the windows for the build and miss the conference the sales will not be lost. The chief executive will visit the clients at a later date to secure the sales; therefore there is no incremental loss in contribution. The chief executive's time is not relevant as he is paid an annual salary and would receive this irrespective of the visit to the clients.

However, should the windows be used for the build, DLW would not be able to attend the conference and be liable to pay the non-attendance fee of $1,500.

Total relevant cost $1,500

7) 400kg of other materials are required for the house build. The incremental cost is $6,000.

8) Fixed costs are not relevant as they will be incurred irrespective of whether the contract is taken or not.

9) Profit mark-up is not relevant as DLW is producing a minimum price quotation to exactly cover the relevant cost.

(b)

When quoting a minimum price for the contract, relevant costing principles are being used. Only relevant costs i.e. those that change as a direct result of the contract decision are included in the quoted cost.

The minimum price will result in DLW making neither a profit nor a loss. This is not a sustainable pricing policy in the longer term as it does not include a contribution to the fixed costs of the organisation.

Relevant costing does not include a profit margin. This is not suitable for DLW in the longer term as the company is planning to expand into different countries and investors will also require a return on their investment.

(c)

Market skimming would be a suitable pricing strategy to launch the houses in the new country. Market skimming charges a high price for the product initially where the product is unique and there are significant barriers to entry for competitors. The price is reduced as new competitors enter the market with a similar product. The strategy aims to maximise the profit from the product.

The high quality materials and unique energy saving technology used in the houses should command high prices from customers keen to have a house with this technology. The house that consumers are willing to pay a high price for, together with the barrier to competitors of the new energy saving technology, make DLW's product suited to the market skimming pricing strategy. This market skimming approach will allow DLW to recover the research and development costs incurred to develop the energy saving technology.

Answer to Question Seven

Rationale

The question examines candidates' knowledge and understanding of transfer pricing together with financial and non-financial divisional performance measures.

The learning outcomes tested are:
Part (a) & (c) D3(b), *discuss the typical consequences of a divisional structure for performance measurement as divisions compete or trade with each other.*

Part (b) D2(c) *discuss alternative measures of performance for responsibility centres.*

Part (d) D3(a) *discuss the likely behavioural consequences of the use of performance metrics in managing cost, profit and investment centres.*

Part (e) C3(b) *discuss the role of non-financial performance indicators.*

Suggested Approach

For parts (a) and (c), candidates needed to carefully read and understand the data provided and assemble the figures to show the profitability of two divisions, with Division C supplying to Division D.

Part (b): candidates needed to carefully read the information in the question and use the appropriate figures to calculate the required performance measures

Part (d): a target ROI of 25% was required. Candidates needed to use their knowledge of the ROI formula to substitute in known values to arrive at a required revenue figure. The value of the external sales could then be taken from this figure to leave the required value of the internal sales.

Part (e) required an explanation of TWO non-financial measures that could also be used to monitor the performance of the manager of Division D against the objectives of CD company. A number of non-financial measures could have been suggested, but candidates needed to read the requirement carefully and explain the relevance of their chosen measure to the objectives of CD company.

(a)

		C $	D $	Working
Sales				
	Internal	2,400,000		1
	External	2,600,000	10,000,000	2
		5,000,000	10,000,000	
Variable costs				
Cans				
	Internal		2,400,000	3
	External	1,600,000		4
Other variable		0	3,000,000	5
Fixed costs		2,400,000	1,750,000	
Profit		1,000,000	2,850,000	

Workings

1)   Transfer price: $0.04 + ($2,400,000 / $40,000,000) = $0.10 * 1.2 = $0.12
         Internal transfers 20,000,000 cans at $0.12
2)   External sales by division C 20,000,000 cans at $0.13
         External sales by division D 20,000,000 canned drinks at $0.50
3)   As per Division C internal sales revenue
4)   Division C variable cost 40,000,000 cans at $0.04
5)   Division D variable cost 20,000,000 canned drinks at $0.15

(b)

	C	D
ROI	$1,000,000/$4,000,000 = 25%	$2,850,000/$12,650,000 = 23%
RI	$1,000,000 − ($4,000,000 x 7%) = $720,000	$2,850,000 − ($12,650,000 x 7%) = $1,964,500

(c)

		C $	D $	Working
Sales				
	Internal	1,520,000		1
	External	3,900,000	10,000,000	2
		5,420,000	10,000,000	
Variable costs				
Cans				
	Internal		1,520,000	3
	External	2,000,000		4
Other variable		0	3,000,000	5
Fixed costs		2,400,000	1,750,000	
Profit		1,020,000	3,730,000	

Workings

1)   8,000,000 cans at $0.13 opportunity cost

    12,000,000 cans at $0.04 variable cost

2)   30,000,000 cans at $0.13

    20,000,000 canned drinks at $0.50

3)   As per Division C internal sales revenue

4)   50,000,000 cans at $0.04

5)   20,000,000 canned drinks at $0.15

(d)

ROI = profit / net assets.

Target ROI required is 25%.

25% = profit / 4,500,000, rearranging the formula gives profit = $1,125,000

Profit = Contribution – fixed costs, here fixed costs = $2,400,000. Therefore:

Contribution = $1,125,000 + $2,400,000 = $3,525,000

Contribution = revenue – variable cost. Here variable cost = $2,000,000. Therefore:

Revenue = $5,525,000

Revenue = Internal sales + external sales. External sales = 30,000,000 * $0.13. Therefore:

Internal sales required = $1,625,000

20,000,000 internal sales. Transfer price should be set at a minimum of $0.08

Alternative solution
Profit requirement: 25% * (4,000,000 + 500,000) = $1,125,000

Therefore, additional $1,125,000 – $1,020,000 = $105,000 profit required

Total transfer price: $1,520,000 + $105,000 = $1,625,000

20,000,000 internal sales. Transfer price should be set at a minimum of $0.08

(e)

Brand awareness percentage. One of CD's stated objectives is to grow its business internationally. A measure of CD's presence in the other countries is brand awareness by consumers. A high brand awareness by consumers could be a lead indicator of increasing sales revenues.

Taste test results from comparison with main competitors. CD aims to grow its brand based on the distinctive taste of its product. A key indicator of potential future success is the measure of consumer preference.

A sample of consumers could be offered the CD soft drink along with that of a competitor. The proportion of sampled consumers selecting the CD soft drink in the taste tests could then measure consumer preference. If consumers favour the taste of the CD drink over competitors, potentially sales revenue will increase as consumers make CD's product their soft drink of choice.
